7/12

W9-CBA-943

THOMAS PENN

Winter King

Henry VII and the Dawn of Tudor England

Simon & Schuster

New York   London   Toronto   Sydney   New Delhi

Simon & Schuster
1230 Avenue of the Americas
New York, NY 10020

First Simon & Schuster hardcover edition March 2012

SIMON & SCHUSTER and colophon are registered trademarks
of Simon & Schuster, Inc.

For information about special discounts for bulk purchases,
please contact Simon & Schuster Special Sales at
1-866-506-1949 or business@simonandschuster.com

The Simon & Schuster Speakers Bureau can bring authors
to your live event. For more information or to book an event,
contact the Simon & Schuster Speakers Bureau at
1-866-248-3049 or visit our website at www.simonspeakers.com.

Manufactured in the United States of America

1   3   5   7   9   10   8   6   5   4   2

Library of Congress Cataloging-in-Publication Data

Penn, Thomas.
Winter king : Henry VII and the dawn of Tudor England / Thomas Penn.
p.   cm.
Originally published in Great Britain by Penguin Books Ltd., 2011.
Includes bibliographical references and index.
1. Henry VII, King of England, 1457–1509. 2. Great Britain—Politics and
government—1485–1509. 3. Great Britain—History—Henry VII, 1485–1509.
4. Great Britain—Kings and rulers—Biography. 5. Tudor, House of.
I. Title
DA330.P46 2012
942.05'1092—dc23
[B]   2011036144
ISBN 978-1-4391-9156-9
ISBN 978-1-4391-9158-3 (ebook)

Acknowledgements

I have met with a great deal of kindness and generosity in the course of writing this book. Staff at the British Library, The National Archives, Cambridge University Library and the Bodleian Library have all dealt with my enquiries with patience and helpfulness. Christine Reynolds facilitated my visits to Westminster Abbey Muniments, while Malcolm Underwood's hospitality and erudition made my time in the archives at St John's College, Cambridge a pleasure.

Margaret Condon, Cliff Davies, John Watts, Adrian Ailes and Samantha Harper have all been generous with their time, and in sharing information and documents.

I am particularly indebted to those who have read though drafts of part or all of the book: Diarmaid MacCulloch and Carl Watkins; Steven Gunn, who also kindly allowed me to look at an early chapter of his forthcoming book on Henry VII's new men; Sean Cunningham and James Ross, who have both been great funds of encouragement and insight; and Rosemary Horrox, whose discernment and attentiveness I have been fortunate enough to enjoy a second time.

I am lucky in the friendship of Michael Peel, Jon Butler, Ed, Linda and Tom Harvey and John Berger. Thanks, too, are due to Tariq Ali, Perry Anderson, and colleagues at Verso: Jacob Stevens, Rowan Wilson, Bob Bhamra, Tania Palmieri, Tamar Shlaim, Sarah Shin and Anwar Fazul.

My thanks to all at Penguin, in particular Simon Winder for his perceptive editing and enthusiastic support; I am also grateful to Jenny Fry, Natalie Ramm, Marina Kemp and Richard Duguid. Charlotte Ridings has been a painstaking copy-editor. I would also like to thank Bob Bender at Simon and Schuster US and, at Aitken Alexander, Anna

ACKNOWLEDGEMENTS

Stein and especially Andrew Kidd, who has been a source of calm advice, reassurance and friendship throughout.

Lastly, I owe more than I can say to my parents, Alan and Jessica; and to Kate Harvey, without whose love and support I could not have written this book.

For Kate

'I love the rose both red and white.
Is that your pure, perfect appetite?'
Thomas Phelyppes,
'I love, I love and whom love ye?' c. 1486

'Since men love at their own pleasure and fear at the pleasure
of the prince, the wise prince should build his foundation
upon that which is his own, not upon that which belongs to
others: only he must seek to avoid being hated.'
Machiavelli, The Prince

Contents

CONTENTS

List of Illustrations

Winter King

England c. 1500

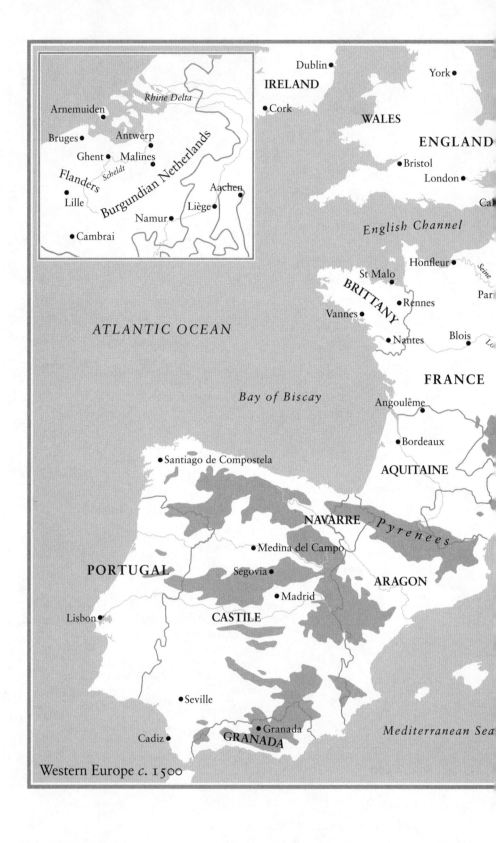

Western Europe *c.* 1500

N

POLAND

●Hamburg

●Munster

HOLY

Guelders

●Wittemberg
●Leipzig

●Cologne

Rhine

Frankfurt am Main
Mainz●

ROMAN

●Prague

BOHEMIA

Speyer●   Nuremberg●

EMPIRE

Augsburg●

●Munich

AUSTRIA

Vienna●

Burgundy

Basle●

A   l   p   s

TYROL

St Johann●

Buda●

HUNGARY

SWISS CON.

on●

●Geneva

SAVOY

Milan●   ●Brescia

VENICE

●Venice

Rhône

Po

●Genoa

●Bologna

Lucca●
Pisa●   Florence●

Arno

A

●Urbino

Siena●

PAPAL STATES

Adriatic Sea

●Ragusa

OTTOMAN EMPIRE

Tolfa●
Rome●

p
e
n
n
i

KINGDOM OF NAPLES

NAPLES

Naples●

n
e
s

High land

100   200 miles

100   200   300 km

Houses of Lancaster and York, and the House of Tudor

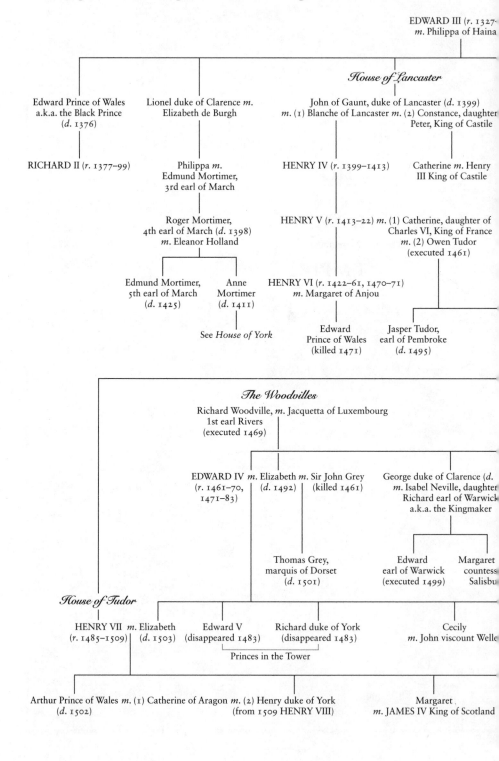

EDWARD III (r. 1327-
m. Philippa of Haina

House of Lancaster

Edward Prince of Wales
a.k.a. the Black Prince
(d. 1376)

Lionel duke of Clarence m.
Elizabeth de Burgh

John of Gaunt, duke of Lancaster (d. 1399)
m. (1) Blanche of Lancaster m. (2) Constance, daughter
Peter, King of Castile

RICHARD II (r. 1377–99)

Philippa m.
Edmund Mortimer,
3rd earl of March

HENRY IV (r. 1399–1413)

Catherine m. Henry
III King of Castile

Roger Mortimer,
4th earl of March (d. 1398)
m. Eleanor Holland

HENRY V (r. 1413–22) m. (1) Catherine, daughter of
Charles VI, King of France
m. (2) Owen Tudor
(executed 1461)

Edmund Mortimer,
5th earl of March
(d. 1425)

Anne
Mortimer
(d. 1411)

HENRY VI (r. 1422–61, 1470–71)
m. Margaret of Anjou

See *House of York*

Edward
Prince of Wales
(killed 1471)

Jasper Tudor,
earl of Pembroke
(d. 1495)

The Woodvilles

Richard Woodville, m. Jacquetta of Luxembourg
1st earl Rivers
(executed 1469)

EDWARD IV m. Elizabeth m. Sir John Grey
(r. 1461–70,   (d. 1492)   (killed 1461)
1471–83)

George duke of Clarence (d.
m. Isabel Neville, daughter
Richard earl of Warwick
a.k.a. the Kingmaker

Thomas Grey,
marquis of Dorset
(d. 1501)

Edward
earl of Warwick
(executed 1499)

Margaret
countess
Salisbu

House of Tudor

HENRY VII m. Elizabeth
(r. 1485–1509)   (d. 1503)

Edward V
(disappeared 1483)

Richard duke of York
(disappeared 1483)

Cecily
m. John viscount Welle

Princes in the Tower

Arthur Prince of Wales m. (1) Catherine of Aragon m. (2) Henry duke of York
(d. 1502)   (from 1509 HENRY VIII)

Margaret
m. JAMES IV King of Scotland

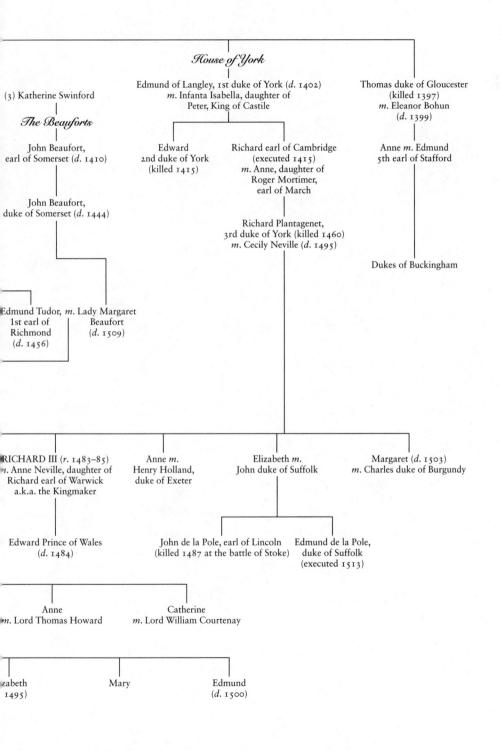

House of York

Edmund of Langley, 1st duke of York (*d.* 1402)
m. Infanta Isabella, daughter of
Peter, King of Castile

Thomas duke of Gloucester
(killed 1397)
m. Eleanor Bohun
(*d.* 1399)

(3) Katherine Swinford

The Beauforts

John Beaufort,
earl of Somerset (*d.* 1410)

Edward
2nd duke of York
(killed 1415)

Richard earl of Cambridge
(executed 1415)
m. Anne, daughter of
Roger Mortimer,
earl of March

Anne *m.* Edmund
5th earl of Stafford

John Beaufort,
duke of Somerset (*d.* 1444)

Richard Plantagenet,
3rd duke of York (killed 1460)
m. Cecily Neville (*d.* 1495)

Dukes of Buckingham

Edmund Tudor, *m.* Lady Margaret
1st earl of   Beaufort
Richmond   (*d.* 1509)
(*d.* 1456)

RICHARD III (*r.* 1483–85)
m. Anne Neville, daughter of
Richard earl of Warwick
a.k.a. the Kingmaker

Anne *m.*
Henry Holland,
duke of Exeter

Elizabeth *m.*
John duke of Suffolk

Margaret (*d.* 1503)
m. Charles duke of Burgundy

Edward Prince of Wales
(*d.* 1484)

John de la Pole, earl of Lincoln
(killed 1487 at the battle of Stoke)

Edmund de la Pole,
duke of Suffolk
(executed 1513)

Anne
m. Lord Thomas Howard

Catherine
m. Lord William Courtenay

zabeth
1495)

Mary

Edmund
(*d.* 1500)

Winter King

Introduction

Henry VII ruled England for almost a quarter-century, from 1485 to 1509. During his reign, the civil wars that had convulsed the country for much of the fifteenth century burned themselves out. By its end, he had laid the foundations for the dynasty that bore his name: Tudor. He was a man with a highly dubious claim to the throne, who seized power and passed it on in the first untroubled succession in almost a century. Yet, wedged between two of the most notorious monarchs in English history – the arch-villain Richard III and the massive figure of Henry VIII – Henry VII remains mysterious, or as his first biographer, the seventeenth-century political thinker Francis Bacon put it, 'a dark prince'.

In English history, Henry VII's reign is still widely understood as a time of transition, one in which the violent feuds of the previous decades gave way to a glorious age of renaissance and reformation. This was the myth that the Tudors themselves built. The later Tudors referred to Henry VII as we now see him: the unifier of a war-torn land, a wise king who brought justice and stability, and who set the crown on a sound financial footing. Nonetheless they were unable to eradicate the lingering sense of a reign that degenerated into oppression, extortion and a kind of terror, at its core an avaricious Machiavellian king who inspired not love but fear. In calling him a 'dark prince', Bacon's emphasis was on the sinister as well as the opaque. Henry VII, he wrote, was 'infinitely suspicious' and he was right to be so, for his times were 'full of secret conspiracies and troubles'. Perhaps the most telling verdict of all is that of Shakespeare, who omits Henry VII altogether from his sequence of history plays – and not for want of material but, one suspects, because the reign was simply too uncomfortable to deal with.

Merely scratching the surface of Henry VII's reign exposes troubling questions about his right to the crown and about the way he held on to it. From the very outset, Henry faced challenges to his rule. Unable to eradicate the taint of illegitimacy that hung around his throne, or to master a world in which the compromised loyalties and political traumas of civil war persisted, he constructed around himself a regime whose magnificence concealed the fact that it was contingent, temporary, a sustained state of emergency. And, sixteen years into his reign, just when he thought that he had laid his demons to rest, a family catastrophe left him newly vulnerable, wrenching the dynasty off the course that he had planned for it, and setting it in a new and unexpected direction, his hopes resting no longer on his first-born son but entirely on his second: the boy who would eventually succeed him as Henry VIII.

Unsurprisingly, when the seventeen-year-old Henry VIII inherited the throne in the spring of 1509, he had a difficult circle to square. His coronation was accompanied by an outpouring of praise which presented him as his father's successor, while at the same time distancing him from the disturbing years that had just passed. Court poets reached for Plato's tried-and-tested idea of the Golden Age: paradise, the first of epochs which, like the seasons, would return. This glorious young prince represented a metaphorical spring, a second coming, seemingly as unlike his father as could be.

It was a model that had been used before – in living memory, in fact. Back in 1485, Henry VII had evoked the Golden Age to define himself against the king he had defeated and called a usurper, Richard III. But in 1509, court poets portrayed Henry's own reign as a sterile landscape, one in which bears roamed and wolves howled, a time in which the natural order had been subverted – but which, mercifully, was rightfully restored in the shape of his son. In other words, if Henry VIII was the spring, his father was the winter.

This is a gripping and largely untold story. The late fifteenth and early sixteenth centuries were a volatile time of change and possibility and, as with periods of flux, its energy and vitality are seductive. The medieval worlds of chivalry and intense piety mingle with new political ideas, spread by the printing press and enforced by gunpowder. Dynasties and states struggle to be born in a war-torn Christendom that is still – in theory – unified by an unswerving obedience to the pope. Fleets of merchant ships, their trade routes to the East blocked by the Ottoman Empire encroaching on Europe's south-eastern frontier, sail west across the Atlantic and discover a new continent.

It is a story which stretches from the remote regions of England to the courts and chancelleries of Venice and Rome. It is traced through merchant banks and accountants' ledgers, courts of law, the pageantry and brutality of court and tiltyard, diplomats' dispatches and the reports of spies and informers. It concerns high ideals and family loyalties; honour, realpolitik and grubby self-interest; deep-rooted traditions and beliefs; and new ways of understanding the roles of princes and governments. All these elements come together and are transformed in the febrile world of Henry VII's household and court.

The last, claustrophobic decade of Henry VII's reign, with an ageing, paranoid king and his dynamic young son at its heart, forms the focus of this book. It is one of the strangest episodes in English history. An atmosphere of fear and suspicion radiated from the royal court into the streets and townhouses of London and throughout England's far-flung estates and provinces. Established forms of rule and government were bent out of shape, distorted in ways that people found both disorientating and terrifying.

But these are also the dawning years of a dynasty. They see the coming of age of Catherine of Aragon, the young Spanish princess who would become Henry VIII's first wife, and of Henry VIII himself – or rather, Prince Henry, as he is here. To explore these precarious years, and to gain a sense of how and why Henry VII behaved and ruled in the way he did, is to reveal much about the house of Tudor, the family that would, over the course of the sixteenth century, dominate and transform England.

Prologue

Red Rose, Avenger of the White

On the afternoon of Sunday 7 August 1485, off the westernmost tip of Wales, seven ships appeared from the south. Heading for the great natural harbour of Milford Haven, they nosed around the headland's sheer, sandstone cliffs and, just before sunset, dropped anchor. Smaller boats came shuttling back and forth, quickly and purposefully, bringing horses ashore, heaving munitions, armour and cannon onto the beach. Many languages and accents could be heard: Scots, Welsh, Breton mixing with French, and English of various dialects. When they swarmed up the hillsides to the small castle commanding the bay, the soldiers found it abandoned, its garrison long gone. Nobody, it seemed, was expecting them – not at that remote place, anyway.[1]

From one boat, a knot of nobles disembarked and waded through the surf. One of them, a wiry man in his late twenties, sank to his knees and clasped his hands in prayer. '*Judica me, Deus*', he began, muttering Psalm 43, 'Judge me, O Lord and favour my cause'. He kissed the Pembrokeshire sand and made the sign of the cross.[2] Exiled first in Brittany, then in northern France, since the age of fourteen, Henry earl of Richmond – or, as the reigning king of England, Richard III, referred to him bitterly, the 'bastard Tudor' – had returned after another fourteen years at the head of a motley band of two thousand political dissidents and mercenaries. With rapidly dwindling support from his French backers, his invasion was furtive and anxious. That he was there at all was an extraordinary circumstance, the latest convulsion in the series of dynastic feuds and turf wars that had torn England apart over the previous half-century, and which would later become known as the Wars of the Roses: the red rose of Lancaster against the white rose of York. This man, who had crossed the

Channel to claim the throne of England and who would father its greatest dynasty, was never meant to be king.

Henry earl of Richmond was born on 28 January 1457 in the fortress of Pembroke Castle, a few miles away from his eventual landing-place. He entered the world during a traumatic time. Sporadic clashes between the armed factions of Lancaster and York were threatening to boil over into civil war. The plague that had ravaged southern Wales late the previous year had carried off his father, Edmund Tudor, imprisoned in a Yorkist dungeon; his mother, Lady Margaret Beaufort, had just turned fourteen. The birth left her damaged. She would have no more children.

England in the 1460s was a mutant, double-headed kingdom. In a raging blizzard on 29 March 1461, Palm Sunday, the two sides had clashed outside the Yorkshire village of Towton: involving some fifty thousand men, it was the biggest battle ever fought on English soil, and one of the bloodiest. Yorkist forces routed the armies of the passive and mentally unstable Lancastrian king, Henry VI, slaughtering nine thousand of them. Three months later, Edward IV, a charismatic giant of an eighteen-year-old, was crowned the first king of the house of York.[3] Both families, Lancaster and York, traced their line back to the great Edward III – but the Yorkists claimed to bear his name of Plantagenet.

For the powerful Lancastrian clans of Beaufort and Tudor, the defeat at Towton was a disaster. The child in whom their families met, the four-year-old Henry earl of Richmond, was now a wealthy prize. Torn away from his mother, his lands parcelled out among the victors, he was presented by Edward IV to a prominent Yorkist, Sir William Herbert, and brought up among the Herbert children at the castle of Raglan in south Wales.

On both sides of his family, the young Henry's lineage was entwined with the house of Lancaster. As half-blood relatives of the Lancastrian kings, the Beauforts shared with them a magnificent forebear, the house's founder John of Gaunt, duke of Lancaster – but their descent was through Gaunt's mistress and they were bastards. The Beauforts were subsequently legitimized – but, as their detractors were quick to point out, they had been barred, by Act of Parliament no less, from ever claiming the English throne. Nevertheless, the Beauforts had gloried in the reign of Henry V, France's reconqueror and the victor of Agincourt, before his son Henry VI had squandered everything. The Tudors had also attached themselves to the house of Lancaster and, despite their tenuous hold, were rising fast: during the troubled 1450s Edmund Tudor, half-brother to Henry VI, had been high in royal favour. The mother they had in common was Henry V's young wife, Catherine of Valois, daughter of the French king. But Edmund's father had been a charming, fast-talking Welsh chamber servant of Catherine's: the pair had fallen in love after Henry V's death and had married secretly. Royal blood, then, ran in the veins of the young Henry earl of Richmond, but it was irretrievably tainted.

Despite the overwhelming victory of Towton, Yorkist rule struggled to take root. With the deposed Henry VI still alive, it was a time of queasy uncertainty, in which self-interested manoeuvring, internecine feuding and struggles for power and land could all be justified by invoking the claim of whichever king best suited people's circumstances. First and foremost, Edward IV had to establish his dynasty, and the great men who had brought him to power now sought to arrange his marriage to a foreign princess, of Burgundy, perhaps, or Castile. But, 'greatly given to fleshly wantonness', Edward wanted a cold, lynx-eyed beauty called Elizabeth Woodville. When she refused to sleep with him, he married her clandestinely and made her his queen. It was unwise. The widow of a Lancastrian knight, Elizabeth was a commoner; her large clan rushed to court, scrabbling for royal favour, titles, land and rich marriages. Pushed to one side, the Yorkist nobles whose ambitions Edward had wrecked through his impulsive marriage watched the arriviste Woodvilles basking in his affections.[4] Gradually, the nobles' discontent and jealousy turned to betrayal, and they joined forces with exiled Lancastrians. In October 1470, Edward IV was forced to flee to the continent, to the Burgundian Netherlands, and the helpless Henry VI was brought out of his place of incarceration in the Tower of London.

To the young Henry of Richmond, his uncle's brief, inglorious second coming was memorable. Taken to London, he was reunited briefly with the mother he had not seen for years, before returning to south Wales, this time in the company of his Tudor uncle Jasper. Six months later Edward IV returned to England, and people again weighed their loyalties in the balance. As Edward's army approached London, Henry VI was paraded, bewildered, through the city streets dressed in an old, faded blue gown, the archbishop of Canterbury leading him gently by the hand. Days later, Edward entered the city unopposed, then, marshalling his forces, exacted decisive revenge in two savage battles: north of London at Barnet and, rampaging into the southwest, in the flood plains of Tewkesbury. Those leading Lancastrians not killed in combat were executed immediately afterwards: they included Lady Margaret Beaufort's cousin the duke of Somerset, hauled out of sanctuary and beheaded, and Henry VI's son and heir. Henry VI himself, reincarcerated in the Tower, was murdered. The house of Lancaster had been all but exterminated.[5]

Still in her twenties, Lady Margaret Beaufort had become an astute political survivor. She and Jasper Tudor, a constant thorn in Edward's flesh over the preceding decade, well understood the heightened significance of her son's half-blooded lineage. That September, Jasper and the fourteen-year-old Henry fled Pembroke Castle, where they had been holed up against the Yorkist armies, across the sea to the traditional Lancastrian refuge of France. Storms took them west, to the north-western tip of mainland Europe, the embattled duchy of Brittany. There, Henry became a pawn in a different game.[6]

Duke Francis of Brittany, who had no sons, received Henry kindly and treated him well. But he also knew the boy's value. As dynastic conflict flared across northern Europe, the French king, Louis XI, was spinning a web round territories that France claimed as its own but which, like Brittany, remained stubbornly independent. Now, in Henry, Duke Francis had a bargaining chip: a commodity desired not only by England but also by France – which wanted Henry in order to keep its island neighbour at bay.

Amid rumours of English and French agents and plots, of kidnap and murder, Henry was transferred from fortress to fortress, never settled, always ready to move at a moment's notice. Dependent on the whims of others, he learned to think like the fugitive he now was: to watch and assess loyalties, to sift information from rumour and, caught in the wash of European power politics, to understand how they affected his own fortunes. He developed an exile's patience, inured to a life in which stretches of empty time were punctuated by sudden alerts, moments of danger in which logical clear-headedness meant the difference between life and death. Once, in November 1476, Duke Francis temporarily succumbed to Edward IV's offers of funds and military aid in exchange for the nineteen-year-old Henry's extradition. But at the port of St Malo, Henry gave his English guard the slip, feigning illness and dodging into sanctuary. When he made it back to the Breton court, Francis was all contrition.[7]

In England, meanwhile, the uncertainty of the 1460s had given way to order under the self-assertive magnificence of Edward IV. He and Elizabeth Woodville had ten children, including two surviving sons, and his dynasty seemed assured. When the forty-year-old king, a man of insatiable and debauched appetites, died grossly fat on 9 April 1483, the older of his two sons, the twelve-year-old Edward Prince of Wales, was named his heir. But Richard duke of Gloucester, the younger brother of the late king, had other ideas. Elizabeth Wood-ville's clan, he felt, had got too close to the heart of power. Arresting and executing leading members of her family, and inveighing against the perversions of his brother's rule, he placed the two princes, his nephews, in the Tower, then crowned himself Richard III in the name of the 'old royal blood of this realm'. That summer the princes, previously observed 'shooting and playing' in the Tower gardens, disappeared into its depths, never to be seen again.[8]

Elizabeth Woodville and her daughters had withdrawn behind the high walls of Westminster Abbey seeking sanctuary. Secretly that summer, on behalf of her son, Lady Margaret Beaufort opened communication through agents – priests, an astrologer the two matriarchs favoured – who were able to pass unchallenged through the heavily guarded gates. A pact was agreed. Henry earl of Richmond would return from Brittany to claim the throne, and he would take as his queen Elizabeth of York, the oldest of Edward IV and Elizabeth's daughters. The families of Beaufort and Woodville – or, if the point was stretched somewhat, the houses of Lancaster and York – would be united; so too would England. Heralds and historians were good at these genealogical sleights of hand. On their brilliantly illuminated parchment rolls, coats-of-arms, badges and portraits were erased and cut out; others appeared in their place. A dynasty that had been eradicated could blossom miraculously like a rose in winter, its lineal descent fully formed, its succession inevitable. Now, with the merging of the red rose and the white, Henry was presented as the successor to Edward IV, the king who had all but obliterated his family and had only narrowly failed to do the same to him. While the logic was flawed, the symbolism was irresistible.[9]

Meanwhile, away in the Welsh castle of Brecon, Richard III's right-hand man, the duke of Buckingham, had been co-opted to the new alliance by the suggestive promptings of a prisoner that the king had unwisely entrusted to Buckingham's care, an experienced political operator, Bishop John Morton of Ely.[10] Conspiracy brewed; agents slipped out of the country to Brittany, working to coordinate uprisings in England with an invasion force led by Henry and backed by Breton funds. That autumn of 1483, Woodville loyalists rose in rebellion along the south coast from Kent to Devon, Buckingham marched out of Wales at the head of an army of retainers, and Henry prepared to set sail from Brittany. But the weather that October was foul, and he left late. Sailing into the teeth of a storm, his fleet was scattered. By the time he appeared off the south Devon coast, there was only one other ship in sight. He turned back.

He was lucky not to have made landfall. Richard III had already quashed the uprisings. Buckingham's forces were routed, the duke beheaded. Besides which, the motives of Buckingham, a vain man with Lancastrian blood, had been opaque; possibly, he had wanted the crown for himself. Pursued by a vengeful Richard III, the leading Woodville rebels fled, in time-honoured fashion, to the continent – to Brittany.

That winter, even in London where gossip and information were rife, people knew little about the shadowy figure who was now claiming the crown as his by right. Arriving in Brittany, the Woodville exiles found a sallow young man, with dark hair curled in the shoulder-length fashion of the time and a penchant for expensively dyed black clothes, whose steady gaze was made more disconcerting by a cast in his left eye – such that while one eye looked at you, the other searched for you.[11] He was, in the words of the Burgundian chronicler Jean Molinet, a 'fine ornament' of the Breton court, a man who worshipped Breton saints, spoke immaculate French and whose courtliness had a distinctly Gallic tinge. The soft politesse concealed a sharp observer, a gleaner of information, cool under pressure and used to having to think several steps ahead: a leader, the Woodville fugitives perhaps sensed – but then again, they had little choice.

Henry's pact with the exiles was sealed in the cathedral at the Breton capital of Rennes on Christmas Day 1483: they pledging their allegiance to him as king, he swearing to marry Elizabeth of York.[12] The dice, though, were still loaded in Richard's favour. While many thought him a usurper, he was nevertheless a crowned king of England. His opponent was a penniless exile who, as one of Richard's proclamations emphatically pointed out, 'hath no manner of interest, right, title or colour, as every man knoweth, for he is descended of bastard blood, both of father's side and mother's side'. Richard embarked on a charm offensive, dangling pardons in front of leading conspirators and offering political rehabilitation. Many refused, but when Elizabeth Woodville herself acknowledged the fact of Richard's rule, agreeing to come out of sanctuary and entrust herself and her daughters to his safekeeping, the resolution of some of Henry's fellow exiles started to crumble.

Travelling to Brittany, Richard's men struck a deal with leading counsellors around the ageing and infirm Duke Francis, pledging money and arms in the duchy's fight against an increasingly menacing France, in exchange for Henry. Warned of his imminent betrayal, Henry fled across the border. At the French court, the embattled faction struggling to retain control of the fourteen-year-old king Charles VIII was delighted to welcome this prestigious English pawn. There, bolstered by new arrivals, fugitives from failed uprisings in East Anglia and Lancastrian diehards escaped from the English enclave of Calais, Henry started to create another story for himself, his half-blooded lineage blurring into legend. No longer a fugitive, he was a king-in-waiting, whose line could be traced back into the mist and rime of British prehistory. No less a king than Cadwallader, forebear of the mythical King Arthur, had prophesied his return, in irrefutable proof of which Henry had added to his arms a red dragon. In his letters into England, meanwhile, his signature of 'Henry de Richemont' was replaced by the poised regal monogram, 'H'.[13]

In the spring of 1485, with the threat from an English-backed Brittany increasing, France proclaimed lavish financial support for Henry's invasion of England. But by early July, as the Breton menace evaporated again, so too did France's enthusiasm, its promises now dismissed with a shrug of indifference. For Henry this was a shattering blow, and more bad news was to come. In an attempt to neutralize the political threat of the Woodvilles, Richard III arranged a marriage between one of his household knights and one of Edward IV's daughters. Indeed, it was whispered that Richard himself was paying close attention to the oldest of them: his sixteen-year-old niece, Henry's betrothed, Elizabeth of York. The rumours 'pinched Henry by the very stomach'. Scrambling to raise loans from financiers, he and his advisers worked to assemble victuals, arms and artillery, horses and transport. He bolstered his sketchy forces with a battalion of French mercenaries who, demobilized from France's recent wars in Flanders, were idly terrorizing the local populace.

At the French court, Henry had exchanged words with the diplomat and political theorist Philippe de Commynes, a man with a lifetime's experience in power politics. Commynes, who had first encountered Henry on his arrival at the Breton court fourteen years before, was unsparing in his assessment. Henry, he wrote, was penniless and his claim to the English throne non-existent, 'whatever one might say about it'. Henry was entirely self-fashioned, his reputation depending not on his lineage, but on his virtues, his 'own person and honesty'. And, he recollected, Henry's conversation was tinged with heaviness and resignation as he described how, since the age of five, his life had been an interminable sequence of suffering, evasion and prison. This was not, Commynes seemed to say, the talk of a king confidently expecting to recover his birthright, but of a man resigned to his fate.[14]

It was not hard to see why. A lifetime spent depending on the caprices and whims of others, the hopelessness and boredom of exile punctuated by false hopes, had culminated in an invasion whose meticulous planning had been thrown into confusion by the scrambled events of the last weeks. But as his small fleet set sail from the northern French port of Honfleur on 1 August 1485, Henry knew that he was, at last, taking his fate into his own hands. Even defeat and destruction were better than the alternative: the slow death of endless, fugitive begging around the courts of Europe.[15]

The battle of Bosworth Field, fought in the English east midlands two weeks after Henry's inauspicious landing at Milford Haven, was in this context a miraculous, God-given, victory. There could be no other explanation. As Henry's forces marched through Wales and into northwest England, the heartlands of his stepfather's powerful Stanley family, the hoped-for support had arrived with reluctance. Lady Margaret Beaufort's third husband, Lord Stanley, an accomplished political trimmer, gave fair words but little commitment: the vast, well-armed Stanley retinues shadowed Henry's route southeast to the battlefield and waited, detached, to see how the chips fell.

Early on the morning of 22 August, they watched Henry's well-drilled vanguard march determinedly towards the massed lines of the king's forces on the ridge above and, as Richard's artillery erupted and the armies engaged, saw them refuse to give ground. They saw nobles apparently loyal to Richard fail to advance against Henry – confused, perhaps, or reluctant to commit – and the king's desperate, impulsive cavalry charge thundering into Henry's household troops. In the carnage, monarch and pretender fought face to face, the heavy, painted canvas standards of Richard's sunburst and boar pitching and yawing against Henry's rougedragon and red rose. Then, as Henry's standard bearer had his legs hacked from under him, the Stanley forces, led by Lord Stanley's brother Sir William, piled in to his rescue. 'This day', soldiers heard Richard shout, 'I will die as a king or win.' He was swept away, battered to death so viciously his helmet was driven into his skull.[16]

By mid-morning, it was all over. Moving busily about the battlefield, Henry's soldiers stripped the dead and dying of their valuables and piled the bodies onto carts for burial. Richard's nearby camp, loaded with fine hangings and ornaments, was looted. On a nearby hill, Lord Stanley, whose chief military action had consisted, ingloriously, of hacking down Richard's defenceless and fleeing troops, placed the dead king's circlet – picked up from where it had fallen, under a thornbush – on his stepson's head, to the shouts of acclamation from his troops. He was King Henry VII.

On 3 September, Henry's torn, bloody battle standards were carried through the suburb of Shoreditch towards London, a city still under curfew, armed patrols silhouetted against its battlemented walls. At Bishopsgate, the mayor and officials waited uncertainly in their scarlet finery to welcome with gifts of cash and gold plate the king they had unceremoniously dismissed weeks before as Richard III's 'rebel'.[17]

Of the details – Henry's flight to France, his invasion plans – there was no mention. Nor was there any detail of his genealogy, of precisely what his claim consisted in. And so it would remain: his fugitive history was chronicled in the haziest of terms by design as much as by accident. That was how Henry wanted it. He had appeared out of nowhere – an avenging king come to claim his kingdom from Richard III, who had murdered his nephews and wrenched the true line of the Yorkist dynasty off course. After the battle, the dead king's wrecked body had been slung over a horse, its long hair tied under its chin, then set on display at Leicester's Franciscan friary, naked except for a piece of cheap black cloth preserving its modesty, before a perfunctory burial – 'like a dog in a ditch', some said.[18] In the first flush of victory, the myths were already being written. 'In the year 1485 on the 22nd day of August', ran one poem, 'the tusks of the Boar were blunted and the red rose, the avenger of the white, shines on us.'[19]

The latest contender in the cycle of violence to be raised up, Henry was now faced with a profound challenge. He had to stop the wheel while he was at its highest point, to keep himself far above the private quarrels and vendettas of nobles, the world from which he had emerged. He had to create a 'new foundation of his crown', one which merged his family's name indistinguishably with the idea of royal authority. Through its power, its magnificence and its justice, his rule would need to ensure that, of all the proliferation of heraldic devices and badges that indicated which lord you followed and where your affinities lay, the red rose commanded instant loyalty and the 'dread' inspired by a sovereign lord who ruled indifferently over all.[20] If he looked, behaved and ruled like a king, perhaps the exhausted, traumatized country of England would come to believe he was one.

At Henry's coronation in 'triumph and glory' at Westminster Abbey on 30 October 1485, Lady Margaret, reunited with the son she had not seen for fourteen years, 'wept marvellously'.[21] Her tears suggested not joy, but apprehension. With a precarious claim to the throne, no large family clan and little hereditary land of his own, virtually no experience of government and heavily reliant on the doubtful allegiances of a group of Yorkists whose loyalties lay with the princess he now courted, there was little to suggest that Henry's reign would last long, or that civil conflict would not simply mutate again. But if Henry knew little of government, his formative years had brought experience of another kind. As he set about creating a new dynasty, Henry would be haunted by the spectres of civil war, real and imagined. They would stay with him all his life and they would define his reign.

PART ONE

Blood and Roses

'Blessed be god, the king the queen and all our sweet children
be in good health.'

Lady Margaret Beaufort, April 1497

'If the King should propose to change any old established rule,
it would seem to every Englishman as if his life were taken
away from him – but I think that the present King Henry will
do away with a great many, should he live ten years longer.'

Venetian ambassador, c. 1500

I

Not a Drop of Doubtful Royal Blood

In early September 1497, two Italian ambassadors left London and, accompanied by a group of English dignitaries and a heavily armed escort in the quartered white-and-green Tudor livery, headed west along the Thames Valley and into Oxfordshire. One was the secretary of the duke of Milan Ludovico Sforza, the other a special envoy from the republic of Venice. The previous June, both men had set out from Italy on the long journey north. Crossing the Alps into the lands of Maximilian, the Holy Roman Emperor, they made their ways along the broad expanse of the Rhine – the river's toll-booths clotted with mercantile traffic and the roads, with their laden mule-trains, just as bad – through the rich trading centres of Speyer and Cologne and west, into the broad river delta of the Low Countries, northern Europe's financial and commercial heart, the patchwork territories ruled over by Maximilian's young, precocious son, Archduke Philip of Burgundy.[1] Meeting in the teeming port-city of Antwerp, the ambassadors swapped notes.

Three years previously, the duke of Milan had allied himself with Charles VIII of France, hoping to harness the might of Europe's most powerful country in the warring that had re-erupted between Italy's city-states. As contemporaries put it, 'he turned a lion loose in his house to catch a mouse'. Aiming to conquer the Spanish-ruled kingdom of Naples, the French army swept down the peninsula, igniting terror, pestilence – a ghastly new venereal disease called syphilis – and revolution. Desperate to halt France's seemingly inexorable advance, Italian states and European powers had overcome their mutual antagonism to form a coalition, a Holy League brokered by the pope,

Alexander VI. The English king Henry VII's inclusion in the coalition was critical to its success, for with its own claims to the French crown, England could menace France's exposed northern border from across the Channel. A dutiful son of the church, Henry had joined the League and France had indeed retreated. But in the face of exhortations to go further, Henry was resolute. He had invaded France once already, five years previously, and the consequences had been disastrous. He was not about to do so again.

The other members of the Holy League were not to be put off so easily. Together with a stream of other European diplomats beating a petitioning path to the English king's door were Sforza's secretary, Raimondo da Soncino, and the Venetian envoy Andrea Trevisano.[2] They had other business, too. As one of England's biggest trading partners, Venice sent galleys packed with wines, spices, silks and other commodities, carrying away English wool and cloth for processing and selling in its vast textile industry in return. It was keen to cement economic and political relations with this English king who, it was rumoured, was enormously rich. He was also, they had heard, in trouble. As all Europe knew, Henry had had his problems. In recent years, his reign had been menaced by a pretender to the throne, a ghost of the English civil wars, who was still at large.

On 22 July, Soncino and Trevisano reached the Flemish city of Bruges. There, amid its canals, markets and counting-houses, they stopped and waited.[3]

The onward journey looked precarious. Their road west to the English enclave of Calais lay through the militarized borderlands of Flanders, over which France and Burgundy had struggled for decades. As it periodically tended to be, the road was closed and reports flooded in of roaming gangs of Frenchmen, plundering and looting.

The ambassadors had also been receiving regular updates from England, dispatches sent via the letter-bags couriered from the London branches of Italian merchant-banks back to their continental headquarters. In these dispatches, rumour and counter-rumour mingled. That June, there had been an uprising against Henry VII. Twenty thousand men had marched the length of the country – from the north, perhaps, or the far southwest – on London, demanding the surrender of the king and his close counsellors, and the king had been beaten and had fled. Then again, a great battle had been fought out-side the city, and the king had won. Meanwhile, there was war in the north. The king of Scotland had invaded England – or perhaps it was Henry doing the invading, his armies advancing in the other direction. Throughout the dispatches, one name was mentioned over and over again: that of Richard duke of York, the 'White Rose' who, many claimed, was the younger of the two princes in the Tower, the sons of the Yorkist king Edward IV, otherwise missing, presumed dead. 'Some say', one dispatch hedged, that the duke of York was in England, 'but no one knew for sure'. One thing alone was certain, it continued. Catastrophe would soon befall England.[4]

By early August Soncino and Trevisano had made it to Calais, accompanied by a detachment of English soldiers. There they waited for the unseasonal storms to abate and for the commander of Calais to check the coast was clear of pirates, before making the short jour-ney across the English Channel. At Dover, a royal reception awaited them: progressing through Kent, they entered London accompanied by two senior officials sent by King Henry himself, and a troop of two hundred horsemen. Days later, summoned by the king, they jour-neyed to Oxford, where they overnighted in the students' colleges; then, the following morning, they made the short journey to the royal manor of Woodstock, where the king's household was in residence for the summer.[5]

Approaching the house across rolling parkland well stocked with game, the ambassadors were escorted through gatehouses freshly painted with red roses, portcullises, greyhounds and rougedragons, the heraldic devices of Henry VII's dynasty. Dismounting, they were led deep into the house, through a succession of galleries and richly decor-ated apartments, to a 'small chamber'. At the far end of this room, hung with exquisite tapestry, were a cluster of advisers in their robes of estate – silks and satins of crimson and purple, trimmed with fur and ermine – among them leading members of the nobility, including six bishops, 'lords spiritual'. In their midst stood the king.

What the ambassadors noted first was his stillness, standing, finger-tips resting lightly on the gilt chair beside him. As they approached, bowing and scraping, the details came into focus. Spare, high-cheek-boned, with dark hair faintly greying around the temples, Henry VII was dressed in a long violet, gold-lined cloak and, around his neck, a collar comprising four rows of 'great pearls' and many other jewels. On his head he wore a black felt cap studded with a pear-shaped pearl which, said Soncino fascinatedly, 'seemed to me something most rich'. As the ambassadors delivered their diplomatic orations, carefully turned in the most fashionable Ciceronian Latin, the king's eyes, small, blue and penetrating, remained fixed on them.[6]

Only when they had finished did Henry stir. Turning aside to a small group of counsellors, he conferred with them intently. A man then stepped forward to give a Latin speech in reply: the king's wizened éminence grise, instantly recognizable in his scarlet robes – the chancellor and archbishop of Canterbury, Cardinal John Morton. Also by the king's side was Prince Arthur, his first-born son and heir. Soncino studied him keenly: this was the boy in whom the future of the English dynasty lay and who was due to marry Catherine, daughter of the Spanish monarchs Ferdinand and Isabella – a sweetener, they hoped, which would induce Henry to ally with them in war against France. The betrothal ceremony, the heart of a new Anglo-Spanish treaty, had been performed only the previous month. With Catherine, aged twelve, still in Spain, the corpulent Spanish ambassador Rodrigo de Puebla had stood in for her. Prince Arthur himself was a year younger but, thought Soncino, tall for his age and of 'singular beauty and grace'. While his father spoke little, the prince was eloquent, 'very ready' in speaking Latin in front of the assembled dignitaries – 'a distinguished son-in-law' for the Catholic monarchs, Soncino opined.[7]

Following the exchange of orations and diplomatic compliments, the ambassadors kissed the hands of Henry and the prince. After dining in state – with 'four lords', said Trevisano, impressed – they were led further into the house, to a smaller, more private room for a confidential chat with the king, servants hovering discreetly in the background. The king talked with deliberation in clear, fluent French, fully in control. As the conversation progressed, the ambassadors, who had come to brief him on Italian affairs, were astonished. He seemed to know all the news even before they had told him: indeed, Soncino reported to his master Sforza that Henry spoke about him as if with the knowledge of an old, familiar friend – except that the two had never met. The ambassadors concurred that the king was wise, 'gracious' and 'grave' with a 'wonderful presence', everything a king should be. 'He evidently has', Soncino concluded, 'a most quiet spirit.'

Before their departure, the ambassadors had time to pay their respects to the queen, Elizabeth. They found her in a small hall, surrounded by ladies and gentlewomen, dressed in cloth-of-gold that offset her mass of strawberry-blonde hair – 'a handsome woman', Trevisano remarked. At her side were the king's mother Lady Margaret Beaufort, a diminutive, sharp-eyed presence, and a six-year-old boy. That Henry and Elizabeth's second son merited barely a footnote in the ambassadors' dispatches was hardly surprising. After all, they could hardly have foreseen the events that would eventually lead him to the English throne.

The Italians were whisked away back to Oxford, where they were 'lavishly entertained' at the king's personal command, and then to London, to await the court's return later that autumn. The whole visit had gone smoothly, and the ambassadors had been flattered, charmed and impressed. The only sign that anything was untoward was the uncharacteristic brevity of their visit to Woodstock.

In fact, the rumours heard by the ambassadors had been true. Fourteen ninety-seven was proving a terrible year for Henry VII. Two months before, thousands of Cornishmen, in protest against swingeing taxation and corrupt officialdom, had swarmed through southern England and had almost reached London's gates, before being defeated at Blackheath. Now, Henry was preparing for what he hoped would be the endgame to another, far more protracted episode. Massing in the grounds at Woodstock, out of sight of the ambassadors' diplomatic visit, were thousands of troops, men and materiel. Throughout his summer hunting and hawking, Henry had been waiting for this spectre to make its rumoured appearance, and indeed, a week after the ambassadors had returned to London, news arrived from the far southwest. A ship bearing the youth who claimed to be Richard duke of York had landed in Cornwall, and he was now marching towards Henry to claim his throne. It was twelve years, almost to the day, since

Henry had won his kingdom, and he had barely had a moment's peace.[8]

○

At Westminster in autumn 1485, the new regime was moving in. An army of craftsmen set about carving and painting its badges and arms on walls and roofs, moulding them on ceilings and glazing scutcheons in windows. In London, Lady Margaret renovated the sprawling Thamesside house of Coldharbour, which her son had presented to her. In it, she installed the eighteen-year-old Elizabeth of York, the daughter of Edward IV and Elizabeth Woodville, whose impending marriage to Henry lay at the heart of England's new political settlement. As Henry courted his future wife – chaperoned by her future mother-in-law – he set about creating his government.[9]

Henry was determined to do things by the book. He would follow rigidly the 'due course and order of his laws', which would allow him to impose his authority swiftly and decisively, to snuff out potential trouble before it could snowball into civil conflict; and also to define and gather the 'rights and revenues' due him, in order to avoid the disaster of having to levy taxes in peacetime. He would reach for the symbols of his royal authority, from proclamations, statutes and newly minted coinage, to the pope's sanction and blessing of his reign, and the papal anathemas that rained down on his enemies. And he would maintain a magnificent household.

The royal household was the regime in microcosm, its beating heart. Below stairs it functioned unseen, a well-oiled machine. Above stairs, awe-inspiring in its spectacular, minutely ordered opulence, was its public face: the hall, and the chamber, with its procession of lobbies, antechambers, closets and galleries. The members of the household were the king's men, their loyalties to him overriding any knotty affinities to noblemen. That, at least, was the theory. During Henry VI's disastrous reign, people had seen in his dysfunctional, spendthrift, faction-riven household all that was rotten about his rule. But the Yorkists had put their house in order and Henry was determined to do the same, while adding some touches of his own. One of his first acts was to create a new French-style security force, three hundred strong: the yeomen of the guard.

At the core of his government, Henry installed his small band of loyalists, those who had proved themselves in exile, from lawyer-clergymen like the experienced Morton and the narrow-eyed Richard Fox – a visiting scholar at the University of Paris when he met Henry, who instantly saw something in him – to the veteran Lancastrian military commander John de Vere, earl of Oxford. But Henry could not rely solely on partisan political loyalties: that way disaster lay, as Richard III's rule had shown. Henry's 'new foundation' had to accommodate everybody: his Stanley relations, whose last-minute arrival at Bosworth had been crucial; those of Richard's men prepared to accept pardons; and the Woodville Yorkists. These last presented a particular problem for Henry. As their support for him rested on their loyalties to his wife-to-be – who, as Edward IV's daughter, had her own claim to the throne – their backing contained a potential threat. If Henry's claim depended on that of his wife, he could effectively be held to ransom. And he had no intention of letting that happen.

That November at Westminster, Henry's first parliament held all these strands in delicate balance. He had extended pardons to all prepared to acknowledge his rule and, at his coronation the previous month, had sworn the usual oaths to be a just king. Now, in parliament, Henry backdated his reign to the day before Bosworth. At a stroke, he had rewritten history: when the battle was fought, Henry was the king and Richard III the usurper; all those who had backed Richard were by definition traitors. If this sent a palpable tremor of unease through the commons, so too did Henry's assertion of his own claim to the throne – in which he sidestepped the delicate issues of blood and lineage and made no mention of the right of his future wife. Woodville supporters found the whole thing overcooked. Rather than citing 'many titles' in support of his claim, wrote one, surely Henry could simply find whatever 'appeared to be missing' – rather a lot, was the implication – in the person of Elizabeth of York, whom the commons petitioned him to marry.[10] Having confirmed the illegitimacy of Richard's reign, however unconvincingly, Henry married Elizabeth the following January. Days after the wedding, 'great enjoyment filled the queen'. She had fallen pregnant.[11]

Henry, it seems, always knew the child would be a son. Invoking the mythical British king from whom both Lancaster and York had liked to trace their descent – the prophet Merlin, no less, had described King Arthur as the fruit of the union of a red king and a white queen – Henry would call his son Arthur, and he would be born in Winchester, the legendary seat of Camelot.[12] In Winchester Castle, at 1 a.m. on 20 September 1486, a squally, windswept night, Elizabeth gave birth. Her son was a month premature – but he was healthy. A *Te Deum* was sung, bonfires were lit in the streets, and yeomen of the crown galloped hard into the provinces with printed proclamations to be read aloud and affixed to church doors up and down the country.

The baby Arthur was the new dynasty incorporated. 'Joyed may we be', minstrels sang, 'Our prince to see, and roses three': red for Lancaster, white for York, and a new rose in which the two colours were intermingled, a rose both red and white.[13]

As the dynasty took its first, uncertain steps, conspiracy had already seeded itself. The signs of instability had come soon after Henry's arrival in London. That September, the sweating sickness, a strange and virulent disease causing 'pain as never was suffered before' – and brought, it was widely believed, by the new king's army – had decimated the city's population. Rumour and ill portents were rife. As one correspondent, writing to his master from court in the wake of Henry's first parliament, noted anxiously, there was 'much running among the lords, but no-one knows what it is. It is said that all is not well among them.'[14] In spring 1486, news came from the heartlands of the old king's support in the north – 'whence all evil spreads', noted a Woodvillite chronicler with a southerner's mixture of contempt and fear – and of noble retinues assembling and arming. But as the caravan of the royal household progressed north, the rebels melted away in the face of overwhelming royal force. It was to be in the following year that Richard III's loyalists found their figurehead.[15]

John de la Pole, earl of Lincoln, was a Plantagenet. His mother was sister to both Edward IV and Richard III, and Richard had apparently named him his heir – and then Bosworth happened. Lincoln remained unreconciled to the new regime. Early in 1487, he fled to the Low Countries, to the Flemish town of Malines and the court of his aunt, Margaret of York, duchess of Burgundy. A focus for disaffected Ricardians, Margaret hated Henry and she detested the new political settlement. The house of York, she felt, could only be restored through a 'male remnant'.

While Lincoln's own claim to the throne was reasonable, he and Margaret knew that the claim of another living Yorkist was better still. In the weeks after Bosworth, Henry's agents had arrested another nephew of Edward IV and immured him in the Tower of London. The last surviving Plantagenet prince descended in the male line, Edward earl of Warwick was a touchstone for Yorkist affections – people still provocatively wore his badge of the bear and ragged staff – and Lincoln understood the galvanizing effect of Warwick's presence at the head of any uprising. Warwick, however, was twelve years old, simple-minded, and inaccessible. Unable to get his hands on him, Lincoln conjured up another Warwick, grooming another young boy to impersonate him.[16]

With an army of German mercenaries, Lincoln sailed to Ireland, which remained a hotbed of Yorkist support, to raise more aid. There, the boy was paraded as the earl of Warwick, newly escaped from the Tower; on 24 May, Whit Sunday, he was crowned king of England in Dublin Cathedral. The following month, Lincoln's invasion force crossed the Irish Sea and landed on the Cumbrian coast, advancing south into the midlands, the child at its head. As England baked under a hot sun, Henry's disciplined, battle-hardened retinues confronted the rebels outside the Nottinghamshire village of East Stoke. Outnumbered and disordered, Lincoln's troops were massacred and Lincoln himself killed, to Henry's frustration. With Lincoln alive, Henry felt, he would have been able to get 'the bottom of his danger', the root of the conspiracy.[17] The young boy, though, was found. He was no earl of Warwick, said Henry's agents, but a fake: the son of an Oxford joiner who went by the name of Lambert Simnel. After the battle, Henry set him to work in an occupation befitting his menial status, as a spit-turner in the royal kitchens.

The battle of Stoke marked an end, of sorts. With the death of Lincoln, a genuine Yorkist contender for the throne, and a decisive victory for Henry, it seemed to draw a line under the resistance of

Richard III's supporters. But old loyalties simmered, and the after-shocks of rebellion rippled on.

◈

In late 1491, a Breton merchant-ship had docked at the southern Irish port of Cork. Among the crew that spilled onto the quayside was a handsome, blond, sixteen-year-old boy dressed, rather incongruously for a ship's hand, in rich silks. It was here, so his confession later had it, that Perkin Warbeck, son of a boatman from the Flemish city of Tournai, was stopped by a group of renegade Yorkists who had returned to southern Ireland to try to revive the plot around the earl of Warwick. They were backed by the French king Charles VIII, who was desperate for a lever to use against an increasingly aggressive Henry – just as some six years previously he had made a show of backing Henry against Richard III. But in Warbeck, who they discovered swanning through the streets of Cork in his borrowed finery, the conspirators found something else altogether. Accosting him, they flattered him and promised to make him a Yorkist prince.

Warbeck later described how the men had tried out a number of identities on him: the earl of Warwick – Lambert Simnel, all over again – and then an illegitimate son of Richard III. Discarding both ideas, they then struck gold. They would groom him to become another kind of Yorkist: Richard duke of York, the second son of Edward IV, the younger of the princes whose disappearance into the Tower had transformed Henry's own prospects from that of fugitive into claimant to the throne.[18]

The reappearance, or re-creation, of Richard duke of York was a masterstroke. The bodies of the princes had never been found. While Henry could take the earl of Warwick out of the Tower and parade him through the streets of London – the same reason that he kept Simnel to hand in the royal kitchens – he could hardly do the same with Edward IV's young sons. Provided he looked and behaved like him, Richard duke of York's second coming could hardly be denied. Turning the political clock back to April 1483, to a time before Richard III's usurpation, it took a wrecking ball to the political settlement that Henry and Elizabeth's marriage represented.

Not only would Richard duke of York be indisputably heir to the throne, but he would also have an undeniable claim on the loyalty of all those who had subsequently transferred their allegiance to his oldest sister Elizabeth and had accepted Henry's rule. Now, they would look again at their genealogical charts and their pedigree rolls, and their loyalties would be torn. The entwined red-and-white roses would be ripped apart. The phantom duke of York's existence, the simple 'what if?', attacked the foundations of everything that Henry was trying to build.

But the full impact of Warbeck, who after his grooming in Ireland had been carried off to the French court, took some time to emerge. In mid-1492, French intelligence officials, quizzing merchants from England on the impact of the 'White Rose', were disappointed at English indifference. Then, that autumn, Henry invaded France.

As he looked outward to Europe, and to the fluctuating dynastic power politics in which as an exile he had once been helplessly thrown about, Henry had followed with concern France's mounting aggression in the constant struggles for domination of the northern European coast. He had been unable to prevent it from swallowing up his former ally, the duchy of Brittany. But he had slowly built an understanding with France's perennial enemy on its eastern border, the tricksy Habsburg king, Maximilian.[19]

War was something the nobility expected of monarchs, and war with France was a rite of passage for English kings who were expected to lay claim to the kingdom they felt was theirs by right.[20] But Henry's abortive expedition of 1492 was a strange episode. The biggest invasion force of the century, involving fifteen thousand troops and seven hundred ships, was assembled, its mobilization had taken much of the year. By the time his armies had crossed the English Channel, however, the campaigning season was all but over. Citing all manner of excuses, from fickle allies – which, given Maximilian's track record, was hardly unreasonable – to their surprise at Boulogne's bristling fortifications, Henry and his counsellors quickly sealed a peace treaty with Charles VIII, who agreed to pay a massive annual pension of 50,000 French crowns. But if Henry felt he had won the peace, he was deceiving himself.

To the English soldiers that trudged back home with barely a shot fired, and then sat grumbling in taverns throughout the country, and to the commons, who continued to pay extortionate taxes for a non-existent campaign, the settlement did not feel remotely honourable. Maximilian, who had been cut out of the Anglo-French treaty and was 'left sitting between two chairs', as one of his commanders put it, was apoplectic with humiliated rage. Little did Henry realize, but Maximilian's means of revenge – and, he hoped, the possibility of placing a rather more compliant English king on the throne – was already at hand.[21]

In the new Anglo-French détente, Warbeck, fearing extradition to England, had fled to Malines in a curious mirror-image of Henry's own flight from Brittany to France. He had been well groomed in his role – well enough, at any rate, for the childless Margaret of Burgundy, desperate for revenge against Henry VII, to accept it wholeheartedly: 'I believed it immediately', she wrote to Isabella of Castile. Maximilian, who was close to the dowager-duchess, was equally enthusiastic. Early in 1493, news of the Yorkist pretender was carried 'blazing and thundering' into England by the merchant ships that coasted around the entrepôts of the Low Countries, and spread like a cancer.

Henry scrambled to make sense of the threat. It was, he stated, beyond all logic, 'completely absurd', 'the height of madness' that people should believe that this 'feigned lad' was who he said he was. Diplomatic efforts with Burgundy and Maximilian were stepped up in order to secure the pretender's extradition, but without success. Relations between England and the Low Countries deteriorated. Henry imposed economic sanctions, refusing to let English merchants trade with Flanders; Maximilian retaliated in kind. In Bruges, the headquarters of the English 'nation' of resident merchants was boarded up; in London, warehouses were piled high with wool and cloth ready for export, gathering dust. Riots broke out; enclaves of foreign merchants, their ships not subject to the embargo, were attacked. Political and economic discontent mingled, and rumour abounded.

Warbeck, it was widely believed, was about to invade. Cells of his supporters were scattered throughout the country. On the road, those who had good reason to travel – merchants of all kinds, pedlars, friars, musicians and performers journeying from town to town and house to house – were suspected of linking up with them, 'artfully and subtly'. There were reported plots to assassinate Henry and his family, including a plan to daub the doorframes and handles of the royal household with a lethal poison. Flybills detailing 'seditions and treacheries and uprisings' were passed from hand to hand. In London, there were co-ordinated flypostings urging the city to revolt; overnight, placards would appear fixed to church doors, including those of St Paul's itself.[22]

Meanwhile, Warbeck's profile continued to grow. In the summer of 1494, Maximilian's father, the Holy Roman Emperor Frederick, died. At his funeral in Vienna Cathedral, in front of the representatives of Europe's foremost dynasties, Warbeck was paraded as the king of England and then brought back through the cities of the Low Countries on a triumphal progress alongside Maximilian's teenage son and heir, Archduke Philip of Burgundy. Henry desperately needed another focus for English loyalties, one which would allow him to take back the title of duke of York and enfold the dangerous Yorkist sentiments within the narrative of his own emerging dynasty. He found this figure in his three-year-old second son, to whom he had given the name of the great kings of Lancaster and his own.

Prince Henry was born on 28 June 1491 at Queen Elizabeth's favourite house of Greenwich, which dominated the expanse of the Thames as it opened out towards the estuary. The family had been fortunate in a succession of healthy births and Henry was their third child, after his sister Margaret. Custom dictated that while the heir was brought up in his father's world, groomed for kingship, the remaining royal children – male and female – were entrusted to the care of their mother. At Greenwich, Elizabeth's household servants organized Prince Henry's baptism in the nearby church of the Friars Observant. Her wardrobers furnished the tapestries that swathed the walls and floors, built a tiered wooden stage, hung it with fine textiles – cloth-of-gold, damask, cypress linens – and placed on it the solid silver font brought from Canterbury Cathedral for the occasion. In front of an audience of dignitaries crammed into the church, the lord privy seal Richard Fox, now bishop of Exeter, immersed the baby boy three times then, as trumpets blared out and torchbearers lit their tapers, swathed him in a mantle of ermine-trimmed cloth-of-gold.[23] With his cluster of wet-nurses and cradle-rockers, the infant prince was moved into the nearby manor house of Eltham. There he spent his childhood with his sister Margaret and the younger siblings, Mary and the short-lived Elizabeth, who would join them soon after.

But by autumn 1494, the three-year-old prince had a new role to play: that of a real, palpable duke of York, in the face of Warbeck's nebulous threat. On 29 October, he rode – unaided, to the astonishment of onlookers – through London's teeming streets to Westminster. The following day, in Westminster Hall, his father dubbed him knight, then lifted him up proudly and 'set him upon the table', in full view of the assembled court. On All Hallows' Day, 1 November, Prince Henry was created duke of York. The heavy formality of his investiture with his symbols of office, cap, sword, rod and coronet, was followed by a celebratory mass in the adjoining chapel of St Stephen's, taken by Archbishop Morton surrounded by eight mitred bishops, to the soaring accompaniment of the Chapel Royal choir. Next came the procession in state in the wavering torchlight, a profusion of purple and crimson silks, jewelled collars, cloth-of-gold. Henry VII, in his robes of estate, was imperious; his small son, tired, had to be carried for much of the time. On the first day of the celebratory jousts that followed, combatants wore the regime's green and white; on the second, they wore blue and tawny, for the young new duke of York.[24]

Amid the feasting and tourneying, Henry had been closing in on Warbeck's English support. His tireless monitoring of networks of retainers – embedding spies in suspects' households, interviewing their servants and the chaplains and confessors to whom they opened their souls – had led him, to his horror, back into the heart of the royal household itself. At the centre of the conspiracy were his two most powerful household officials, the head of the 'below stairs', his lord steward Lord Fitzwalter, and, most disturbingly of all, his lord chamberlain, the man who controlled access to the chamber, the public and private apartments, Sir William Stanley.[25]

Brother to Lady Margaret Beaufort's husband Lord Stanley, Sir William and his men had turned the tide for Henry at Bosworth. But he was a former loyalist of Edward IV and for him, as for so many, questions of allegiance and self-interest mingled. Moreover, despite the recognition he had received under Henry, Sir William had never felt entirely settled in his favour. For his own part, Henry was all too aware of the Stanleys' history of changing sides, while their family retinues, who provided his military backbone, tended to arrive late to the party – as indeed they had done at Bosworth and Stoke. When Sir William was arrested and brought before the king in the first days of 1495, Henry's display of wounded astonishment masked the fact that, as both men knew, he had been watching Stanley's retainers for well over a year. Stanley was tried and beheaded. When Henry's men arrived to take possession of his castle of Holt, among the stuff they inventoried was a Yorkist livery collar studded with white roses and sunbursts, and £10,000 in cash: enough to bankroll an army.[26]

As the Stanley plot unfolded, the royal household became more rigorously controlled. Officials carrying lists of servants receiving 'bouge of court' – wages and board – carried out identity checks; at night, heavily armed yeomen paced the household's galleries and chambers with extra vigilance. The king, hedged about by security, became more distant, more remote. People were increasingly afraid to talk openly, looking over their shoulders, lowering their voices. Henry's relationship with his leading subjects began to change.

Warbeck was still at large. The next years saw him flitting around England's borders, moth-like, never settling. In June 1495, his invasion force, backed by Maximilian, finally materialized off the coast of east Kent. Henry's men were waiting, hidden in the sand dunes of Deal Beach, and an advance party of Warbeck's soldiers, lured ashore, were massacred in the shallows. But the pretender himself stayed on board ship and Henry's grasp closed around thin air.[27]

For several months his trail went cold. Neither his sponsors nor Henry, whose ships ceaselessly patrolled the western reaches of the Channel and the Irish Sea, knew of his whereabouts. Then, late in the year, he resurfaced at the court of James IV of Scotland. At twenty-two, a year older than Warbeck, James was ambitious and adventurous, desperate to impose himself and his nation on the European stage – and he had plans for the pretender. Lavishing on him attention, gifts and a wife – Katherine Gordon, the beautiful young daughter of a Scottish nobleman, whom Warbeck married with all the splendour of a royal wedding – James set him up as the king of England and, in September 1496, the men moved southwards at the head of an army, crossing the border together. But the incursion into England was neither the triumphal progress of a returning Yorkist prince nor a Scottish invasion – though to English eyes, the burning, plundering and pillaging made it look suspiciously like the latter. Encountering resolute resistance, it petered out after six days. Henry, however, was on the warpath. His prolonged and excessive response would result in the biggest crisis of his reign to date.

The following month, his council started drawing up meticulous plans for a military offensive and authorized a loan of £120,000, to be repaid by general taxation, a decision ratified by an anxious parliament.[28] Meanwhile, border garrisons were bolstered and martial law declared, arms dumps overhauled and, in the fertile recruiting grounds of Flanders, Henry's agents indentured battalions of Swiss and German mercenaries. Out at the firing ranges of Mile End, east of London, expert Dutch gunners put the latest European artillery and handguns through their paces. In the late spring of 1497 columns of men, horses, carts and munitions streamed north towards the Scottish border. All the while, Henry's tax collectors continued to work zealously, in the face of widespread resentment, and nowhere more so than in the deep southwest of England in the small Cornish parish of St Keverne, where Michael Joseph – known locally as An Gof, the Blacksmith – rounded on one of the king's tax collectors, accusing him of corruption and refusing to pay.

Headed by An Gof and Thomas Flamank, a local lawyer, rebellion exploded out of Cornwall, just as retinues loyal to Henry were heading north. Thousands strong, the insurgents moved through southern England with frightening speed. London, terrified by reports of the ravaging Cornishmen, bolstered its defences; Queen Elizabeth, Lady Margaret and the royal children were moved into the Tower. Skirting the city to the southeast, the rebels made their camp at Blackheath, the time-honoured ground of popular rebellion, and prepared for a final assault. The whole kingdom was in chaos, reported one ambassador: if the king had lost, he would have been 'finished off and beheaded'.[29]

But London clung on. Royal troops frantically recalled from their northern deployment arrived. Torn between confrontation and negotiation the rebels hesitated, and their cause was lost. An Gof and Flamank were hanged, drawn and quartered. Their heads, boiled and tarred, were jammed on spikes on London Bridge; their body parts were dismembered, some nailed to the city gates, others sent southwest to be displayed in towns of dubious loyalty.[30]

That summer, James and Warbeck planned another assault. This time, Warbeck would sail from Scotland to the southwest of England to capitalize on inflamed Cornish resentments; James, meanwhile, would co-ordinate his attack with another cross-border invasion. But James's military campaign, menaced by an English army sent north to confront him, hit the buffers. As Soncino and Trevisano arrived at Woodstock, the Scots and English diplomats were seated round the negotiating table. Warbeck was on his own.

In the end, it was no contest. Although sympathies still lingered and Warbeck, amassing Cornish support, swept out of the peninsula, Henry's vastly superior forces were prepared. Outside Taunton, the pretender's army scattered, and he fled to sanctuary at Beaulieu on the south coast, from where he was extracted. Finally, Henry had the 'feigned lad' in his hands. But while Warbeck had failed to bring down the dynasty, he had, inadvertently, succeeded in transforming its nature.

That autumn, the Italian ambassadors settled into a comfortable life in London. In a stream of confidential dispatches, they painted a picture of a kingdom that was calm and tranquil. Henry, Soncino wrote, had been extraordinarily merciful. His dealings with Warbeck bespoke a regal confidence. Rather than lock him up, Henry put the pretender on display at court, a curio, a plaything for people to marvel and point at, and make fun of: *levissimus*, the least of men.[31]

Further acquaintance with the king and his court only impressed the visitors more. He was surrounded by finely dressed nobles and intellectual, politically sophisticated advisers whose knowledge of foreign affairs was so impressive that, Soncino wrote, 'I fancy myself in Rome'. Henry cultivated Italian merchant-bankers – the Florentines, in particular, 'never stop giving the king advices' – and loved to employ foreigners, from high-ranking Italian diplomats and Dutch craftsmen to the French and Breton servants who hovered around him, much to the 'diabolical' envy of the English.[32] Then there was the other talking-point that autumn, besides Warbeck. Sailing west into uncharted seas with a group of Bristol merchants, the Venetian fugitive-adventurer Zoane Caboto, John Cabot, had returned to England with reports of a New Found Land, a discovery that, as Henry hoped – and as the Spanish feared, writing agitated dispatches to Columbus himself about the arrival in London of *'uno como Colon'* – would rival recent Spanish discoveries of a New World. At court, Cabot rustled about in silks, armed with rolls of maps, followed by a trail of admirers who 'run after him like mad'. Henry had plans for Cabot. He would fund a fleet of ships and pack them with 'all the malefactors' in English prisons. Then, they would cross the Atlantic and form a colony.[33]

Money seemed no object to Henry. His Thameside houses, renovated in the latest Burgundian fashions, were visions in red brick, imported glazing and gleaming cupolas; inside, their chambers and galleries were well ordered and opulent. He knew how to entertain 'magnificently', and Soncino took full advantage: 'I put in three hours at table twice a day for the love of your excellency', he wrote to Sforza. But as he grew acquainted with the English court, his view of the king began to change: still 'most wise', but 'suspicious of everything'. Yes, he was rich, but he had built up an 'immense treasure' because 'he has no one he can trust, except his paid men at arms'. Beneath the poised regality was not the 'quiet spirit' that Soncino had originally divined.[34] To those foreign observers who bothered to raise their heads from the loaded plates in front of them and look behind the ostentatious wealth and the carefully ordered ceremonial, there seemed something distinctly odd in the state of Henry VII's England.

One such was Pedro de Ayala. Previously the Spanish envoy to Scotland, he had arrived at the English court in late 1497, as Anglo-Scottish relations had begun to thaw. Henry, he wrote, liked to give the impression of being very rich, but he was not as rich as he said he was. He liked to be much spoken of, 'highly appreciated by the whole world', and to be thought of as a 'great man' – although in de Ayala's opinion he wasn't, because his love of money was 'too great'. People didn't love him, either: they feared him. Henry's government, too, appeared strange. It was neither one thing nor the other, a kind of halfway house. He was 'subject to his council', but he had 'already shaken off some, and got rid of some part of this subjection'. His rule was, de Ayala thought, remarkably hands-on. When not in public, indulging his passions of hunting and hawking or in discussions with his counsellors, he was closeted away, 'writing the accounts of his expenses with his own hand'. Searching for a way to sum up what he found, he wrote that Henry wanted to govern 'in the French fashion' – but that he could not. De Ayala had expressed it imperfectly, but he was right. Henry was not playing by the rules people expected; or, rather, he was trying to change them to suit himself.[35]

Increasingly private and distant, Henry's rule was taking on his own character. At the centre of the glittering carapace of the royal household lay an institutional black hole: a complex of private apartments known as the 'secret' or privy chamber, which was separated from the presence chamber, where the king's throne stood under its cloth of estate, by a heavily guarded door. Earlier in the decade, when Henry discovered that conspiracy had penetrated to the core of the household, the privy chamber's functioning had changed. Previously, its workings had been laid out as part of the meticulous 'ordinances' or protocols that ordered the wider household, and its servants had shuttled easily between the public and private worlds. But from 1494, all reference to the privy chamber was eradicated from official directives. Written rules no longer governed it. Its servants were specified simply as men who would 'best content the king'. Serving his meals, bathing him, strewing fresh rushes on the floor, making the royal bed and rolling on it to check there was 'none untruth therein', these most select of personal servants, answerable directly and only to the king, handled his personal expenses and undertook confidential missions. They were also Henry's first line of security, discreet, watchful, ever present.[36] Their relationship with the king was encapsulated by the secret chamber's head, an imperturbable west-countryman named Hugh Denys. As 'groom of the stool', Denys looked after the king's commode, presiding over him while he sat. As close to the king as he could possibly be, his position gave him an unparalleled, intimate perspective on the realities of power.[37]

From his privy chamber, Henry presided over another change, one that was entirely characteristic of the way he had started to govern. Traditionally, the chamber treasury controlled the king's private wealth – which was, more or less, income from his lands. But Henry was obsessed with having quantities of ready cash to bolster the regime's security and authority. During the emergencies of the 1490s, the chamber treasury's remit had started to creep inexorably into the realm of public finance and the exchequer offices, channelling and rerouting public income – taxation and customs – into the king's own coffers. All of this was facilitated by a coterie of servants and counsellors that, as Perkin Warbeck had pointed out in a proclamation that accompanied his invasion, were not noblemen but 'caitiffs and villains of simple birth', and who, as de Ayala said, had a 'wonderful dexterity in getting other people's money'.[38]

Accusations of low-born, venal administrators clustering round the king were as old as the hills; besides which, Warbeck had particular reasons for fuelling nobles' grudges and resentments against the king. Henry certainly needed noblemen and their retinues, and he counted them among his trusted advisers: men like the earl of Oxford, Thomas Howard, earl of Surrey, and his new chamberlain Giles lord Daubeney. But Warbeck did have a point. Traditionally, the 'might of the land' rested in the 'great lords', and then the king's officers. But Henry's natural suspicion of great lords, intensified by the events of the 1490s, had changed all this. In his regime, as people were discovering to their bewilderment, power and status were not the same thing at all.

As everybody from Soncino to Warbeck discerned, Henry was surrounded by a small circle of men: the likes of Cardinal-chancellor Morton and Richard Fox, now bishop of Durham; the king's bruising chief financial administrator Sir Reynold Bray, and Sir Thomas Lovell, the square-jawed treasurer of the king's household.[39] These were men whose wealth and power derived entirely from their service and loyalty to Henry. So too did their identity: some, like Lovell and the king's jewel-house keeper Sir Henry Wyatt, even dressed like him, in sober but costly black. They formed the small, informal councils in which Henry liked to do business, and they were at the centre of a practice that he was increasingly using to define his relationship with the country: the rigorous enforcement of his prerogative rights and powers through a system of suspended financial penalties or bonds. Such bonds were part of the fabric of life, used to guarantee business deals, to acknowledge debts owed and to ensure good behaviour. But during the upheavals of Warbeck, Henry and his agents had started to reach for them instinctively, at the first sign of disorder.

It was in the king's account books – the same accounts that de Ayala had spotted him spending so much time with, closeted away in his secret chamber – that everything came together. They listed income and expenditure, but they also listed bonds and debts, painstakingly entered by the king's accountants under the practised eye of his chamber treasurer, John Heron, and countersigned with the king's spindly monogram. The chamber accounts were turning into a tool of surveillance, of political control: as Henry totted up his books, he was mapping and monitoring the offences, and the loyalties, of his subjects. After the near-disaster of the Cornish uprising, Soncino had remarked on the king's 'clement' response to the rebels. If he had seen Henry's account books, he might have thought otherwise. In one of them was neatly listed the dedicated network of spies that Henry had deployed in the region, gathering intelligence on potential troublemakers and providing a flow of information on which his law-enforcers could act.[40]

During the civil wars, back in the 1460s, the chief justice and political commentator Sir John Fortescue had described the difference between English rule – which he extolled – and the 'evil things' of French rule. In France, Fortescue explained, the king's will was law. In England, however, the king was bound by law. He was part of a 'body politic' – the 'ruling part' to be sure, but nevertheless still a part – a compact between the king and his subjects that Magna Carta had formalized back in the early thirteenth century. But Henry's rule, based on a relentless gathering of information and forensic interpretation of the law, was centred increasingly on his personal control. It was not exactly French – but it was hardly surprising if, to the likes of de Ayala, it looked like it.[41]

Running through all this was the perpetual question of legitimacy and loyalty. In the aftermath of Blackheath, an intelligence report landed on the desk of Henry's administrator Sir Reynold Bray. Reporting an exchange between two men who had fought for Henry against the Cornish rebels, it revealed the unease that permeated the minds even of those loyal to the regime. One had urged the other to pray for Henry VII. The reply was evasive: 'we need not pray for the king by name', he said, 'but *pro rege nostro tunc*' – just, 'for our king'. Asked to explain what he meant, he elaborated: ''tis hard to know who is righteous king.' His dilemma summed up Henry's deepest fear. Even those keen to uphold the status quo didn't know, deep down, who should embody it.[42]

Late in the evening of 9 June 1498, Trinity Sunday, Warbeck climbed through an unlocked window in Westminster Palace and fled upstream to the Charterhouse at Sheen, where he claimed sanctuary. The following day he was turned over to royal guards. The circumstances of his escape were puzzling. A Venetian dispatch probably came closest, reasoning that it was a put-up job, and that Henry's own servants had seeded the idea of escape in Warbeck's mind. Warbeck's living quarters had been in the wardrobe of robes, which housed the king's clothes and personal belongings, and which was sited directly below the privy chamber. His gaolers were two of the king's privy servants, William Smith and James Braybroke and, in the resulting inquiry into Warbeck's flight, both got off scot-free. Henry wanted a reason to move him out of sight and – he hoped – out of mind; so he created one.[43]

After his recapture, Warbeck's treatment changed. Publicly pilloried in London, he was then moved into the Tower and locked in a windowless cell. Towards the end of July, Henry took ambassadors from Flanders, sent to agree to newly normalized trade relations between England and the Low Countries, to visit the prisoner; also present was the Spanish ambassador, Rodrigo de Puebla. When Warbeck was brought in, shackled and chained, his appearance had, de Puebla reported, been 'much altered', his princely good looks so savagely disfigured 'that I, and all other persons here, believed his life will be very short'. That, de Puebla concluded briskly, was that: 'He must pay for what he has done.'[44]

But the disturbances continued. The simple fact of Warbeck's existence, and that of Edward earl of Warwick, now in his early twenties, seemed to be motivation enough. In January 1499 a fresh plot was uncovered in Cambridge. It involved a young university student named Ralph Wilford who, groomed by a local priest to believe that he too was the earl of Warwick, had experienced a series of dream-visions in which he was anointed king. Brought to London, Wilford was hanged the following month, his body left on a gibbet on the Old Kent Road, the main south-eastern approach to London. For Henry the episode, which bore so many hallmarks of the Lambert Simnel case twelve years before, was traumatic. Outwardly calm, his body betrayed him. He seemed to age twenty years in two weeks.

Henry's preoccupation with what the future held began to seem coloured by his own ill-health. There were telltale signs, such as the £2 paid to 'a stranger of Perpignan that showed quintessentia', the fabled water of life that could cure everything from gout to tuberculosis, poisoning and 'troubles from devils' – and, into the bargain, restore youth to old men and convert base metals into gold. He frequently resorted to prophecy, the practice that he himself had made illegal in one of the first acts of his reign, and whose ban was stringently enforced. In the months after Wilford's execution, he summoned a Welsh priest who had foretold the deaths of Edward IV and Richard III and who, among 'many other unpleasant things', advised Henry that his life was in danger and that there were 'two parties of very different political creeds' in the kingdom. Yorkist conspiracy, in other words, was alive.[45]

In the middle of the year, royal agents began to pick up whispers of old plots, resurrected in a sequence of meetings in secret houses across London, involving an assortment of city merchants, opportunist hangers-on looking for a chance to make money and, disturbingly, four of Warbeck and Warwick's warders, who acted as go-betweens with their two charges. Fuelled by the inevitable astrological consultations, the plot coalesced into a plan to seize the Tower, steal its treasure, blow up the magazine of explosives there, and smuggle the pair out of the country in a ship filled with a cargo of woolcloth. The conspirators would make their move that summer when the city was quiet and the king and his household on progress in the country; he would, they swore, never return to London alive.

Oddly, neither Warbeck nor Warwick seemed particularly engaged. Warbeck, very probably, had been tortured to the point of uninterest; either way, after a lifetime of assumed identities, he barely seemed to know who he was any more. Indeed, it was Warwick, the gentle, bewildered prince who it was said could not tell a goose from a capon and who had spent the last fourteen years in the Tower, who was the more enthusiastic: he simply seemed glad of the attention. The two were given pep talks and constantly prompted with encouraging news and the small change of conspiracy: secret tokens, a book of cipher, and a file and hammer for Warbeck to break his shackles. Mingling with the genuine conspirators were royal agents provocateurs, pushing and shaping the plot, incriminating the two prisoners, giving them enough rope to hang themselves. In early August, one of the plotters, filled with a sense of creeping unease, got cold feet and, announcing that Henry knew everything, bolted to the safety of sanctuary. Still the king and his counsellors waited, for another three weeks. On 25 August, the conspirators met for a final time. Then the net closed.[46]

That October, an Italian astrologer known by his anglicized name of William Parron presented to Henry his prognostication for the year ahead. *De Astrorum vi fatali*, *The Fateful Meaning of the Stars*, concerned why it was that the innocent should die – indeed, why sometimes it was necessary for them to do so. If people were born under bad stars, natural law decreed that, even if they were utterly innocent of any crime, they were destined to die unnatural deaths of one kind or another: beheading, hanging, poverty or disease. Parron's treatise went on to demonstrate how unlucky were the stars of two men and, although the pair were not named, the reference was clearly to Warbeck and Warwick. These ill-starred people infected the country and, until they died, they would continue to be a focus for revolt – but die they surely would, because they were ill-starred. It was a satisfyingly closed logic, and it satisfied Henry's conscience.

Saturday 23 November 1499, St Clement's Day, was the first day of winter. That year, autumn had blown itself out with gales and storms, but even the foulest weather could not prevent Londoners from turning out in numbers for an execution. Lining the badly paved streets, out through the suburbs of Holborn and west through the fields, they watched as the twenty-five-year-old Warbeck bumped along behind a horse, lashed to a wooden hurdle. At Tyburn, amid the crowds and assembled dignitaries, he was hauled up a ladder to the scaffold. There, with the noose round his neck, he confessed. He was not Edward IV's second son – in fact, he had no Yorkist blood at all – but was just a 'stranger', a foreigner, the son of a boatman from Tournai. Begging absolution from the king and 'all others he had offended', he composed himself 'meekly'. Then the ladder was whipped away and he jerked downwards, his body convulsing violently, then twitching, then limp.[47]

Five days later, on the other side of the city, the ambassadors were present at another execution, this one a private affair, as befitted a true nobleman. If Warbeck's trial had been perfunctory, Warwick's was a farce. At his hearing in London's Guildhall, as utterly confused now as he had been by the plot to free him, the earl had to be 'compelled to answer'. The records of his trial were locked away in a cupboard with three locks, the keys allocated separately to three unnamed royal officers. Under louring skies, lightning and thunder, with rain driving in off the Thames, Warwick was led out to his place of execution on Tower Green, and beheaded.

Henry VII had been on the throne for fifteen years and three months. Only now, with these two executions, did he feel safe.[48]

As the new century began, the Spanish ambassador Rodrigo de Puebla posted a dispatch from London to Ferdinand and Isabella of Spain. He expatiated on England's tranquillity and obedience. There had, he wrote, 'always been Pretenders to the crown'; more than that, there had been a number of contesting claims to the English throne, 'and of such quality that the matter could be disputed between the two sides'. Now, however, 'it has pleased God that all should be thoroughly and duly purged and cleansed'. There remained 'not a drop of doubtful royal blood'. The only royal blood in the kingdom was the 'true blood' of Henry VII, his queen, Elizabeth, and 'above all' their first-born son Arthur, prince of Wales and heir to the throne. The civil wars, he said, were over.

De Puebla's mood was skittish; he really should, he added breezily, stop harping on about the two executions, as he was aware that he had written 'so often' about them recently. The way was now paved for a spectacular royal wedding between England and Spain, one which would set the seal on Henry VII's dynastic ambitions. It was a dispatch intended specifically to communicate a sense of closure to the Spanish monarchs, to show that England possessed a dynasty fit for an infanta of Spain. The wedding preparations could begin.[49]

2

Richmond

In the early afternoon of Friday 12 November 1501, the sixteen-year-old Catherine of Aragon and her retinue, 'in most sumptuous wise apparelled', reined in their horses in front of London Bridge, on the Southwark side of the Thames. Awaiting her, on the north bank, the city dominated a sweeping arc of the river, fringed by the entanglement of wharves, quays, jetties and shipping through which flowed London's immense mercantile wealth. From the foursquare royal Tower on the city's eastern edge to the Dominican monastery of the Blackfriars in the west, its skyline a forest of spires and belltowers. Above them all soared the greatest spire, five hundred feet high, which topped the Gothic bulk of St Paul's Cathedral, where Catherine and Prince Arthur were to be married two days later.[1]

Through its fortified stone gate, Catherine could see London Bridge itself, its twin-towered portcullis and drawbridge topped with the heads of traitors, its houses crammed precariously on either side, and in its midst a riot of colour: the first of the six extravagant pageants celebrating the Spanish princess's arrival in and ceremonial progression through the city to St Paul's.[2] At her side was the slight, carrot-haired ten-year-old who had been assigned a crucial role in the festivities. Detailed to attend on the princess closely, to accompany her through the city and down the aisle, was the king's second son, Henry duke of York.

Prince Arthur's marriage to Catherine, younger daughter of Ferdinand of Aragon and Isabella of Castile – the pious, re-conquering 'Catholic monarchs', as the pope had entitled them – was the culmination of all Henry VII's ambitions. First brokered back in the spring of 1489, it had survived the violent fluctuations of European dynastic

WINTER KING

politics and a convoluted dance of negotiation between Henry and
Ferdinand, two equally suspicious monarchs: pulled one way by Henry's abortive invasion of France and the tension-filled years of
Warbeck's conspiracy, and another by France's own expansionist tendencies, which Henry's right-hand man John Morton, archbishop of
Canterbury, had described as its 'unbridled rage for domination' and
which filled both monarchs with alarm.³ Twelve years and numerous
subsequent treaties, proxy marriages and ratifications later, the day
was finally at hand.

A fortnight long, the planned celebrations were of an unparalleled
splendour and complexity. Following Catherine's reception and marriage, the festivities would move west along the curve of the Thames,
past the large bishops' palaces whose gardens lined the water's edge,
and the cloistered inns of court which churned out the country's finest
legal minds, to Westminster. Finally, they would culminate at Henry
VII's new palace of Richmond, rushed to completion in time for
Catherine's arrival.

Two years in the making, the ceremonies would, so the king was
determined, break new ground. Henry and his planners had delved
into the archives, scouring precedents from previous royal celebrations. They cherry-picked the most dramatic features from the
all-conquering triumphs of Henry V, and the glamorous tournaments
of Edward IV, whose close links to that epicentre of chivalric sophistication, the ducal court of Burgundy, were an inspiration; and they
cast a thoughtful and creative eye over the most spectacular European
court celebrations of recent times. The result would be a supreme cultural articulation of sovereignty, spelling out a very clear message.
Henry VII and his descendants, and they alone, were the rightful
monarchs of England: all-powerful, a dynasty that presided over the
'common wealth' of the state with a benevolent and omnipotent
hand.

All of which could hardly mask the fact that the wedding plans had
their roots in division, discord and blood. For it had been on 19
November 1499, the same day that the earl of Warwick, bewildered,
backward and harmless, had made his forced confession in front of a
tribunal of Henry's counsellors in London's Guildhall, that the city

42

corporation had met in the same building to start planning Catherine's lavish civic reception.[4]

○

Over the centuries, London's relationship with the crown had settled into an uneasy symbiosis, their interests increasingly intertwined. In return for massive corporate loans from the city, the unofficial royal bank, a perennially cash-strapped monarchy ceded to it privileges of self-government and trade protection. And as the royal household grew more unwieldy and less mobile, it settled into its houses strung out along the banks of the Thames, within easy reach of Westminster, the centre of law, government and administration, and London, its most reliable source of funds. Royal servants became part of the fabric of city life, renting and acquiring property, accumulating business interests, mingling with the mercantile elites, who were themselves familiar figures at court. Under Henry, the relationship had, more or less, continued to prosper.[5]

There was, though, an undertow of friction between a city that jealously guarded its own political and economic liberties and a crown which sought to control and manipulate them. Cracking down on the habitual sharp practices indulged in by the city's merchants and financiers, Henry had made examples of prominent Londoners with a series of punitive fines, while he and his counsellors constantly played off the city guilds against each other, favouring one, then another, in a process of divide and rule. During the height of the Perkin Warbeck conspiracy, Henry's embargo on trade with the Low Countries had wrecked London's economy, with merchants unable to export goods to the great commercial centres of Bruges and Antwerp, a ban reinforced by sporadic harassment and intimidation by royal officials. To the consternation of the city guilds, when trade officially restarted in 1496 Henry himself chose the new governor of the English merchant adventurers in Bruges, a privilege previously reserved to the city. Conspiracy had continued to linger: merchants' trade routes were arteries for information and espionage, and London's citizens had been among those caught up in the Warbeck plot. Highly suspicious of the city's independent-mindedness and covetous of its wealth, Henry was always looking for opportunities to tighten his grip.[6]

But in general, Henry and his counsellors were alert to London's importance in raising funds and maintaining order, and cosy relationships developed between city leaders and members of the king's inner circle of counsellors. London was the chief sponsor and organizer of royal triumphs and receptions, the dramatized public processions which communicated the crown's magnificence and power to the crowds who flocked to such occasions from far-flung corners of the country and from abroad.[7] Kings tended to leave the arrangements in the hands of the city. After all, it was paying. But in November 1499 Henry informed the city corporation of a change to the customary plans. The mayor was ordered to appoint an eight-person committee to communicate with 'diverse of the king's council' about Catherine's reception into London. The planning and creative input would come personally from Henry and his counsellors, down to the last detail. They would tell the city what to do, and when. London was in effect being treated as a sub-department of the royal household – and it would be required to foot a huge bill for the privilege.[8]

The pageants that the king and his advisers had in mind would, following usual custom, be strategically placed at prominent sites along the route to St Paul's, constructed on multi-storey wooden stages over the crenellated stone conduits that, supplying London's fresh water, stood solidly in its main thoroughfares. Weaving together history, myth and prophecy, a series of dramatic tableaux would depict the dynasty's rule as inexorable, inevitable; no accident of history, nor the chance product of deaths, tenuous bloodlines and last-gasp victories, it was, rather, written in the stars. Such a royal extravaganza in England's capital was doubly significant in light of the security operation that had, the previous summer, forced out the deep-rooted network of Yorkist recidivists from its dense warren of back streets. London, the 'steadfast, sure chamber of England', the country's window to the world, had been thoroughly cleansed. So confident were the king and his counsellors that, with an eye to maximum visibility, the forthcoming wedding would be held not in the customary venue of Westminster Abbey, but in St Paul's, one of the greatest cathedrals in Europe, and London's largest public space and commercial centre to boot.[9]

To co-ordinate this vision Henry turned to a man who knew his mind better than most. Having assumed a leading role in the hard-fought negotiations over Arthur and Catherine's wedding, Richard Fox, now in his early fifties, took control of its preparations. He drew up summaries of the duties of all those who were to participate, a close-knit circle of Henry's leading counsellors and household officers, from the lord chamberlain Giles Daubeney to the comptroller Sir Richard Guildford, an able engineer and an aficionado of jousts and tournaments.[10]

The reception and wedding would highlight Henry's chief source of political capital: his sons. In the world of dynastic politics, charismatic royal children, as one contemporary observer had once remarked of Edward IV's ill-fated boys, 'surpassed all else' at court festivities.[11] In Prince Arthur, the groom-to-be, and his younger brother Henry duke of York, Henry VII had two highly contrasting focal points. Taking after his father, Arthur seemed to come into his own in the more restricted spaces of court and household, where his classical education and grooming for kingship manifested themselves in a slightly distant graciousness.[12] His brother, on the other hand, was proving a master of the defining public gesture, with a natural feel for the big occasion – at the age of three, after all, he had ridden through London's crowds on horseback, behaviour that both his father and mother seemed to delight in. But Prince Henry's charisma was not the only or even the main reason for the most prominent of roles assigned him at Catherine's side. With both Warbeck and Warwick dead, his presence alongside the young Spanish princess would be a reminder to London and the world that York, and the house of Plantagenet, embodied in this young, chivalrous prince, had been successfully assimilated into the new dynasty. Prince Henry's appetite for the limelight would play to the London crowds and help set Catherine at ease. Arthur, meanwhile, would be presented in the role to which he was becoming accustomed: Henry VII's heir, made in his own image, regal and detached.

By the spring the preparations were well under way. On Fox's direction the Fleet Street printer Richard Pynson produced a commemorative pamphlet of the orders for Catherine's reception, which circulated throughout the city and the courts of Europe.[13] That June, Henry's summit meeting with the twenty-one-year-old Archduke Philip of Burgundy, the glamorous heir to the Habsburg Empire, in the English enclave of Calais, served further to ramp up expectations.

Making the short journey across the Dover Straits, the English court met Philip and his posse of young knights in a glittering reception amid tight security in the church of St Peter's outside the town – Philip would not, he insisted, set foot in the town itself – 'richly hanged with arras' for the occasion.[14] Philip, whose family had once extended such support to Warbeck, seemed to prove rather more tractable than either his father, Maximilian, or the dowager Duchess Margaret of Burgundy. He acclaimed Henry as his 'patron, father and protector' and, during the course of a 'rich banquet', the two chatted about a possible Anglo-Habsburg marriage alliance between Prince Henry and Eleanor, Philip's infant daughter.[15]

At Calais the archduke and his entourage were neatly co-opted into the unveiling of another stage in the wedding festivities: a succession of jousts, to take place at Westminster in the week following the ceremony. The tournament challenge was proclaimed resoundingly in the name of Edmund de la Pole, earl of Suffolk. Brash, hot-tempered and 'readily roused to anger', Suffolk was a member of the Order of the Garter and one of the most accomplished jousters at Henry's court. What was more, he was a full-blooded Yorkist – son of Elizabeth Plantagenet, sister to Edward IV and Richard III, and a younger brother of John de la Pole, earl of Lincoln, the man who had masterminded the abortive Lambert Simnel rebellion thirteen years previously. In mid-1499, Suffolk had left the country without royal licence, heading first to Calais and then east into the archduke's territory, before finally being persuaded to return to England that October. Now, Henry was using the tournament challenge to tell the world – and especially Philip – that Suffolk was well and truly under his thumb.[16]

Sixteen at the time of his brother's death at the battle of Stoke, Edmund de la Pole was next in line to inherit the family title of duke of Suffolk. The problem was that a chunk of the Suffolk estates had already been in Lincoln's possession and, forfeited by his treason, they were now in the hands of the king. Title and income went hand in hand. You had to be able to maintain a standard of living appropriate to your rank – and Edmund de la Pole, as Henry pointed out to him, didn't now have sufficient estates to support a dukedom. Henry then agreed to grant his inheritance and the lower title of earl, but on typically onerous terms: a fine of £5,000. The king, as Suffolk knew, was deliberately degrading him, and making him pay for the privilege.[17]

Suffolk seemed to realize what was demanded of him. He took a conspicuous role in Henry's invasion of France, fought the Cornish rebels at Blackheath in 1497 and jousted with distinction in court tournaments. But none of it got him very far; perhaps, in part, because Henry held a low opinion of his abilities, but, increasingly, during the tension-filled 1490s, because of who he was.[18]

In autumn 1498, Suffolk and a group of courtiers had been involved in an argument outside Aldgate, on London's eastern edge, which spilled over into a mass brawl in which three men were killed. Suffolk, who had already failed to turn up to one legal hearing earlier in the year on unrelated charges, was hauled before the judges of King's Bench, the royal criminal court in Westminster Hall, and indicted for murder. On the face of it, this seemed a display of the efficiency and impartiality of royal justice but, even setting aside Suffolk's outrage at being charged for the killing of a commoner, there were several curious things about the case. First was the involvement of one of Henry's closest counsellors, Sir Reynold Bray, who had personally delivered the indictment against Suffolk. Then came the detailed coroner's inquest, which made no mention of Suffolk having struck a fatal blow. And finally, courtiers of far lesser rank, favoured jousters such as Roland de Veleville and Matthew Baker, regularly got away – quite literally – with murder. Meanwhile, Henry was forcing Suffolk to beg for pardon.[19]

Highly sensitive to this perceived slight on his honour, Suffolk refused to do so. Instead, he left England. His timing could not have been worse. With the Warbeck endgame being played out amid reports of unrest in East Anglia, and with John de Vere, earl of Oxford, Henry's chief man in the region, uncovering a similar plot to groom a pretender in Cambridge, Suffolk's flight to the Habsburg-controlled Low Countries must have looked suspiciously like a re-run of Lincoln's own plot twelve years previously.

Henry took it very seriously indeed. His response was to threaten a repeat of the economic sanctions that had so destabilized the Netherlands during the 1490s, and which Philip of Burgundy badly wanted to avoid. With Suffolk himself, Henry's approach was delicate: he could not risk the earl's departure turning into outright rebellion. He afforded Suffolk the honour of a diplomatic visit headed by Sir Richard Guildford, complete with an official communiqué to be shown to the recalcitrant earl. In the customary private briefing issued to Guildford, Henry instructed him to talk to the earl as it were off the record, as if 'without the king's knowledge'. Seeming to speak with Suffolk's own well-being at heart, Guildford was to persuade him to see sense. Henry wanted Suffolk to return, not as his captive, but of his own free will, as Henry's loyal subject, which would best stand with the king's 'great honour, both within his realm and without'. If he did so, then he could 'in time' regain favour and 'enjoy that [which] he had when he departed'. If not, well, 'he may never look to recover nor come to again'. Any further disloyalty could only bring about his 'utter clear destruction'. Suffolk came back.[20]

So when, at the Calais summit meeting, Garter king-of-arms John Writhe threw down the gauntlet on Suffolk's behalf in an impeccably turned expression of fealty to Henry VII, Philip, who had welcomed Suffolk as a fugitive the previous year, would not have missed the point. Neither would the ambassadors assembled from the courts of Europe, nor the people of Calais, a town of unpredictable allegiances. For Henry, the conventional protestations of service and loyalty to the crown took on a particularly satisfying resonance. Suffolk, proclaimed Writhe, 'humbly begged' Henry to let him and a select team of companions joust in honour of the king and the forthcoming marriage 'and', he stressed, 'for no other cause or intention'.[21] For good measure, copies of Suffolk's challenge, in French, were given to Archduke Philip, to the French herald for Charles VIII of France, and dispatched to James IV of Scotland, another erstwhile sponsor of Warbeck; in addition, the Spanish ambassador sent a copy to Ferdinand and Isabella. Henry had, it seemed, successfully corralled Suffolk into his dynastic plans.

Underneath the pomp and ceremony of the English court's progress to Calais there had been a pervasive sense of panic. An epidemic of plague was sweeping London and the southeast, and mortality rates were staggeringly high. The London chronicler Robert Fabyan, an influential draper and city alderman, put the total deaths at twenty thousand – between a third and a half of the city's entire population. It may have been the plague that carried off the infant Prince Edmund, Henry and Elizabeth's youngest child and third son, who died on 19 June and was buried in state three days later at Westminster Abbey.[22] Another victim may have been Henry's chancellor, John Morton, who died that September at the age of eighty. Almost to the end, this supreme architect of Henry's reign, with his 'deep insight in politic worldly drifts', had remained an ever-observant presence at the king's side. For Henry, the loss was immense. Lawyer, politician, administrator, archbishop and cardinal, Morton had navigated the dynastic changes of the past half-century with a considered daring, his adaptability matched by his resolute belief in strong, forceful kingship. Of all Henry's small group of close advisers, his chancellor, a generation older than the rest, had perhaps been the most influential, his mild appearance belying a precise ruthlessness. Henry had learned much from him.[23]

These losses were tempered by the coming wedding. Late in 1500, another proxy marriage was enacted now that Arthur had reached the legitimate marriageable age of fourteen, the Spanish ambassador de Puebla again acting the part of the absent bride with great gusto. The pair exchanged vows, the contract *per verba de praesenti* required by canon law. The marriage was now legally indissoluble and the wedding itself confirmed for the following September. After much wrangling, the conditions and method of payment for Catherine's marriage portion, or dowry, were finalized, and the list of Catherine's Spanish servants who would remain with her as part of her new, English, household agreed upon. As he described the tortuous conclusion to the negotiations, de Puebla's customary optimism acquired a brittle edge. That December, Henry had summoned him to his privy chamber with 'all sweetness'; then, his mood clouding over, had turned on the harassed ambassador, blaming him for having held up the marriage through his 'shifts and evasions'. Dealing with the calculating English king over Catherine's dowry had, de Puebla sighed to Ferdinand and Isabella, been a 'nightmare'.[24]

The scale of the marriage plans had produced a contradictory reaction in the pious Queen Isabella. Professing herself delighted at the magnificence of the preparations and the consequent honour done to her daughter, her fastidious asceticism nevertheless baulked at their luxury. Perhaps finding Henry and Elizabeth's ambitions for wedding glamour a touch vulgar – they had implored Isabella that the Spanish ladies accompanying Catherine to England should be beautiful, or at the very least that 'none of them should be ugly' – she begged Henry to 'moderate the expenses'. There was nothing wrong with rejoicings, she wrote, but the 'substantial part of the festival should be his love ... the princess should be treated by him and by the Queen as their true daughter'.[25]

As the time for Catherine's departure grew near, misgivings may well have crept into Isabella's mind. Of her six children, her eldest daughter and two sons had died, and two of her remaining three daughters had already been married off. Catherine's eldest sister, the beautiful but fragile Juana, was beginning to show signs of mental deterioration following her high-profile wedding to Archduke Philip of Burgundy five years previously. Catherine, cloistered but with a natural resourcefulness, was made of sterner stuff. But Isabella knew well the brutal realities of such marriage negotiations, and she wanted her daughter to be more than a political trophy: to be treated humanely and with kindness by her new family.

Spring 1501 brought further delays. Uprisings continued to flare in newly reconquered southern Spain, and Ferdinand had his hands full in quelling Moorish resistance in the Andalucian hill-town of Ronda. After shaking off a stubborn fever, Catherine finally departed from Granada in May, her party crossing the high plateaux of central Spain en route to the northern port of Laredo.[26]

By July, with the household on its summer progress, Henry had moved downstream to Greenwich. Here, in the seclusion of his wife's favourite residence, he finally caught up on some correspondence, including a reply to a number of letters from his mother Lady Margaret Beaufort. His own letter mainly concerned business, but in a postscript riddled with apologies he allowed himself a rare lapse into a more intimate tone, one that betrayed fatigue and illness. Promising his mother that he would 'hereafter, at better leisure', devote more time to her affairs, he apologized for burdening her with such a long letter – though given how seldom he wrote, he added, it was necessary. And again he asked her pardon, 'for verily Madame my sight is nothing so perfect as it has been, and I know well it will impair daily'. He hoped that Margaret would not be put out if he 'wrote not so often with mine own hand, for on my faith', he concluded, 'I have been three days ere I could make an end of this letter.'[27] The Olympian distance he so carefully cultivated was shot through with genuine exhaustion. Workaholic and overburdened with affairs of state, he had evidently written the letter in snatched moments between other matters. More alarming was the physical effort it had cost him to write a note whose contents fitted comfortably on two sides of paper. Still, for all his weariness, Henry was hoping that quieter and more stable times lay ahead. In fact, matters were about to take a drastic turn for the worse.

That August, as Catherine prepared to embark on the long sea journey to England, a ship slipped unobserved out of the port of London and down the Thames estuary towards the North Sea. It was carrying Edmund de la Pole, earl of Suffolk and a small band of supporters. The Yorkist who Henry believed he had successfully co-opted into the high-profile celebrations at Calais had fled a second time. In his softly-softly approach, Henry had been too clever by half; in Suffolk's case the white rose would not graft so easily onto the red after all.

If, almost two years before, Suffolk had returned to court in the expectation of regaining his dead father's title and lands, he should have known better. Henry was happy to wheel him out on great occasions of state, when his flamboyant chivalry added lustre to the court, but Suffolk, quite clearly, remained under a cloud. Monitoring the activities of the earl and his associates closely, Henry began to attack Suffolk's authority and standing in his East Anglian backyard, forcing his retainers into financial bonds for good behaviour and intervening in his legal proceedings. The backdrop to Suffolk's starring role in Calais was another lawsuit brought against him in the court of King's Bench at Westminster where, only a month previously, royal justices had ruled in favour of his opponent.[28]

Things were, Suffolk felt, getting worse. His decline in East Anglia was exacerbated by the rise of Thomas Howard, earl of Surrey. On the losing side at Bosworth, Howard had worked tirelessly to prove his loyalty to the new regime; now, back from his successful campaigns in the north of England against the Scots and in great favour with Henry, he was looking to recover his own family's inheritance, encroaching on Suffolk's sphere of influence in the region. Perhaps the final straw was the emergence at court of Edward Stafford, the young duke of Buckingham, who cut an aggressively fashionable figure, keeping a lavish household and a sensational wardrobe. Commentators reached breathlessly for superlatives to describe his clothes and style. Buckingham and Suffolk were almost invariably paired together, and Suffolk, the lower-ranked earl, invariably came second.[29] All of which served to trigger a tangle of more deep-rooted resentments.

As his membership of the Order of the Garter and his noble title brought home to him, Suffolk owed loyalty and service to the crown. But in the recent past, there had been plenty of accusations and instances of Henry's oppressive misrule, of which the execution of the earl of Warwick, Suffolk's cousin, was the most recent and emphatic example. Suffolk was only too aware of his own family's sense of entitlement. Back in the 1450s, his Yorkist forebears had challenged the ruling house of Lancaster in the interests of reform, justice, and the public good – and, of course, a belief in their own superior royal lineage. Similar thoughts, it was clear, fuelled the de la Poles' attitude to the Tudors.

For any noble or knight, the ownership of genealogical rolls describing, confirming – and, sometimes, inventing – their family's glorious ancestry was de rigueur. The earl of Lincoln had one which, after his death, may have passed to Suffolk. Unfurled, the long sheet of sewn strips of parchment reveals brightly illuminated images of Edward IV and Elizabeth Woodville, who turn, gesturing, to the lineage and royal claim of Richard duke of York and the de la Poles, whose line concludes in a coloured medallion of the earl of Lincoln and his descendants. It was the kind of document that could have been produced after Richard III's own son had died, when he had apparently nominated Lincoln his heir. But some time after the battle of Bosworth, there had been an addition. Squashed in the right-hand margin, the name of Henry VII has been added, and above it, back through the roll, a thick black line has been crudely drawn, tracing his descent from, derisively, 'Owen Tudor, a chamber servant'. The meaning was all too clear: the Tudors, the brash upstarts, were a diversion from the natural order of things in which the de la Poles, nobles of the blood, were destined to be kings. Lincoln, of course, had acted on this, and the impulse lingered in his brother's mind. Whether he wanted the throne or simply wanted his dukedom back and his pre-eminent place at court confirmed, whether he was scared that, with his brother dead and cousin murdered, he would be next, or whether life had become intolerable or a mixture of all of these things, it was time, he felt, for a 'revolution'.[30]

After Suffolk's first indiscretion, Henry's counsellors had warned him that the earl was being worked on by the king's enemies. Pre-emption was the key: Henry should act with 'rigorous severity' in making an example of him. Otherwise, Suffolk, seeing Henry's for-giveness and restoration of favour as weakness, would become even more wilful and uncontrollable: 'he would again', they said, 'engineer some dangerous assault against the state.' They were proved right. With the chutzpah of Warbeck and the lineage of Warwick, Suffolk was Henry's worst nightmare, the spectres of the past rolled into one loose Yorkist cannon, roaming the courts of northern Europe seeking political and military support for an invasion of England. As the enor-mity of the situation bore home, Henry could not believe that he had spared Suffolk, and 'began to fear fresh upheavals'.[31] To the king's advisers, Suffolk's flight came as no surprise at all. And as they had intimated, he was not acting alone. Henry's intelligence network scrambled to discover the extent of the conspiracy. What it found was that rebellion was once more being fuelled by a combination of for-eign powers and enemies within.

Preoccupied with renewed concerns about security, Henry turned to the forthcoming wedding ceremonies with redoubled obsession. Suffolk's disappearance had ratcheted up the significance of the fes-tivities; more than ever, they were needed to drive home the message of dynastic magnificence, power and permanence.

Through the late summer of 1501, the plans were worked over exhaustively. In practical terms, Suffolk's absence had to be accom-modated. As announced in Calais, he had been due to captain one of the two teams participating in the forthcoming tournament. Now, casting around for another appropriate noble to lead these stylized expressions of chivalric loyalty to the crown, the king promoted a member of Suffolk's original team – the twenty-four-year-old Thomas Grey, marquis of Dorset, extrovert grandson of Elizabeth Woodville and cousin to Queen Elizabeth. Dorset's father, whom Henry had always mistrusted after his vacillating support in exile, died on 1 September. It was the perfect opportunity for Henry to throw a paternal arm around the young marquis in a gesture of familial inclusiveness, creating him a knight of the Garter to boot. Dorset's team would include the foremost of the young generation of nobles who adorned the court: Henry Bourchier, earl of Essex and William Courtenay, heir to the earldom of Devon. All three were close friends and companions-in-arms, a tight-knit group.[32] And all were advertisements for the stability of the reign. Dorset and Essex were Woodvillite Yorkists while Courtenay, from a staunch Lancastrian family, was married to one, the queen's sister Katherine. Together, they had become leading lights of Henry's court. Essex and Courtenay, moreover, had played key roles in crushing Warbeck's army in 1497.

In a characteristic fit of micro-management, Henry overhauled arrangements for the reception – one of a stream of organizers trooping down to Richmond to confirm plans was Garter herald John Writhe, who took a boat from London in order to 'have the king's mind' on the colour of Prince Arthur's trumpets – and the after-dinner entertainments. The two men initially entrusted with looking after these revels 'in the best manner they can' were deemed inadequate to requirements. In their place, Henry summoned one of the household's outstanding talents. William Cornish, master of the children of the Chapel Royal, had burst on to the court's consciousness during the twelfth night celebrations of 1494, when around midnight, dressed as St George, he had led into Westminster Hall a pageant consisting of a 'terrible and huge red dragon, the which in sundry places of the hall as he passed spit fire', then recited courtly verses of his own making before breaking into song, backed by a bravura performance by his well-drilled choir.[33] The extrovert Cornish, Henry had decided, was the man capable of sprinkling stardust over the wedding entertainments. In place of the original, vague instructions, Cornish was closely briefed to produce a sequence of 'disguisings', dramatic tableaux and dances that would incorporate the latest European cultural fashions in an emphatic message of Anglo-Spanish political unity. Over the next months, he would visit the king, outline his plans, and draw substantial sums from the chamber treasurer, John Heron, for his services.[34]

Henry and his counsellors decided that something more was needed in the wake of Suffolk's flight. Sir Reynold Bray, one of the king's inner circle and a familiar and unwelcome face in London's corridors of power, strode into the Guildhall to demand a major change to the plans. The customary wine fountain, positioned outside St Paul's on the wedding day to keep the crowds in good voice, should be transformed into another pageant, the most spectacular of them all. An artificial mountain studded with jewels and covered with red roses, wine gushing forth ceaselessly from its depths, this 'Rich Mount', a play on Henry's family name of Richmond, would be an emphatic statement – and the city, Bray stated, would foot the bill. Outraged, the city leaders pointed out that they had paid for all the other pageants and a lavish present of gold plate for the Spanish infanta, and refused point-blank, unmoved even by Bray's uncompromising bluntness. The king's household grudgingly covered the cost.

Finally, as October drew to a close, Henry received word of Catherine's delayed arrival in England. Her first attempt to make the trip had met with 'great hugeness of storm' so severe that it ripped the ships' masts out of their sockets, and she had been forced to turn back. When she set out again, the long journey through the Bay of Biscay and up the Atlantic coast had been a miserable one. Landing at last in Plymouth, 'far in the country of the west', Catherine made stately progress through southern England, welcomed on the borders of every county by regional notables under the co-ordination of the king's lord steward, Lord Willoughby de Broke. The king had waited a long time for this moment. Now it was in view, he could contain himself no longer. On 4 November, in the late afternoon, he rode out from Richmond Palace to meet Catherine, lodging that night with Prince Arthur at his manor of Easthampstead.

Two days later, they encountered Catherine's representatives outside the village of Dogmersfield on the Hampshire plains, where the princess's party was lodging in the sprawling house owned by the bishop of Bath and Wells, the king's former secretary Oliver King. Leaving Arthur behind, Henry reached the house by mid-afternoon. The princess's servants fussed around; she was, they protested, in siesta. Henry brushed the excuses aside. He had, he said, come to meet his daughter-in-law, and was not to be denied, even if she were in bed. In the middle of her flustered attendants, Catherine was poised and correct. She and Henry met with 'great joy and gladness'. Barely an hour later, Arthur arrived and was introduced to his future bride. The teenagers faced each other, exchanging courtesies in mutually comprehensible Latin: Arthur elegant, formal and deprecating; Catherine petite, auburn hair tightly framing a snub-nosed, doll-like face.

Through persistent autumn rain, the Spanish retinue continued its slow journey towards London. As they descended the Surrey hills towards the village of Kingston-upon-Thames, they were confronted by a mass of uniformed men, four hundred strong. Detaching themselves from this 'great company', a cluster of richly dressed riders advanced towards the princess, led by the duke of Buckingham, florid and blue-eyed, who recited Latin verses in welcome. He and his private army, all dressed in the Buckingham black and red, would accompany her on the last stage of her progress. It was a magnificent assertion of noble power – or rather, as a royal herald travelling with the party preferred to put it, an example of the quality of the 'assistants of the realm of England' that Henry could call upon. Swollen with Buckingham's retainers, the retinue moved on to the archbishop of Canterbury's palace at Lambeth, where Catherine would spend the night before her reception into London.[35]

On the morning of Friday 12 November, Catherine set out from Lambeth through the suburban meadows and market gardens of the Thames's south bank to St George's Fields. Awaiting her was the horsebacked group of English lords, 'spiritual and temporal', who would parade with her through London, Buckingham pre-eminent. With him was Henry's military mastermind, Thomas Howard, earl of Surrey, thin-lipped and beak-nosed; the mitred and croziered archbishop of York; and an array of younger nobles and their hangers-on, slickly groomed in coloured silks and plumed headdresses, and heavy with ornaments and jewelled chains, exchanging cool glances with the ladies of the queen's household. At the head of the party, in a cloak of crimson cloth-of-gold and attended by a hundred retainers in gowns of tawny and blue, was Henry duke of York. As they met for the first time, Catherine would have been struck by the marked difference between the brothers, physically and temperamentally. In contrast to Arthur's constrained politesse, Henry, half a decade younger, ruddy-cheeked and blue-eyed, was a bundle of barely suppressed energy. Their horses stamping and steaming in the November cold, the English party paired up with their Spanish equivalents and set off through Southwark and the Borough to London Bridge.[36]

Greeted by the mayor in his robes of scarlet satin, and the twenty-four aldermen in scarlet velvet, the party moved slowly onto the bridge, clattering across its lowered drawbridge and into the tunnel of houses whose gabled upper storeys met overhead. They then emerged into the bridge's open square, with its chapel of St Thomas of Canterbury jutting out into the Thames, and into a profusion of dynastic symbolism. Two great gold-painted wooden posts, adorned with the king's escutcheons, badges and emblems, bracketed a two-storeyed wooden tabernacle. Covered with canvas painted to resemble stonework, it was hung with coloured cloth and images of the Order of the Garter inset with the red rose. On each floor of this tableau sat a costumed figure, portraying saints Katherine and Ursula respectively.[37] Each in turn stepped forward to address Catherine.

Previewing the young princess's imminent journey through the London streets, they figured forth an allegorical world of epic scale, in which reality and myth merged inseparably, with Catherine and Arthur at its heart. The pageants to come would, they said, lead her on a quest for worldly honour and immortal glory, which would culminate in her marriage. Honour, St Ursula expounded, was only obtainable through a combination of virtue and nobility. Over the course of the six pageants this narrative would, as St Ursula described it, be woven into a cosmology in which Catherine's husband-to-be was both the second coming of King Arthur, the unifying king of legend, and the embodiment of Arcturus, an astrological constellation which, according to the Commentaries of Gregory the Great, signified the epitome of the Christian life of virtue. The verse speeches proclaimed by the two saints were so bafflingly complex that their elaborations sailed over the heads of even the most learned observers. Catherine probably had to rely on the condensed summaries, in Latin, painted on boards hanging from the side of each pageant. The general gist, though, was crashingly obvious: Catherine, the pageants said, was about to become part of something very special indeed.

As Catherine progressed away from the river and into the heart of the city, the tumult of feast-day London pressed in on all sides. Lining the streets – freshly sanded for the benefit of horses and to absorb the evil-smelling mud that seeped through the cracked paving – people surged forward to get a glimpse of the cavalcade. Onlookers filled every available vantage point, leaning from windows, balanced precariously on rooftops, as dislodged tiles skittered down under slipping feet. Tapestry and arras, cloth-of-gold, satin and velvet were hung from the houses lining the route, fine drapery whipped in the autumn winds.[38] Separated from the crowds by wooden barriers, members of London's guilds stood dressed in the various 'liveries and hoods of their manor'. Halfway up Gracechurch Street, at the road's widest point, the second pageant soared into the air – a battlemented, turreted castle, covered with more of the dynasty's emblems and badges and, hovering above it, a huge red dragon. Standing in the castle's gatehouse, a man dressed as a Roman senator addressed the princess and the assembled multitudes. His name, he said, was Policy. Among the stock allegorical figures, the pageant deviser had managed to insinuate a character resembling nothing so much as one of Henry's lawyer-counsellors who represented good and accountable government, with his 'eye on the commonwealth'. Policy was evidently meant to send out a reassuring note to the onlooking subjects: Henry's counsellors were not an unaccountable cabal; rather, they were tireless servants of the public interest. It was a touch typical of Henry VII – or perhaps of the reception's co-ordinator, Richard Fox.[39]

Moving slowly up Gracechurch Street, the party then turned left, down Cornhill, the city's financial heart. The next three pageants enacted elaborate astrological variations on the marriage. As Catherine and her retinue approached, each in succession came alive:

musicians playing, cogs whirring, mechanical constellations operated by costumed children puffing around treadmills. Constructed over Cornhill's barrel-shaped conduit, the Tun, the third pageant, of the moon, was the most ingenious, extravagant and costly of the set-pieces, featuring lengthy prognostications of nuptial bliss expounded by Catherine's ancestor, Alfonso X. But the going was so slow that the short November afternoon had already begun to wane. Having 'well aviewed the goodly device', the princess had to leave the orating Alfonso behind, and move on, past the Stocks Market and up the great commercial thoroughfare of Cheapside, whose goldsmiths were, according to one Italian visitor, mouth agape, more impressive than 'all the shops in Milan, Rome, Venice and Florence put together'. Here the last three pageants were waiting, together with Henry VII and Prince Arthur, who had 'somewhat privily and secretly' taken a vantage point halfway up the street.[40]

During the reception and wedding Henry's carefully calibrated public appearances would present him as the wellspring of honour, justice and power, the unknowable, all-seeing sovereign who, as the Milanese ambassador Soncino nicely observed, appeared in public 'like one at the top of a tower looking on at what is passing in the plain'.[41] Henry had done exactly this at Exeter in 1497 when, in the wake of Warbeck's failed invasion, he had received the submission of captured rebels while lodged at the treasurer's house on the cathedral green. With half the trees on the green cut down so that he could enjoy the view, and standing at a 'fair large' window knocked through for the purpose, he watched, imperious, as the commons of Devon, in only their shirts and with halters round their necks, knelt with 'lamentable cries for our grace and remission', before lecturing them on the obedience he expected of them.[42]

Now, rejecting the usual arrangement of a grandstand, he had commandeered the house of a rich London haberdasher, one of a number of wide-windowed multi-storeyed merchant houses that lined the south side of Cheapside.[43] Henry's elite security force, the three-hundred-strong yeomen of the guard, had secured the area. With their spiked, bladed halberds, and white-and-green jackets stamped with the red rose, they swarmed all over the house, taking up positions 'in windows, leads, gutters and battlements'. Surrounded by a cluster of his close counsellors, including Arthur's godfather the earl of Oxford and Richard Fox, Henry stood at the window in 'open sight', lifted above the crowds, remote, untouchable.[44]

At the king's side, the royal chronicler documenting proceedings noted the first indications of Catherine's approach: the expectant shifting of the crowds, and the royal heralds pushing them back. Then came the young lords and their attention-seeking gallants, 'making gambads', pirouetting their decorated horses to shouts of approbation from the onlookers.[45] Following them, surrounded by a mass of footmen, rode the animated Prince Henry and, alongside him, Catherine. A tiny, upright figure on muleback, she wore a hat of deep red, her auburn hair falling down about her shoulders. Bringing up the rear came the ladies of Queen Elizabeth's household paired with Catherine's. The spectacle seemed to convince even the most coolly appraising of London's bourgeoisie, including the sceptical, ascetic young legal student Thomas More. More wrote to his former schoolmaster John Holt that everything about the reception was superb, apart from Catherine's ladies-in-waiting who, he sneered, looked like 'refugees from hell' – Isabella had evidently not seen fit to prioritize Henry and Elizabeth's pleas for comeliness. But when it came to the princess herself, More was positively dreamy: 'Take my word for it, she thrilled the hearts of everyone; she possesses all those qualities that make for beauty in a very charming young girl. Everywhere she receives the highest of praises, but even that is inadequate.' He concluded, though, on a slightly hesitant note: 'I do hope this highly publicized union will prove a happy omen for England.' It was as if, in their staggering magnificence and heaping up of favourable portents and astrological conjunctions, More felt that the festivities were somehow tempting fate.[46]

The procession came to a halt in front of the house commandeered by the king, and the fifth pageant. Built over the Standard, another of London's conduits and a notorious place of punishment, the tableau was a stylized heaven in which mellifluous choirs of angels – Cornish's highly trained child singers – surrounded an enthroned godlike figure dressed entirely in gold. A second character dressed as a bishop, gesturing towards the onlooking Henry VII, compared him with the costumed deity: 'Right so,' he declaimed, 'our sovereign lord the king/ May be resembled to the king celestial/ As well as any prince earthly now living.' Looking from one to the other, the onlookers must have been struck by the uncanny resemblance: the costumed god of the pageant was made up to look like Henry himself. Under the king's approving eye, the enthroned actor showered the princess with bene-dictions, blessing 'the fruit of your belly'. Kingliness, as embodied by Henry VII, was next to Godliness.[47]

At the top of Cheapside, Catherine reached the final pageant. The Little Conduit, in front of the church of St Michael Le Querne, marked the eastern entrance to St Paul's churchyard. Here, the costumed fig-ure of Honour showed Catherine that she had reached the end of her quest, indicating as he did so two vacant thrones, containing crowns and sceptres, on either side of him, awaiting the happy couple. Receiv-ing gifts of gold and plate from London's dignitaries, the party then progressed around the streets bounding the churchyard before enter-ing the cathedral where, giving thanks and making offerings, Catherine was blessed by the archbishop of Canterbury. When she emerged, the procession broke up, Catherine and her retinue withdrawing to the bishop of London's palace on the north side of St Paul's churchyard. Prince Arthur headed southwest, where the city shelved steeply towards the river in a tangle of backstreets, to his lodgings at the Great Wardrobe, one of the inner-city royal houses.[48] Prince Henry, meanwhile, overnighted at the bishop of Durham's great house on the Strand. The various nobles, servants in tow, retired to their 'places, lodgings and inns' scattered throughout the city.

The following day, Saturday, the king received the Spanish ambassa-dors at Baynard's Castle, his lavishly rebuilt residence on the Thames, east of Blackfriars.[49] With the two princes at his right and left, he listened as the ambassadors itemized the terms of the forthcoming marriage, in particular, the 'assureness' of Catherine's virginity. As the afternoon wore on, Catherine was brought down the hill to Baynard's Castle for an introduction to Queen Elizabeth, in whose frank brown-eyed gaze, cupid's-bow mouth and strawberry-blonde hair so charac-teristic of the Plantagenets Catherine would have immediately seen the resemblance to the boy who had accompanied her through London's streets the previous day. The queen and young princess immediately clicked. Formalities over, the afternoon dissolved into something altogether more relaxed: conversation flowed, unforced; Elizabeth called for 'disports', music and dancing. Late in the evening, 'with torches lit to a great number', Catherine was conveyed through the dark, silent streets back up the hill to her lodgings.[50]

Mid-morning on Sunday 14 November, the gates of the bishop of London's palace swung open. Through them, surrounded by a multitude of English and Spanish nobility and with Prince Henry at her side, Catherine emerged, a vision in white satin, Spanish style, along a wide carpet of blue cloth. She wore a hooped, pleated dress and a headdress of white silk bordered by gold and precious stones, her face veiled. Henry VII's courtiers, meanwhile, had dressed to impress – and impressed the onlookers duly were, London's merchants pricing everything they saw. The highlight was, predictably enough, Buckingham, whose gown, worth a staggering £1,500 – the cost of all the pageants put together – elicited gasps from the crowd. Trumpet fanfares blared out as the party paraded across the square and up the broad steps to the cathedral's west door, where the marriage agreements, including the paperwork for the long-negotiated dowry, were exchanged between the English and Spanish dignitaries.[51]

Inside, the cathedral's cavernous interior was transformed, its walls hung with massive tapestries.[52] Under its stained-glass rose window, the high altar glinted with gold plate, ornaments and relics encrusted with precious stones. And from the west door, an elevated walkway covered in fine red cloth stretched the length of the cathedral, some six hundred feet, to a stage in the round where the ceremony was to take place and which created an effect 'like unto a mountain'. Together with Queen Elizabeth, his mother Lady Margaret Beaufort and a number of his counsellors and servants, the king, who 'would make no open show nor appearance that day', had concealed himself in a closet adjoining the stage, reached by a door specially knocked through for the purpose. Barely visible behind the closet's latticed windows, they stood 'secretly to see and apperceive the form and manner of the ministration'.[53]

While all eyes were on Catherine and Prince Henry as they paraded slowly down the walkway, Arthur had appeared on the great stage.

There, surrounded by the archbishop of Canterbury, eighteen bishops, and attendants dressed in coloured silks and cloth-of-gold, the three children met; Henry gave up the princess to his older brother. As the three-hour-long ceremony drew to a close, the brass section, positioned high above the west door of the cathedral, struck up. The newlyweds, hand in hand, turned to north and south, presenting themselves to the multitudes packed within the cathedral. In the middle of this sea of colour, the two slight figures in white satin saw 'nothing but faces'.

Following a celebratory mass, and after wine and refreshments had been served, Arthur left as he had arrived: by a side entrance, to greet his new bride at the bishop of London's palace. Catherine and Prince Henry retraced their steps down the walkway to the west door. Emerging, they were confronted by a green mountain covered in precious metals: the king's towering monument to Tudor kingship, his contentious Rich Mount. On its summit stood three trees, against which were positioned three kings dressed in armour. In the middle, flanked by the monarchs of France – to which England, of course, still laid claim – and Spain, was King Arthur; from his tree, covered with red roses, sprang a snarling red dragon. As the couple watched, a constant stream of people filed through a gate in the surrounding picket fence to help themselves to the wine that flowed continuously and, it seemed, by magic, from a spring in the mountain's core.[54]

The wedding feast was a suitably sumptuous affair, stretching on until five in the evening and followed by drinking and entertainments. At between seven and eight o'clock Arthur was dragged away from his companions and their 'goodly disports' by the earl of Oxford, overseer of the nuptial arrangements. Accompanied to the bedchamber by a group of clergy and courtiers, Arthur found Catherine, surrounded by her attendants, stretched out in the carefully prepared marriage bed. After he had lain down beside her, the pair and the bed were blessed, prayers offered up, censers wafted and holy water liberally sprinkled. Then all withdrew, and the just-married teenagers were left alone.[55]

The next day, Monday 15 November, everything was still. The bishop's palace was 'under silence', and Catherine stayed in her chamber together with her ladies and gentlewomen; 'no access utterly' was to be had to her and the only person admitted was the earl of Oxford, bearing a loving note from Catherine's new father-in-law. Earlier Arthur had, apparently, emerged from the bridal suite with a 'good and sanguine complexion' and an air of awkward bravado. He called one of his body servants, Anthony Willoughby, the son of Henry VII's lord steward, to bring him a cup of ale, 'for I have this night been in the midst of Spain'.[56] On Tuesday, the 16th, Henry VII and his two sons, accompanied by five hundred members of the royal household and Catherine's retinue, processed back to St Paul's. The new bride was 'secretly conveyed' to the closet, high up in the cathedral, from where the king had scrutinized proceedings two days previously. Catherine stood alone, watching as Henry VII gave thanks that 'this noble and excellent act' had been brought to its most 'laudable conclusion'.

That afternoon, an armada of forty barges conveyed the royal party and London's civic dignitaries some two miles downstream to Westminster Palace. Abutting the abbey, from whose sanctuary it was separated by a high wall, and the seething lanes of its cramped satellite town, the palace was prepared for a week-long programme of sporting and dramatic entertainment. Security details had searched all the tenements within the abbey grounds and Canon Row, the narrow lane whose houses gave on to the palace yard's north wall, submitting a written report of their findings; their inhabitants had all been ordered to clean and decorate their homes. Open to the river at its southern end, the expanse of the yard had been gravelled and sanded for the sure footing of the horses; in it had been erected a temporary stadium, ready for a series of jousts. The low-slung bulk of Westminster Hall, in term-time swarming with the business of London's law courts, stood decorated, prepared to receive the wedding party.[57]

A torrential downpour having finally abated, expectant crowds thronged the palace yard. Londoners filed in, mingling with lawyers and students from the nearby inns of court, many of whom had been ordered to attend on pain of royal displeasure – and to pay a hefty 12d entrance fee into the bargain. Onlookers craned out of the overlooking houses, so many 'that unto sight and perceiving was no thing to the eye but only visages and faces without appearance of their bodies', straining to catch a glimpse of the Spanish princess as the royal party, some hundreds strong, took their seats in a purpose-built gallery.[58] The atmosphere built to fever pitch. Trumpets announced the chief challenger, Buckingham, who emerged from Westminster Hall, fully armoured and on horseback, inside a white-and-green satin pavilion on wheels, scattered with red roses. Followed by his team, he circled the yard slowly, milking the thunderous applause, before doing obeisance to the king. Half an hour later, the five 'defenders' appeared through the opposite entrance: Lord William Courtenay, in blood-red plate armour, riding a red dragon led by a giant carrying a tree; the team captain, the marquis of Dorset, in a suit of coal-black armour, horsed, in a pavilion of cloth-of-gold. One of the 'answerers' on the opposing team, Lord Rivers, topped the lot, arriving in a ship firing cannon, 'which made a great and an huge noise'. The 'Rich Mount' made another appearance, this time on wheels as the earl of Essex's 'pavilion'; sitting atop it was a young woman in white, hair flowing around her shoulders. Such entrances, said an eyewitness, had not been seen 'in very long remembrance'.[59]

Poring through his big book of jousts, bought from the widow of Edward IV's king-of-arms, Garter herald John Writhe had devised an elaborate world of stylized violence to rival the famed tournaments of the Yorkists and which bore comparison with the matchless displays of Burgundian chivalry.[60] At Calais the year before, Writhe and Henry VII's tournament-planner, Sir Richard Guildford, had been close and interested observers of Archduke Philip and his knights. Now, conjuring up a world of chivalric make-believe, dream landscapes, damsels in distress, wildmen and unicorns, the pair had created a supreme articulation of political loyalty to Henry VII. In a last-minute adjustment to the Tree of Chivalry standing in one corner of the palace yard, both teams' escutcheons hung together in a solid expression of unity. The previous arrangement, in which the shields of the teams led by Buckingham and Suffolk were to have faced each other in aggressive opposition, would have sent out entirely the wrong signals. The inconvenient fact of Suffolk's rebellion had been thoroughly effaced.

Fantasy heroes within a securely Tudor universe, the combatants thundered together, 'striking, cutting and lashing at each other ... Some of their swords were broken of 2 pieces, and some other their harness [armour] was hewn off from their body.' Guildford, the experienced referee, ensured that the violence stayed within reasonable limits; Writhe kept score. In the grandstand, Henry sat like a Solomon, watching and judging, leaning forward with an aficionado's keenness, conversing with Guildford and sending messages of encouragement and approbation out to the nobles who jousted in his honour. Following each round, the jousters trotted up, dismounted and climbed the pavilion stairs to do obeisance. At the end of the week, in a prize-giving ceremony, the king's blue eyes searched the faces of the participants as he congratulated them and distributed precious stones, tokens of his favour. Buckingham received a diamond of 'great virtue and price'. Dorset, the opposing captain, was presented with a rose made of rubies inset with a diamond: the red-and-white rose was, Henry seemed to say, a highly appropriate prize for the loyal jousting of Suffolk's replacement.[61]

By night, the focus shifted to Westminster Hall, its walls hung with tapestries and at its western end a cupboard, seven shelves high, on which quantities of gold plate winked and glittered in the torchlight. In front of this display, on a raised dais, Henry and Elizabeth sat enthroned under their cloth of estate. Surrounded by the newlyweds, the royal family and the assembled court and household, they watched, enrapt, as William Cornish's disguisings unfolded before them. One night, a succession of wheeled pageant cars, some eighteen feet high, swayed and creaked out of the gloom of the hall's eastern end and ground to a halt before the royal company.[62] In one scene, actors played out an allegory of Arthur's wooing of Catherine, in which two English ambassadors descended from a ship, fully rigged and crewed, to pay court to ladies peering from the windows of a Spanish castle. After the performers had come together in a sequence of intricately choreographed dances, the assembled company looked on as the bride and groom danced in succession. Then, last of all, Prince Henry descended from the dais with his fourteen-year-old sister Margaret. They performed two slow bass dances, as the others had done. But the heavy formality of it all chafed at the ten-year-old prince who, feeling weighed down by his clothes, 'suddenly cast off his gown and danced in his jacket'. In one stroke, he had shattered the gravitas. And everybody loved it, including the king and queen, to whom it gave 'right great and singular pleasure'. He had stolen the show.[63]

After the week-long revelry at Westminster, Friday 26 November was, as the official chronicler put it, a day of business and pleasure. The royal household packed itself up with practised efficiency as it prepared to move some eight miles upriver to Henry VII's house at Richmond for the final stage in the festivities. Tapestries were rolled up, plate and furnishings were loaded into myriad 'great and huge standards, coffers, chests, cloth sacks, with all other vessels of conveyance', then heaved onto carts and wagons, boats and wherries. After lunch, the wedding party emerged from Westminster Palace and crossed the palace yard to Westminster Bridge, the broad landing stage that extended far out into the river. There, the Thames was thick with some sixty boats waiting to transport the dignitaries, festooned with pennants, flags and tapestries, many 'rowing and skimming' as they waited their turn to dock. The wedding party boarded the barges that were the royal family's usual method of transport through London and the flotilla moved off upstream, in its midst the king's barge with its red dragon prow, accompanied by the 'most goodly and pleasant mirth of trumpets, clarions, shawms, tabors, recorders, and other diverse instruments, to whose noise upon the water hath not been heard the like'. Landing several hours later at the small village of Mortlake, the party transferred to horseback and, 'very late, in the silence of the evening', rode into Richmond, their way lit by the yeomen of the guard carrying flaming brands.[64]

If the 'Rich Mount' in front of St Paul's had figured forth the dynasty's magnificence, Richmond was the real thing. Rising sheer from the Thames, the red-brick palace, with its onion-shaped domes, glassfilled bay windows, covered galleries and pleasure gardens, was an overwhelming testament to the new dynasty. Everything was light, clean and airy, designed after 'the most new invention and craft'. Observers wondered at the plumbing, with its running water and taps 'that at the will of the drawers of water openeth and is closed again'. Henry had scoured northern Europe for the finest in interior design. The hall was hung with tapestries of great battles; at intervals stood statues of the renowned English kings of history, in which, naturally, Henry's likeness also appeared – though set somewhat higher than the others. The chapel royal dripped with plate, saints' relics, jewels and cloth-of-gold. And everything, from the great cistern in the palace's courtyard to the roof timbers, was scattered with red roses. A 'paradise', the 'beauteous exemplar of all proper lodgings', Richmond was an apotheosis.[65]

The party drifted through Richmond as if in a dream. The sculpted gardens contained topiaried mythical beasts and trees laden with exotic fruit. Everywhere was entertainment: chess, backgammon, cards, dice, billiards and a purpose-built sports complex – 'bowling alleys, butts for archers and goodly tennis plays' and 'other goodly and pleasant disports for every person as they would choose and desire'. A Spanish acrobat performed on a tightrope forty feet in the air, juggling with iron chains and engaging in imaginary single combat with a sword and shield. Late on the final evening, as the customary 'void' – spiced wine and sweetmeats – was served, more elaborate disguisings in the great hall culminated in the release of a flock of white doves.

Finally, on Monday 29 November, the party was over. Catherine had, as negotiated, been allowed to keep some of her Spanish retinue; the rest, laden with gifts, left to begin the long journey home. The young princess felt their departure keenly, 'annoyed and pensive of their said miss and absence'. The reaction of her new father-in-law displayed genuine sensitivity – empathy, even. Henry took Catherine and her ladies on a tour of the library with which he had equipped Richmond, showing her 'many goodly pleasant books of works full delightful, sage, merry, and also right cunning'. Catherine would hardly have noticed, in the bulky, intricately illuminated manuscripts, the inherited Yorkist volumes overpainted with sprays of blooming red-and-white roses and emblems. Then Henry produced his trump card: a collection of rings made specifically for the occasion, 'desiring her to oversee them and behold them well, and after that to choose of them one such as she liked best.'[66]

In recent times, Henry had rarely seemed so relaxed, so attentive. To his new daughter-in-law he had indeed shown the 'love' that Catherine's mother had so earnestly desired. The festivities had gone as smoothly as could possibly have been hoped, and the new princess of

Wales, becoming accustomed 'unto the manner, guise and usages of England', would with her 'most dear and loving husband' set the reign on a new dynastic footing. Arthur, for his part, wrote to his new in-laws that he had 'never felt so much joy in his life as when he beheld the sweet face of his bride'. Some days later the couple left for Arthur's distant seat of Ludlow, in the Welsh Marches. Abandoning his initial plans to keep Arthur and Catherine with him at court during the first year of their marriage, the king had been enthusiastic, and adamant in the face of protests from Catherine's parents, that the couple should go.[67] It was a decision that would haunt him for the rest of his life.

3

He Seeks in All Places to Destroy Me

Late in the evening of Monday 4 April 1502, a boat docked at the landing stage at Greenwich, where Henry, Elizabeth and the royal household were in residence. It carried a messenger with urgent dispatches from Ludlow, under the seal of Prince Arthur's chamberlain, Richard Pole. Henry had retired for the night and the house was quiet; close counsellors opened the letters. The news was devastating. The prince of Wales had died forty-eight hours previously, in his chamber at Ludlow Castle. He had been taken ill nearly two months before, at Shrovetide, but his decline, when it came, had been swift and brutal. The likely cause, a 'pitiful disease' that 'with so sore and great violence had battled and driven, in the singular part of him inward' was the sweating sickness, the lethal flu-like virus whose symptoms included a raging temperature, convulsing intestinal pain, asphyxiation and acute kidney failure.[1] The counsellors summoned Henry VII's confessor, one of the severe, grey-habited friars at the adjoining convent of Franciscan Observants. The following morning, 'somewhat before the time accustomed', he knocked discreetly on the door of Henry's privy chamber. Entering, he told all the servants present to leave, then turned to the king and broke the news: his dearest son was departed to God.[2]

Henry's first instinct was to send for Elizabeth who, seeing her husband in 'natural and painful sorrow', comforted him. Her response was reassuring and rational. Henry should, she said, remember that he still had a 'fair and goodly' prince, and two fair princesses. Besides which, he still had her, and they could have more children: 'we are both young enough'. Finally calming, Henry thanked his wife, who returned with her ladies to her own apartments, where she broke down. The scene was replayed in reverse: now, it was Henry who came to console Elizabeth in 'good haste', out of 'true, gentle and faithful love', and who reminded her of the advice she had just given him.[3]

Prince Arthur's death was as unexpected as it was shattering. Life was precarious, and death close, but familiarity did not desensitize. In an exercise book written a few months before Arthur's death, an Oxford schoolboy described how for a long time after the death of his brother, 'my mother was wont to sit weeping every day'. There was, the boy added, 'nobody which would not be sorry if he had seen her weeping'. Henry and Elizabeth's reaction to the loss of their beloved son was deeply human. But there was no mistaking, too, the disastrous political impact of Arthur's death.[4]

Over the last decade and a half, England had gradually grown accustomed to the idea of Henry and Elizabeth's first-born son as heir to the throne, something spectacularly consolidated by his marriage the previous November. Aged fifteen, on the threshold of adulthood and moulded in his father's image, Arthur had embodied the fragile confidence of the dynasty's future. As Elizabeth had said, they did have another son. But Prince Henry was only ten years old. Meanwhile, away in the Low Countries, there was another pretender: Edmund de la Pole, earl of Suffolk.

During the previous eight months, Henry's agents had been unpicking the knot of Suffolk's conspiracy. Through the late summer and autumn of 1501, behind the preparations for Arthur and Catherine's wedding, they had moved fast to counter this new threat to the dynasty. What they discovered bore disturbing parallels with the Warbeck plot of the 1490s. Although Suffolk had fled with a mere handful of co-conspirators, he had powerful continental backing, and a network of support that extended deep into the royal household.

Suffolk, it transpired, had fled England with a plan. From the port of London, his ship had taken him down the Thames estuary and across the North Sea to one of the ports on the Dutch coast, from where he rode east and south, towards Austria and the court of Maximilian, the Holy Roman Emperor. What was more, he had been invited.

Aquiline, with the pronounced jawline for which the Habsburg dynasty was already renowned, Maximilian was a man of capricious brilliance, a builder of prodigious – and half-finished – castles in the sky. Machiavelli, echoing the common view, thought him impossibly fickle, rarely taking counsel before deciding on a plan of action, then, when doubts were aired, dropping it and moving on to something else. Henry thought much the same. 'How I wish,' he once said through gritted teeth, 'that the emperor would not undertake any enterprise except through mature consideration.'[5] The hare-brained scheme of Maximilian's that had almost brought Henry's regime to its knees was his backing of Warbeck, in conjunction with Margaret of Burgundy. And now, apparently, he was at it again.

That September, at St Johann in the Austrian Alps, Maximilian listened with sympathy to Suffolk's indignant description of Henry's crimes, and how he 'intended to have murdered him and his brother', before regretting that he could not aid Suffolk openly, given the treaties in place between his son Philip of Burgundy and Henry. But he gave the earl license to stay, safe passage throughout the imperial territories and a guarantee of military backing, and packed him off to the city of Aachen. There, Suffolk started to plan.[6]

The small group of supporters with Suffolk included his younger brother Richard, a mixture of his household servants – including his indefatigable steward Thomas Killingworth – and Yorkist backsliders such as Sir George Neville, a face all too familiar to Henry's agents. Feelingly referred to in official dispatches as 'the bastard', Neville was an illegitimate member of one of the most powerful of England's noble families. A body servant to Richard III, he had become reconciled to Henry after Bosworth, before fleeing England in the 1490s to become a member of Perkin Warbeck's small court-in-exile. In Scotland, one of James IV's chief advisers had seen Neville for the political butterfly he was: declaring for Warbeck one minute, hoping to make up with Henry the next, his loyalties seemed to tie themselves in knots. Although, finally, he had drifted away from the pretender and, pardoned by Henry, returned to court, his loyalties remained skin-deep, and Suffolk's plot had proved too good an opportunity to resist.[7]

Others came from Suffolk's stamping ground of East Anglia: men with long-held ties of affinity to the de la Poles, like the Norfolk knight Sir John Wyndham and his son Thomas, whose Yorkist loyalties had been reignited by their own personal resentments and quarrels. When, following Suffolk's first flight, Henry had kept a beady eye on the loyalties of his supporters, Thomas Wyndham had failed to answer a summons to London to report to the king and his council, and had been bound for £200 as a result. Another local family who fell under suspicion were the Tyrells of Gipping in Suffolk. The Tyrells provided a link in the chain of conspiracy which led south, across the Dover Straits, to the English colony of Calais.[8]

A low-lying, marshy enclave stretching eighteen miles along the coast and pushing some eight to ten miles inland, the Pale of Calais nestled between French Picardy to the west and, to the east, the imperial-dominated territories of Flanders. Inland, its borderlands were policed by the hulking fortresses of Guisnes and Hammes. On the coast, facing England across the Dover Straits, sat Calais's heavily fortified port town, its capacious harbour guarded by the Rysbank Tower and by Calais Castle. Calais was a constant drain on crown resources. It maintained one of only two standing royal armies – the other being at Berwick, on the Scottish border – of around five hundred men; its defences, meanwhile, required constant upkeep and renovation, as the sea seeped into the walls and foundations of town and castle, rotting timber and eroding stone. But it was worth it, for Calais was one of the 'principal treasures' of the crown, of both strategic and economic importance. It was home to the staple, the crown-controlled marketplace for England's lucrative textile trade, whose substantial customs and tax revenues flooded into Henry's coffers. During the civil wars, Calais had acted as a base for rebel invasions. When in 1484 the captain of Hammes Castle, Sir James Blount, defected to Henry with his garrison and his Lancastrian political prisoner John de Vere, earl of Oxford, it was a significant boost to Henry's cause. Conversely, the following year, as Henry ascended the throne, some two hundred pro-Yorkist troops had deserted to Maximilian. On a constant state of alert, the town's walls were silhouetted with sentries and guards, while its narrow streets swarmed with troops, merchants, diplomats and ambassadors. And it fully upheld its reputation as a hotbed of disaffection and espionage.[9]

Early in his reign, Henry had given Calais's chief military command to one of his most trusted officers, Giles lord Daubeney. He also needed men experienced in the unique vagaries of Calais's government, and that had meant reappointing people like Sir James Tyrell, captain of Guisnes Castle and formerly one of Richard III's lieutenants. After Bosworth, Henry had imprisoned Tyrell but then, reassured perhaps by his family connections – he was Daubeney's brother-in-law – had restored him to his post. Tyrell had remained loyal to Henry during the 1490s, when the town was riddled with sedition and when members of his own family had become entangled in Warbeck's conspiracy. Then, in the summer of 1499, after his first flight abroad, Suffolk had travelled through Calais on his way back to England, and had dropped in at Guisnes, where he stayed as Tyrell's guest.[10]

On the face of it, there was no reason why he should not have put Suffolk up. Following his chat with Henry's emissary Sir Richard Guildford, Suffolk was returning to England of his own free will and, with his East Anglian connections, Tyrell was an obvious port of call. Neither did the episode provoke any immediate response from Henry. Tyrell ostensibly continued in favour and some months later was co-opted on to one of the planning sub-committees for Arthur and Catherine's wedding. But in the autumn of 1499, at around the same time that Henry started to put the screws on Suffolk and his retainers, he issued Tyrell with a financial bond for allegiance of £300, then confiscated one of his lucrative royal estates, leasing it instead to a group of local farmers for an inflated rent. Henry never missed a chance for a quick profit – but, characteristically, it was also a warning shot. Tyrell's consorting with Suffolk had been noted.

By the summer of 1501 Tyrell was simmering with resentment. If, previously, his welcoming of Suffolk had been innocent, his long-dormant Yorkist loyalties had been provoked: Guisnes declared for Suffolk. And there was more bad news from Calais. Sir Robert Curzon, captain of the neighbouring fortress of Hammes, had gone over to Suffolk as well. Not only that, but it was, apparently, Curzon who had brokered Suffolk's flight to Maximilian.[11]

Part of the jousting set at court, Curzon, like Tyrell, was one of Henry's household knights, another ex-Ricardian whom Henry had grown to like – they played tennis together, Henry tended to lose – and, in 1498, he had appointed Curzon captain of Hammes. The following summer, around the time Suffolk turned up in Calais, Curzon applied to Henry for a licence to leave his post and go on crusade against the Ottoman Turkish army which, cutting a swath through the Balkans, was currently encroaching on the south-eastern border of the Holy Roman Empire. Curzon, in other words, was going to fight for Maximilian. To Henry, it seemed like a good idea. He and the emperor were in their period of post-Warbeck détente and, at a time when Maximilian was badgering him for large financial loans, it was a cost-effective way of showing his friendship – as well as gaining a reliable line of information at his erstwhile enemy's court.[12]

The plan backfired. In early 1500 Curzon had arrived at an imperial court awash with talk of the recent executions of Warbeck and Warwick. His own dormant allegiances had perhaps been stirred, for he regaled Maximilian with stories of Henry's 'murders and tyrannies'. He then put forward 'the proposal of my lord of Suffolk against king Henry to recover his right'.

Maximilian had listened, a gleam in his eye. After Warbeck, here was a fresh opportunity to turn England to his advantage, a handle in his own foreign adventures. If, Maximilian told Curzon, he 'might have one of king Edward's blood in his hands, he would help him to recover the crown of England and be revenged upon Henry'. He knew perfectly well what effect Yorkist pretenders had on the English king, and on his kingdom.

In summer 1501, as soon as Henry had got wind of Suffolk's destination, he dispatched two diplomatic veterans of the Warbeck crisis to open negotiations with the emperor's representatives. William Warham, one of Henry's brightest civil lawyers, and his head of security, the vice-chamberlain Sir Charles Somerset, were instructed to persuade Maximilian to expel Suffolk from his territories – and to do whatever it took.

As Maximilian's protracted support of Warbeck had petered out, Henry had, he thought, finally worked out how to deal with him. The stick of economic sanctions and trade embargoes had failed to make the emperor see sense, but the promise of financial aid – *hilfsgelder* – which

Henry waved in front of Maximilian concentrated his mind wonderfully. Constantly impecunious, he had 'long time desired' from Henry a loan of £10,000 towards his 'crusades against the Turks' – or rather, his expensive wars against the French and his ambitions in Italy, not to mention his long-planned journey to Rome to be crowned Holy Roman Emperor, which he had been unable to afford. In 1499, in place of a loan for his crusade, Henry had sent him Curzon. And now Maximilian had a new bargaining chip in Suffolk.[13]

At first, Warham and Somerset's embassy seemed to go well, with the emperor of 'resolute mind'. But as the negotiations went on and on, Maximilian kept shifting the goalposts. A weary tone crept into the ambassadors' dispatches. They had no idea what Maximilian was minded to do, and 'marvelled' at his inconstancy. He also had a habit of muttering asides to the counsellors around him that prompted sycophantic gales of laughter, in front of the English diplomats who stood uncomprehending and stony-faced. In private, Maximilian's advisers sympathized with the situation Warham and Somerset found themselves in – they too had 'to change their minds' when the emperor changed his, which was often. Instead of agreeing to the terms laid down by Henry for Suffolk's banishment, Maximilian now proposed that they should apply only to his hereditary Habsburg lands – 'far countries to the which your subjects seldom or never have any resort', Warham and Somerset told Henry. Maximilian was terribly sorry, but he could not give any such guarantees to Henry regarding the free imperial cities, the autonomous entities dotted throughout the imperial lands, for the electors would never commit to such an agreement. Maximilian probably anticipated Henry's request, for he had sent Suffolk to just one such city: Aachen. And he took Henry's £10,000.[14]

Calais's fortifications were strengthened, with a 'great substance of timber' shipped over, and England's coastal defences checked, from the south-eastern ports to Berwick on the Scottish border, whose captain, Sir Thomas Darcy, was ordered to employ a team of masons and labourers 'continually in occupation for the reparations' there.

In Kent, Sussex and the Channel ports, Sir Richard Guildford's men sifted loyalties; so too did those of Sir Reynold Bray. Information and tip-offs flooded in of suspicious behaviour, stolen ships and people slipping out of the country. In October 1501, as Catherine's flotilla fought its way through the Atlantic storms, a plot was uncovered at Beaulieu Abbey on the south coast, where Perkin Warbeck had once sought sanctuary. The abbot's porter, one Baskerville, and ten of the sanctuary men in his custody, tried to commandeer a ship to join Suffolk and were intercepted in the act, 'even at the point of going'. Under torture, Baskerville confessed and 'cursed much' two other men who, in a related plot, had stolen a ship full of Cornish tin, which they had intended to steer across the Channel. The insecurities of Warbeck had, it seemed, reignited. Each and every disturbance seemed to be construed as part of Suffolk's plot.[15]

As he moved to prevent events spinning out of control, and to assess and monitor the extent of Suffolk's support, Henry turned to the bonds and financial sureties that he and his administrators entered meticulously in his various books of accounts. In fact, his reliance on this system was intensifying markedly. Towards the end of 1499, after Suffolk's first flight, he had ordered officials in chancery to enrol – formally record – all names of both 'subjects and strangers', Englishmen and foreigners, who had been involved in cases of treason and of misprision – failing to report, or actively concealing, suspects – and who had been bound for sums of money. Armed with these lists and books of names, offences and fines, Henry and his counsellors had started to trawl through all cases of people who had been issued with bonds of various kinds – for debts owed, or for allegiance, 'good abearing' – whether recent or way back in the past, whether they had in fact committed an offence or not. In the wake of Suffolk's second flight, they started to use bonds systematically, not just to punish offences, but to guarantee loyalty: or, to put it another way, as a method of pre-emption.[16]

That summer, the king's administrators took an unprecedented series of bonds: in the standing garrison of Berwick, where Darcy was bound for £4,000 for the security of the town and castle, along with a number of the king's household knights, and across the country in Carlisle. In October, the preparations for Arthur and Catherine's wedding were being finalized, royal officials moved into East Anglia, armed with lists of the 'names of such persons as were servants of our rebel'. In his fortress of Headingham on the Essex–Suffolk border, Henry's point-man in the region, the earl of Oxford, took bond after bond from those associated with Suffolk: tenants and clients, yeomen, esquires, knights and lawyers. Anybody who failed to appear was deemed guilty and, when found, would be committed to prison 'till they find security'.[17]

Henry continued to spin his web. He played the long game, waiting and waiting, steadily assembling information as if nothing were untoward. Contemporaries all said the same thing. He would, said one, proceed 'circumspectly and with convenient diligence'; another, that he would 'always grope further', always with 'good await and espial' to those under surveillance. Almost invariably, few – even his closest servants – could tell anything from the king's outward appearance. Henry's method was to proceed with '*suaviter ac saeviter in modo*', a calm demeanour masking a savage intensity. Soncino, the Milanese ambassador, put it well. 'As the English say', he wrote to his boss Ludovico Sforza, describing Henry's pursuit of Warbeck, ' "Where can I go from your spirit? Where can I flee from your presence?" '[18]

Sometime in early 1502 a confidential discussion between two men took place in the Tower of London. One, William Hussey, was the younger brother of Sir John, one of Henry's financial administrators. The previous year, William had become caught up in some unspecified trouble, and had been forced to sign over his lands to leading royal officers – among them Sir Reynold Bray, Sir Thomas Lovell and his own brother – to be administered on behalf of the crown. Somehow, he had ended up in the Tower. And he was obviously rumoured to have connections to the earl of Suffolk, because he had got friendly with somebody – a fellow inmate, perhaps – who had asked his advice about the best way to defect. Hussey's friend never gave his name. His report of the conversation, though, ended up on the desk of one of Henry's spymasters.[19]

Hussey had spoken like somebody who knew what he was talking about. He urged the man to be upfront: to go direct to Suffolk and offer him 'true and faithful service'. His interlocutor agreed wholeheartedly, saying that this was what he had planned to do. The conversation was larded with the usual conspiratorial talk about astrological portents, while Hussey gave the man tokens that Suffolk would recognize as his, and that would accordingly lend credence to the defector.

But the exchange was not quite what it seemed. Access to many areas of the sprawling complex of the Tower – part royal palace, part armoury, part open prison – was for the most part relatively straight-forward. Only the privy lodgings and the maximum security quarters in its bowels, into which people disappeared and rarely came out again, were difficult to get to. In 1499, the plotters trying to release Warwick and Warbeck had found it easy enough to contact them. And in the murky world of counter-espionage, this arrangement could work both ways. Then, there had been much to suggest that a number of the plotters were royal agents provocateurs, egging the two reluctant Yorkist captives on to their deaths. The constable of the Tower Sir Simon Digby, and his deputy Sir Thomas Lovell, one of Henry's most intimate counsellors, had watched everything, waited, and then pounced.

As old allegiances stirred again, the same tactic was, it seems, being used. The man seeking William Hussey's advice was a plant – a royal spy posing as an adherent of Suffolk's, trying to inveigle himself into the exiled earl's household in order to find out the extent to which the conspiracy had taken root in England, and what was being planned. As he reported, Hussey clearly knew exactly what had gone on when Suffolk had absconded the previous summer. Hussey named times, places – and, above all, he named names.

Less than a week before Suffolk fled, according to Hussey, the earl had 'privily' hosted a dinner for a small group of close friends in London. The guests were high profile indeed. They included the young marquis of Dorset Thomas Grey, Henry Bourchier, earl of Essex, and Lord William Courtenay, heir of the earl of Devon. Essex and Courtenay were close companions of Suffolk. Essex had fought alongside him at Blackheath, while Courtenay had been caught up in the affray that had led to Suffolk's indictment for murder. All three had been named in Suffolk's team in the tournaments for the forthcoming wedding.[20]

Then, around the time of his flight, Suffolk had invited Courtenay's father, the earl of Devon, and an East Anglian gentleman, Sir Thomas Green, a friend of the Tyrell family, to dinner in a house in Warwick Lane, just around the corner from St Paul's. An onlooker – a servant in Suffolk's own household, maybe – reported how the earl himself came to the house's outer gate, to welcome his guest 'with great reverence', a sign perhaps that the earl of Devon knew all about Suffolk's impending flight. All this, Hussey said to the spy, had already 'come to the king's knowledge'.[21]

If this was the case, Henry had reacted to the news of potential conspiracy and betrayal with no outward change of demeanour. Throughout the wedding celebrations, as observers noted, he remained unruffled, the picture of poised majesty. The festivities, indeed, were the perfect opportunity to watch the behaviour of those whose loyalties had been called into question. This was precisely what Henry had done back in the autumn of 1494 when, amid the banqueting and tournaments for Prince Henry's creation as duke of York, he had scrutinized his rogue lord chamberlain Sir William Stanley and his associates until he was ready to move against them fast. In 1501, at the Westminster jousts, the moment when he rewarded Dorset's performance with a red-and-white rose of rubies and diamonds may have been a question, as much as a confirmation, of the young marquis's loyalty.

The spy's report of his conversation with Hussey had a sequel. In it, the spy recounted how he had made his way to Aachen and had succeeded in talking with Suffolk himself. Telling Suffolk how much the king already knew about the circumstances of his flight, the spy tried tentatively to draw the earl out on the allegiances of his fellow diners: 'in many men's minds', he said, the fact that they had been seen just before the flight made them suspect. Also, he said, it was widely rumoured that the earl of Devon was 'agreeable' to Suffolk's plans to flee and, when Suffolk returned to England with his invasion force, for him to land on the south Devon coast. Was this true?

Suffolk was hot-headed, proud and in many respects obtuse. But his reply was canny, deliberately preying on the king's doubts over his subjects' loyalties. He shrugged off the significance of the diners. He, Dorset, Essex and Courtenay were 'often times in such company together', he said, stressing that his guests knew nothing of his plans to flee. It was plausible enough. All were companions-in-arms, men of the same generation who had bonded at court and in the tiltyard. It was perfectly normal that they should dine together. When the spy persisted, Suffolk said simply that 'there is many pretty castings of eyes made to any countenance that was showed me' – people were bound to look askance at anybody associated with him before he fled. But, he continued, 'no force': it was not his problem. Henry's spies, counsellors, and the king himself, could 'judge by outward counten-ance what they will' – they could construe whatever they wanted from such behaviour. Suffolk, in other words, confirmed nothing, and denied nothing. His reply left a broader, unspoken, question hanging in the air. Was the king chasing shadows – or was he chasing a genu-ine, dynasty-threatening conspiracy? It was, went Suffolk's equivocal reply, up to Henry to find out.[22]

Henry and his counsellors worked hard to disentangle rumour from evidence. The king continued to block off potential European bolt-holes for Suffolk, negotiating extradition treaties – all backed up with hefty financial inducements – with the countries bordering Maximil-ian's territories, from the kingdom of Hungary to the prince-bishopric of Liège, the small city-state bordering Suffolk's refuge of Aachen.

Across the Channel, in Calais, the situation remained tense. In October 1501, as Henry reinforced the security of his major fort-resses, he had ordered a senior Calais official, its porter Sir Sampson Norton, to occupy Tyrell's stronghold of Guisnes. Norton failed to do so, and Tyrell and his garrison remained holed up. The overall com-mander of Calais, Henry's lord chamberlain Giles lord Daubeney, and Henry's master diplomat Richard Fox became involved in protracted correspondence with Tyrell, sending 'fair words' requesting him to come to England and explain his conduct before the king's council. If he did so, they promised, all would be forgiven. Tyrell, however, was an old hand. He stayed put.

Then, sometime in February 1502, the black-clad figure of Sir Tho-mas Lovell materialized in Calais. In his capacity as one of the king's chief financial officers, Lovell made regular trips over to the Pale, supervising the collection of the annual pension due to Henry in danger money from the French crown, and the substantial customs revenues from Calais's wool trade, paid directly into the treasure chests of the king's chamber. But Lovell was up to something else, too.

Strange things tended to happen when Lovell was around. Some years earlier, he had been in Calais when Henry's former household steward, Lord Fitzwalter, who had been imprisoned in Calais Castle for his part in the Warbeck plot, was caught trying to escape – a put-up job, so rumour had it – and unceremoniously beheaded. And Lovell had, of course, been lurking in the background when Warwick and Warbeck were caught up in the plot to break them out of the Tower in 1499. Now, Lovell made his way out to Guisnes Castle for a friendly chat with Tyrell. Whatever he said was convincing. Leaving his son Thomas in charge of Guisnes, Tyrell made his way with Lovell back to Calais harbour to take ship for England.[23]

As they sailed into the open waters of the Channel, Lovell's pleasant demeanour changed. Seizing Tyrell, he threatened to throw him overboard unless he sent word to his son to surrender Guisnes to the king's officers. There was nothing Tyrell could do. Together with two other suspects, Sir John Wyndham and a servant of Tyrell's called Robert Wellesbourne, Tyrell and his son were brought back to London and thrown in the Tower, where they were visited by members of the king's council, to whom treason cases were entrusted. Henry, very probably, took a hand in the questioning too.[24]

It was normal for kings to interrogate suspects, and Henry was no exception. Payments for 'bringing up of prisoners' litter his chamber accounts, and after Warbeck's failed invasion at Deal in 1495, he cross-examined many of his captured supporters under threat of death. Henry's method of questioning is well documented, from his probing of Warbeck in the Tower, to his cross-examining of the many people that brought him information. As with his way of assembling intelligence, it was gentle, meticulous and logical: perfectly clear, so that people could understand what was being asked of them, leaving no room for evasion. If they then started twisting and turning, he then snapped, 'suaviter ac saeviter' as Soncino had said. It was the kind of interrogation technique that left people trembling in apprehension, wondering when the storm would break.

Whether or not Henry himself had people tortured is unrecorded, though if not, he would be unique among monarchs of the age. The characteristic secrecy with which he operated is a more ready explanation. His officials, in the usual way, resorted to torture – 'straight handling', or 'some pain' – at the drop of a hat, as soon as a suspect showed signs of resistance or 'stomach' or was overly 'crafty in making his answers'. Methods of applying pain were many and ingenious, in particular the ways of twisting, stretching and manipulating the body out of shape, normally falling under the catch-all term of the rack, or the brakes. Often, these machines were customized and named according to the twisted imaginations of their practitioners: in the Tower in the 1450s, there was a brake called 'the duke of Exeter's daughter'.[25] Whatever happened to Tyrell and his associates in the Tower that March, somebody talked.

Amid rumours of an imperial-backed invasion by Suffolk, and as the earl and his right-hand man Sir Robert Curzon were anathematized by bell, book and candle at St Paul's Cross, the country remained on a state of high alert. In March, a detachment of Sir Reynold Bray's men swooped on Portchester Castle, whose strategic position on the Hampshire coast made it a crucial link in England's defences, and whose garrison had, apparently, been infiltrated by Suffolk sympathizers. The suspects were arrested, taken to nearby Winchester and, on 19 March, amid a city preparing for the Palm Sunday festivities, summarily beheaded. One of the ringleaders, the castle's constable, Charles Rippon, had history. Years before, he had been caught up in the Stanley conspiracy and, as Henry's net closed, he had been arrested, then pardoned. He had subsequently fought for Henry against the Cornish rebels at Blackheath in 1497 – but that, it seemed, was hardly a guarantee of loyalty: so too had Suffolk. As Henry trawled through his lists of suspects, Rippon, like so many, had again fallen under suspicion.[26] Then, in April, came the catastrophic news of Arthur's death. After that, things started to snowball.

On 18 April Venetian dispatches from England reported that the king was 'in trouble' and 'had ordered the arrest of one of his chamber attendants', a yeoman usher called Matthew Jones.[27] Although Jones's role in

the conspiracy was obscure, his arrest indicated a horribly familiar phenomenon: disloyalty deep within the king's household. Around the same time, another far more prominent attendant was seized by Henry's guardsmen as he did his 'daily diligence to the king' and carried away to the Tower: Lord William Courtenay, son of the earl of Devon and Queen Elizabeth's brother-in-law, and one of those who had 'banqueted privily' with Suffolk in the days before he fled. With him was Suffolk's youngest brother, William de la Pole, who as a Plantagenet could not be allowed to remain at liberty any longer. News of the pre-emptive detentions, 'for favour which they bore unto Sir Edmund de la Pole, as the fame then went', swirled around London.[28] The capital was tense. On 30 April, two unnamed men, one old and one young, imprisoned for 'certain slanderous words spoken by them of the king and his council', were taken to the Tun at Cornhill, the barrel-shaped stone conduit over which the third pageant of Catherine's reception had been constructed the previous November, and locked in the pillory on top of it. After standing there for an hour being pelted with rubbish and stones, their ears were hacked off. They were then sent back to prison.

The following Monday, 2 May, London's Guildhall was the scene of a high-profile show trial. After some two months in the Tower, Sir James Tyrell, his servant Robert Wellesbourne, Sir John Wyndham and a shipman were hauled before a judicial commission. The same day, they were convicted of treason and sentenced to be hanged, drawn and quartered. Four days later, their sentences commuted to a quicker, less agonizing death, Tyrell and Wyndham were beheaded away from public view in the seclusion of Tower Hill. From his walk-on part in Suffolk's conspiracy, Tyrell's role was to assume greater dimensions beyond the grave. Not long after his execution, it was being said that he had confessed to murdering Edward IV's sons, the princes in the Tower. A decade on, Thomas More had transformed Tyrell into the archetype of the over-ambitious courtier, a man whose heart 'sore longed upward', who organized the princes' deaths at Richard III's behest. By the end of the sixteenth century, following More, Shakespeare immortalized Tyrell as the perpetrator of 'the most arch deed of piteous massacre/ That ever yet this land was guilty of.'[29]

Tyrell's servant, Robert Wellesbourne, 'remained in prison abiding the king's grace and pardon'. It soon became clear why. The following

Saturday, in the White Hall of Westminster Palace, Tyrell's son Thomas, Matthew Jones and Sir Robert Curzon's pursuivant, or courier, were paraded in a carefully staged indictment: the key witness was their co-conspirator Wellesbourne. Jones and the courier were sentenced to death and shipped back across the Channel to Guisnes, where they were executed as an example to Tyrell's recalcitrant garrison.[30]

Wellesbourne's testimony had been crucial. Jones had probably been arrested on his evidence, so too Rippon and his colleagues at Portchester, all events that had occurred after Wellesbourne's arrival in England. Whether he had been a double-agent all along – Welles-bourne's family had strong connections with Tyrell, but also with Sir Thomas Lovell – or had been turned by Henry's agents is debatable, but it was probably the latter. The king had long had a reputation for being able to intimidate, flatter and turn conspirators into useful lines of royal intelligence – Warbeck had denounced, in rather prim tones, the 'importunate labour' of Henry and his agents to 'certain of our servants about our person, some of them to murder our person, and other to forsake and leave our righteous quarrel.'[31] Wellesbourne, 'alias Hodgekinson', was only the latest in a long and dishonourable line. Towards the end of May, he received a royal pardon for services rendered, and was retained by the king on the comfortable half-year's salary of 60s 10d. The following month, he seems to have been back in the Low Countries, where he managed to get access to the earl of Suffolk's confidential correspondence, copying letters and sending them back to Henry. These would not be the last of his services.[32]

Over this rash of punishment and execution loomed the shadow of Prince Arthur's death. His coffined body, disembowelled, embalmed, spiced and wrapped in waxed cloth, was placed in his chamber at Ludlow Castle, until 23 April, St George's Day, by which time the royal mourning party had arrived from London with orders for the funeral ceremonies. As custom dictated, the royal family was absent. The entourage, which included Garter king-at-arms John Writhe and a number of prominent nobles, was headed by Thomas Howard, earl of Surrey. Surrey's appointment as principal mourner was significant. Having completed his political rehabilitation, this former supporter of

Richard III had been chosen over a more obvious candidate: the duke of Buckingham, higher in rank than Surrey and the greatest landowner in the Welsh Marches after the crown. Buckingham, though, had royal blood. His presence in the funeral entourage risked connecting him with the succession, particularly now that the Tudor dynasty hung by a thread. The choice of burial place was significant, too. Arthur's body would not be buried in Westminster Abbey, but in Worcester Cathedral.

It was a practical choice. Lying in the region subject to the council in the Marches, Worcester was associated with Prince Arthur; that it was the site of another royal tomb – that of King John – also counted in its favour. Besides which, the spring storms that year made the roads practically impassable. When, after a funeral ceremony in Ludlow parish church, the cortège set off on 25 April, it was in driving rain and violent winds: 'foul', grumbled John Writhe, and the road 'the worst way that I have seen'; the carriage bearing Arthur's coffin was repeatedly stuck in mud, and oxen were brought to haul it. But there was, perhaps, another reason for Arthur's burial in the English mid-lands, away from London and the glare of domestic and international attention. The disaster of Arthur's death was something Henry wanted to play down, rather than play up.[33]

For all this, the funeral rites were on a scale befitting the size of the tragedy, involving some 550 people and costing the best part of £900. Nearly 2,400 yards of black mourning cloth were allocated to the mourners, varying in quality, quantity and cut according to the wearer's status; over 6,000 pounds of candle wax were burned. Over the coffin, draped in black cloth-of-gold embroidered with a white cross, through the wind and rain, was carried a canopy of purple damask sprinkled with golden flowers. Inside Worcester Cathedral, the coffin was transferred to its hearse, a vast, storeyed, wooden structure, painted black and adorned with heraldic escutcheons, badged pennants or 'pencels', silk standards of St George, banners of the royal arms of England and Spain, and of Arthur's various titles, from Wales to Pon-thieu in Normandy. Over it hung a cloth of estate, with a woven picture of Christ and the four evangelists, trimmed with valences decorated with the ostrich feathers of Wales and Arthur's motto. In the gloom of the cathedral, all this glittered in the light of over a thousand candles. It was, said Writhe, the best funeral he had ever seen.[34]

Following a night-long vigil, the ceremonies approached their climax. As a requiem mass was sung in the cathedral, through the west door and the crowds of mourners came a man on horseback. Wearing Arthur's own plate armour and gripping a poleaxe, blade downwards, the man-at-arms rode an armoured, black-caparisoned courser up the nave and into the choir; there, in front of the bishops, abbots and officers-of-arms, he dismounted and presented the horse to the gospel reader. After Arthur's coat-of-arms, shield, sword and helmet, the symbols of his earthly roles, had been offered up by the attendant nobility along with palls of cloth-of-gold, his coffin was lowered into the open grave. William Smith, bishop of Lincoln and head of Arthur's council, 'sore weeping', cast holy water and earth onto the coffin. Then, as custom dictated, the prince's household servants broke their staves and rods of office in two, and threw them into the grave; among them was Arthur's herald, Wallingford pursuivant Thomas Writhe, the eldest son of Garter king-of-arms. Arthur's household was now disbanded, the dead prince's servants bereft, masterless: 'to have seen the weepings when the offering was done', commented the funeral account, 'he had a hard heart that wept not.'[35]

Kicking his heels in Aachen, Suffolk was not slow to grasp the significance of the situation. When news reached him of Arthur's death, he fired off an urgent dispatch to Maximilian. The emperor, he wrote, should know of the danger that his friends in England were in – Suffolk was evidently unaware of the recent slew of executions – a danger that increased daily as the king's security forces closed in on them. With the regime reeling and newly vulnerable, now was his chance to return to England and to confront the king, but it was, he stressed urgently, a race against time: 'I have been warned in no uncertain terms, that King Henry is seeking in all places, and through all kinds of people that he can buy off with gold and silver, to destroy me; and moreover', he added, 'the longer I stay out of England, the stronger King Henry will become, and the worse it will be for me.'[36]

Over the past months, the emperor had proved evasive and inconsistent, and Suffolk had a hunch that something was up. As he grumbled
to his steward Thomas Killingworth, who was representing Suffolk's
interests at the imperial court, he was fed up with the way he was
forced to 'dissimulate' to Maximilian in order to earn his goodwill and
a meagre supply of credit. Suffolk, though rarely quick on the uptake,
suspected – correctly – that one of the people taking Henry's gold and
silver was Maximilian himself.

Henry was indeed spending inordinate amounts of money on bribes
and intelligence. Throughout the civil wars of the fifteenth century,
espionage had been a constant drain on the crown's resources: in one
year alone, Edward IV had spent well over £2,000 on 'certain secret
matters' concerning the kingdom and, as Warbeck had noted, Henry
was willing to stretch his budget to an almost infinite degree, by offering 'large sums of money' to 'corrupt the princes in every land and
country and that we have been retained with'. Already, Henry's pursuit of Suffolk was involving financial transactions on a massive
scale – and as it turned out, this was only the beginning.

Soon after Arthur's death, Henry continued his reshuffle of Calais officials, with the appointment of Sir John Wilshere as comptroller, or chief
financial officer, of the enclave. A London merchant-turned-household-
official, Wilshere had been one of the gentleman-ushers of Henry's
chamber. Loyal, watchful and experienced, he also had a head for figures, knowledge of international markets and a raft of contacts in the
city and the commercial centres of the Low Countries. He was, in short,
Henry's kind of servant. In keeping watch on Calais's finances, Wilshere
acted as another line of information, ordered to keep his account books
separately from the Calais treasurer so that Henry could check both,
compare – and contrast – for corruption and peculation. But the new
comptroller had other roles, too, for which he was perfectly suited.[37]

Wilshere, a confidential brief stipulated, was to be one of the chief
nodes of Henry's espionage network, a control in touch with all the
existing agents and 'enterprisers' working out of Calais against Suffolk and his circle. He was to employ more spies, as many as he saw
fit, on the crown's behalf, and he was to keep them motivated and

loyal. He was also instructed to try and turn Suffolk's men, promising them royal pardons on the understanding that they named names and provided other credible intelligence on the earl and his conspiracy. Wilshere would report to a 'Messire Charles'. This, almost certainly, was Sir Charles Somerset. A member of Lady Margaret's Beaufort clan, he was cousin to the king and one of his inner circle, a powerful presence in the royal household where he was captain of the guard and vice-chamberlain, one of the people Wilshere would have answered to in his previous role as gentleman-usher. Somerset, too, wore another hat: that of high-level diplomat, entrusted with the most delicate of negotiations, and spymaster. Along with the likes of Lovell, Fox, Bray and Guildford, he lurked behind the activities of Henry's 'flies and familiars'.[38]

Wilshere's role as intelligencer merged seamlessly with the world of high finance. He was to be kept fully briefed on the vast bribes that Henry was paying to Maximilian, transferred to the emperor through the London branches of international merchant banks, in order that he could co-ordinate activities on the ground. As soon as Wilshere heard the relevant instalments had been processed, he was to ensure that Maximilian – who had, finally, added his signature to the new extradition treaty – stuck to his side of the bargain. Wilshere's men were to monitor the proclamation banishing Suffolk and his men from imperial territories, checking that it was correctly announced and published in all towns and cities 'where the king's said rebels might be', in exactly the wording specified 'in French and Latin by the king's council', together with a comprehensive list of the 'names and surnames of the king's rebels that they may be banished'. For good measure, Wilshere was to send a German translation of the proclamation to the emperor.[39] Henry was determined to get full value for his £10,000. All this activity, however, only served to confirm what Henry and Maximilian both knew: that with Arthur's death, Suffolk's value – and the emperor's bargaining power – had increased exponentially.

Suffolk knew it too. In a separate note to Killingworth, he instructed the steward to impress upon the emperor the enormity of the new situation. The only figure that now remained between Suffolk and his claim was King Henry's second son – and if he should 'happen to die', there would be 'no doubt' whatsoever of Suffolk's title.

Nor could there be any doubting the significance of Suffolk's words – or what he meant when he talked of his 'title'. In the event of Prince Henry's death, Suffolk, as a Plantagenet, was well placed to inherit the English throne. Even alive, the eleven-year-old prince barely seemed an obstacle. Prince Henry, he sneered, 'will pose no kind of a threat'.[40]

Back in Ludlow, Catherine had not accompanied the funeral cortège to Worcester. Grieving, she was herself dangerously ill. She was carried slowly back to London, still weak, in a litter of black velvet sent by a solicitous Queen Elizabeth. By early May, she was convalescing at Lady Margaret Beaufort's Thameside palace of Croydon, west of Richmond, where she received a stream of messengers from Henry and Elizabeth, and wrote to her parents, reassuring them that she was herself well out of danger, and removed from the 'unhealthy situation' at Ludlow.

Apart from a natural concern for the young widow, there was another reason for the solicitous attention shown her: the possibility that she might be carrying her dead husband's child. If she were, and if she had a boy, that child would be heir to the English throne; Catherine, as his mother, would continue to occupy the honoured place within the new dynasty that her wedding reception had signified. Catherine, however, was not pregnant – and therefore, she was no longer part of her dead husband's family. Prince Henry was heir to the throne.[41]

Ferdinand and Isabella, meanwhile, sent a stream of urgent dispatches to Rodrigo de Puebla, varying wildly in tone from the assertive to the querulous. They 'confidently' expected that Henry would 'fulfil his obligations' to their daughter, which included giving Catherine her dower lands – the estates due to her as a widow – so that she could pay her household expenses. They were sure that the king of England would not break his word 'at any time, and much less at present whilst the Princess is overwhelmed with grief'. This rather overemphatic confidence in Henry's probity betrayed that they fully expected him not to keep his promise.

In fact, they had been alarmed to hear that people in England were already advising Catherine to borrow money against the gold, jewels and silver that she had brought with her as part of her marriage portion, because Henry was hardly going to provide for her. De Puebla was to instruct Juan de Cuero, Catherine's wardrober, to keep the treasure secure, in case she started selling or pawning it. And Catherine herself, Ferdinand and Isabella commanded, should be sent straight home to Spain on the next available ship: 'We cannot endure that a daughter whom we love should be so far from us when she is in affliction.'[42]

But as Ferdinand and Isabella wept crocodile tears, they were also playing a game of double bluff. Catherine remained a highly valuable commodity in the world of international politics, and now she was evidently not pregnant, she was free to marry again. Far from wanting their daughter shipped back, her parents were very keen indeed that she should wed the 'Prince of Wales that now is' – 'without delay'.[43]

The Spanish monarchs, in fact, were more desperate than ever to have England onside. Back in 1499 the new French king, Louis XII, had picked up where his predecessor had left off. Re-invading and re-occupying swathes of northern Italy, his armies were once again on the warpath against Spanish-ruled Naples. Fearing complete French domination of the peninsula, Ferdinand and Isabella were now trying to hustle Henry into a new marriage alliance that would, again, force him to commit to war against France – or, at the very least, put quantities of his fabled wealth towards it. If, as they wrote to de Puebla that August, the new betrothal and its accompanying treaty could be arranged, 'all our anxiety would cease, and we shall be able to seek the aid of England against France'.[44]

Eager to show they had a card to play, Ferdinand and Isabella offered to exert pressure on Maximilian to give up the earl of Suffolk. The Spanish monarchs had a strong presence at the court of the emperor's son, Archduke Philip of Burgundy, who had married their daughter, Catherine's sister Juana of Castile. The coterie of Castilian diplomats at the Burgundian court, they reasoned, might be able to pull some strings. It was a lame offer, and Henry knew it.[45]

Henry temporized. Here, at least, he was in a strong position to negotiate – and he was unwilling to rush into anything. By the autumn, the tone of Ferdinand and Isabella's letters was subdued, far from the bullishness of earlier in the year. They told their ambassadors not to mention anything to Henry about France, in case it put him off the idea of a betrothal, adding plaintively that, were the betrothal to take place it 'might chance' that Henry's friendship 'might prove an advantage to us'. Once the paperwork was in place, they reasoned, they could continue lobbying Henry about military intervention.[46]

As 1502 wore on, changes were afoot at Eltham, as Prince Henry's little household began to transform itself into an establishment fit for an heir. And Queen Elizabeth's consoling words to Henry had been proved right. She was pregnant again.

4

Now Must You Supply the Mother's Part Also

On Christmas Day 1502, Henry made his customary procession, crowned and in a gown of purple velvet lined with sable, through Richmond's public chambers and galleries to the Chapel Royal, surrounded by a thicket of lords temporal and spiritual dressed in their robes of estate, his way lined with halberd-bearing guards pushing back anybody 'so hardy' as to approach. There, before the high altar, as the choir's voices soared upwards to the blue, star-flecked ceiling, Henry knelt and made his offering of a 'noble in gold', 6s 8d. After him, his eleven-year-old son stepped forward to make his offering of five shillings, not as the duke of York, but, for the first time, as 'my lord prince'. At the centre of things, too, was the reassuring sight of Elizabeth. Cheeks flushed, heavily pregnant, she heard the children of the Chapel Royal sing William Cornish's new setting of a carol, and on Boxing Day, she settled down to endless games of cards, gambling away a hundred shillings.[1]

As usual that Christmas, the solemn liturgies and crown-wearing processions were interwoven with the feasts, the endless processions of extravagantly dressed and spiced dishes borne out of the royal kitchens, the distribution of largesse to heralds and winter clothing to the household servants, and the entertainments: a succession of tumblers, singers, carollers and minstrels, interludes and plays. Weaving through the festivities on his hobby horse pranced the mocking master of ceremonies, the lord of misrule. Pursued by his band of gaudily dressed, painted fools, he supervised the programme of revels and 'rarest pastimes to delight the beholders', with its satirical upending of the established order – kitchen servants strutting around with the airs, graces and clothing of great men; household officers acting as

93

menials – all to be done, of course, 'without quarrel or offence'.[2] Behind this temporary upside-down world lurked a sense of the fragility of things, that the lurching wheel of fortune which raised people up could as quickly overturn them. Riches, honour, wealth, and life, could disappear in an instant.

On New Year's Day, servants queued to present the king and queen with gifts from their masters: large sums of money from Henry's close counsellors and, from others, fine foods and exotic fruits – pomegranates, branches of oranges, figs – and a snarling leopard, with which Henry was clearly delighted, rewarding the giver liberally with £13 6s 8d.[3] Among the gifts was a small Latin manuscript entitled 'The Book of the Excellent Fortunes of Henry duke of York and his Parents'. The composer of this fulsome horoscope was William Parron, the Italian astrologer who had carved out for himself a role at court as a semi-official peddler of prognostications, which he combined with a sideline in cheap printed almanacks. The fashionable classical allusions which Parron sprinkled over his predictions may have given them a certain superficial authority, but he made sure to tell Henry what he wanted to hear: his most notorious moment to date had been his advocacy of the judicial murder of Edward earl of Warwick back in autumn 1499. Now, in the wake of Arthur's death, Parron's horoscope for 1503 predicted the glowing futures of Henry, Elizabeth and Prince Henry, who received his own personalized copy, dedicated to him in his new role as prince of Wales. This time, though, Parron had overreached himself. Elizabeth, he forecast, would live to the age of eighty.[4]

Late in January, the royal household moved downriver, to the Tower. Elizabeth was carefully ferried in her barge, reclining heavily on cushions and carpets, burning braziers filled with sweet herbs to mask the smells of the freezing Thames, her twenty-two oarsmen rowing with particular care. At the Tower, the rituals of childbirth began with a ceremonial mass in the chapel of St John the Evangelist, followed by a 'void' of spiced wine and sweetmeats. Then, surrounded by her ladies and gentlewomen, her mother-in-law Lady Margaret Beaufort at their head, Elizabeth went into confinement.

Following ordinances drawn up by Lady Margaret, the chamber

in which Elizabeth would give birth had been meticulously well appointed. Above the heavily carpeted floor, the ceiling, walls, 'windows and all' were swathed in blue arras peppered with gold fleurs-de-lys, signifying kingship and that paradigm of motherhood, the Virgin Mary. One window only was left uncovered to admit light. The room had a cupboard gleaming with plate, two cradles standing in readiness and a 'rich altar' encrusted with relics of the saints. Below their velvet, gold and ermine canopies of estate worked with embroidered red-and-white roses stood the bed on which the queen was to give birth, and at its foot a pallet, half-throne, half day-bed, with furnishings of velvet and cloth-of-gold and counterpanes of ermine-fringed scarlet. In this opulent, womblike environment, in which the events crucial to the dynasty and the country would unfold, the queen's status was exalted, almost sacred. The furnishings, too, were designed with tranquillity in mind, the simple patterns of the fleurs-de-lys preferred to more elaborately designed arras with 'images', so as not to overstimulate 'women in such case'. And while Alice Massy, Elizabeth's favoured midwife, was in attendance, there were as usual no physicians. The presence of men in this all-female environment was forbidden – besides which doctors, it was thought, only served to cause anxiety to women in labour.[5]

On 2 February, the household celebrated Candlemas. Of all the great feasts of estate, Candlemas was one of the most distinctive. Forty days after Christmas, its candles emphasized the light brought into the world by the new-born child. In the depth of winter they symbolized, too, rebirth and renewal, bringing a sense that the first faint signs of spring could not be too far away. On that day, barely a fortnight into a confinement intended to last a month, Elizabeth was convulsed by sudden and violent contractions.[6]

The traumatic and premature labour was badly handled, and Elizabeth became feverish. Soon, she had a raging temperature and was slipping in and out of consciousness. Waiting with mounting anxiety outside his wife's apartments, Henry frenziedly sought medical advice. Messengers rode through the night into Kent and the west country to summon specialists. Nothing worked. On 11 February, her thirty-seventh birthday, Elizabeth died. Her sickly baby daughter, hastily christened Catherine, followed soon after.[7]

Nobody, those around Henry reported, had ever 'seen or heard' the king in such a state. Anguish ruptured the poised regality in which he had sublimated all his anxieties. Years before, in exile, rumours of Elizabeth's betrothal to Richard III had 'pinched him to the very stomach'; now, her death provoked in him a visceral response.

As his wife's newly coffined body lay in the chapel of St John the Evangelist, bathed in the light of innumerable candles, and attended by her mourning gentlewomen and the 'great estates' of court, the king left the funeral ceremonies in the hands of Lady Margaret Beaufort, Thomas Howard, earl of Surrey and Sir Richard Guildford. Commanding six hundred masses to be sung in London's churches, Henry, surrounded by a clutch of his close servants in mourning black, 'privily departed to a solitary place to pass his sorrows and would no man should resort to him'. His barge slid away from the Tower and up the wintry Thames to Richmond. There, he disappeared, up flights of stairs, through the succession of public chambers and galleries into the building's heart, his privy chamber, where he collapsed.[8]

On Wednesday 22 February Queen Elizabeth's funeral procession snaked through London's crowded, silent streets, from the Tower to her place of burial at Westminster Abbey. Bells tolled and priests stood in church doorways with swaying censers, the pungent smell of incense drifting over the cortège as it passed. With a vanguard of horsebacked lords, among them London's mayor and Garter king-of-arms John Writhe, the hearse was drawn by eight warhorses caparisoned in black velvet. On it rested a painted, intricately modelled effigy of the late queen, clothed in her crown and robes of estate, bejewelled hands clutching her sceptre. The hearse was accompanied by two hundred poor men, their presence believed to be a powerful act of intercession with Christ, bearing lighted tapers. Following them came the queen's gentlewomen, eight ladies of honour riding black palfreys, the rest in two carriages, each drawn by a team of six horses. Chaplains, squires, knights and aldermen rode alongside, black gowns draped behind, their mourning hoods pulled down obscuring their faces. The orders of friars patronized by Elizabeth, the Carmelites in their white habits and the Augustinians in black, joined the king's chapel choir in the singing of 'solemn anthems'. Then followed representatives of London's guilds and the city's foreign mercantile and banking communities: Spanish, French, Dutch and Germans, Venetians, Florentines, Lucchese and Genoese.

On that dark February day, the overwhelming impression made on the London chronicler was one of light. From the manor of Blanch Appleton on the city's eastern edge to Temple Bar in the west, the city was illuminated. Over 4,000 flaming torches lit the streets through which the procession passed, while the main streets of Cornhill and Cheapside, 'garnished thoroughly with new torches', were lined with white-clad men holding burning brands. At Fenchurch Street and the top of Cheapside stood groups of thirty-seven virgins, one for each year of the late queen's life, dressed in white, holding lighted tapers.[9]

Though founded on pragmatism, Henry and Elizabeth's marriage had nevertheless blossomed throughout the uncertainty and upheaval of the previous eighteen years. This was a marriage of 'faithful love', of mutual attraction, affection and respect, from which the king seems to have drawn great strength – indeed, it was the kind of marriage that their second son, Prince Henry, would spend his whole life trying to find. With Elizabeth's burial, the lights went out all over Henry VII's court. The reign was plunged into crisis. Henry, shattered, would never be the same again. For his young, vulnerable son, so recently saddled with the burden of impending kingship, it was a traumatic loss.

Beautiful, serene and able, through all the crises of the reign Elizabeth had been the embodiment of reconciliation. A focus for the loyalties of many who had accepted Henry's rule, she had produced six children, the stuff of a new dynasty, and had been a charismatic counterpart to her increasingly suspicious, controlling husband. In life, nobody had a bad word to say about her and, as the outpouring of grief on her death testified, she was genuinely loved. Her serenity was sometimes mistaken for passivity, as by the Spanish ambassador Pedro de Ayala, who reported acidly that she was 'beloved because she was powerless'. But Elizabeth's true quality lay in an apparently

artless graciousness, which was thrown into relief by the close proximity of the king's sharp-elbowed mother.

Deeply pious and a stickler for protocol, Lady Margaret Beaufort
ran her own household with a rod of iron. If she was a bit of a nag –
even her saintly confessor, John Fisher, remarked on how she tended
to repeat the same moralizing stories 'many a time' – the appearance
of her slight form, clad in black gown, mantle and wimple was faintly
intimidating. She had, Fisher noted, a particular gift for 'bolting
out faction', for sniffing out suspect loyalties among her household
servants.[10]

Royal mothers tended to busy themselves with the affairs of their
sons and daughters-in-law – but at a distance. Lady Margaret Beaufort, however, was very much more hands-on. Adopting the airs and
graces of a queen, she was constantly at Elizabeth's shoulder – literally
so, walking a mere half-pace behind her in public ceremonials. In
some royal houses, her apartments were next to the king's own; at
Henry's Oxfordshire manor of Woodstock, they shared an intercon-
necting 'drawing chamber', to which they could retreat to discuss
politics or play cards. The upheavals of the 1490s only served to
increase her influence. In 1499, after separating from her husband
Thomas Stanley, earl of Derby – whose family remained under a cloud
following their involvement in the Warbeck conspiracy – she altered
her signature to 'Margaret R': possibly an abbreviation of 'Richmond', it also looked like the queen's 'Elizabeth Regina'. At court, on
progress, or through her servants who, like the powerful Sir Reynold
Bray, had become members of the king's household, Margaret was
constantly watching, observing, organizing. It felt to one Spanish
envoy as though she kept Elizabeth 'in subjection'. Others agreed.
One irritated petitioner, trying to gain access to the queen, suggested
that Margaret was, more or less, her gatekeeper: he would, he said,
have spoken more with Elizabeth 'had it not been for that strong
whore, the king's mother'.[11]

If Elizabeth resented Lady Margaret's intrusion on her territory, she
kept her thoughts to herself. It was, after all, only natural that the
reign's self-styled matriarch should have taken the younger woman
under her wing. There was, too, much to suggest that as Elizabeth
settled into her role as queen, this became a relationship of equals. If

Lady Margaret paraded her spirituality across the full spectrum of visible acts of piety – punctiliously observed daily rituals, devotion to cults of saints and any number of good works, from the giving of alms to the endowment of chantries – so too did Elizabeth. Early in the reign, Lady Margaret had commissioned the printer William Caxton to publish the romance *Blanchardin and Eglantine*, apparently in honour of the love-story that was Henry and Elizabeth's marriage; later, Margaret and Elizabeth together commissioned from Caxton *The Fifteen Oes*, a highly popular prayer sequence whose fifteen prayers, each beginning 'O blessed Jesu' – hence the title – underscored their devotion to the fashionable cult of the Name of Jesus.

Henry, too, spoke of them in the same breath. When in 1498 he wrote to the Scottish king James IV to postpone the wedding between James and his daughter Margaret, then nine years old, he cited intensive lobbying by 'the Queen and my mother'. When, in the run-up to Prince Arthur and Catherine's wedding, Lady Margaret drew up a list of the queen's attendants, there were spaces for names to be included – after discussion with Elizabeth.

Elizabeth was a discreet, persuasive lobbyist on her own account. London's key politicians and merchants cultivated her assiduously; so too did foreign diplomats. They did so not because she was 'powerless', but quite the opposite. Beneath the emollience was a steeliness, glimpsed in the brisk letters she wrote intervening in legal affairs, and in petitioning her husband for favours on behalf of her servants. When Pope Alexander VI requested that his representative in England be given the vacant bishopric of Worcester, Henry wrote back apologetically, explaining that his queen had already bagged the post for her confessor. Elizabeth could, it seemed, put her foot down. During the preparations for Arthur and Catherine's wedding, the Spanish ambassador de Puebla handed over letters in duplicate to the queen from Catherine of Aragon and from her parents. Henry wanted copies of each 'to carry continually about him'. Elizabeth refused. One set, she said, was for Prince Arthur, and she 'did not like to part with hers'; the resulting marital tiff was played out in front of Lady Margaret and the watching de Puebla.[12]

Elizabeth combined a strong sense of family loyalty – including a love for her siblings which was, according to Henry VII's chronicler Bernard André, '*ferme incredibilis*', truly extraordinary – with a strong awareness of the new political dispensation that she represented.[13] In early 1495, in the face of Warbeck's continued threat and the recent upheavals within the royal household, she had brokered and funded high-profile marriages for her younger sisters, Anne and Katherine, in the process binding two noble families further into the regime: Anne's husband was the oldest son of Thomas Howard, earl of Surrey; Katherine, meanwhile, married Lord William Courtenay, son of the earl of Devon. As her extended family became entangled in the various crises of the reign, Elizabeth's quietly emollient role continued to dovetail with Henry's policies. After the flight of her cousin the earl of Suffolk in August 1501, she arranged accommodation for his unfortunate wife Margaret who, having been under surveillance for two years as a result of her husband's intriguing, had her lands and revenues annexed by the crown – the proceeds flowed into Elizabeth's own coffers. When in spring the following year Elizabeth's brother-in-law William Courtenay was tainted by association with Suffolk and incarcerated in the Tower, she sent him a care package of clothes: shirts, a gown and a 'night bonnet'. The Courtenay children, meanwhile, were securely looked after at the queen's Essex house of Havering-at-Bower.[14]

Elizabeth's household staff mirrored that of her husband. Among her gentlewomen were the wives of Henry's counsellors and intimate servants, who were themselves regularly around, bringing messages and gifts from the king: in January 1503, the privy chamber servants Piers Barbour and James Braybroke were first on the queen's list of New Year's rewards. She also employed them on her own account. On one occasion she instructed the head of the privy chamber, Hugh Denys, to tip a foreigner who had brought her a pair of clavichords, the first set of keyboards known in England; on another, the urbane Richard Weston, travelling abroad on the king's business, picked up a set of expensive, ornamented devotional girdles – fashionable pregnancy wear – on the queen's orders.[15] Entertainers and musicians, too, made their way between the two households: one man regularly in demand with both Elizabeth and Lady Margaret was Henry Glasebury, marshal of the king's minstrels and a composer of entertaining doggerel verse. And her household had an engaged, enquiring openness about it – the kind of easiness that had attracted the king's mother's hawklike attention – which took its tone from Elizabeth herself.

One of Elizabeth's last appointments seemed to sum up the tone of her household. By autumn 1501 her half-brother, Edward IV's bastard son, had entered service as her cupbearer. With the distinctive auburn hair and bulky frame of his family, Arthur Plantagenet was solid, companionable and unaffected, with a fondness for jousting and fine wine; his easy-going nature led a friend later to describe him as 'the pleasantest man in the world'. He was, too, a gifted correspondent: decades later, his letters from Calais as Viscount Lisle would prove one of the most enduring windows on to the world of 1530s England.[16]

The atmosphere of Elizabeth's household permeated the small satellite establishment that its staff also served, that of Prince Henry and his sisters Margaret and Mary, at Eltham in the Kent countryside. A stone's throw from Elizabeth's favourite house of Greenwich, Eltham was especially prized by the children's grandfather Edward IV. In 1480 he had built a glorious new great hall, whose balance and lightness made it one of the triumphs of English domestic architecture, its entrance surmounted by the Yorkist *rose en soleil*, carved in stone.[17] The worlds of Elizabeth and her younger children were from their infancy intimately linked, their staff shuttling between the two households. In 1494 Elizabeth Denton, one of Elizabeth's gentlewomen, was appointed head of the children's nursery, looking after the three-year-old Prince Henry and his five-year-old sister Margaret, while continuing to draw a salary as one of the queen's attendants. Later, Arthur Plantagenet's appointment as Elizabeth's cupbearer may well have been made with one eye on providing the young duke of York with suitable role models: Henry VIII would later recollect his uncle Arthur as 'the gentlest heart living'.[18] It was in this relaxed world that Prince Henry was exposed to formative influences that would remain with him all his life.

Henry and Elizabeth were highly ambitious for their children's education. In combining a cutting-edge classical curriculum with physical training and the skills needed for a life of government, they borrowed heavily from the impressive programme of learning drawn up for Elizabeth's own ill-fated brothers, Edward IV's young princes. But in Prince Arthur's case, Henry VII had made one crucial adaptation. The post of the prince's 'governor', the overall supervisor of his education and mentor, had formerly been occupied by a high-level aristocrat, and it was a role that could quickly become politicized, with disastrous consequences. The young Edward V was reportedly traumatized following the summary execution of his governor, his charismatic, highly cultivated uncle Anthony Woodville, Earl Rivers, in one of the defining acts of Richard III's usurpation. Henry, unsurprisingly, did away with the role completely.[19]

Prince Arthur, of course, had his own carefully vetted council and his own discrete household, headed by its chamberlain, the king's cousin Sir Reginald Pole. In the absence of a governor, the status and influence of the grammar master who oversaw Arthur's primary education rose accordingly. Chosen for him by his father and close advisers, John Rede, the former head of Winchester College, was no political animal but a solid, sober professional educator – just the kind of person who could be trusted around the heir to the throne.[20]

The same went for Henry duke of York's education. As in everything, it was his mother and Lady Margaret who, as he grew and his little household expanded, chose the people who moulded and shaped his world, from his 'lady mistress' Elizabeth Denton to childhood companions such as his cupbearer, the boisterous, quick-thinking Henry Guildford – son of the king's close adviser Sir Richard Guildford and Elizabeth's gentlewoman Anne – and his tutors. And the first grammar master they chose for him was poles apart from the expert, but perhaps rather worthy, John Rede. The man who exploded on to the young Henry's consciousness in the late 1490s was no career schoolmaster, but a rhetorician and poet – and no ordinary poet at that. Swirling behind him his bay-green laureate's cloak with the name 'Calliope', the muse of epic poetry, garishly picked out in gold embroidery, was the self-proclaimed genius of English letters, John Skelton.[21]

Then in his late thirties, Skelton was an irrepressible, unstoppable, creative force. A torrent of words – English, French, Latin, Castilian –

poured out of him, a jumble of languages, in every possible form and combination: lyrics of courtly love and foul-mouthed humour, devotional verse, interludes, educational writings and religious treatises.

Skelton's route to the young duke of York's schoolroom at Eltham had been circuitous. On a visit to Oxford University in 1488, Henry VII had conferred on him a laureateship. This fashionable degree in classical Latin rhetoric, common in the avant-garde humanities departments of prestigious Italian and northern European universities, had never before been awarded in England. For Skelton, the first English poet laureate, it was the defining moment in his career, and he set about making it the centrepiece of his own personal mythology: his poem *Garland of Laurel* comprised 1,600 lines in praise of himself. But if he thought it would be a gateway to the salaried job in the royal household that he hankered after, he was to be disappointed. The laureateship was more about making Henry look like a cultivated European monarch than it was about Skelton. While his Latin was good, it was already out of date, overtaken by the new, sophisticated and conversational style perfected and practised in the courts and chancelleries of Europe. More to the point, Skelton didn't have what Henry looked for in his men-of-letters: the contacts-books, international connections, political and diplomatic know-how that scholars like the Italians Giovanni Gigli, the king's resident ambassador at the papal court in Rome, and his Latin secretary Pietro Carmeliano brought with them.

But what Skelton did have going for him, apart from unswerving self-regard, was a command of the English language which, as he never failed to point out, made him the direct literary descendant of Chaucer. Taking the time-honoured route of aspiring men-of-letters, he hovered on the margins of court, writing fulsome verses to people who might put in a good word for him in high places. Drifting around Westminster, he made the acquaintance of William Caxton and his Dutch colleague Wynkyn de Worde, who published his poems in cheap editions and employed him as a literary translator. In the preface to his 1490 English translation of Virgil's *Aeneid*, dedicated to Prince Arthur, Caxton gave Skelton a glowing public testimonial, praising his critical abilities and his translations from Latin into English, not in 'rude and old language but in polished and ornate terms'.[22]

At Cambridge, meanwhile, influential academic friends pulled strings. Not to be outdone by Oxford, the university gave him its own laureateship, which brought him to the attention of its great benefactor, Lady Margaret Beaufort. Skelton, too, had other irons in the fire.

For some years, he had been a familiar figure around the household of Elizabeth countess of Surrey, wife to the powerful Thomas Howard, where he carried out secretarial and administrative duties with decorous formality, perfected his courtly skills, and acted as an outrageously flirtatious tutor to the countess's daughters and their friends. When in 1495 the Howard family's rehabilitation into the regime was made complete with the wedding of their first son, also Thomas, to the queen's sister Anne, Skelton was ideally placed. With his laureateships, his university connections, his friendships with the printers favoured by royalty and associations with noble ladies – foremost among them the queen's new in-law, the countess of Surrey – he ticked all the boxes for preferment. A ladies' man through and through, Skelton was perfectly suited to the female environment of Prince Henry's household. Elizabeth and Lady Margaret, casting around for somebody to teach the prince his 'learning primordial', and having perhaps read Skelton's recent encomium on the prince's creation as duke of York, evidently thought so too.

Skelton now held a post of considerable importance. As Prince Henry's 'creancer' or mentor, he had power over the development of the young prince's mind. Appointed the prince's chaplain in 1498 – he was ordained for the purpose – he also had influence on his soul.[23] The educational works he wrote for Henry are a snapshot of the curriculum of the age. They include a 'new grammar in English', a Latin grammar with English instructions, and a translation of 'Tully's Familiars', a work by the classical politician-philosopher Cicero, whose Latin prose style was regarded as the ideal model.[24] Added to these were treatises on manners and courtesy ('the book to speak well or be still'), and on government. A flavour of these works – their titles preserved only by Skelton's obsessive documenting of his own canon – lingers in his surviving *Speculum Principis*, a 'mirror for princes', or guide to behaviour, presented to the young prince at Eltham in late August 1501, which he was instructed to 'read, and to understand/ All the demeanour of princely estate'.[25] But the *Speculum Principis* shows why Skelton, for all his pride in his role, was ultimately too self-absorbed to be the perfect teacher. A set of second-hand moral exhortations, it has the air of a rushed job, something distractedly thrown together. Among the commonplace, sententious maxims are hints of Skelton's own vocation: the route to kingliness, it suggested, was through the arts. 'Do not be mean ... Love poets: athletes are two a penny but patrons of the arts are rare.' Wisdom was to be found in chronicles and histories, which Henry duke of York should commit to memory. He should not take 'vain pride in riches', but pursue 'the glory of virtue'. Skelton was among the first to drum such self-interested advice into the young prince. Many more would follow.[26]

All the while, Skelton wrote and wrote. The grave tutor and chaplain was also the self-styled 'wanton clerk', charming, provocative. He revelled in female company, portraying himself as that must-have accessory, the parrot, 'with his beak bent and little wanton eye' fixed lasciviously on the courtly ladies cooing over him and pushing sweetmeats through the bars of his gilded cage. Skelton's talent, too, began to unfurl in the world of the king's household, where he was mentioned in the same breath as the man who set many of his lyrics to music, William Cornish. And if his parrot summed up life among 'great ladies of estate', another of his characters, Dread, exposed the dark underside of life at Henry VII's court.

The power politics and intrigue, the edginess and uncertainty of the late 1490s infused the brooding allegory of Skelton's masterpiece, *The Bowge of Court* – 'bouge' being the salary, board and lodging granted regular servants. In it, Dread has a dream: welcomed aboard the good ship of court by a great lady of estate, Dame Sans-Peer, he is so scared and disorientated by the plotting and 'doubleness' of the courtiers he encounters that he throws himself overboard – before waking up. The poem may have come in a long tradition of satire that painted the court as a hell on earth but, printed in 1499, the year of the Warbeck endgame and Suffolk's first flight, there was no mistaking its topicality. Skelton undoubtedly realized this. In the disclaimer that concluded the poem, he wrote that no reader was to be 'miscontent' and that its context was strictly fictional – any resemblance to persons living or dead was, he might have added, purely coincidental. But nevertheless he could not resist adding, with typical audacity, that 'ofttime such dreams be found true'. 'Now construe you what is the residue', he challenged his reader.[27]

In his carefree existence out at Eltham, this was a world from which Skelton's young student, Prince Henry, was for the moment insulated. But as the prince grew, there was a crucial dimension to his education that Skelton could not supply. By 1499 Elizabeth was looking for another kind of mentor for her son, an educated, worldly, well-rounded nobleman tutored in the ways of that 'school of urbanity', the court – somebody, in other words, like her uncle Earl Rivers, but without the political power and the familial baggage. Then in his early twenties, William Blount, Lord Mountjoy, the prince's neighbour at Sayes Court, a few miles from Greenwich and Eltham, fitted the bill perfectly.[28]

Charming and cultivated with a hint of chivalric steel, Mountjoy came from a noble family with a spotless record of service. His grandfather Walter had been close to Edward IV and the Woodville family, while his uncle and guardian Sir James Blount had joined Henry in exile, bringing with him the garrison of Hammes Castle and his influential political prisoner, the earl of Oxford. Mountjoy's stepfather, the earl of Ormond, meanwhile, was chamberlain to Queen Elizabeth, and it was Elizabeth who was the driving force behind Mountjoy's appointment as Prince Henry's intellectual mentor. Her own cultural tastes may have been conventional enough, but she had an enquiring mind and recognized talent when she saw it. And it was Mountjoy who, as the fifteenth century turned into the sixteenth, provided Prince Henry with the gateway to a new world of learning.

Mountjoy had a passion for intellectual culture. After fighting against the Cornish rebels in 1497, he had left for Paris accompanied by his tutor, a young don of Queens' College, Cambridge called Richard Whitford. There, he immersed himself in a programme of classical learning under the guidance of a former Augustinian monk turned international man-of-letters, the brilliant Dutch scholar Desiderius Erasmus.

On returning to England in 1499, Mountjoy invited Erasmus to accompany him. Ever susceptible to the charms of attractive, well-connected and rich young men, Erasmus had been smitten by his English protégé. 'Lord Mountjoy', he swooned, 'swept me away ... Where, indeed, would I not follow a young man so enlightened, so kindly, and so amiable? I would follow him, as God loves me, even to the lower world itself.'[29] But, it seemed, there was little danger in following his former pupil. Back in England, it was now that Mountjoy took up a post in Prince Henry's household as his 'study companion', as Erasmus put it.

From his townhouse south of St Paul's in Knightrider Street, among the Bordeaux wine merchants of the cobbled thoroughfare of La Ryole that sloped steeply down towards the Thames, Mountjoy was a familiar presence in the city's cultural life.[30] Through the summer and autumn of 1499 he guided Erasmus through the city's townhouses, as well as the cosmopolitan intellectual atmosphere of Doctors' Commons, the civil lawyers' club on Paternoster Row. What Erasmus found amazed him. As he recollected, he encountered 'so great a quantity of intellectual refinement and scholarship ... profound and learned and truly classical, in both Latin and Greek'. The learning that Erasmus described was that of the *humanae litterae*, the study of classical poetry, oratory and rhetoric reinvigorated by the discovery of long-lost ancient manuscripts which, buried for centuries in the dusty libraries of monasteries and cathedrals, had been brought westwards in the baggage of refugees fleeing the advance of the Ottoman Turks, and whose circulation was given impetus by the printing press. Erasmus had been desperate to go to Italy, the crucible of this rebirth or Renaissance of learning, and where this refocusing on the transformative power of classical letters – which, humanists felt, could be used to reform and reshape society anew – was at its most intense. But then, arriving in England, he changed his mind: 'I have little longing left for Italy.'[31]

Four names in particular made a profound impression on him. Presiding over the quartet was the benevolent Oxford don and Greek scholar William Grocyn. A generation younger, Thomas Linacre and John Colet had recently returned from extended tours in an Italy ripped apart and traumatized by the French invasion of 1494.

A classical scholar and medical doctor of firecracker brilliance, Linacre was now kicking his heels in London, short of money and looking for jobs. Introverted, ascetic and with a contempt for money and careerism that only the truly rich and privileged could affect, John Colet had no such concerns. Son of the powerful London mercer and twice mayor Sir Henry, he had gone abroad, Erasmus said, in search of knowledge like an acquisitive merchant, and had returned fired by the learning of the Florentine thinkers Marsilio Ficino and Pico della Mirandola, men who had fused Platonic philosophy with exploration of the Bible in its original Greek, in writings of mystical, interiorized spirituality. There was something radical and dangerous about these thinkers. Mirandola cultivated a Dominican friar, Savonarola, whose millenarian visions had provoked revolution: in the wake of France's invasion, he had inspired a popular uprising in Florence, its ruling Medici family replaced by a people's republic. Colet had been bitten by the bug, too. At Oxford, he had delivered a coruscating series of lectures on St Paul, fulminating against the corruption of the clergy and the abuses of the church.[32]

The fourth member of the group was Thomas More. By far the youngest at twenty-one, he already seemed its focus. Grocyn was his 'creancer', Linacre taught him Greek, and Colet, whose intense piety fascinated More, was his spiritual guide.[33] More had grown up in the household of Henry VII's late chancellor, Archbishop Morton, who, recognizing his precocity, had dispatched him to Oxford aged fifteen. Returning to London to follow in the footsteps of his father, a prominent city lawyer, More had instead fallen under Colet's spell. He had, much to his father's annoyance, ducked out of his legal education and instead immersed himself in a programme of religious learning, taking up residence at the Charterhouse, the Carthusian monastery on the city's north-western edge.

It was very probably the Hertfordshire knight Sir William Say – who as well as being an acquaintance of Archbishop Morton and More's father Sir John, was Mountjoy's father-in-law – who had provided the young More with an introduction to Mountjoy, with whom he became firm friends. The Say family, indeed, joined all the dots: Sir William was half-brother to Elizabeth countess of Surrey, and among the queen's gentlewomen was his sister, Anne. Here was a skein of relationships that led to the heart of the queen's household – and to that of her son, the duke of York.

○

When More and Erasmus met in 1499 they formed an instant bond – though Erasmus, typically, fell more quickly for the younger man: 'What has Nature ever created more sweet, more happy than the genius of Thomas More?' One early autumn afternoon, More called on Erasmus at Sayes Court, and the pair strolled over to nearby Eltham to visit Mountjoy, who was with the royal children. Erasmus remembered the meeting, framed in his mind's eye: the children assembled in Eltham's great hall, Prince Henry at their centre, already looking 'somehow like a natural king, displaying a noble spirit combined with peculiar courtesy'.[34] It was a scene carefully choreographed by Mountjoy and More, to show off the cultured young prince as a master of that peculiarly Renaissance art of constructed spontaneity, *sprezzatura*. And, as Erasmus recollected, the encounter left him squirming with embarrassment.

As they were presented to the eight-year-old Henry and his household, More produced a gift of writing for the prince. It was a deliberate and – for one supposedly so 'sweet' – curiously calculated display of one-upmanship, for Erasmus had come empty-handed. His humiliation was compounded when, at dinner, Prince Henry produced a note to Erasmus, challenging him to write something. In the next few days, Erasmus cobbled together a ten-page ode to England, *Prosopopoeia Britanniae Maioris*, in which he lauded Henry VII and his children to the skies. In an accompanying dedicatory letter, he wrote that he would have felt it necessary to urge the prince to the pursuit of virtue, 'were it not that you are thither bound already of your free choice; and that you have a bard of your own in Skelton, the great light and ornament of English letters, who can not only inspire but perfect your studies' – the emphasis being strictly on Skelton's English, rather than his Latin. Given his non-existent English, Erasmus, unable to read a word of Skelton's, had undoubtedly been briefed. What he really thought of Prince Henry's 'creancer' is indicated in a later, 1507, edition of the *Prosopopoeia*, by which time Skelton had left royal service:

his name had been deleted.[35] Erasmus always had a particularly economical attitude to flattery.

As Erasmus's dedication implied, however, there were no job opportunities in the prince's household – or, for that matter, anywhere else. That autumn, away from the serene picture at Eltham, the regime was tense, with Suffolk loitering in Calais and Warbeck's conspirators plotting feverishly; the king's counsellors, their hands full, barely afforded Erasmus a second glance. As October drew on, the delights of England started to pall. Fed up with trying to ingratiate himself with 'those wretched courtiers', as he sniffily put it, Erasmus was desperate to leave. Thanks to the 'recent flight of a certain duke', however, with the Channel ports on high alert and Kent crawling with soldiers on the lookout for infiltrators, travelling in safety was impossible. Particularly, he might have added, given his Dutch accent, clerical appearance and lack of English, which would have shouted 'spy' to any suspicious militiaman.[36]

Erasmus's enforced sojourn, however, was to prove transformative. Retreating to Oxford, he did a crash course in Greek with Grocyn and discussed theology with Colet: both experiences which in the next years would have a profound impact on his work and thought. But if Erasmus appreciated English scholarship, he was less enamoured of its officialdom. When, in early January 1500, he finally reached Dover, customs officers relieved him of the gifts of money he had been given, amounting to a healthy £20 – despite Mountjoy's blithe assurances to the contrary, there was no taking hard currency out of the kingdom – before sending him on his way. It would be another four years before Erasmus returned hopefully to England. There would be no repeat then of the cosy familial scene he had witnessed at Eltham.[37]

Erasmus's account of his Eltham visit was, of course, designed to portray Mountjoy, his sometime student and hoped-for patron – and by implication himself – in the best possible light. But its portrayal of the gracious, cultured atmosphere of the prince's household was accurate enough. His emphasis on Mountjoy's influence, too, was not misplaced. A conduit to the prince, he was a principal path to Elizabeth's favour as well: in 1501, she appointed him her new chamberlain.

The humanists' growing influence over the prince's education was evident in the reshuffle in his household that took place after Prince Arthur's death in April 1502. This seismic change in the prince's life coincided with a natural educational progression in which, around the age of twelve, he moved on to a more advanced programme of studies. Skelton was pensioned off – or perhaps, unable to face the increasingly claustrophobic atmosphere of the king's court, he jumped before he was pushed, retreating to the Norfolk benefice of Diss, to which he had been presented by Lady Margaret as a reward for his services. The appointment of his replacement, the progressive Chichester grammarian John Holt, had More's and Mountjoy's fingerprints all over it. Previously an employee of Archbishop Morton, Holt was More's ex-teacher and a firm friend. A few quiet words from More in Mountjoy's ear undoubtedly worked wonders.[38]

By late June that year, when Holt received his first payment as schoolmaster, Prince Henry – now 'my lord prince' – was at the centre of a world that his parents had decided to disrupt as little as possible. His educational re-orientation had started to take place, but in the familiar environment of Eltham, with the reassuring faces around him that he had known since infancy.

On 11 February 1503, in his last action before retreating from public view, the king dispatched Sir Richard Guildford and Sir Charles Somerset with words of comfort to the household of his dead queen, together with assurances that its staff would be looked after, places found for them elsewhere. It was probably through them, too, that Prince Henry received what he later described as the most 'hateful intelligence': news of the sudden death of the mother who had shaped his world.

Among the many verse epitaphs that hung, painted on boards, around Elizabeth's tomb in Westminster Abbey, was a poem by Thomas More, as well placed as any to describe the impact of her death. A work of heartfelt, spare simplicity, More's 'Rueful Lamentation' was a soliloquy, a farewell address from the mouth of the late queen herself. Lamenting the unexpected 'strange reckoning' that had befallen her, she warned of the frailty of worldly joy and prosperity – and, in a scathing aside, of the 'blandishing promise' of 'false astrology' which Elizabeth's death had so emphatically disproved: 'The year yet lasteth, and lo now here I lie.'[39]

The passing of the glories of the world, the instability of life and the permanence of death: all the themes of More's poem were conventional enough. But they drove home emphatically the fragile foundations on which the reign now rested. In speaking of the fleeting nature of earthly things, More's Elizabeth summoned up the most visible signs of royal power – precisely those architectural projects into which Henry had poured so much money: 'Goodly Richmond', his proud dynastic symbol, and 'that costly work of yours', the new chapel attached to Westminster Abbey on which work had started only the previous month, following Henry's initial downpayment of £30,000. Consciously or not – and with More, things were rarely unwitting – he had struck at the heart of the matter. With Elizabeth's death, the edifice of power that Henry had so painstakingly built was crumbling.[40]

As she bade farewell to her family, a ghostly repeated refrain of 'adieu . . . adieu' fading into eternity, More's fictional Elizabeth saved her most direct advice for Henry, her 'faithful love', her 'dear spouse'. Formerly 'were you father' but now 'must you supply/ The mother's part also.' Not only did the king have to raise an heir, he had to nurture a son.

Henry, though, was in no position to do anything. His retreat from the world to a 'solitary place' had been announced as a willed period of private mourning; in fact, his reaction to his wife's death was altogether more uncontrolled. As was increasingly the case, his inscrutable reactions to the vicissitudes of his reign were betrayed by his body. For the next six weeks, he was shut away. As well as the tubercular condition that had struck him down in previous winters, brought on by the February cold and damp, he had developed a quinsy, an acute, pustular tonsillitis. Feverish, his lungs infected, he lay close to death. For days he was unable to swallow or even open his mouth.[41]

Since Henry's first major illness in 1499 at the height of the Perkin Warbeck denouement, intermittent talk at court had revolved around what would happen in the event of the king's death, with both his sons then in their minority. Now, with his queen dead, with the succession depending solely on his twelve-year-old son, and with Suffolk at large, the situation was infinitely worse. It was vital that word of his illness did not leak out.

He was surrounded by his 'secretest': his small group of intimate body servants. Among them were Richard Weston, James Braybroke and Piers Barbour, the Breton Francis Marzen and the page of the wardrobe of robes William Smith. Presided over by the impassive groom of the stool Hugh Denys, they ensured that, with the dynasty's future in the balance, security around the ailing king was tight. Lady Margaret moved into Richmond, ordering in medicines and necessaries for her son and liberal supplies of sweet wine for herself, rewarding the king's physicians, his secret servants and their wives, along with the reassuring presence of Arthur Plantagenet: during that uncertain time, Elizabeth's dependable half-brother was close at hand, possibly as a confidential line of communication between Richmond and Eltham. And, as Lady Margaret tended her son and directed his servants, all the time she watched, peering over her gold-rimmed spectacles.[42]

Through February and March, the king slipped in and out of delirium. Then, as the days grew lighter and the chill of winter subsided, he emerged, thin and drawn, dressed in mourning black.[43] But the mask was back in place. By the end of the month, he was convalescing in the Essex countryside. Something in Henry, though, was altered, intensified : there was, perhaps, a greater sense than before of his detachment from those around him, his implacable drive for control, over himself and over his kingdom. Few around him, including his closest counsellors, would 'see or hear' anything of the private man ever again. And he set his mind to reconstructing the future of the kingdom around his second son, a child whom he barely knew at all.[44]

In early April, as correspondence between England and Spain on the subject of the new marriage shuttled back and forth, rumours reached Catherine's parents of a new and disconcerting development: the king had turned an appraising eye on Prince Arthur's widow as a possible bridal candidate for himself. It was, Isabella stuttered, 'a very evil thing ... we would not for anything in the world that it should take place.'[45] 'Talk in England' remained just that, but for all Isabella's disapproving tone, the Catholic monarchs were more than ever desperate to conclude a new Anglo-Spanish marriage treaty – just not one that involved the king. Over-extended in their ruinous war against France for supremacy on the Italian peninsula, with French troops massing on the northern border of Spain, and needing to bind Henry more closely into Spanish affairs, they offered him instead the hand of Ferdinand's niece Giovanna, the twenty-five-year-old dowager queen of Naples.

The rumours dissipated. But in the precarious aftermath of his wife's death, Henry, who had previously temporized over the prince's proposed betrothal of Catherine, called in his son to see him. One of the counsellors standing in the background, Richard Fox's protégé Nicholas West, an authority in matrimonial law, later remembered the scene, the young boy standing mutely in front of his father, the king's speech formal and stilted: 'Son Henry,' he said, 'I have agreed with the King of Aragon that you should marry Catherine, your brother's widow, in order that the peace between us might be continued.' Do you, he asked his son, want this to happen? The prince, submissive, deferred to his father.[46]

For Catherine, Elizabeth's death also came as a blow. There had been signs – Elizabeth's learning of Spanish and her solicitude toward her bereaved daughter-in-law following Prince Arthur's death – of a growing relationship, that of mentor and protégée, between the two. Now, installed with her household at Durham House on the Strand, Catherine waited anxiously. With widowhood, her status as princess of Wales had lapsed, and with it her independence: she was, once more, an unmarried Spanish infanta, under the domineering, self-aggrandizing governance of her duenna, Doña Elvira Manrique.

Since she had first set foot in England, Catherine's entourage had been trouble. Squabbles between her household officers had emerged as outright faction, headed by the Spanish ambassadors resident at Henry's court, Pedro de Ayala and Rodrigo de Puebla, who hated each other. To the likes of de Ayala and Doña Elvira, de Puebla seemed to have gone native; worse still, he was servile and low-born and – the ultimate offence, in de Ayala's eyes – he was 'not a good Christian' but a *converso*, a converted Jew. De Ayala, though, had since left England to take up a post at the Burgundian court, while de Puebla's ally in Catherine's household, her confessor, was recalled to Spain under a cloud. But the infighting between de Puebla and Doña Elvira continued and the Spanish were unable to present a united front – which was precisely what Ferdinand and Isabella, concerned that the divisions would impede negotiations for the new marriage, were afraid of.

In fact, although the squabbling continued, all parties were keen for the betrothal to go ahead. Whatever qualms Catherine may have had about marrying her dead husband's brother were dispelled by a desperation to get out from under her duenna's thumb and resume the status – and with it, the income – of an English princess. That spring, things were, it seemed, looking up. In a spasm of unaccustomed largesse that April, Henry had authorized an extra £100 over and above her normal household allowance, remembering to scribble 'for this time only' in the margin of his chamber accounts. So desperate were Ferdinand and Isabella to proceed that they deliberately avoided the knotty questions of Catherine's income and her dowry. By 23 June, a new marriage treaty was signed and sealed.[47]

Two days later, Prince Henry and Catherine were betrothed in a ceremony at the Bishop of Salisbury's Inn, south of Fleet Street. It was only a start. There would have to be another engagement ceremony when the prince reached the marriageable age of fourteen. And before that, papal authorization would have to be obtained for the match to proceed. As Item 1 of the draft treaty outlined, such a dispensation was necessary because Catherine's previous marriage had been 'solemnised within the rites of the Catholic Church' and 'afterwards consummated' – as Prince Arthur had boasted when he emerged after his wedding night announcing to his servants what 'good pastime it is to have a wife'.[48] As a result, Catherine was related to her intended spouse in the first degree of affinity. Both Henry VII and Ferdinand would have to negotiate the labyrinthine world of papal politics, whose venality and corruption had assumed baroque proportions under the rule of the Borgia Pope Alexander VI, who even his greatest admirer admitted 'never did anything else, nor thought about anything else, than to deceive men'.[49] Both monarchs, though, had reason to feel confident of success.

Henry placed a premium on his relationship with Rome. In the absence of other forms of legitimacy, he had from the beginning held papal validation of his reign – and papal condemnation of his Yorkist rivals – as being of prime importance. Ostentatiously parading his devotion to the church, he basked in the lustre of close relations with the papacy, constantly dangling the carrot of substantial financial backing in front of perennially bankrupt popes. But although Henry put his hand in his purse when occasion demanded, in general fine words and displays of piety were about as far as it went. In England, his administrators and lawyers attacked church jurisdiction – an obstacle to royal authority – at every opportunity, while the fruits of his exorbitant taxation of the church, and fees for appointments to bishoprics, tended to disappear into his coffers rather than making their way to Rome. Once, when a papal representative opened a collecting box installed at Henry's court, he found at the bottom a measly £11 11s – along, no doubt, with a few cobwebs. But Henry also knew the value of warm diplomatic relations and good intelligence. By mid-1503, his agents and legal representatives in the papal curia seemed well placed.[50]

In favouring the well-connected, politically and culturally sophisticated Italian merchants and diplomats who regularly arrived in England on curial business Henry killed two birds with one stone, gratifying popes by the attention and respect shown to their intimates, and employing them as his own eyes and ears at Rome, along with a number of highly educated permanent English representatives there. By mid-1503, as Henry and Ferdinand prepared to petition Alexander VI for the dispensation, the first-named among Henry's diplomatic staff at the papal curia was a confidant of the pope himself.

Arriving in London in 1488 as a papal mediator in the ongoing conflict between England and Scotland, Adriano Castellesi had immediately come to Henry's attention. Steeped in classical scholarship and sliding easily through the treacherous waters of curial politics, Castellesi embodied everything that Henry looked for in his diplomats. The king 'much fantasied' his political know-how and contacts, his precise, measured speech, and his willingness to put his talents at the king's service. Castellesi was showered with grants and offices, including the bishopric of Hereford, a see from which he was almost always absent. As collector of papal taxes in England, he became the king's 'creature' as much as the pope's, in the process becoming close to the shrewdest of all Henry's diplomats. Immediately recognizing the ease with which Castellesi moulded his considerable talents to fit the king's desires, Richard Fox showed him 'all good will and affection'. Henry and his advisers had backed the right horse, for in 1497 Castellesi became private secretary to Pope Alexander VI.[51]

In autumn 1501 Castellesi had helped secure the bull anathematizing the earl of Suffolk; the following year he helped ratify the marriage of Henry's daughter Margaret to Scotland's James IV. When, in 1502, Castellesi sent a deputy to London to look after his affairs, he selected his agent with typical discernment and a shrewd awareness of the king's interests. Polydore Vergil was a promising young historian from Urbino, one of the fortified hilltop towns perched in the jagged spine of the Italian Marches, whose court under the famed Montefeltro dukes had become a byword for intellectual culture. Henry received him with the courtesy and kindliness that he always reserved for foreign men-of-letters whose skills he might be able to put to political use – and he was to take a particular interest in Vergil's literary abilities.

By summer 1503, and now a cardinal, Castellesi was in Rome trying to engineer the papal dispensation for the new Anglo-Spanish marriage. On 6 August he invited the seventy-eight-year-old Alexander and his implacable son Cesare Borgia, so remorseless that even his father was scared of him, to a banquet at his gleaming new palazzo near the papal enclave in Borgo. Dinner went on late into the balmy summer evening; the table talk, fuelled by fine wines, would undoubtedly have taken in the political situation in Italy, where Aragonese forces had pushed the previously rampant French armies back up the peninsula, retaking Naples the previous month. The subject of the papal dispensation, too, would have come up. The Aragon-born Alexander, constantly playing off French and Spanish interests against each other to his own and his son's advantage and aware of Henry VII's full coffers, must have been delighted at the bargaining chip with which he was now presented. But it was to be the last dinner the Borgia pope ever ate.[52]

Whether, as was widely rumoured, Alexander was poisoned, or whether he died of disease, is unclear – though the fact that both Castellesi and Cesare Borgia were both dangerously ill in the days following the banquet perhaps tells its own story. Alexander VI died on 12 August, to widespread rejoicing in Rome. Following a disorderly funeral, at which fights broke out, Alexander's bloated, decomposing body, its complexion 'foul and black', was unceremoniously rolled up in an old carpet and jammed into an undersized coffin by six labourers who made blasphemous jokes about the corpse as they did so.[53] His successor, the decrepit Pius III, died within twenty-six days of his election; in his place came Julius II, the 'terrible', the warrior pope, who harboured an implacable hatred of all things Borgia.[54] All those who had gone in fear and trembling under Borgia rule were delighted; Henry and Ferdinand were less so. They would have to recalibrate their approach – and so too would the former Borgia favourite Adriano Castellesi.

Eager to push things forward, Ferdinand now changed his story. Although the new Anglo-Spanish treaty had indeed stated that Catherine and Prince Arthur's marriage had been consummated, it was not in fact the case. Doña Elvira, who had superintended Catherine's preparations for her wedding night, and who had doubtless found out as much detail as she could about what had gone on, was resolutely insistent that she was still a virgin – something Ferdinand was now more than prepared to accept.

Henry, though, insisted otherwise. His reasons for doing so were not hard to fathom: they were, typically, financial. According to the previous marriage contract between Arthur and Catherine, if the marriage were consummated Catherine's parents would have to hand over the outstanding 100,000 crowns of the marriage portion to Henry before he, in turn, released any of Catherine's dower – the lands and revenues due to her in the event of her husband's death.[55] Ferdinand was not in a position to argue. He wrote to his ambassador in Rome that the princess was still a virgin, 'as is well known in England'. But, he shrugged, as the English wanted to argue the case, it would be better to humour them and proceed according to the wording of the treaty drawn up by Fox and his colleagues – as if, in other words, the marriage between Arthur and Catherine had indeed been consummated. In his rush to get the papal documentation completed, and the English onside, Ferdinand had muddied the waters still further. The question of the finance was now thoroughly confused – and so, as it would transpire, with ultimately seismic consequences, was the question of Catherine's virginity. But that autumn, as a new round of papal lobbying began, Henry had other things on his mind.[56]

In little over a year, Henry's best-laid plans for the security and succession of his reign had been brought crashing down around him. Over time, and through constant political upheaval, people had become reconciled – or resigned – to the fact of his rule. But with Arthur's death, that idea had been shaken; with Elizabeth's, it all but disintegrated. The political settlement that Henry and Elizabeth's marriage represented had been practically torn up. Many of those who had accepted Henry as king had done so out of their loyalty to Edward IV's children: were Henry to remarry and have further offspring, they would embody something quite different.

In theory, that loyalty could be transferred to Elizabeth's one remaining son. But with the king's ill-health patently obvious, the question of succession, embodied by Prince Henry's youth and vulnerability, was now starkly exposed. The memory of events following Edward IV's death, whose aftershocks had reverberated throughout the first fifteen years of Henry's reign, were still raw – and Edward's son had been about the same age as Prince Henry was now. The spectre of political instability began to loom.

PART TWO

Change of Worlds

'I saw a knife hid in his one sleeve,
Whereon was written this word: Mischief.'
                    John Skelton, The Bowge of Court

'There be many lords that cannot play the lord
But I that am none can play it royally.'
                    A Fifteenth Century School Book

5

No Sure Way

On 3 July 1503, a week after Prince Henry and Catherine's betrothal, seven men were arraigned at a hearing in the great hall at London's Guildhall. All were indicted with treason for conspiring with Edmund de la Pole, earl of Suffolk. Their trial was perfunctory. The following morning, they were found guilty as charged by a panel of judges, and sentenced to be hanged, drawn and quartered. The seven had, it seems, been in prison awaiting trial for over a year, having been rounded up during the arrests in Calais and the royal household in the spring of 1502. The man who supplied the key evidence for their conviction was Robert Wellesbourne, 'alias Hodgekinson', the shadowy turncoat whose information had condemned Tyrell, Wyndham and their colleagues the year before.

Among the condemned were two shipmen, and two men whose names carried disturbing resonances: one 'Pole', the bailiff of Thurrock, a port town on the Thames estuary in the low-lying Essex marshland; and Oliver St John, a member of Lady Margaret Beaufort's extended family. These four were duly executed, their heads spiked and displayed on London Bridge. But three others escaped death and had their sentences commuted. One, Robert Symson, had friends in high places. A wealthy Kentish landowner, he was a retainer of Henry's trusted counsellor Sir Richard Guildford, one of the king's inner circle, whose men maintained royal influence in Kent. By November, Symson had been pardoned – and, in the increasingly idiosyncratic way Henry's justice worked, he paid heavily for it. Both the king and his counsellors did well out of the deal. Guildford paid the king £100 for Symson's pardon; in turn, Symson had then been forced

to sell his lucrative estates to Guildford and a syndicate of royal counsellors for the knockdown price of £200.[1]

With the king about to go on progress, the trials and executions
were deliberately timed. That summer, Henry decided, he would
accompany his thirteen-year-old daughter Margaret on the first stage
of her journey to Scotland, where she would cement the Tudor–Stuart
alliance in a marriage to James IV. Prince Henry would remain behind,
at Eltham. As his father was well aware, summer progresses, with the
king away from London, were an ideal time for unrest to brew: in
1499, Warbeck's men had plotted their conspiracy with a leaked copy
of Henry's summer itinerary to hand. Now, with the kingdom insecure, and with Prince Henry taking his first, tentative steps as heir to
the throne, the executions were intended to send out a message of
uncompromising royal authority to any would-be plotters on behalf
of Suffolk.

In early August, as London's half-emptied streets baked, two royal
officials sat in a room in the Tower with a suspect who had been
hauled in for questioning. The case was serious. Confronting the
accused were Brian Sanford, one of the Tower's senior commanders,
and the clerk of the royal council, Robert Rydon, who sat at a table
minuting the interrogation in detail, quill scratching busily over
parchment.[2]

Alexander Symson, a sawyer, had been drinking heavily in a pub in
Erith, a booming port town on the south bank of the Thames estuary,
where ships unloaded their goods for the short onward journey overland to London, and in whose streets foreign accents and languages,
predominantly Dutch and French, were commonplace. Symson had
got talking to the 'good man of the house' and, increasingly inebri-
ated, had poured out a complicated scheme in which he proposed to
abduct a local boy and flee by boat to France or Zeeland, the coastal
region around Antwerp, where he would groom the boy as a pretender, a 'great inheritor and next unto the crown'. He had a proposal
for the landlord: if he could arrange a ship for them, he could earn
forty shillings a year. It was then that Symson's evening came to an

abrupt halt, for the landlord was not the landlord at all. Thomas Broke, a man from the nearby village of Crayford, was – for some reason – standing in for the evening. He reported the conversation to the local authorities, who had brought Symson into London under armed guard and had given their own statement of events to Sanford and Rydon.

Symson's ramblings were the kind of talk about which Henry had good reason to be concerned. It was grooming of this sort that had produced the two royal pretenders Lambert Simnel and Perkin Warbeck. In 1487, Suffolk's older brother, John de la Pole earl of Lincoln, had used the twelve-year-old Simnel's impersonation of Edward earl of Warwick as a front for his own designs on the English crown – and twelve years later, the Cambridge student Ralph Wilford, also brainwashed into believing he was Warwick, acted as a rallying cry for Yorkist dissidents in Suffolk's own East Anglian backyard. Warwick himself was now dead, but the pattern was familiar: to the king, this was the kind of scheme that had Suffolk's fingerprints all over it.

Henry was concerned for another reason, too. Through his informers, his household men, his administrators and their agents, he had tried to extend his reach far into the provinces, to bind and control the influence of powerful families, local big men and their retainers, backed up by his increasingly ruthless system of financial penalties. Different regions presented different challenges, from the power vacuum of Northumberland, whose earl was too young to govern for much of the 1490s, to the northwest, where the huge retinues of the powerful Stanley clan, Henry's step-family, had provided much of his military muscle from Bosworth onwards. Henry had rewarded the family with political office and a position at the heart of power – until Warbeck had caused doubt to seep into Sir William Stanley's mind and Henry's whole relationship with the family had changed. Now, the appearance of Suffolk and the regime's new vulnerability cast local vendettas and grudges, resentments and grievances against the king and his counsellors in an altered light. In Kent, a particularly toxic blend of dynastic instability and local lawlessness was brewing. Sir Richard Guildford was at its heart; and hovering on its periphery, connected by loose strands of allegiance and affinity, was Alexander Symson.[3]

Symson's name would have rung a bell with his interrogators. Another prisoner in the Tower, his namesake Robert, was the Londoner with Kentish connections who had been convicted of treason just weeks before. Not only did the Symsons share a name, they shared a master. Robert Symson had narrowly avoided death through Sir Richard Guildford's personal intervention with the king. Now, as Alexander Symson recounted his own version of events, it turned out that he too was connected to Guildford. What was more, when detained in Erith, he had been on his way to report to the man himself. In fact, as he recounted to his perplexed questioners, he was a royal spy, recruited by one of Guildford's own retainers, and he had just returned from the Low Countries, where he had been sent to infiltrate Suffolk's household. Symson had news that would be deeply troubling both to Guildford and to Henry: Guildford's spy network was rotten.

Symson started his story from the beginning. He lived in the Kentish village of Cranbrook, squarely in Sir Richard Guildford's territory, and had been recruited by a man called Walter Roberts, a man of considerable local standing and one of the Guildford family's most trusted retainers in the area. But, standing in front of the two officials in the Tower, Symson accused his control, Roberts, of being of a double-agent, who was working not on behalf of Guildford and the king, but of Suffolk. In fact, Roberts took up so much of Symson's testimony that Rydon, the clerk, scribbled at the top 'Deposition contra Robertum': 'against Roberts'.[4]

Symson had, he told Sanford and Rydon, been in Walter Roberts' service for a long time, had 'belonged' to him for over twenty years 'for the more part'. Early in 1503, Roberts had been casting around for recruits to supplement the crown's information network, presumably on Guildford's behalf. Symson's recruitment began that Easter, in a meadow outside Cranbrook, when Roberts casually asked Symson whether he could be trusted. Yes, came the reply, he could. Things then fell quiet. Their next contact was about five weeks later, and Symson remembered the time precisely: it was in the Rogation days, when locals processed around their parish boundaries amid a riot of brightly coloured religious banners, ringing handbells, chanting litanies invoking God's blessing on the fields, and drinking prodigious quantities of beer.[5] Symson, meanwhile, was among a group of workers weeding a pond belonging to Roberts, who took him aside and briefed him on his assignment: to go to Aachen, make contact with Suffolk, and try to find out what kind of backing – and from whom – he was expecting 'for his coming into England'. At this point in the inquisition Rydon, with clerical precision, looked up from his note-taking. How did Roberts refer to Suffolk: as 'duke' or 'earl'? The former would have been a telltale sign of Roberts' sympathies. Symson couldn't recall.

Symson had clearly been jumpy about his mission from the outset. On the morning of 4 June, Whit Sunday, he had attended matins in Cranbrook church. After the service, most of the congregation had filed outside into the late spring sun. Lingering behind, Symson waited for Roberts, who possessed the elusiveness of spymasters through the ages. Appearing suddenly in the gloom of the church, he asked Symson whether he was ready, gave him his expenses, and sent him on his way, urging him to 'be secret' and not to reveal his true identity.

Landing on the Dutch coast, Symson made his way southeast to Aachen without any difficulty and, lodged in the city, started making enquiries. News of the inquisitive Englishman reached Suffolk's right-hand man Sir George Neville, 'the bastard'. Their encounter was, initially, a bruising one. Neville produced a knife and, threatening to cut off Symson's ears, demanded to know what his business was and who had sent him. Terrified, Symson blurted out Roberts' name, which, to his surprise, transformed the atmosphere: 'after that he had showed by whom he was sent thither, he was neither evil dealt with neither evil said to'. Neville grew thoughtful, acknowledging that he knew and respected Roberts. As Symson told his interrogators in the Tower, having been detailed to find information on Suffolk's English supporters, he was aghast to find that they included Roberts, his own control.

Retracing his steps to Antwerp, he took a boat down the Scheldt estuary to the port of Arnemuiden, hitched a ride back to Erith on a barge loaded with salt fish, and returned to Cranbrook. But knowing what he now knew about Roberts, Symson was desperate to avoid him. Staying only one night with his wife, he went back up to Erith, winding up in the tavern where he was arrested. Rather than report to Roberts, he said, he had been going to take his information right to the top: to Sir Richard Guildford himself.[6]

There was much about Symson's story that didn't add up. Perhaps Sir George Neville had been playing a clever game: implying Roberts' disloyalty, and sending the gullible Symson back to sow seeds of mutual suspicion and doubt among Henry's intelligence network. But Symson's abortive mission had proved him a useless spy, naming names at the drop of a hat – so bad, in fact, that it appeared less like a cock-up than a conspiracy. It looked for all the world as though Symson's mission to make contact with Suffolk was undertaken for different reasons: that he, too, was part of the group of plotters intriguing on Suffolk's behalf, and that, having been arrested, he was now looking for a plea-bargain by incriminating his superior, Roberts. And then there was the question of what on earth a casual labourer was doing working as a spy in the first place.

Whatever the case, for the royal officials in the Tower, and for Henry himself, trying to unpick the skein of tangled loyalties, the story took on wider implications for the kingdom's security. Henry was well aware that, over the past years, Sir Richard Guildford had been losing his grip in Kent. If the likes of Symson and Roberts, Guildford men through and through, were – inadvertently or otherwise – sending out the message that all was not well with Guildford's affinity, then Henry, too, had to think again. There was another big man in the region, one who had been flexing his muscles in a series of increasingly violent encounters with Guildford's retainers. Not only was this man a Yorkist, he was Suffolk's cousin.[7]

Throughout the troubled fifteenth century, violence in the volatile county of Kent had presaged wider conflict. In 1450, Jack Cade had marched on London at the head of five thousand Kentish insurgents in protest at Henry VI's disastrous inability to rule – an uprising that had foreshadowed the country's rapid descent into civil war. Kent's strategic proximity to the Low Countries, Calais and London had made it a focus for repeated invasions, Yorkist and Lancastrian. Then came the Woodville-led uprisings against Richard III in 1483, in which the Guildfords and their man Walter Roberts had played a major role.[8]

After 1485, as Henry built up networks of royal influence in Kent, he turned to those who had already proved their loyalty during the turbulent years of exile and rebellion. At their apex was Sir Richard Guildford, with close links to Queen Elizabeth, to Sir Reynold Bray, to Lady Margaret Beaufort and to the king himself. But Guildford's rise meant the eclipse of the region's two most influential noblemen: John Broke, Lord Cobham and his brother-in-law George Neville, Lord Bergavenny. Both men, allies of Richard III, had been active in putting down the 1483 insurgency and, when Guildford and his fellow Woodville supporters fled into exile, had consolidated their power. But neither had been particularly happy with the rewards and opportunities offered them by Richard. They had stayed away from Bosworth, indifferent and aloof, and, with the opportunism of the age, seemed perfectly prepared to transfer their loyalties to the new regime.

To Henry, though, the very name of Neville spelled trouble. It was intimately associated with the house of York, whose matriarch, Cecily Neville, dowager duchess of York and mother to Edward IV and Richard III, remained a focus for insurgency: her household was closely linked to both the Warwick and Warbeck conspiracies until her death in 1495. Among those who had been involved with Warbeck and who subsequently fled with Suffolk was another Neville: Sir George, 'the bastard'. Meanwhile, in 1492 the cool, calculating Lord Bergavenny died, and Henry had to deal with his young son and heir. Not only did the aggressive twenty-three-year-old come with all the wrong kind of dynastic and family baggage, but he was bound to be associated in Henry's mind with Warbeck. For if Warbeck was really Richard duke of York, then the new Lord Bergavenny was his cousin.[9]

From the outset, Henry made it clear that he was watching the young noble. In 1492, as Bergavenny joined the king's abortive invasion of France, Henry bound him over to guarantee his return – presumably to prevent him sloping off to join the brewing conspiracy. Warbeck's attempted landing of 1495 didn't help, either: in his search for local support, Bergavenny would probably have been one of the first names on his list. Bergavenny, though, appeared to keep his head down. He attended court ceremonies dutifully, and played a seemingly decisive role in the defeat of the Cornish insurgency at Blackheath in 1497 – fighting alongside his cousin, the earl of Suffolk.

As Henry's uncovering of conspiracy in the mid-1490s made him fall back on servants of proven loyalty, Guildford's position was reinforced, both in the royal household and in Kent, where his retainers manned the coastal defences and kept a sharp eye on disturbances and potential disloyalties in the region. The stream of royal favour flowed decisively in Guildford's direction; he and his wife were popular at court, and his younger son became one of Prince Henry's closest friends.

But Guildford had one fundamental flaw. He was a terrible businessman, utterly incapable of managing his own money – or for that matter, the royal household's. When in 1494 Henry appointed Guildford as comptroller, the officer who vetted the household accounts, it seemed a barely conceivable promotion for somebody who had already been caught putting his hand in the royal coffers to service his own debts – though at that stage, in the middle of the Stanley conspiracy, Henry may have valued proven loyalty over financial probity. By the late 1490s Guildford's investments in wardships and the land market had gone badly wrong. Defaulting on repayments for a string of 'great charges', he took out further loans. Despite the support of the king and of Guildford's good friend Sir Reynold Bray, things got so bad that Henry was forced to appoint him a personal debt manager, the abbot of Battle. As Guildford's fortunes declined, so did his ability to maintain his authority in Kent – and, by extension, the king's influence too. It was no coincidence that, at the same time, Bergavenny's influence started to spread.

Fuelled by an ingrained personal loathing for Guildford, the man whose regional dominance had eclipsed his own, Bergavenny started building up his power base, his men appearing more frequently in areas under Guildford's control, handing out livery clothing, badges, colours and the promises that came with them: job opportunities, money, and the less tangible rewards that constituted a big man's 'good lordship' – protection, influence, help with a lawsuit, or arranging a marriage.[10] Trouble began to flare in towns and villages on the borders between Guildford and Bergavenny territory. Henry tried to keep a lid on the intensifying violence: between 1497 and 1503 he instigated over a dozen special commissions to provide rapid justice and attempt to snuff out the trouble at its source. But with Bergavenny poaching Guildford's servants, the map of power in Kent was changing fast.

At Easter 1503, as Roberts and Symson had their first wary exchange, the confrontation between Bergavenny's and Guildford's retinues escalated dramatically. On Easter Monday, Sir Richard Guildford's son George was presiding over the local court sessions at Aylesford, where he was steward, when a gang of Bergavenny's men walked in, assaulted him, beat up his constable and bailiff, and made a bonfire of the court records. The following Monday, the same group went on the rampage, steaming through the local fair at Maidstone. In the inquests that followed, accusation and counter-accusation tumbled over each other: Bergavenny's men said that Guildford had started it, deliberately provoking trouble by swaggering about in Aylesford – which was, after all, Bergavenny's manor.[11]

As much as Suffolk's conspiracy, it was this local turf war, with its packs of aggressive retainers, that was the context for the arrest of the drunken Symson in Erith that summer. The clash of allegiances, in fact, may have lain directly behind the encounter, for the landlord who plied Symson with beer before reporting him to the local authorities, Thomas Broke, was almost certainly one of Bergavenny's men. Broke came from the village of Crayford, some two miles south and inland from Erith. Lying near Dartford on the main London to Canterbury road, it fell squarely within the territory of Lord Cobham, who was close to Bergavenny, his son-in-law, and was increasingly in his shadow. Thomas Broke was very probably a retainer of Cobham's; he may also have been related to a ward of the same name that Bergavenny bought from Cobham a few years later. Financial motives were bound up in his informing, too: this was the chance to make some quick cash, spinning Symson's drunken tall tale into a case of genuine sedition 'for to have a bribe'.

Symson's arrest, and his subsequent deposition against Roberts – a tale of doubtful loyalties, tangled affinities and local vendettas – drove home to Henry what he already knew.[12] Guildford, the king's man, was losing control in Kent – and consequently, so was the king.

Bergavenny's influence, on the other hand, was everywhere. Faced with a disastrous breakdown of authority in the region, a situation amplified by the presence of Suffolk just across the Channel, Henry had to choose between Guildford, one of the dwindling number of loyal servants who had been with him in exile and who had served him resolutely, and Bergavenny, with his dubious lineage, who he did not trust an inch. But the facts on the ground had changed, and Henry had to change with them. Guildford's demise was not long in coming.

Kent was not Henry's only concern, by a long chalk. With his dynasty hanging by a thread, he looked askance not only at those, like Bergavenny, who had much to gain from a change of regime, but those nobles who might expect to form part of a new dispensation; indeed, who had aspirations to the crown themselves. Two such men were at the forefront of the emerging generation of aristocrats. They had spent most of their lives growing up as wards of court, incubated at the very heart of the king's family. And it did not seem to have done them much good.

Born a year apart, and in their early twenties, the duke of Buckingham and the earl of Northumberland cut dazzling figures at Henry's court.[13] Both men had similar axes to grind. Their fathers had died when they were young. Buckingham was five years old when in autumn 1483 his father, a focus for the abortive uprising against Richard III, had been captured and beheaded. Later, he was cast as a pro-Tudor martyr, although his impulses for rebelling appear to have been prompted more by his own royal ambitions – as a direct descendant of Edward III – than by any particular inclination towards Henry. Six years later Northumberland's father, the fourth earl, had been trying to collect taxes on Henry's behalf in the restless northeast of England when he was assaulted and stabbed to death by resentful locals. His retainers, apparently, had quietly stood aside and let it happen – revenge, it was said, for the earl's own inaction at Bosworth, when he left Richard to the mercy of Henry's forces.[14]

As minors, Buckingham and Northumberland both became royal wards: Buckingham was raised in Lady Margaret Beaufort's household, Northumberland in the king's. Their sweeping family lands – Buckingham's estates in the Welsh Marches and Gloucestershire made him the greatest landowner in the country – were given into the custody of royal officials, and the revenues from them flooded into Henry's coffers. During the Warbeck years the young nobles were paraded at court as magnificent but obedient subjects, and their fortunes became increasingly entwined. They became brothers-in-law after Henry, always unable to resist a sale, had arranged Buckingham's marriage to Northumberland's sister for £4,000, and they were both admitted to the Order of the Garter in the same year. But if Henry hoped that their upbringing at the heart of the regime would have instilled in them a sense of their proper place in it, and their loyalty to it, he was to be sorely disappointed.

While they grew up, Henry's administrators had been busily eating away, termite-like, at their estates and their authority. As they approached their majorities, both men looked for signs that they would gain the pre-eminence and responsibility as the king's 'natural' counsellors that their rank, and their fathers' sacrifices on the regime's behalf, demanded – as well, of course, as the lucrative crown offices and titles that they believed were theirs by hereditary right. Northumberland was broodingly conscious of his family's role as great lords in the traditionally unstable northeast; Buckingham, meanwhile, hankered after the office of Constable of England, a title that Richard III had withheld from his father – one of the factors that had tipped him into rebellion.[15] All of which left Henry singularly unimpressed. As a contemporary commentator put it, for the king to confer high office and political power on noblemen 'of his free disposition' was 'laudable' – but, he warned, lords should 'not presume to take it of their own authority, for then it will surely choke them'.[16] It was for nobles to display good service and loyalty, and for the king to reward it, not the other way round. As Henry watched the young nobles parading themselves at court – Buckingham, in particular, was turning out to be a 'high-minded man' with a reputation for quick-tempered vindictiveness, who spoke 'as in a rage' – he probably convinced himself that these were not men who were suitable for political responsibility. Running under this, however, was his awareness that both nobles were due to inherit vast independent lordships; and, too, the perpetual question of allegiance – particularly as far as Buckingham was concerned. For, as everybody knew, he had a royal claim of his own.[17]

All of which lent a certain inevitability to what followed. Both lords had to go through the process of reclaiming their lands from the crown, and 'suing livery', as it was termed, rarely came cheap. As he had done with the youthful Suffolk, Henry took every opportunity to ratchet up the charges. Exploiting legal technicalities and irregularities in Buckingham's paperwork, Henry managed to squeeze a total of £6,600 out of the young duke in fines and bonds. While Buckingham was still a minor, Henry made him pay £2,000 on his mother's behalf for remarrying without the king's licence – which, Buckingham grumbled, was 'against right and good conscience' – and pocketed his wife's dowry for good measure. Financially harassed, and borrowing huge sums off Italian bankers to meet his repayments – and to sustain the lavish lifestyle which his rank demanded – Buckingham was already simmering with resentment by the time he regained his estates.[18]

Very little by way of royal favour was forthcoming. At court, Henry treated both men as courtly clothes-horses. But even here, Buckingham presented a threat, parading himself with a glamour and arrogance that was troubling even as it added lustre to Henry's court. On horseback, admirers noted, he resembled a 'Paris or Hector of Troy', while the spectacular outfits that had attracted such admiration at Prince Arthur and Catherine's wedding trod a fine line along the careful distinctions of rank and fabric made by contemporary sumptuary laws. In sheer cloth-of-gold tissue, purple and sable, Buckingham maintained his exalted status as the greatest noble in the land. He dressed in semi-regal fashion – almost as though he felt, as his father had done, that in the event of a contested succession he might make a good king himself. It was hardly surprising that, after Prince Arthur died, he was not invited to the funeral.[19]

Though Buckingham had the good sense to keep his mouth shut, he detested Henry and his administrators. And, away at his Gloucestershire seat of Thornbury, he steadily recruited men from his sweeping estates in the west country and the Welsh Marches into what was already a huge affinity. Capitalizing on a loophole in Henry's retaining laws, he invented non-existent jobs, 'much studying to make many particular offices in his lands, to the intent that he might retain as many men by the said offices as he could.' Or, in other words, to build up an army. As people started to whisper quietly, he was beginning to look like a king-in-waiting.[20]

In the decade that Northumberland had spent growing up at court, the political landscape of his own region had changed dramatically: north of the River Trent, the traditional domain of the Percy family, England was crawling with royal officials. As lieutenant of the North during the 1490s, parachuted in from his native East Anglia, Thomas Howard earl of Surrey had made his mark; so too had administrators like Sir Reynold Bray's man William Sever, the bishop of Carlisle. Now, there was a royal council in the North, headed by the archbishop of York, Thomas Savage, and many of the plum jobs that Northumberland had expected to fall into his hands, in order to distribute to his own men, had been hoovered up by royal servants – many, indeed, were held in Prince Henry's name, in his capacity of duke of York.[21]

When, during that summer of 1503, Northumberland had accompanied Princess Margaret on the last stage of her journey north to Edinburgh, he met her party outside York at the head of a glittering retinue, seated on a horse draped in crimson velvet scattered with his coat of arms, wearing a gown of the same crimson, his cuffs and collars encrusted with precious stones, gold spurs on his feet.[22] Beneath the ostensibly loyal splendour, he, too, was recruiting – and not so quietly. And as far away as the southeast of England, in increasingly unstable Kent, stories of his independent-minded petulance were doing the rounds. People gleefully related the insolent excuse that he had given the king for failing to appear at court: he couldn't, he said truculently, find a farrier to shoe his horses.

In towns across Yorkshire, including York itself, in place of the 'red roses of silver' distributed by the king's representatives, men wore the Percy blue-and-yellow livery and its crescent badge, and walked the streets looking for trouble. Royal officials reported intimidation and beatings; those who refused to recognize Northumberland's pre-eminence were subject to 'sundry misdemeanours, enormities, injuries and wrongs'. It had to be said, however, that the men encroaching on what Northumberland saw as his personal jurisdiction were no angels, either. Many of the household officers whom Henry employed in the regions tended to use the royal authority with which they were invested to advance their own interests, pursue personal grudges and settle scores. In the northeast, the household knights Sir John Hotham and Sir Robert Constable were bywords for violence and corruption: both had run-ins with Northumberland. Hotham tried to drag him into a dispute over land, a quarrel behind which – as in so many cases – was the hidden hand of the king, testing, probing, controlling and undermining the authority of his greatest subjects. Constable, meanwhile, was described simply as 'dangerous' by one court of law.[23]

Northumberland's real bête noire was Constable's boss: the head of Henry's council in the north, Thomas Savage, archbishop of York. An Italian-trained civil lawyer who had helped broker the original marriage treaty between Arthur and Catherine back in 1489, Savage wore his title of king's commissioner like a badge of nobility. He was also a flamboyant, worldly sophisticate, a keen hunter and a keeper of peacocks, with an unholy penchant for taking the Lord's name in vain.[24] His corruption, too, had a distinctly Italian flavour. A nepotist of the highest order, he exploited his position to the full, twisting the law in favour of friends and family. Underscoring all this was a deep-seated inferiority complex, born out of the fact, as he later stressed to Henry, that he was 'of little substance, but a poor gentleman and a younger brother', who owed not only his living but his very existence to the king – it was as though 'his highness had made him out of clay'. Northumberland and Savage, the wilful hereditary peer and the new man moulded by Henry, were like chalk and cheese. With every clash between the earl's men and royal retainers, tensions mounted. Finally, on 23 May 1504, they boiled over.

In late afternoon, Northumberland left the town of Fulford, outside York, accompanied by a small escort of thirteen riders. Not long before, Archbishop Savage had passed the same way with eighty armed men on horseback, having been at a boozy reception with York's mayor and corporation. Throughout the day, the two parties had crossed each other's paths; on each occasion, there had been provocation. Now, on the road out of Fulford, Northumberland encountered about a dozen of the archbishop's men, who had hung back, two of whom rode deliberately between the earl and his servants; Northumberland's horse stumbled and fell to its knees. 'Is there no way, sirs, but over me?' he snarled, grabbed one of the horsemen and punched him in the face. As swords were drawn and blows exchanged, the main body of the archbishop's force charged back and surrounded them, crossbows levelled, shouting abuse at the earl: 'traitor' and 'whoreson'. One of Savage's men aimed his bow at Northumberland; another, thinking quickly, cut the bowstring before he could fire. As the earl, dishevelled, clothes ripped, struggled in the grip of the archbishop's men, Savage asked him, blandly, 'What needs this work, my lord of Northumberland? I know well you are a gentleman, and I am another.' Northumberland's noncommittal reply riled the archbishop, who again prompted: 'Yea, I say am I, and that as good a gentleman as you.' Northumberland stared at his feet: 'Nay, not so.'[25]

When tempers cooled, both men were genuinely apprehensive about the king's reaction. They and their retainers were ordered down to London later that year and hauled in front of a panel of counsellors at Westminster. Despite Savage's insistence that Northumberland had started everything, the king punished both with equal severity, forcing them to enter into bonds for £2,000 to keep the peace.[26]

Henry was livid about the fracas – and about Savage's role in it as much as Northumberland's. Back in 1489 Northumberland's own father had been murdered during a popular uprising behind which, Henry feared, Yorkist conspiracy lurked. At a time when the shock of Warwick's extrajudicial murder continued to linger, Northumberland's killing in suspicious circumstances, by a royal servant, would have been incendiary, setting a match to local rivalries and tensions, and sending shockwaves through an already volatile country. Besides which, Henry always welcomed the opportunity to impose his authority – and to make a profit into the bargain.

The career of Savage, formerly so energetic both on the king's behalf and his own, entered a gentle downward path, ending in his death three years later. But for Northumberland, the incident was only the beginning. Fuelled by a lifetime of perceived slights and thwarted entitlement, and hungry for the restoration of his family's authority north of the River Trent, he embarked on a career of criminality and riot, almost as if he were trying to see how far he could push the king. Henry would crack down hard.[27]

In June 1503, as Prince Henry and Catherine were betrothed and Alexander Symson made his clandestine way to Aachen, the king continued to overhaul security at Calais. Alongside Sir John Wilshere, who doubled as comptroller and spymaster co-ordinating Calais's operation against the earl of Suffolk, another new face was Prince Henry's mentor Lord Mountjoy, who the king appointed as captain of the border fortress of Hammes, previously the stamping-ground of Suffolk's right-hand man Sir Robert Curzon.

After the debacle of Suffolk, Tyrell and Curzon, Henry badly needed loyal men with strong local connections in Calais – and, given his family's long association with the Pale, Mountjoy was a logical choice. His own reaction to the appointment, though, was probably mixed. Exchanging his unhurried but influential role at Eltham – a role which had acquired far greater significance since Prince Henry had become heir to the throne – for the remote boredom of the frontier garrison was, on the face of it, hardly an ideal career move. But his presence would not be required all the time – a deputy could do much of the donkey work – and besides, jobs at Calais were often stepping stones on a career path leading to great office. There were, too, opportunities to dabble in the lucrative textile trade on the side. What shocked Mountjoy, however, were his terms of employment.[28]

Of all the financial bonds that Henry imposed during his reign, Mountjoy's were among the most complex and extensive. His conditions of office – keeping the castle secure, reporting to the king and council on reasonable written notice – were enforced by a pledge of £10,000, backed up by guarantors providing securities for the same sum. Although Mountjoy was well connected, it was hardly a surprise that his friends could, between them, only scrape together pledges for a little over half the amount.[29]

While indentures of office regularly included financial pledges for doing the job properly, the size and scale of those attached to Mountjoy's new role were unprecedented. What lay at the root of these conditions of office was Henry's increasing obsession, verging on paranoia, with allegiance to the regime – even in the case of people like Mountjoy, who had proved themselves time and again. After all, even household men like Tyrell and Curzon, whose loyalties had been thought secure, had been fallible. By binding Mountjoy and his guarantors so closely to the regime, Henry aimed to remove any similar temptation, should it arise. Soon after Mountjoy's arrival, an incident at Calais would illuminate how precarious and strained the allegiances of even the most loyal of Henry's servants were becoming.

In 1504, 'about the last day of September', five men gathered in a small, private room at the house of Sir Richard Nanfan, acting head of Calais during the prolonged absences of the enclave's overall commander Lord Daubeney, whose duties as chamberlain of the royal household and as one of the king's inner circle kept him at court. The meeting included the master porter and military expert Sir Sampson Norton and Sir Hugh Conway, the new treasurer of Calais. All three were long-standing members of the king's household: experienced, loyal political veterans. With them were two younger men, Nanfan's son William, and John Flamank, his son-in-law and a member of the Calais garrison, both of whom were there to be seen rather than heard.[30]

The atmosphere was fraught. As the men settled, Nanfan, clearly on edge, turned to his son and to Flamank and, producing a Bible, swore them to confidentiality, not to repeat anything 'that is now here spoken'. The three senior men then discussed the perennial problem of Calais's security, Nanfan a moderating voice between Conway's agitated concern and Norton's blunt, straight-talking scepticism. It was Conway, scared and insistent, who led the conversation.

On disembarking at Calais three months previously to take up his new appointment, Conway had immediately smelt disloyalty in the air. Sniffing around, he picked up hints of a plot to murder Nanfan, and a sense that of the six-hundred-strong Calais garrison, the 'greater part' that had been recruited by Lord Daubeney could not be relied upon: they 'will never love none of us', Conway said, gesturing at his colleagues. What was more, he added, this factionalism stretched all the way into the royal household where, in his role as lord chamberlain,

Daubeney was responsible for vetting and appointing its chamber servants. The household, Conway said, was crawling with Daubeney's men – you just had to look at the king's security force, the yeomen of the guard, the 'most part' of whom were drawn from his own retinues. Daubeney, Conway insinuated, was manoeuvring for position, right under the king's nose.[31] In the event of Henry's death, both Calais and the royal household would be packed with men whose primary loyalties would be not to the young prince, but to Daubeney himself.

This was, on the face of it, a staggering claim. Daubeney's relationship with Henry had been forged in exile and in battle. He was one of the king's trusted right-hand men, a member of his inner circle, one of the very few who had traction with him. His disloyalty was inconceivable – and, indeed, everybody in the room hastily agreed that nobody was casting aspersions on his trustworthiness. But then Nanfan interjected. Thinking about it, he ruminated, back in the summer of 1497 the chamberlain had been 'very slack' in redeploying his forces, which had been en route to the Scottish border to fight James IV, against the Cornish rebels swarming towards London. If he had followed orders with more alacrity, the insurgents would have been destroyed long before they were in sight of the city. Henry, Nanfan said, had been 'discontent'. Daubeney's commitment to the regime, he implied, was distinctly shaky.

As everybody knew, Conway continued, the king was 'a weak man and a sickly, not likely to be a long-lived man'. Henry's increasingly frequent illnesses could hardly be kept secret for long: his chamber accounts betrayed how, on progress around his hunting lodges, the court would come to a halt in one place for weeks on end, a sure sign that he had relapsed. Conway recounted how on one such occasion, when Henry lay ill at his manor of Wanstead in Essex, he happened to be in the company of 'many great personages' who were discussing how things would play out on the king's death. Some had thought the duke of Buckingham would make a 'royal ruler'; Suffolk's name had also come up. 'None of them', though, 'spoke of my lord prince.' And, as Conway said meaningfully, 'it hath been seen in times past that change of worlds hath caused change of mind'. In other words, even though people remained loyal to Henry VII while he lived, there was no guarantee that they would transfer those loyalties easily to his young and vulnerable son.

Troubled by this talk, Conway had resorted to prophecy. Poring over a book of astrological prognostication to determine what the future held, he found that the stars were ill-omened indeed. The king would shortly die: 'my book', he told his colleagues, 'shall declare the same to you plainly to be as I have said and spoken'.

Unimpressed, the sergeant-majorly Norton told Conway to pull himself together, and to burn his book for good measure. But Conway's talk continued to circle the events of the recent past, scratching a persistent itch. It was impossible to know what people were really thinking – and therefore imperative that he and his colleagues looked after themselves first: 'see to our own security'. After all, it was what everybody else was doing. Conway recounted recent chats with two of Calais's other senior military officials, Sir Nicholas Vaux, lieutenant of Guisnes and Sir Anthony Browne, lieutenant of Calais Castle. Both men had waved his anxieties away with the smug certainty of those who knew they had 'good holds to resort to' in the event of instability: they would be fine, 'how so ever the world turn'.

Responses like these only increased Conway's growing sense of unease. But the real problem in his view was not Browne, but his wife, Lady Lucy, who 'loveth not the king's grace'. Lady Lucy was yet another member of the extended Neville clan, another of Suffolk's cousins. And she had her eye on the main chance. At the first sign of instability she would open up the castle gates to Suffolk and his men, and would give him all the help that she could. In such a scenario, with the garrison and town riddled with subversive elements who 'never loved the king's grace nor never will do', Conway feared that he and his loyalist friends would all be murdered in their beds. And once the rebels had Calais, he said, England would be open before them. Just across the Channel was that hotbed of instability, Kent: 'remember what alliance they be of there'.

Conway then ran through a number of names in Kent whose loyalty could not be counted on. All were men with strong connections to key Calais figures. Astonishingly, these included Sir Richard Guildford himself and Sir Edward Poynings, a knight of the Garter and one of Henry's chief military men who, like Guildford, was a paragon of loyalty. But Conway's point, again, was not about their loyalty to the king – it was about what might happen should he die while the prince was still young. For Poynings, who had previously been one of Daubeney's deputies, was cousin to Sir Anthony Browne; Vaux, meanwhile, was Guildford's brother-in-law. If, on Henry's death, loyalties to his son unravelled fast, a return to the turbulent family feuding of the civil wars was, Conway felt, entirely possible.[33]

The conversation in Nanfan's house summed up the mentality, anxious and restive, that permeated the country in the months and years following the deaths of Prince Arthur and Queen Elizabeth: from Northumberland to Calais, Lancashire to East Anglia and Kent. And the threat of political instability was exacerbated by the insecurity that rippled out from the wellspring of power, the royal household. To experienced hands like Conway, well used to watching for the faintest, barely detectable signs of conspiracy – the whispered conversation, the note passed from hand to hand – the source of this insecurity was, without a shadow of a doubt, the king himself. What was more, it was quite deliberately done.

Norton, forthright, had told Conway to put up or shut up. He should take his concerns about the Calais garrison straight to the top, to the king. But Conway's response was equally emphatic. He would do nothing of the sort, 'nor never would do'. Henry would never believe him, but would immediately suspect that he was talking out of 'envy, ill-will and malice'; he would have only 'blame, and no thank, for his truth and good mind'.

Conway knew what he was talking about, he said, because he had been in a similar situation years before, soon after Henry had ascended the throne. Then, he had gone to the king's right-hand man Sir Reynold Bray with information that Yorkist rebellion had been stirring. Bray had passed it on to the king, who summoned Conway to explain himself. Ushered into the king's presence he knelt and repeated his story, which he swore was true. No, Henry told him, it couldn't be, then methodically pulled the story apart, piece by piece – 'always to the contrary of my sayings', Conway recalled – and, after he had laid bare its inconsistencies, demanded Conway's source. When he pleadingly refused, trying to explain that he had sworn not to reveal his informant's identity even if he were 'drawn with wild horses', Henry's anger had been terrifying. Having gone to the king through his own 'goodwill', Conway had ended up with the finger of suspicion pointing directly at him. There was no way he would ever go through an experience like that again, as long as he lived.

To Nanfan, the story had a horrible familiarity about it. A while back, both he and Norton had gone to the king and council with their concerns that James Tyrell was intriguing with the earl of Suffolk. The reaction had been the same: scepticism shot through with suspicion – of them. Certain royal counsellors had even put it about that Nanfan, 'for malice', had been deliberately trying to ruin Tyrell's reputation. Another time, he had written to Henry about the machinations of Perkin Warbeck's right-hand man, Sir Robert Clifford, in Calais, only to receive 'sharp writing' from the king, demanding proof. Luckily for Nanfan, he had managed to get Clifford to repeat his treasonable words in front of a witness, 'otherwise I had likely to be put to a great plunge for my truth'. Nanfan was, presumably, exaggerating about being hanged by way of punishment for rumour-mongering – but like Conway, he decided not to go to the king with any further allegations. Just in case.

As it turned out, all the information that the king was so unwilling to believe – about the rebellion of 1486, about Clifford's disloyalty, and Tyrell's – had been proved correct. And, as they swapped stories of their uneasy encounters with the king, it was Norton who summed things up best. 'It was a pity', he mused, 'that the king did not trust his true knights better.' Henry really should give his loyal servants 'credence in such things as they should show for his security'. This lack of trust on the king's part, he concluded, had the potential to produce 'great hurt'.

This, of course, went to the heart of the problem. As household knights, placed in positions of trust and responsibility and expected to be the crown's eyes and ears – men 'by whom it may be known the disposition of the countries' – Nanfan, Conway and Norton were all simply trying to do their jobs, along preconceived ideas of service. But since the mid-1490s, when Henry's chief household officers, his chamberlain Sir William Stanley and steward Lord Fitzwalter, had been found wanting, so, in their various ways, had a number of other household knights – Clifford, Curzon, Tyrell, to name but a few. Each time, Henry had been reluctant to believe ill of them, and had been profoundly shaken when they had proved disloyal. Slowly but surely, however, trust had evaporated.

In his reforming treatise on the laws of England, written in the queasy 1460s, the common-law judge John Fortescue had stressed that 'the beginning of all service is to know the will of the lord whom you serve'.[34] What was glaringly obvious in the conversation among the Calais knights, who genuinely wanted to serve the king, was that they didn't know Henry's will at all – or rather, the only thing they could rely upon was the unpredictability with which he reacted. In the process, as Norton's comment revealed, normal relationships of service and trust were being undermined. Something else was taking their place.

Some time after the Calais meeting, Nanfan sent his son-in-law and servant John Flamank to Sir Hugh Conway with a letter from the cocksure lieutenant of Guisnes, Sir Nicholas Vaux. It evidently contained up-to-the-minute intelligence from the royal household, for Conway read it thoughtfully, then, in a gesture of confidentiality, took Flamank by the arm.

'Now you may see,' he said, flourishing the letter, 'that other men' – he meant the likes of Vaux and Browne – 'can have knowledge daily of every thing or great matter that is done in England, and we can have no knowledge of nothing, but by them. This,' he continued, 'is not good, neither no sure way for us.' What Conway and his colleagues needed, as he told Flamank, was a reliable, direct source of intelligence at court, a 'sure and wise man' who they would pay – 'at our cost and charges' – and who 'may all times send us how the world goeth'.[35] Feeling horribly out of the loop, about to be overtaken by events, unable to trust traditional chains of command, or to have a frank dialogue with the king and his counsellors, the Calais officials had resorted to the method that everybody else was using to gain information: they employed a spy and sent him into the royal household.

Conway, as it turned out, had confided in the wrong man. The only reason we know about these anxious, clandestine discussions in Calais is because, some months later, Flamank wrote an 'information', an informer's report, to the king, in which he detailed the conversations – including his own confidential chat with Conway – and in the manner typical of spies at the time, itemized its key points in a list for good measure.

Flamank's own motives for betraying these confidences were unhealthy. They were coloured by a recent spat with his father-in-law Nanfan, his own unpopularity among his colleagues in the Calais garrison and a self-seeking ambition. His report was, in other words, precisely the kind of rumour-mongering that Henry might have been expected to dismiss, as having been made out of 'envy, ill-will and malice'. For Henry, however, the problem was the uncertainty, the ambiguities and fence-sitting that pervaded everything and everybody: from the evasive testimony of Alexander Symson in the Tower and the turf wars of Kent, to Northumberland and Buckingham's sullen acquiescence, to the loyalties of Daubeney's men in the household, the arrangements made by Vaux and Browne, and Conway's desperate attempts to find out the truth through espionage. Flamank's report provided not answers, but yet more questions about allegiance: known unknowns.

It was as John Skelton's protagonist Dread had described in his nightmarish vision of court, confronted by doubleness and inconstancy at every turn, people creeping just out of his eyeline, whispering in corners as they looked him up and down, unable to be sure of anything or anybody. A kind of terror had settled on the royal household. And it stemmed from the king himself.[36]

Writing less than a decade later, Machiavelli, inevitably, described it best. Discussing the knotty question of whether it was better for a prince to be loved or feared, he wrote that, in an ideal world, 'one would like to be both one and the other'. But, Machiavelli continued, the world was not ideal. It was difficult to inspire both qualities, so if you had to choose one, it would be fear. The problem with love was that it was sustained by a 'chain of obligation', of service, which, 'because men are a wretched lot, is broken on every occasion for their own self-interest'. Fear, though, was different. It was sustained by a constant dread of punishment, by a sense of the prince's all-encompassing power.

Fear, Machiavelli concluded, worked better because 'men love at their own pleasure, and fear at the pleasure of the prince.' The wise prince should build his foundation on what belongs to him, not on what belongs to others. Faced with profound instability, that was exactly what Henry had done. Looking into the void of dynastic uncertainty, he was perfecting a system, idiosyncratic and terrifying, that would allow him unprecedented control over his subjects. He would describe this plan in terms that were an uncanny foreshadowing of Machiavelli's own. It was designed, he said, to allow him to keep his subjects 'in danger at his pleasure'.[37]

6

Council Learned

As the latest round of executions of de la Pole's confederates took place in summer 1503, Henry VII and his older daughter Margaret, together with a 'great multitude of lords and other noble persons', set out from Richmond and progressed north on the first stages of her journey to Edinburgh, where she would marry the Scottish king James IV. By early July, the household had arrived at Collyweston, Lady Margaret Beaufort's Northamptonshire palace and the centre of royal power in the east midlands. Set in rolling parkland, with water meadows, orchards, ponds and summer-houses, Collyweston had undergone months of improvements in preparation for the visit: the main gate had been newly crenellated and a new lodging built, with four large bay windows glazed with the Beaufort portcullis and clusters of daisies or 'marguerites'. After two weeks of entertainments, Lady Margaret hosted a select gathering in the great hall – only those related by blood to the family were admitted – to bid farewell to the young girl, Henry pressing into her hand a book of hours and telling her to write. The forthcoming marriage may have been key to Scottish peace, but both the king and his mother appeared reluctant to let go of the fragile thirteen-year-old, whose departure seemed to compound the recent family losses. Margaret, too, was his oldest surviving child. Should anything happen to Prince Henry, she would be heir – and the English throne would on her death pass to the Stuart kings of Scotland. Exactly a century later, on the death of Henry VII's granddaughter Queen Elizabeth, this was precisely what would happen, as Margaret's great-grandson James VI of Scotland became James I of England.[1]

As Margaret's party made its way with appropriate pomp towards Scotland, minstrels and trumpeters playing 'in all the departings of the

towns and in the entering of the same', Henry and his household progressed as far as Nottingham, where news came of another hammer
blow: Sir Reynold Bray, Henry's chancellor of the duchy of Lancaster
and the mastermind behind his financial policies, was dead. As the
king's household turned back, Henry took stock. Heading southwest,
he reached the duchy of Lancaster estates at Tutbury by 31 August; a
week later, he moved south to Merevale Abbey. There, he paid for the
new stained-glass depiction of his favoured Breton saint, Armel, a
belated commemoration of his victory at nearby Bosworth. Little
would have remained of the battle site, ploughed over for the last
eighteen years, but the time of year and the ripening cornfields, which
his forces had once trampled down as they advanced steadily towards
Richard III's armies, perhaps prompted memories of his fugitive past
and of the carnage that had yielded his God-given victory, and the
sense that his dynastic ambitions were, now, just as uncertain as they
had been then. The death of Bray, one of the chief architects of his
reign, only added to the sense of insecurity.[2]

Of Henry's small group of intimate advisers, Bray was the man of
whom he had earliest memories. Aged eleven, growing up in Raglan
Castle in the care of his Yorkist custodian Sir William Herbert, Henry
had received a visit from the thickset, shaggy-haired son of a Worces-
tershire bone-setter and blood-letter who was then his mother's
indefatigable steward, and who had presented the young boy with a
bow and a quiverful of arrows. During Henry's exile, Bray had worked
on behalf of Lady Margaret, supplying information to the insurgency
and, crucially, raising finance for the invasion through his network of
contacts in the city of London. In the first cash-strapped years of the
reign, Bray's financial acumen had been critical. Appointed chancellor
of the duchy of Lancaster, the crown lands that the king ran as his
own private estates, his brutally efficient methods of management and
revenue-collection were quickly extended throughout Henry's government. He was trusted implicitly by the king and his mother, and
remained a vital channel of communication between them.

Over the years, Bray had become pre-eminent among those in Henry's inner circle. It was said that, in their long, private conversations

in the privy chamber, the abrasive, straight-talking midlander even contradicted the king; that he could, as an observer succinctly put it, 'do anything' with Henry. On one occasion, the ever-impecunious Sir Richard Guildford, loitering around the privy chamber in the hope of waylaying Bray in order to borrow money from him, was summarily dismissed to entertain Catherine of Aragon until Bray and the king had finished talking business. Later, when Guildford returned, Bray, 'so multifariously charged' with the king's affairs, had vanished.[3]

A snapshot of Bray's omnicompetence comes in a memorandum that he drew up late in 1502, as the regime recovered from the shock of Prince Arthur's death. This wide-ranging to-do list shows exactly how far his remit extended. In it, he reminded himself to fine gaolers for escaped prisoners; to process the sales of royal wardships and marriages; to investigate customs offences (a shipload of tin had been impounded at Southampton docks 'to our behalf'; Venetian shippers owed import duties on a thousand butts of sweet wine, which as far as Bray could make out, London's customs officers 'must answer for'); and the inevitable actioning of financial bonds. At the head of this list he had itemized 'three great matters in especial': running the rule over details in the king's will; conducting an audit into the household accounts and 'setting some good order therein'; and carrying out a wide-ranging investigation into all the 'revenues and receipts' of the king's lands that had not been properly accounted.

All of which confirms what everybody knew: all roads led to Bray. With no formal office, no formal appointment by letters patent, he sat at the top of the tree, the king's chief executive. As the many ingratiating letters to him attested, the highest nobles in the land trod the well-worn path to the door of their 'loving friend' Bray, knowing that a few words from him in the king's ear could unlock the door to royal favour, plunge people into a lifetime of debt – or release them from it. For one petitioner, the son of Henry's steward Lord Willoughby, Bray was behind only the king and Prince Henry in the pecking order of loyalties: 'next to the king's grace and my lord prince', he wrote to Bray, he was bound 'to owe you my service and [that of] all the friends I can make.'[4]

In his remorseless pursuit of the king's interests, Bray had made himself enormously rich. The ways to profit from his position were legion, and he was good at all of them. He acquired plum crown offices, and, as the man who oversaw the king's finances, knew best where the good deals were. He sold – on Henry's behalf, naturally, although he took his cut – leases of crown lands, marriages to rich heiresses in the crown's charge, and the custody of wards (the investment market in propertied minors, and widows for that matter, was booming). He received pensions, or financial retainers for access to royal favour, from several noblemen, and, indeed, the king of France. Then there was the sale of justice, in the form of fines and pardons for offences, or bonds whose conditions had, he and his colleagues had found, been broken. He bought up a vast portfolio of estates, which arced through eastern and southern England, much of it compulsorily purchased. He played the administrator's trick of trapping people in debt to the crown, then setting fines so high that people were unable to pay them; he took over their debts in exchange for their land, sold to him at knockdown prices. He built houses and palaces, employed thousands of staff, and kept a fine wardrobe. His most prized possession was 'a gown of crimson with the hood lined with white sarcenet of the order of Saint George', his robe of the Order of the Garter, into which he had been elected along with the likes of Sir Thomas Lovell; Bray's coat of arms still scatter the ceiling of the Garter's spiritual home, St George's Chapel in Windsor Castle, into which he ploughed funds. Not only was Bray more powerful than most nobles; he looked like one too. The crucial difference was that he owed everything he had to the king. Bray, in short, did what all Henry's counsellors and servants were doing – only he did it best.[5]

Bray had played an instrumental role in the development of Henry's peculiar system of government. Over the years, his influence, and that of his duchy of Lancaster staff, had spread inexorably into the flexible, protean committees, offshoots of the king's council, which hunted down and exploited the king's prerogative rights, which sliced through the intractable meanderings of the common law courts like a hot knife through butter – and which helped generate the revenues that flooded into Henry's chamber treasury, bypassing the grindingly slow process of the exchequer. By 1500, Bray's name had become synonymous with one such tribunal, which enforced the king's rights with a zealous rigour and which would become the most infamous expression of Henry's rule.[6]

The tribunal's name, in a sense, said it all. The phrase by which it referred to itself, and by which it came to be known by its victims, the 'council learned in the law' – or 'council learned' for short – was a generic term used to refer to a body of lawyers retained by a nobleman to arbitrate on cases within their private jurisdiction, or by a rich merchant to provide legal advice. The council headed by Bray, therefore, didn't really have a name. It didn't have a fixed membership either: consisting generally of a small quorum of between six and nine of the king's counsellors, specialists in law or administration, its composition constantly mutated. And it was never legally constituted.

The council learned's presence, unsurprisingly, was elusive. Its minute books rarely recorded the dates of its sessions, or names of attendees.[7] Sometimes it met in the warren of government offices housing the exchequer and chancery that led off Westminster Hall; sometimes in the duchy of Lancaster's rooms at St Bride's on the western edge of the city, between Fleet Street and the Thames, and conveniently near the duchy's favoured place of incarceration a few minutes' frogmarch away from its offices, the Fleet prison. More often than not, it met simply where a few of its members happened to be gathered – at Greenwich or Richmond, or wherever the king was in residence. Given that its clerk, William Heydon, didn't even know where the council learned was convening half the time, it was unsurprising that defendants hauled before it didn't, either: one man who had travelled down from Nottingham in answer to a summons protested to the council that he had been in London for a week and 'could not have knowledge where he should appear'.

The methods by which it worked were equally opaque. It was fed by a constant stream of information supplied by a well-entrenched network of retainers, agents and informers. Its subpoenas – consisting of a summons stamped with the privy seal, or a 'sharp letter' from the king or one of his counsellors – could be delivered by anyone, even an anonymous messenger. These writs rarely, if ever, stated a precise

charge – simply a demand that the defendant should turn up in
response to some unspecified accusation: 'to answer to such things as
shall be objected against him'.[8] And because the council learned was
not a recognized court of law, and its writs were not formally enrolled
when they were issued, the defendant had to appear clutching the sub-
poena that he had been served. A process that filled people with fear,
frustration and rage, it bypassed and overrode the common law
courts, plucking people out of the normal workings of the legal system and hauling them straight in front of a panel invested with the
king's ultimate judicial authority. Henry himself never attended the
council's hearings, but then he didn't have to. It was the perfect expression of his will, and of his personal rule – with Bray at its head.[9]

In a royal household which, underneath the carefully calibrated magnificence, was suffused with uncertainty and watchfulness, Bray's men
were everywhere, eyes on the lookout, ears pricked for loose talk. Sir
John Mordaunt, a grizzled Middle-Temple lawyer who had fought for
Henry at Bosworth, was increasingly prominent. So too was the duchy
receiver-general John Cutt, a man with a no-nonsense attitude to
interrogation: suspecting one of his household servants of stealing, he
had dragged him into a privy and put a knife to his throat, stating
bluntly that if the servant didn't produce the stolen goods there and
then, he would kill him. Then there was the auditor Robert Southwell,
one of the small group of men who helped Henry cross-check his
accounts, and another assiduous supplier of intelligence reports on
flaky loyalties.[10]

Bray also had friends among the king's secret servants, including
William Smith, a man who worked closely with Bray and the council
learned as a revenue-collector and financial enforcer. Wearing his
other hat, Smith was page of the king's wardrobe of robes, the personal wardrobe in which the king's clothes were stored in a carefully
organized sequence of racks, shelves and presses, and which was connected with the king's privy chamber via a back stair. In this capacity,
he was constantly about the king: brushing, storing and preparing his
clothes, dressing him, handling petty cash and buying necessaries.[11]
As one of Perkin Warbeck's keepers, Smith had turned provocateur,

enticing him into trying to escape and providing Henry with the excuse he needed to lock the pretender in the Tower and to disfigure and mutilate him so that he no longer resembled the Yorkist prince he claimed to be.

If, as the Calais treasurer Sir Hugh Conway had feared, Lord Daubeney's men were 'strong in the king's court', so too, in their different way, were Bray's. As a landed noble, Daubeney brought into the king's service retainers from his own regional estates, men whose loyalties, in the final analysis, lay with him. Bray's men were among those who, in John Skelton's words, stood in small groups in the corridors of power 'in sad communication', who 'pointed and nodded' meaningfully, who strolled through the galleries and chambers in constant motion so as not to be overheard, who 'wandered aye and stood still in no stead'.[12]

One of the regular faces on the council learned was Bray's right-hand man Richard Empson. A Middle-Temple-trained lawyer and career bureaucrat, Empson had been the duchy's attorney-general under Edward IV, before being sacked by Richard III – possibly owing to his connection with Anthony Woodville, Lord Rivers, whom Richard had summarily executed in 1483. Bad associations under Richard III, however, tended to be good ones in the new regime, and Empson was reappointed the same day as his new boss, Bray. Like his mentor and colleagues, Empson combined tireless service to the crown with tireless self-advancement. A suave, able networker – 'he maketh his friends', as one observer put it – his political career burgeoned. In 1497, he gained the dubious distinction of being named by Warbeck as prominent among the king's 'low-born and evil counsellors'.[13]

In one of the long-running legal battles characteristic of the age, Empson had tried to disinherit the Yorkshire knight Sir Robert Plumpton in favour of his own daughter, aiming to land some prime pieces of real estate for himself in the process. No angel himself, Plumpton wilted in the face of Empson's sustained campaign of intimidation and perversion of the course of justice, leading one of Plumpton's relatives to condemn the counsellor's 'utter and malicious enmity, and false craft'. One of Empson's associates, accompanied by a group of servants, assaulted a bailiff of Plumpton's, battering him almost to death before making him sign a statement in their favour. At a hearing at the York assizes in 1502, Empson appeared with a powerful display of muscle. Among two hundred servants, all wearing the red rose badge, were a number of Henry's household knights and members of the king's own security forces, the yeomen of the guard, who showed Empson exaggerated respect, holding the counsellor's stirrup as he swung himself down from his horse. Suitably cowed, the jury returned in Empson's favour, plunging Plumpton deep into debt. With these liveried retinues, Empson was behaving more like a member of the high nobility than the government lawyer he was. His appearance, Plumpton bitterly recalled, would have been more fitting for a duke.[14]

The all-pervasive influence of Bray and his men was evident in an anxious letter to Plumpton from one of his legal advisers, written the following year. Having been stitched up by Empson at the York assizes, Plumpton was now desperately trying to appeal to the king's council. The Lincoln's Inn lawyer George Emerson, hanging around the Westminster law-courts monitoring his case, sent him some judicious words of advice.

Should Plumpton gain an audience with the king, Emerson wrote, he would very likely ask Plumpton to propose the names of counsellors 'which you would should have examination of your matters'. But, Emerson insisted, Plumpton should name nobody. The king would immediately assume that any names he mentioned would be biased in Plumpton's favour – and, more to the point, his own allies at court would be revealed: 'your friends should be known'. Emerson's portrait of Henry's counter-intuitive methods was one that courtiers from Soncino to Conway would have instantly recognized: the benevolent demeanour masking a relentless probing for weakness and information. In the face of this, the only thing to do, Emerson said, was to play a straight bat. Plumpton should tell the king that he would be happy with any counsellors that the king chose to judge his case – except any of those 'belonging to Mr Bray', who would be sure to conclude the case in Empson's favour. It was advice that spoke volumes for Bray's dominance: nobody, however influential, wanted to be known to be intriguing against one of his men.[15]

Plumpton did well to listen, because his own friends at court were influential indeed. In February 1504, he wrote a Valentine's-day letter to his wife from a wintry London, where he was trying vainly to move his 'matter' forward. Things were still stuck, but he was reassured by the king's behaviour, and that of his own 'good friends': the bishop of Winchester and lord privy seal Richard Fox, Sir Thomas Lovell, Sir Richard Guildford and Richard Weston. Although Guildford's influence was fast waning, Fox and Lovell were perhaps the closest of the king's advisers after Bray, while the pleasant, courteous Weston was one of the king's secret servants. Behind the scenes, Plumpton's matter was raised. Words were spoken in the king's ear and counsellors were discreetly lobbied. Plumpton was granted immunity from arrest for his debts and could breathe again.

At first glance, it might seem surprising that Fox, Lovell and Guildford should have moved against Empson, a man with whom, along with his master Bray, they had worked since the beginning of the reign. But by 1504, when Henry's select committee of counsellors met to judge Plumpton's case, Bray was dead and as people circled, looking for opportunity, Empson was on the rise. Perhaps Plumpton's 'good friends', long-established advisers and servants, looked askance at Empson's hunger for power and influence. Then again, perhaps they just didn't like him.

The death of Bray, the man who had come closest to understanding the workings of the king's mind and who held the mechanisms of law-enforcement, security and fundraising in a fine balance, left Henry with a problem. With the cumulative crises of the past years, he was more wary than ever of the political nation, even of the counsellors around him, to whom he was increasingly disinclined to listen. His illness, too, had left him more withdrawn, exacerbating this remoteness. Henry's relationship with the world around him seemed more than ever a financial one: where trust was replaced by contracts and the bonds of allegiance by the monitoring of behaviour, backed up by the ever-present threat of financial penalties. It seemed that written bonds and fines, the physicality of hard cash, jewels and plate, were more secure, more real to Henry than the intangible vagaries of men's minds.

Henry seemed increasingly obsessed by the equation of security and money. His chamber system, informal and flexible, had developed to allow him personal control over the ever-increasing quantities of cash and financial sureties generated by the activities of Bray and his fellow counsellors. Sitting in his offices behind the high walls of Westminster Abbey sanctuary, the chamber treasurer John Heron and his small team of clerks recorded the receipt and expenditure of massive quantities of cash, written bonds and debts, their account books personally audited by the king, his spidery monogram adorning the bottom of every page – and, when in particularly obsessive mood, every accounting entry. Heron, too, supervised the siphoning-off of tens of thousands of pounds in gold into the king's coffers, chests and strongboxes in the Tower, the treasury at Calais, the jewel house and other closely guarded 'secret places' where he accumulated cash and treasure, the fruits of Bray's meticulous revenue-collection.

But even Heron didn't know everything that went on. Much of the time, the king processed accounts himself. In the front of Heron's book of receipts, he scribbled in a fluent, elegant hand pages of closely written description of monies accumulated from various sources: revenues from the Calais wool staple; from his French pension; a tranche of Prince Arthur's marriage portion; speculations on the European currency markets handled by his favoured broker, the Bolognese financier Lodovico della Fava. His hands delving into bags of cash, Henry recorded money in Flemish gold, Spanish gold and silver, 'Romish' guilders and guilders from Utrecht, French Louis d'or and 'crowns of soleil'. He examined hard currency with an intimate care, feeling in his hand the substance of each type of coin: 'light crowns', he noted, 'good crowns', and, most approvingly, 'old weighty crowns'.[16] These were the actions, not of a miser, but of a sophisticated financial mind; a king with a complex, all-consuming obsession with the control, influence and power that money represented, both at home and abroad.

Henry had taken a close personal interest in enforcing his rights. But now, at a time when he was stepping up the use of his financial sureties, he was physically unable to sign and oversee everything. With his Bosworth advisers dying off – and others, like Guildford, proving themselves inadequate – Henry needed people who would answer to him unconditionally, and whose work he could control. Characteristically, rather than hand over Bray's all-encompassing role to another counsellor, he decided to split it up, portioning it between a number of administrators. At the centre, he could hold the strings himself.

The first signs of this reshuffle came towards the end of 1503, when the lawyer and financial specialist Robert Southwell started to take charge of the auditing duties, together with another colleague, the bishop of Carlisle William Sever. Like Southwell, Sever had worked closely with Bray as the king's financial enforcer in the north of England. He was well used to spotting opportunities that might be manipulated 'to the king's advantage' – the delicate phrase, beloved of Henry's administrators, which belied a multitude of exploitative practices. Sever, who had a bleak sense of humour, put the reality rather better: in a note to Bray he once described his role as that of a ravening dog taking a bone from two others while they distractedly tore lumps out of each other.[17] Under Southwell and Sever, the auditing process soon hardened into another informal tribunal, invested with the authority to oversee, vet and approve accounts – and, if there were evidence of malpractice or corruption, to follow it up with the council learned. In fact, given that both men were members of the council learned, they could simply put on their other hats and judge the case themselves.

At around the same time, Henry appointed a dedicated master of the wards. Bray had run this big and lucrative income stream with considerable success. Now, the job of buying and selling the legal control of minor heirs, their property and revenues, and sniffing out other opportunities for the crown to intervene ('idiots' mentally unable to manage their property, widows with no legal rights) was hived off to John Hussey, a bluff ex-colleague of Bray's who had not long before displayed a dubious aptitude for the task by selling wardships for substantial backhanders. Hussey had been caught, fined and hit with the ubiquitous bonds into the bargain, something which, Henry may have felt, now made him all the more compliant a servant.[18] That he was the son of one of Henry's chief justices, was an ex-employee of the king's mother, and had just married his son to Sir Thomas Lovell's niece was all grist to the mill.[19] There remained, however, a

big, Bray-sized gap at the heart of Henry's system. In the autumn of
1503 he found his man.

A sharp, silver-tongued and intellectually curious lawyer in his early
forties, Edmund Dudley was from a good Sussex family, but – for him
at least – one whose glory days were behind it. Though his grandfather was a baron and his uncle a bishop of Durham, his own father
had been the younger son, meaning that for Edmund nobility, spiritual and temporal, had remained tantalizingly close but just out of
reach. It was this, perhaps, as well as his fascination for the intricacies
of law and a hungry ambition that simmered beneath his affability,
which had driven his rise through the legal ranks. Enrolling at Gray's
Inn, Dudley had been shrewd enough to focus his work on one of the
obscure – but, to the king, highly lucrative – prerogative statutes. In
1495, the year that Henry had started to take a sustained interest in
his prerogative rights, Dudley had displayed his aptitude in a series of
forensically brilliant readings; a year later, he took a job as under-
sheriff in the London law courts. His appointment was a testament to
his networking skills as well as his legal ability: relentless lobbying by
'all the friends he could make' led the city to overlook the fact that he
was, as its chronicler disparagingly put it, a 'poor man' who did not
possess the requisite wealth needed to maintain the dignity of such an
office.[20]

During his six years working in London's courts of justice, Dudley
became intimately familiar with the city's workings. He knew its corridors of power, its Guildhall politics, its major players – wealthy
merchant-politicians like Sir Henry Colet and Sir William Capel – and
the intricate web of rivalry, opportunism and mistrust that linked the
city's guilds and companies, from the the mercers and drapers to the
goldsmiths and haberdashers. He understood, too, the mechanisms of
commerce, international banking and trade, and the rampant sharp
practice and corruption that flourished, from the coin-clipping and
proliferation of illegal exchanges to the import-export rackets that
the customs officers down at London's port tried vainly to track – or,
more commonly, to turn a blind eye to, or participate in. All of which
made him familiar with London's alien communities, from the

Thamesside ghetto of the Hanse Steelyard, whose high, fortified walls contained a whole German- and Dutch-speaking world – houses, gardens, warehouses bursting with fish, timber, furs, wax and Rhenish wine – to the Italian merchant-bankers, dominated by the great Florentine houses of Frescobaldi, the Bonvisi of Lucca, and the Genoese Grimaldi.

Dudley, in fact, seemed particularly drawn to the Italian merchant-bankers. Clustered around Lombard Street and their religious and commercial centre of Austin Friars, whose precincts formed the centre of London's international trade and which swarmed with 'sharp spies' from 'all parts of the world', their luxurious palazzi exuded wealth and international political influence. Crammed with fine imported soft furnishings and interior features that reminded them of home – under-floor heating, Roman baths, hot-and-cold running water – these informal ambassadorial residences figured forth the power of the banking houses that they represented and the vast capital flows they controlled. Dudley could have hardly helped notice, too, the tensions between London's companies and the foreign merchants – especially the Italians, who seemed to get all the best contracts, supplying the royal wardrobe with silks, satins and cloth-of-gold – and between the Guildhall and the king.[21]

Though he may have been poor, comparatively speaking, Dudley had his connections. The head of the great wardrobe, the man who handed out fat contracts on the king's behalf and who handled an annual budget of thousands of pounds, was his brother-in-law, Sir Andrew Windsor. And there was another family friend who had a particular influence on his career: Sir Reynold Bray.[22]

While still a London under-sheriff, Dudley had first started working for Bray, investigating and enforcing the king's rights in his home county of Sussex; he had, too, popped up in Kent, taking bonds with Sir Richard Guildford. In Dudley, Bray saw a valuable combination of legal sharpness and worldly know-how – particularly as far as London was concerned. Of late, the king's relationship with the city, always one of guarded suspicion, had moved into a more aggressive mode. Dudley, Henry and Bray felt, could be a key to unlocking the city's closely guarded independence once and for all.

When Dudley resigned from his post of under-sheriff to further his legal career, he was given a golden handshake by a grateful city, which was undoubtedly aware that he was destined for great things. But in autumn 1503, about to take up a prestigious post as sergeant-at-law, one of the highest legal offices in the land, he abruptly changed course. A parliament had been called for the following January, and Dudley had been chosen as Speaker.[23] Though elected by the commons, the Speaker was nominated by the king and was a mark of considerable favour. It was, as Dudley knew, a gateway to the sunny uplands of royal service, as a glance at the previous incumbents under Henry VII, all common lawyers, showed: they included Thomas Lovell, John Mordaunt and Richard Empson. The parliament of January 1504 would be a testing baptism for Dudley and a watershed for Henry's reign. It would also be the last parliament the king would ever call.[24]

On 25 January, Parliament assembled in the Chamber of the Cross in Westminster Palace, crowded with magnates and bishops, with Henry enthroned under his cloth of estate. The new archbishop of Canterbury and chancellor, William Warham, stepped forward to preach the opening sermon that set the tone for the parliament. Neither his theme of justice, nor his selected text – a verse from the Book of Wisdom beloved of lawyers everywhere – was particularly novel, but then, tradition and authority were precisely what Warham wanted to evoke. Weaving together quotes from Cicero, Aristotle and Augustine, he painted a comforting picture of society, stressing the importance of the nobility and landowners in the natural order, everything in its right place – all held together by the law. For without justice, he said, citing Augustine, 'what are kingdoms but great bands of robbers?'[25] This made what followed all the more alarming. Henry, it quickly became clear, was fundraising with a vengeance. And he was doing it in a way that involved a sweeping extension of royal power into the lives of his subjects. It was no wonder that Dudley, with his encyclopaedic knowledge of the prerogative, was in the Speaker's hotseat.

When kings came to Parliament to ask for taxes, it was as compliant as they got. Taxation provoked widespread resentment and, often, unrest. For that reason, taxes were generally granted in and for exceptional circumstances: for defence of the kingdom, or for war. If a king asked for taxes in peacetime or for other reasons, it was a clear sign of his lack of financial prudence – and, if he did so repeatedly, it almost invariably backfired on him. Ever since Henry VI's hopeless inability to manage his money in the 1450s, kings had soothed Parliament's anxieties by promising not to overburden it with demands, while at the same time exploring ever more creative ways to squeeze money out of their subjects. This, in particular, was what Parliament found disconcerting about Henry: it was not just about how much money he asked for, but how he wanted to levy it.

From early in the reign, the king's commissioners had trawled the country assessing individual wealth, something that people used to the fixed tax rates, in place for over a hundred and fifty years, resented hugely. This new, invasive system became known as 'Morton's Fork', after Henry's chancellor: if you looked wealthy, then you could obviously afford to pay up; if, on the other hand, you had a frugal lifestyle, you probably had money salted away. Henry had trod a fine line. Like Edward IV, he had levied a tax for a war, in 1492, which he never fought – his commissioners continued to collect money even after he had returned home having pocketed a massive French pension. Five years later, the aggressive demands of his collectors triggered the Cornish uprising, which fell just short of toppling his regime.[26]

Now, in his latest demand for a tax, Henry dusted off an ancient prerogative right called a feudal aid. This was a goodwill tax, a 'benevolence' given by the king's subjects to cover major royal events – in this case, to cover the costs of Prince Arthur's knighting way back in 1489, and his daughter Margaret's marriage to James IV. No king had asked Parliament to help out with expenses like this for over a century – and even then, in 1401, when it had been levied for the first time in living memory, it had met with widespread anger. But it was entirely typical of Henry's persistence in sniffing out his rights, as attested by the 'note to self' he had scribbled in the margin of his accounts, next to the payment for his daughter's wedding, reminding himself to claim it back. Arthur's knighting, meanwhile, had taken place fifteen years ago; besides which, he was dead. Although the demand was technically legal, it was, to say the least, a tenuous way of raising cash. And its repercussions were potentially huge.

For, in asking for the feudal aid, Henry was effectively seeking

Parliament's approval to deploy his fiscal agents in a new, comprehensive round of information-gathering needed to levy the tax – information that could then be used in all sorts of other ways in the future. The commons knew exactly what was going on. The aid, they said, 'should be to them doubtful, uncertain and great inquietness'. Parliament erupted.[27]

Looking on interestedly at the robust exchanges that followed was one of Henry VII's secret servants. A trusted administrator, well equipped to follow the cut-and-thrust of recondite legal debate, William Tyler had evidently been briefed by the king to report on progress. The eloquent resistance of one young MP in particular was said to have caught Tyler's eye. Now enrolled at Lincoln's Inn, the twenty-six-year-old Thomas More had abandoned his plans to take holy orders and was following in his father's footsteps as a London lawyer; he had, too, been elected to his father's parliamentary seat of Gatton in Surrey. As his son-in-law and biographer William Roper later recounted, More made 'such arguments and reasons' against the feudal aid that the bill was 'clean overthrown'. After the vote, Tyler took himself off to the king, to tell him that 'a beardless boy' had 'disappointed all his purpose'.[28]

Roper, whose hagiographic account portrayed More's life as one long preparation for his eventual martyrdom, had particular reason to glorify this otherwise undocumented episode. But there was a perfectly good reason why More should have waded in. The king's manipulation of his rights looked suspiciously like the 'exquisite' – or exceptional – 'means of getting of good', against which the eminent common lawyer Sir John Fortescue had warned kings back in the 1470s – which was probably what the young More thought, along with the rest of the commons.

Parliament eventually granted Henry's tax – but crucially, and pointedly, it shifted the goalposts. Defined as a defence tax rather than a feudal aid, it was to be levied in the traditional way, with no chance for the king to let his financial agents off the leash. The commons had slammed the door in his face.

Henry, of course, had first-hand experience of how taxation could get out of hand. With his anxieties over Suffolk, over the disturbances in Kent and elsewhere, and with the spectre of the Cornish rebels lingering in his mind, he acquiesced gracefully. And towards the end of March, as the parliament drew to a close, he announced that he did not intend to call Parliament again 'for a long tract of time'. The reason he gave was the 'ease of his subjects' – and the commons, no doubt, were relieved. Parliament was, for most, an expensive, time-consuming process in which MPs were expected to stay in London for months, and pay Westminster's inflated prices. For Henry, it was an obvious crowd-pleasing gesture. But there was another, more pertinent reason, too. The king had in place a system that would allow him to extract money from his subjects. If Parliament would not allow Henry to raise funds on his own terms, he would simply go round it. And he had marked Thomas More's card, too.[29]

June came, and with it the hottest summer in living memory: three months without rain. After years of bad harvests, men watched anxiously as rivers and ponds receded and dried up, and cattle were driven miles in search of water; a relentless sun burned pasture and meadow.[30] Late in the month, Henry finally settled on Bray's replacement as chancellor of the duchy of Lancaster: not Richard Empson, but his colleague John Mordaunt. Around the same time, Empson was up to his old tricks.

That month, the king's chapelman William Cornish was waylaid and beaten up by Empson's men and immured in the Fleet, the notorious debtors' prison sandwiched between the city's western wall and the river from which it took its name, the sluggish open sewer that seeped out into the nearby Thames at Blackfriars. Cornish was not formally charged. His crime, though, seems to have been the spreading of rumour – 'false news' or, as he put it, 'false information' – a serious, statutory offence, against which Henry had legislated early in the reign. Cornish pleaded his innocence, in a poem that he addressed to the king himself.[31]

In 'A Treatise between Truth and Information', Cornish took the court poet's typical precaution of veiling his complaint in allegory – as Skelton put it, 'metaphora, allegoria withal' was the poet's 'protection, his pavis and his wall'.[32] But there was no mistaking Cornish's message. He had, he wrote, been the victim of a travesty of justice. His poem, riddled with fear and bewilderment, hinted at the palpable atmosphere of unease that hung over the royal household. What he – or rather his allegorical narrator, Truth – had tried to do was to speak out against an injustice perpetrated in the king's name, one that the king would surely right if only he knew about it.

The scene of the poem was Cornish's own stamping-ground, the Chapel Royal, where the choir were performing one of the soaring polyphonic masses for which Cornish and his colleagues were renowned, sung from the chapel's elaborate illuminated songbooks. But one of the choristers, Truth, was finding the music difficult to follow. It was burdensome, badly written 'with force' and 'lettered with wrong'; what was more, his voice was weak and hoarse, people couldn't hear it. After 'a day or two' off resting his voice and eating sugar candies to soothe his vocal cords, Truth took his place among his colleagues, determined to sing out 'true and plain'. But there were those who hated what he was singing, who had 'spite' at his song, and would do whatever they could 'to have it sung wrong'. Chief among them was another singer called Information, who was 'so curious in his chanting' that his loud, over-intricate variations turned Truth's melody into a cacophony, distorting, stifling and twisting his 'true plain song'.

Cornish's nightmarish musical vision was the same world that Conway, Nanfan and Norton's anxious conversation had figured forth: of suspicion and rumour, where true loyalties had been displaced by something else, and which was dominated by informers who, in Cornish's words, 'disgorge their venom'. In this warped universe, he wrote, false information ruled truth, and people believed that 'the righteous shall do wrong'.

There were shades, too, of Emerson's warning to Plumpton to keep his causes and his friends secret. Cornish had 'sounded out' influential support, trying out his music on 'both knight and lord', but 'none would speak'. Inadvisedly, he had gone it alone and spoken out. If only he could have a proper hearing, and the due process of law, he could prove his case.

Cornish was of course drawing on a rich literary tradition that portrayed the court as hell, much as Skelton had done in his *Bowge of Court*. But reality tore through Cornish's allegorical veil. He had been beaten up and imprisoned by Empson; he had written the poem in desperation to plead his case to the king. Somehow, Cornish got his message across. That July, he managed to have the verses smuggled out of the Fleet and carried downriver to Henry at Greenwich, where the household was preparing to go on summer progress. And Cornish, like Plumpton, evidently had good friends. Shortly after, Henry gave Empson a taste of his own medicine. He bound the counsellor to the tune of £500, constraining Empson to keep the peace against Cornish, and that 'the same Cornish take no bodily hurt neither by the same Sir Richard neither by no one other by the consent, assent, procuring, abetting or stirring of the same Sir Richard'.[33]

What exactly Cornish had said or written to provoke Empson's brutal response can probably never be known. There seems little doubt, though, that he had got caught up in the power politics of court, and in particular with interests opposed to the ever-increasing influence of Empson and his fellow financial counsellors. One name suggests itself: Henry Percy, earl of Northumberland, who, weeks before Cornish had been thrown in prison, had narrowly escaped being shot by Archbishop Savage's men. Northumberland had a taste for literature and, whether or not he had had anything to do with Cornish's poem, its vision of a duplicitous court governed by false information spoke strongly to him: he ordered his secretary to copy it painstakingly into a manuscript of collected verse.

Henry's bond against Empson was a slap across the wrist of the kind he was fond of, a warning shot against those who were too free in wielding the power he had invested in them. But while Cornish had escaped, the dangers of voicing healthy criticism of the king's counsellors were all too evident – and the beating-up and incarceration of one of the high-profile cultural mouthpieces at court had its effect. Cornish would think very hard before speaking out again, as for that matter would others. Gradually, the pressure-valve of dissent and satire, through which court voiced its criticism, would be shut off. When the inevitable explosion came, it would be all the greater.

That August, messengers rode out from Westminster into all parts of the country, carrying with them copies of a royal proclamation, the king's elaborate scrawl in the top-left-hand corner, the signatures of counsellors at the bottom and the heavy wax disc of the great seal attached, to be proclaimed in marketplaces and affixed to church doors throughout the country.[34] In it, after a preamble stating his love for his subjects and his desire for justice, Henry stated that anyone who could 'reasonably and truly' claim that they had been wrongfully indebted to the king, that their property rights had been violated, or that the crown had otherwise done them 'any wrong', could submit a complaint in writing at any time in the following two years, up to Michaelmas 1506, to any of seven named officials: Fox, the king's secretary Thomas Ruthal and Geoffrey Symeon, dean of the chapel royal, all civil lawyers, and the common lawyers Thomas Lovell, the two chief justices, and the chancellor of the duchy of Lancaster John Mordaunt.[35]

The proclamation seems to have been prompted in part by one of the periodic fits of spiritual conscience to which Henry, acutely aware of his failing health, was increasingly prone. Not long before, he had ruefully acknowledged in a letter to his pious mother that most of his appointments to the bench of bishops had been motivated by distinctly temporal impulses. William Warham, his new archbishop of Canterbury and a man whose attributes included 'cunning and worldly wisdom', was the latest in a long line of lawyers and diplomats – men like Morton and Fox, the venal Savage, Adriano Castellesi – whom Henry had favoured with rich bishoprics. Warham's promotion had been, the king baldly explained, more about doing 'us and our realm good and acceptable service' than about his spiritual qualities.

Now, as Henry wrote to Lady Margaret, he planned the rapid promotion of her devout, ascetic confessor, John Fisher, to the bishopric of Rochester for very different reasons: 'for the great and singular virtue that I know and see in him'. Not that it was a particularly grandiloquent gesture – one of the poorest sees in England, Rochester was hardly an attractive office with which to reward people of influence – but Henry was anxious about the state of his soul, and about his legacy. All this appeared to chime with Henry's proclamation: a slate-cleaning exercise, an expression of the king's justice, mercy and good government, and an act of repentance and remorse. It seemed, almost, as though he were already preparing to meet his maker. But, as always with Henry, there was a flip side. Issued alongside the king's ever more constricting programme of investigation, surveillance and enforcement, and the tribunals that applied the 'due order and course of his laws' in direct and punitive ways, the proclamation allowed Henry to have his cake and eat it. Having salved his conscience, the king was about to put in place the latest piece in his jigsaw of finance and security.[36]

On 11 September 1504, as he wrote on the first leaf of a new account book, Edmund Dudley entered royal service. He had been made a royal counsellor, drawing a substantial annual salary of a hundred marks. This simple title, though, hid the extraordinary role that he had been given.

The king had made it quite clear what he required of Dudley. Henry, he later wrote, wanted 'many persons in danger at his pleasure ... bound to his grace for great sums of money.' Dudley was to sniff out every and any legal infraction, any opportunity for applying the law 'to the king's advantage'. He was then to punish such violations by 'a simple bond absolute payable at a certain day, for his grace would have them so made'. In other words, Henry was giving him a free hand to do what Bray, Lovell and his other financial administrators had been doing – but Dudley's new role had a particular intensity and focus. He had been made a kind of chief financial enforcer, with a free hand to sniff out all potential sources of revenue due under the king's rights. Although he would work alongside the nebulous council learned, Dudley had been given a roving brief. He would operate on his own – and report directly to Henry himself.[37]

Rummaging through the assorted books, parchment rolls and bundles of indentures detailing old debts and fines, bonds taken over years, decades, long-forgotten and never chased up, the king handed them over to Dudley to investigate, and to action. On one book, a list of suspended fines taken in the court of King's Bench stretching back to the beginning of the reign, Henry scribbled that 'Dudley hath taken charge, to make our proof of all those [debts] that be unpaid.'

From the king's privy chamber, from John Heron's treasury offices in the shadow of Westminster Abbey, Dudley and his clerk John Mitchell carried away bags and boxes of legal and financial documents. Heron sat at a desk, itemizing the files that Dudley had taken away to 'keep and pursue unto the use and behove of our sovereign lord': in this unregulated and unaccountable system, there was no way Heron was going to get caught without a paper trail. All this work, moreover, would be done not from government offices, but from Dudley's own house in Candlewick Street, deep within the city of London.[38]

Dudley set to work with a will, sifting through pages and pages of suspended fines, looking at who had defaulted, or broken the conditions under which the fines had been made. Henry and Dudley would discuss individual cases, heads together, Dudley's account book open in front of them. Then, they would decide on an appropriate financial penalty; the king signed each page of Dudley's book. Still an esquire, and in his early forties – young, compared to the Bosworth generation who comprised the majority of Henry's close financial advisers – Dudley had, quite suddenly, become a mini-Bray. Invested with direct sovereign authority, this ambitious London lawyer was answerable to nobody but the king. It was a meteoric, heady rise.

It was easy to understand what the king saw in the pleasant and intellectually sophisticated Dudley. He had a creative way with the penal laws and statutes in which he was expert, deploying the obscure, semi-French patois of the common lawyers – a 'barbarous tongue', as the sixteenth-century lawyer Thomas Starkey put it – with a precise smoothness. Like most common lawyers, he believed strongly in the supremacy of the king's law, and was keen to show Henry how it could be made to do what he wanted it to. Then, too, there was Dudley's London background: his awareness of the 'large profits and customs' that could be gained from trade and his ability to action them. Dudley, as it would transpire, was more than a lawyer; he also knew how to cut a deal.[39]

In Dudley, too, the impulse of service was concentrated. Parachuted into a position of exceptional influence, he was not about to speak truth to power in the direct way that somebody like Bray, his relationship with the king forged in adversity and tempered over decades of service, had done. Dudley may have been experienced in the ways of the courtroom, of city-hall politics and the grubby world of financial corruption, but now he was exposed to a rarefied, intoxicating atmosphere: that of proximity to the king, to sovereign power. He was not going to start advising Henry, as Bray had done, that it was better that certain lines should not be crossed, or, as Lovell did, that it was occasionally worth 'respiting' people.[40] Grasping immediately what the king wanted to achieve, that his 'security standeth much in plenty of treasure', Dudley would go out of his way to provide it, by any means necessary. He was now a royal servant, his new post held at the king's pleasure – and his own career path, his future success and wealth lay in 'studying to serve'. He was hardly about to start examining his conscience. Ultimately, he was a yes-man. And that, increasingly, was how Henry liked it.

In fact, as Dudley would later write, there were plenty of servants who, in pursuing the king's causes, would go 'further than conscience requireth ... oftentimes to win a special thank of the king' – all the while lining their own pockets and pursuing their own private vendettas, 'their own quarrels, grudges or malice'. Dudley, though, would prove even more zealous than his colleagues in the pursuit of the king's interests, and of his own. Henry, undoubtedly, had noticed that Dudley possessed the tireless willingness of the attack dog.[41]

On the same day that Dudley entered royal service, John Mordaunt died unexpectedly, after a short illness. That October, Sir Richard Empson received the call that he had been waiting for: Henry handed him the seals of the duchy of Lancaster, and with them the ultimate responsibility for enforcing the king's rights, presiding over the council learned in the law.

As 1504 drew to a close, Empson and Dudley had emerged among the leading group of Henry's lawyer-counsellors. With them came the full flowering of a system which, intended for efficient administration and swift justice, was beginning to resemble something very different, with its twisting and distorting of law and the exploitation of legal technicalities, the indiscriminate suspension of due process and, above all, the imposition of financial penalties in all shapes and sizes: bonds, recognizances, obligations.

The only person who was really sure how this curiously contingent form of government worked was the king, in whose hands the various threads – the court of wards and audits, the council learned, the counsellors who came together in small groups to take bonds and fines on the king's behalf, Dudley's financial freelancing – all came together.

The way Henry's councils functioned was legal – indeed, it was founded on forensic research into and rigorous application of the law – but it was not normal or customary, and nor, for the most part, was it just. Its processes were extrajudicial, existing outside courts of record, and they depended entirely on the king's personal control. A system which encouraged and thrived on informers, which functioned by the arbitrary use of 'sharp letters' and subpoenas, and which was enforced with punitive fines, it was unpredictable, unaccountable, unchallengeable and terrifying. Edmund Dudley himself summed it up in a nutshell. It was, he said, 'extraordinary justice'.[42]

But over all this hovered the unanswered – and unanswerable – question, posed by the officials at Calais, by the great lords, and discussed in lowered voices in taverns and households throughout the land. If the king died before the prince was of an age to rule, what then?

7

Our Second Treasure

In the hot, dry June of 1504, Prince Henry and his household came to court. They arrived at Richmond in time for midsummer. The Nativity of St John the Baptist, on the 24th, was one of the great days of estate: processions, masses in the Chapel Royal, feasting and, in the evening, a 'void' involving wine, a spice-plate and sweetmeats. It was, too, the solstice, midsummer night, marked with pageants and passion plays, and by the great bonfire scented with branches of birch and fennel, built by the pages of the hall, its flames leaping into the dark. In the privy garden, the king's secret servants kept watch in their doublets and gowns of black satin and damask. It was a time that, despite the ordered ritual and liturgy, still resonated with magic and unruliness, disorder and instability. Whatever the prince felt about it that June – excitement and anticipation, probably – it would come to trouble him; 24 June, he noted decades later, was a date associated with 'sundry occasions of evil'.[1]

His arrival had been deliberately planned. Turning thirteen on 28 June, he was on the threshold of *adolescentia*, the age when boyhood merged into adulthood. Since his mother's death over a year previously, through the rumours, alerts, arrests and executions, he had remained with his sisters out at the backwater of Eltham, apart from the occasional visit to court. Now, however, things were changing. He was moving into the royal household, where he would live with the father he hardly knew.[2]

Henry's reasons for leaving his son at Eltham had been pragmatic. The repeated crises of the past years had left him with his hands full, at a time when he was battling constantly with illness. And, very probably, he was in a quandary about precisely how to bring the boy up.

By the age of seven, Prince Arthur had had his own independent household and council in the Welsh Marches, and was already gaining the hands-on experience deemed so necessary for kingship. From afar, the king had kept in constant touch with the prince's council, who reported on his progress and on anything untoward, including any 'unprincely demeaning' on Arthur's part – and on the behaviour of members of his household. Since Elizabeth's death, he had been doing the same for Prince Henry, gradually reshaping his son's household from the establishment of his infancy into one fit for an adolescent heir to the throne. He did so in conjunction with that stickler for organization, his mother, and the prince's grandmother, Lady Margaret Beaufort.[3]

In the intervening years, the prince's household had taken on a new tone. His footmen and personal servants were now dressed, not in the blue and tawny of the duke of York, but in tawny and black: royal colours.[4] The female-dominated atmosphere of his early years had changed, too. His lady mistress Elizabeth Denton, the woman who had been like a second mother to him, had had her wages paid up and left the prince's service to become a gentlewoman in Lady Margaret's household. Several new, male, servants joined him. Many of them, in their late teens and early twenties, had spent the greater part of their lives in royal service, like the devout Welshman William Thomas, previously one of Prince Arthur's close attendants, and Ralph Pudsey, a groom of Henry VII's chamber who became the prince's waiter and keeper of his jewellery. Among them was a man called William Compton. A ward of court from the age of eleven following the death of his father, a minor Warwickshire landowner, Compton had been brought up among the menial servants of the royal household, learning how to serve. It was an education that, now aged twenty-two, he had fully absorbed, knowing when to speak and when to keep quiet and still, to blend into the background.[5]

Presiding over the prince's household was his chamberlain, Sir Henry Marney. Now in his late forties, from an old Essex family, Marney had become a royal counsellor early in the reign. He was cut from the same cloth as many of Henry's closest advisers: a hard-nosed, ambitious administrator who could back up his words with judicious force, he had fought at Stoke and against the Cornish rebels at

Blackheath. Marney had been a familiar face around the prince's household as early as 1494, when he was knighted at the prince's creation as duke of York, while his son Thomas and daughter Grace were among the prince's servants at Eltham. As the king and Lady Margaret cast around for somebody to head the prince's household, Sir Richard Pole, previously Arthur's chamberlain and a member of the Beaufort family might have been an obvious choice. But Pole was, very probably, already sickening with the illness that would kill him in October 1504. More to the point, Marney was familiar. The king trusted him and so too did Lady Margaret: she would make him one of the executors to her will, alongside Fox, Lovell and the saintly bishop of Rochester, John Fisher.

In early 1504, nearly two years after his brother's death, Prince Henry was formally created Prince of Wales. After Parliament had stripped him of his title and lands of the duchy of York – whose management and lucrative revenues duly reverted to the crown – and invested him with those of Prince of Wales, his creation was performed on 23 February.[6] His period of stasis at Eltham was coming to a close: finally, his father had decided on a plan. While the prince was still duke of York, while his brother was still alive, the king had contemplated setting him up independently; he had even acquired a home for him, Castle Codnor in Derbyshire, and planned for the expansion of his household. But now, after what had happened to Arthur in Ludlow, and after the repeated shocks of the previous years, he had changed his mind.

Henry would keep his son close, the prince's household and council absorbed within his own. The likes of Sir Richard Empson, prominent about the king, would sit on Prince Henry's council, while Richard Fox, the man who had christened and baptized the prince, could also keep a close eye on him. That summer, as the prince and his retinue arrived at court, Sir Henry Marney received a present of a hundred marks from the king, a 'golden hello'. And, at the top of the king's wage bill, drawing the handsome quarterly salary of £6 13s 4d, appeared the name of 'Master Arthur'. Henry's incorporation of the prince's beloved uncle, Arthur Plantagenet, into his own staff spoke volumes. Henry clearly valued his wife's affable, trustworthy half-brother, who had been a reassuring presence following Elizabeth's death, and wanted him around. Besides which, this Yorkist offshoot had – for Henry – the inestimable advantage of bastardy, with no difficult issues of lineage to complicate things. The king, it seemed, was determined to play a full role in his son's future development – and that included sharing his servants.[7]

The prince was not entirely wet behind the ears. He had, after all, been on display from the moment of his birth, born into the rhythms and rituals of court life. His natural presence and his appetite for the big occasion had been evident from an early age, and the hiatus of the last years had undoubtedly left him itching to take his place on the biggest stage of all. Court, of course, was a stage. Thomas More talked about power politics as 'kings' games, as it were stage plays, and for the most part played upon scaffolds'. More being More, the pun on scaffold as both stage and gallows was fully intended.[8] But, as Henry VII was fully aware, there was an audience ready and waiting to watch and scrutinize the young prince: his appearance, his behaviour, who he called to his side, whose company he preferred, who he spoke to kindly, and who he ignored. In short, people would be considering what kind of heir he might make, when the time came – and what they could get out of him.

Moreover, although the prince had a certain precociousness, he was sheltered, dutiful and pious, immersed in the rich, complex patterns of traditional religion by which people understood and ordered their lives. In this, he followed his mother and, of course, that model of devotion, his grandmother Lady Margaret Beaufort, with her relics, books of hours and patronage of fashionable religious cults such as the Holy Name of Jesus and the Five Wounds of Christ.[9] All of which is evident from a 'bede roll' – a portable aid to prayer – that he carried around with him.

Five inches wide and eleven feet long, the parchment roll unfurls to reveal delicate, richly coloured illuminations: the red-and-white rose and other royal emblems giving way to the Blessed Trinity, a crowned God the Father flanked on his right by the Holy Ghost and on his left by Jesus; then a Christ crucified, his sacred blood spurting from his five wounds onto a mortuary sheet held by two hovering angels. More images follow: the three nails of the passion, hammered into Jesus' feet and hands; the Virgin and child; and six saints, including St George and Henry VII's favoured St Armel. Punctuating the images, Latin prayers and rubrics instruct on its use. The repetitious, incantatory exercises – kneeling, making the sign of the cross, concentrating fixedly on the images while reciting endless Pater Nosters, Ave Marias and Credos – could bring the reciter impressive spiritual benefits: one particular daily exercise alone yielded 52,712 years and 40 days off time in purgatory. Another, if performed correctly and daily, guaranteed seven gifts. The reciter would not die a 'sudden death', nor would he be 'slain with sword or knife' or poisoned; neither would his enemies overcome him. He would have sufficient wealth all his life and would not die without receiving the sacraments. Meanwhile, he would be defended from 'all evil spirits, pestilence, fevers, and all other infirmities on land and on water'. All this had a magical quality; indeed, the roll itself was a charm, an amulet. The very act of carrying it would ward off evil.

Who gave Prince Henry the bede roll, and when, is unclear. He might have inherited it from his brother, as he inherited everything else: the roll contains both the prince of Wales's ostrich feathers and Catherine's crown of Castile. Later, he would give it to his servant William Thomas – his prayer companion, perhaps, the two genuflecting, crossing and half-whispering half-muttering the mantras over and over – writing on it laboriously: 'William Thomas, I pray you, pray for me, your loving master Prince Henry.' That he believed fervently in its power, its ability to protect, is undeniable – which was just as well, because he needed all the help he could get.[10]

In coming to court, the prince was entering his father's world. At Eltham, he had been more or less insulated from the instability of recent years – another reason, perhaps, why the king had kept him secluded for so long. But now, he would be exposed to the tensions and politicking of the royal household, where the uncertainties of the time were distilled into faction, and for which he was, increasingly, the focus: from the anxieties, voiced by the Calais servants, that he would not be able to compel loyalty on his father's death, to nobles like Buckingham, for whom the young figure of the prince only served to reinforce their own sense of superiority and entitlement. Even among his own circle of companions there were those who looked at him with resentment. A year younger than the prince, Henry Pole was the eldest son of Sir Richard Pole, formerly Arthur's chamberlain. But his mother, Margaret Pole, was a full-blooded Plantagenet, older sister of the earl of Warwick, executed on trumped-up charges by Henry VII. In the decades to come, as members of his family became Henry VIII's most bitter enemies, Pole would state how he had 'never loved' him 'from childhood'.

Henry had planned the timing of his son's arrival at court for another reason, too. For the first time, the prince would join him on the summer progress, the extended hunting holiday that doubled as a political tour of the regions. By the end of July, the court had moved down to Greenwich, from where the 'riding' household, scaled down to around half the size of the standing household of around 1,500 servants, prepared to depart.[11]

Contrary to recent years, when the travelling household had shuttled between the royal houses along the banks of the Thames, that summer's progress seemed a throwback to the early years of the reign, when Henry had travelled widely to assert royal power in the far-flung regions of his new, highly insecure kingdom. Published, as was customary, in June, the 'gests' or itinerary mapped out a route southeast, deep into Kent, where political instability, local feuding, rumours of the king's impending death and challenges to his son's succession had come together in a combustible mix, and where the king's presence was urgently needed. The household would stop off at the manors of all the region's big men – John Broke, Lord Cobham at Dartford, Lord Bergavenny at Birling, Sir Richard Guildford at Maidstone and Sir Edward Poynings at Westenhanger. Being chosen to accommodate and entertain the king in this way was a great honour, but such signs of favour were rarely entirely straightforward. It was a chance for Henry to take the political temperature, to assess the atmosphere in the houses he stayed in, and to impress his subjects. It was, then, highly significant that he should take his son with him. The prince was, it seems, beginning to develop into a reassuringly solid physical presence who could safely be shown off as heir to the throne.

As well as getting a first-hand introduction to government in the restive provinces, this would be an extended holiday for the prince and his previously absentee father. On progress, the politics, lobbying and petitioning focused on the hunt – and hunting was a sport to which both Henry and the prince were addicted. That summer, too, they were constantly in each other's company for the first time. It was a chance for the king to get to know his son and heir better, and to lavish very public attention on him.[12]

The prince's coming to court that summer coincided with a dispatch from Rome, where negotiations over the dispensation for Catherine's remarriage had dragged on interminably. While Alexander VI, the Borgia pope, may have been a byword for nepotism, the new incumbent, the belligerent Julius II, was proving no slouch on that front himself, packing the curia with his relatives from the Tuscan city of Lucca. The head of the English ambassadorial team and former Borgia favourite, Adriano Castellesi, had been lobbying frantically to ingratiate himself with the new papal regime, and to stay in Henry's good books. He was, he wrote to the king, '*ex toto anglicus*', English to his core, and was 'your creature and the work of your hands'. He stressed his loyalty and commitment by decorating his lavish new palace in Rome with England's coat-of-arms and making it over to the king as an embassy – thereby cementing his own position – and by laying out a detailed programme for obtaining the dispensation. Castellesi's plan largely involved showering the new pope's Della Rovere clan with sweeteners in the form of cash, lucrative offices and honours, including conferring the Order of the Garter on Duke Guidobaldo of Urbino whose cultured court acted as a back-channel to the papal curia. All of which appeared to do the trick. When, on 20 May 1504, the English embassy arrived in Rome to profess obedience to the new pope, the deputation was headed by Castellesi. His uneasiness, however, would prove entirely justified.[13]

On 6 July, Julius wrote to Henry VII protesting that he had never intended to withhold the dispensation, and that the delay was simply due to his desire to 'consider the case more maturely'; he would, he stressed, take the affairs of England under his 'special protection'. He was delighted, he added casually, that the king had chosen as his Cardinal Protector the pope's nephew, Galeotto della Rovere, and he took the opportunity to drop in a few more names of those whose advancement might further Henry's cause in Rome. Castellesi's name was notable by its absence. But among them was another of the pope's extended family, Silvestro Gigli, on whom Julius heaped praise for his efforts on Henry's behalf.

Intrigue ran in Gigli's blood. His uncle Giovanni, born in the Netherlands of Lucchese parents, had moved to England decades previously, joining the London branch of the family merchant-banking firm. A cultured man of letters, he had become the first resident English ambassador at Rome and, on his death, had been succeeded by Castellesi. Silvestro, also a merchant-financier and a member of Henry's diplomatic team, was given his uncle's bishopric of Worcester. Silvestro, though, had his eye on Castellesi's job. Now that Julius II was in power, he saw his opportunity. As the king's two chief diplomats at Rome scrambled for his favour in their race to obtain the dispensation, their mutual antagonism would have unexpected side-effects. In the months and years to come, it would crystallize into faction between Henry's counsellors and would ripple out into the houses of London's intelligentsia and, ultimately, into the household of the prince himself.[14]

In the last week of July, preceded by the harbingers who rode ahead, checking that accommodation was ample and correctly allocated according to rank – as well as for warning signs of disease and 'perilous sickmen' in the towns and villages through which the court passed – the household moved out of Greenwich and along the main London–Canterbury road, through apple orchards and fields of wheat and barley parched with lack of rain, horses straining at carts piled high with coffers and trunks. With his son at his side, and the brief for the marriage dispensation just arrived, Henry was in expansive and solicitous mood. On 4 August he dispatched one of his privy servants with a letter to Catherine, who had fallen seriously ill at Greenwich; her fever, racking cough and stomach problems were exacerbated by a hamfisted doctor whose laboured efforts to bleed her resulted in 'no blood'. Rather than accompanying the court and her betrothed on progress, she had returned to Durham House with her household to convalesce. Henry promised her the best physicians he could find. He loved her, he stressed, 'as his own daughter', and told her to ask him for anything she wanted.[15]

But it was Henry's demonstrative affection for his son that attracted most attention. Travelling with the court, the Spanish ambassador Ferdinand Duque – sent to bolster, and keep an eye on, the activities of the Anglophile Rodrigo de Puebla – remarked warmly of the king's parenting skills in a letter to King Ferdinand. 'It is quite wonderful', he wrote, 'how much the king likes the prince of Wales' – and with good reason, for the prince 'deserves all love.' 'Certainly', he commented approvingly, 'there could be no better school in the world than the society of such a father as Henry VII.'

Ferdinand Duque had no reason to disbelieve the evidence of his own eyes, and indeed, Henry's delight in the prince was entirely consistent with his behaviour on the rare occasions that the pair had previously been seen together. The king did love his son – who was, after all, the embodiment of everything he had fought for over the previous quarter century. Besides which, the boy probably reminded Henry of Elizabeth.

But Duque also mentioned something else, a topic that was evidently the talk of court that summer. Previously, the king had never taken his son on progress, in order 'not to disrupt his studies'. Henry, he continued, was so wise, and attentive to everything regarding his son's upbringing: 'nothing escapes his attention'. Indeed, Duque concluded, if the king were to live ten years longer, he would leave the prince 'furnished with good habits, and immense riches, and in as happy circumstances as man can be.'[16] For the first thirteen years of Prince Henry's life, he had barely inhabited his father's world. Suddenly, in Duque's portrait, they had been thrown vividly, closely together; Henry, hawklike, watching over his son's security and development.

The situation in which Henry and the prince now found themselves was, however, highly unusual. Every heir to the throne in living memory, and many more before that, had been trained in adversity – or at the very least in a separate household, away from their parents. Henry himself, as he was always at pains to point out, had been hardened in the refugee's struggle for sheer survival – and besides, he had won his battles. At the age of ten Prince Henry's grandfather, Edward IV, was marching on London at the head of an army ten thousand strong.[17] Everybody understood that the first requirement of kingship was to lead by example – and that meant by fighting and military leadership. When, back in the 1460s, the lawyer Sir John Fortescue lectured the Lancastrian heir Edward, prince of Wales on the importance of studying law, he took it for granted that kings knew how to fight, which was ironic given that his pupil's father, Henry VI, was the only king in living memory who had not distinguished himself in battle; indeed, his helpless diffidence – which Henry VII was now reinventing as a saintlike passivity – had plunged the country into civil war.

So, at the age when Prince Henry might have been expected to be exposed to the world around him, and to acquire responsibility for his actions, his father wrapped him in cotton wool, his independence restricted, his every move tightly controlled. Contemporary educationalists would have been concerned. One, writing in 1500, believed that the offspring of rich families were spoiled brats, ill-equipped for life, because they were 'lost nowadays in their youth at home, and that with their fathers and mothers'. There was, he believed, a point in a child's development where the tender-hearted indulgence of mothers, with their 'weeping and wailing' over the slightest scratch sustained by their beloved offspring, simply got in the way. The king, of course, was hardly one for cosseting of this kind. But, given the situation he now faced, it was the only option. Forced to keep his son at his side, Henry VII was belatedly 'playing the mother's part'. He would make a virtue of necessity.[18]

Duque's comment about the prince's education was not, or not only, a platitude. Although the prince's study-companion, Lord Mountjoy, was increasingly preoccupied by his duties in Calais – the financial sword of Damocles suspended over him undoubtedly helped him keep his mind on the job – he was still heavily involved in the prince's educational development, in particular the modish classical curriculum in which he was now well advanced. When John Holt, the prince's grammar master, died in June 1504, Mountjoy's fingerprints were all over the appointment of his replacement, William Hone.

Cut from the same cloth as his predecessor – when Holt was appointed the prince's tutor, Hone succeeded him as master of Chichester prebendal school – Hone was an obvious choice. But Holt's death, which had by all accounts been sudden, had come just as Prince Henry had arrived at court, where there was another figure who might have been expected to play a major role: Prince Arthur's former tutor, a blind, black-clad Augustinian canon from Toulouse called Bernard André. That André was notable by his absence from the prince's education spoke volumes.

Introduced to Henry in exile by Richard Fox, André had been a fixture at court since Bosworth. He was high in royal favour, friends with highly influential figures like Lady Margaret and Richard Fox, and had by his own account given Prince Arthur an exemplary classical education, following which he had been put out to grass with a wealthy benefice and the post of court historian, receiving a handsome annuity for a succession of saccharine eulogies and supine annual chronicles of the year's major events. When, in 1502, John Skelton had left Prince Henry's service, there had been a good reason why André had not been appointed in his place: the prince's education was still overseen by Queen Elizabeth and by Mountjoy, then her chamberlain. But now André, still only in his early fifties and apparently in good health, was an obvious choice, particularly as he seemed still to be actively involved in tuition, giving lessons to the likes of Henry Daubeney, son of the king's chamberlain. What was more, a comparison between André's reading list for Prince Arthur and Holt's set texts for Prince Henry revealed much the same curriculum.[19] It ranged in both cases from Cicero, the pre-eminent classical icon of political thought, and ancient historians such as Caesar and Livy to the iconoclastic fifteenth-century Italian humanist Lorenzo Valla, who had singlehandedly demolished one of the key documents of papal supremacy, the Donation of Constantine, when he exposed it as a fake. Neither was there a great deal of difference in their methods of teaching. But while there seemed little wrong with André, instead the prince got an obscure grammarian who, while effective, was unknown at court and in international literary circles.[20]

Part of the reason for this was, perhaps, in order that the prince might be taught ancient Greek, the avant-garde language of choice for humanists, in which Hone was an expert. But there was, undoubtedly, a political subtext. Mountjoy and his intellectual friends detested André who, years before, had decisively terminated the prospects of one of their number: Thomas Linacre had hoped to get a job as one of Prince Arthur's tutors, André had spoken against him to the king, and that was that. So aggressively and successfully did André guard avenues to royal favour – he was on good terms not just with the likes of Fox but also with Francis Marzen and Matthew Baker, two of Henry's French privy chamber servants – that Erasmus later christened him 'Cerberus', after the dog who guarded the entrance to Hades. If André had gained the post of tutor to Prince Henry, one of the Mountjoy circle's vital routes to the prince would have been severed – and it was a line of influence that they were determined to keep open. They were in luck. Henry wanted his son to have the best possible classical education, and Mountjoy had undoubtedly proved himself an excellent supervisor. His proposal of William Hone as the prince's tutor stood. That, though, would not be the end of the matter.[21]

Although Henry VII had a healthy respect for the latest classical scholarship, recognizing the prestige it brought him and his family, he remained a distant admirer. French, which he spoke like the native he almost was, remained his literary language of choice, and he preferred the classics in translation. Notably, the biography of the fashionable Florentine intellectual Pico della Mirandola that later turned up in the royal library was not Thomas More's acclaimed Latin version, but another – in French. It was, as much as anywhere else, in the library's lavishly illuminated Franco-Burgundian volumes, the books of chivalric romance and, especially, history – which as Erasmus recalled both he and his son loved 'above all' – that Henry's and the prince's minds met.

In early 1504, perhaps with his son's impending arrival in mind, Henry had expanded the library staff, taking on the printer, scribe and book-importer William Faques to supplement the skills of his long-standing librarian, the engagingly named Quentin Poulet. Both men were from northern France, and were calligraphers and illuminators of considerable talent. Poulet had been in his post for over a decade, stocking the royal library with the latest printed volumes from Paris and the Low Countries, and transcribing books for the king. As a 'limner', he added the delicately traced sprays of red-and-white roses that blossomed in the books' margins and title pages – often obscuring the badges of Edward IV and Richard III underneath – and painted in brightly coloured scenes of courtly love and chivalric adventure. And, around the time of Faques' arrival, Poulet was busy at work on one of the king's prized manuscripts, *L'imagination de vraie noblesse*, adding to it the crown and ostrich feathers of the prince of Wales. The royal library, Henry made sure, was somewhere where the prince could browse to his heart's content, guided in his programme of reading by another Frenchman who had come with him from Eltham, Giles Duwes.[22]

Starting life at court in the 1490s as teacher of French and librarian to the royal children – in which capacity Henry VIII would continue to employ him – Duwes was also a lutenist of rare quality and an outstanding music teacher. In the prince and his younger sister Mary, he had willing and able pupils. By the time the prince arrived at Richmond, he was already proficient in the musicianship for which he would become celebrated, in 'singing ... playing at recorders, flute, virginals, and in setting of songs, making of ballads'. Although he also had a 'master at pipes', it was Duwes, his 'Master to Lute, French', who played a key role in the prince's transformation from schoolboy into sophisticated courtier. The king, too, recognized his value. Whether in acknowledgement of Duwes' influence on his son's education, or whether he simply liked listening to him play, on his son's arrival at court Henry added 'Giles luter' to his own payroll, just below Arthur Plantagenet, on the handsome half-yearly salary of £6 8s 4d.[23]

Amid the atmosphere of instability and insecurity, the arrival of the prince and his attendants in the royal household prompted a subtle but palpable recalibration, one encapsulated by a young chamber servant, Stephen Hawes. Hawes was one of the thirty or so grooms of the chamber who carried out routine domestic duties – cleaning, dusting, setting up the moveable 'boards' or trestles at mealtimes for the household to dine on, and doubling as security staff. With a salary of forty shillings a year, it was a good, though not particularly privileged, position; it did, though, give Hawes an opportunity to get himself noticed. Like all chamber servants, he was presentable, decorous, trained in the ways of the court. He was also a flourishing young poet, a talent that, just occasionally, was his passport into the most exclusive company, to provide entertainment and 'pastime' for influential members of court and their guests.[24]

Despite his assiduous copying of John Skelton, Hawes had none of his genius. Written in the florid aureate style of the time, his ploddingly conventional verse dealt with the formulaic topics – service, etiquette, the virtues of chivalry, the romance of courtly love – in an entirely predictable way. It was, in short, the kind of middle-of-the-road, crowd-pleasing stuff that people lapped up. Bringing him popularity at court and beyond, it also attracted the attention of Wynkyn de Worde, Caxton's former apprentice, who had taken over his Westminster print-shop and who had an appraising eye for a bestseller. Sometime after Prince Henry arrived at court, Hawes presented a new poem to the king – which de Worde then rushed out in print. But while *The Example of Virtue* was dedicated to Henry VII, it also had one eye on his son. Larded with lines lifted from Skelton's poems, its dedication included a fulsome reference to 'our second treasure/ Surmounting in virtue and mirror of beauty'. On closer inspection, moreover, *The Example of Virtue* was entirely about the prince, for it was written specifically with his education in mind.

Hawes' poem was one of the many treatises, manuals of 'nurture', manners, practical education and instruction for life in polite society that were 'very utile and necessary unto all youth' – including children of 'blood Royal' – which household servants churned out on a regular basis. Most of these works had literary pretensions of one sort or another, written in (often execrable) rhyme, or garnished with authoritative classical tags, but Hawes went one better. Sugaring the educational pill, he wrote his poem in courtly rhyme royal, and cloaked his sententious advice in a chivalrous romance, in which a horsebacked Youth goes on a quest; finally, through his 'good governance', he kills a three-headed serpent, and is transformed into the 'noble veteran', Virtue.[25]

It was hardly a blinding insight of Hawes to predict that tales of chivalric derring-do would be a good way to teach Prince Henry how to behave. Hawes had seen what everybody at court had also noticed: the prince was absorbed by chivalry, and by his own place in it. Indeed, it would have been stranger if he hadn't been, given that he was surrounded by reminders: from the histories and romances in which he immersed himself, to the tapestries, statues and paintings of kings from Arthur to his own father, 'visaged and appearing like bold and valiant knights', that adorned the royal houses. At every turn, the prince was encouraged to place himself in this world of history and myth, to think of his life as that of a hero on a quest, or as a new Alexander the Great or his glorious Lancastrian forebear, Henry V. But it was not only the history that the prince was interested in. He was proving remarkably good at the practice as well.

With adolescence came a heightened emphasis on the young noble's military training. Theorists recommended a varied regime, from running and swimming to weightlifting, hawking and hunting – 'a plain recording of [training for] war', as one educationalist approvingly put it. Pre-eminent among these sports were the chivalric martial arts: fighting with axes – Prince Henry had his own 'master at axes' – swordplay and, the most glamorous discipline of all, jousting on horseback. If the prince could not earn his spurs as a war leader, if he could not maintain his own independent household, then he did have one outlet for self-assertion. The king, who knew the political value of his son's chivalric education, thoroughly approved.[26]

Around his older son, Henry VII had encouraged the building up of a loyalty-inducing Arthurian cult, one that had had to be unceremoniously ditched after his untimely death. He had done something similar with Prince Henry's creation as duke of York, which was explicitly intended to head off Perkin Warbeck's claim to that title. Now, with his son shadowing him at court, the king would create a renewal of chivalric activity, centred on the prince. In doing so, Henry would kill several birds with one stone. He himself had always been disinclined to joust, a result, perhaps, of lack of opportunity during his refugee's upbringing in Brittany, or because of the exceptional danger of this ultimate contact sport – or simply on account of his poor eyesight. As one jousting practitioner put it, self-evidently, 'I cannot think that anyone who cannot see can joust well.'

Henry had turned his lack of participation into a virtue: the remote, regal Solomon who judged tournaments from a lofty distance. Now, increasingly ill, he was aware that his ability to fulfil this visibly magnificent role was diminishing rapidly. The prince's palpable enthusiasm for chivalry reinforced his status as an heir the political nation could believe in, somebody who embodied the traditional qualities of military leadership and prowess expected in a king. In providing his son with the company of 'sons of nobles, lords and gentlemen', Henry forced the younger generation of nobles to attend court, where he could see them. And, with the prince surrounded by the king's own counsellors, and in his own household, he could curb any 'unprincely demeaning' or potential independent-mindedness on the part of his son.[27]

On 21 July 1504, less than a week before Prince Henry's inaugural progress with his father, four young men were added to the household's payroll. They were called, simply, 'spears', and their military function was evident from the basic fighting unit that each brought with them: a 'costrel' or attendant, a page, and two archers. Like all household servants these king's spears, as they became known, had to swear, on oath, not to be retained by anybody except the king, and to be constantly alert to suspicious – particularly, treasonable – activity. Henry VII already had his three-hundred-strong yeomen of the guard. But while the spears evidently provided another layer of personal security, they had another role, very different from that of the yeomen. Moreover, the timing of their formation makes it clear that they were designed expressly with the prince in mind.

Unlike the yeomen, the spears were richly dressed men of good birth. They were not simply menial servants but courtiers and jousters, and, as well as adding a dash of youthful glamour to the prince's first appearance on progress, they would form part of a renewed chivalrous culture at court. The prince had his study-mates; now, he would also have his companions-in-arms.

In selecting them, Henry turned to the source of many of his most trusted servants, his mother's household. Lady Margaret was a particularly energetic supporter of chivalry and all that it represented. She knew as well as anybody its binding force, the loyalty it engendered, and its combination – at least, in theory – of valour and piety; she had, too, a fiercely crusading mentality. Book of hours to hand, this small, energetic, wimpled lady persistently egged on her son to respond to the papacy's increasingly urgent calls for a crusade against the Ottoman Turkish Empire that was rapidly expanding through south-eastern Europe and the eastern Mediterranean. She repeated to anybody who would listen that she would go with the crusaders and 'wash their clothes, for the love of Jesus', if only she could. Henry himself shared her inclinations – though, as it turned out, he had a rather more worldly idea of the realpolitik that lay behind the heightened aims and ambitions of papal crusades. Meanwhile, Lady Margaret participated in all things chivalric. A member of the Order of the Garter – its last female member until Queen Victoria – she attended tournaments and encouraged the more courtly members of her household to do the same, paying their expenses. She was, too, a proud, doting grandmother with a sentimental side – two years previously, just before Prince Arthur's death, she had presented both her grandsons with garters of damascene gold. Delighting in Prince Henry's evident enthusiasm for and ability in martial arts, she would prove a formative influence on his transformation into one of the chivalric icons of the age.[28]

Two of the four spears came directly from Lady Margaret's staff. One was her great-nephew Maurice St John, who had been an intimate attendant of Prince Arthur, one of the select group that had seen him on the morning after his wedding night as he emerged with teenaged bravado demanding ale. In June 1504, Lady Margaret had waved him off with a handsome tip of ten marks 'towards his costs and charges in preparing of himself as a man of arms in the king's service'. Although St John was formally joining the royal household, it was the prince, just as much as Henry VII, whose service he was entering.

Henry's plans for this revival of chivalry, with his son at its centre, were plainly evident in the most exclusive club of all, the Order of the Garter. Membership of the twenty-four-strong Garter was a rare honour, one coveted by nobles and kings across Europe: recent members included the king of Naples and Emperor Maximilian. With its rituals and sacred oaths to the king, it was a potent weapon of royal control – and Henry, unsurprisingly, had a healthy respect for it. Knights of the order included members of Henry's inner circle: his chamberlain Giles lord Daubeney, and aspirational counsellors like Bray and Lovell; the Garter's prelate was another architect of his regime, Richard Fox. They rubbed shoulders with glamorous noble jousters of more uncertain loyalty: Buckingham, Northumberland, Suffolk – who had been unceremoniously turfed out of the order following his flight – and Henry Bourchier, earl of Essex, whose involvement in Suffolk's conspiracy had been suspected, but never proved. In the year that Prince Henry came to court, changes in the Garter's membership were quite clearly made with him in mind.

In April 1504 the longstanding Garter king-of-arms John Writhe died. Garter was the senior, most prestigious heraldic office and Writhe, who had held it under Edward IV, had fulfilled it to perfection – not least, as far as Henry was concerned, in resigning from his post under Richard III. Writhe had combined the herald's pedantic obsession with protocol and genealogy with an appetite for that other key heraldic function, diplomacy. Ten years before, on a mission to Margaret of Burgundy's court at Malines at the height of the Warbeck affair, he had stood outside her palace bellowing out a denunciation of the pretender's claim to all who cared to listen. Following Writhe's death, Henry was minded to confer the post on another highly experienced herald, Roger Machado, a Portuguese who had joined Henry in exile, and whose public role as Clarenceux king-at-arms merged with the twilit world of misinformation and espionage.[29] But when the ageing Machado declined, probably feeling that Garter herald was a younger man's job, Henry settled on Writhe's son Thomas. As Wallingford pursuivant, Thomas Writhe had been principal messenger to Prince Arthur, and then to Prince Henry. But the rank of pursuivant was below that of the most junior herald. The following January, Thomas Writhe was parachuted into the office of Garter king-of-arms. His promotion, which undoubtedly put noses out of joint among the heraldic community, had evidently involved some kind of arrangement with Machado, who pocketed a large slice of his salary.[30]

Henry, though, knew exactly what he was getting in Thomas Writhe. He was a chip off the old block, a meticulous compiler and documenter of pedigrees and precedents. He was, too, a keen draughtsman, and developed a burgeoning workshop of artists and painters, based in the family home in Cripplegate, in the north of the city. Over the next decades, his studio would churn out the paraphernalia of heraldry that formalized the Tudor regime, from brilliantly illuminated pedigrees and tournament rolls to the armorial decorations of the great royal ceremonies at court.

Thomas Writhe was, too, perfectly attuned to Henry VII's upwardly mobile regime. He seemed to have a particularly sophisticated sense of his role, not just in codifying traditions and creating new ones, but in creatively manipulating them, manufacturing the convincing family pedigree that transformed a thrusting arriviste into a permanent, highly respected member of the political elite. One of the first people he made over in this way was himself. Once installed in his new post he changed his surname, because he 'disliked the shortness of it'. After a few experiments, he settled on Wriothesley, a name that seemed to him to have the appropriate gravitas, and which his contemporaries found as entertaining as it was unpronounceable. He then retrospectively conferred it on his forebears, for whom he contrived a new lineage, knighting his deceased father for good measure. Wriothesley, in other words, was a herald for the emerging generation, the perfect candidate to create and document the chivalric revival around the prince.[31]

Henry's efforts to bolster his son's profile were evident, too, in his wardrobe accounts. On 1 February 1505, he ordered a new set of clothes for the prince: an arming doublet of black satin, with fashionable detachable sleeves, and with it an arming partlet or under-collar, pairs of arming spurs and arming shoes, and two dozen silk points or laces. Henry was fitting out his son for the tiltyard and for the jousts in which, the prince hoped, he would soon take an active part. There was more to it than that, though. Arming doublets, heavily padded jackets stuffed with horsehair, were worn tightly laced under plate armour as a first layer of protection. But they were, too, worn on their own – and, increasingly, as a courtly fashion statement. This was how the prince's black satin doublet was intended to be seen. Henry VII was not just indulging his son's passion for sport; he was making him look like a chivalrous leader, at the centre of a group of loyal knights. With the doublet and its accessories came an order for a matching saddle and harness in black velvet, with gilt buckles and pendants, in the latest 'Almain' – German – fashion. It was the kind of thing Henry would never have been seen in, but that he was all too happy to buy for his son.[32]

The prince's arrival did indeed seem to bring a new vigour to court. When, in April 1505, Henry selected two new Garter knights from the nominees put forward, he chose young noblemen in their mid-twenties, cousins to the prince: Lord Henry Stafford, the duke of Buckingham's impecunious younger brother, and Richard Grey, the delinquent young earl of Kent, whose very name provoked rueful head-shaking and rolling of eyes among the king's administrators. Henry, typically, had little use for both men in government, but as enthusiastic jousters they could add to the lustre of his court and learn loyalty to his son – more to the point, he could keep an eye on them. That same month, the celebrations of the feast of St George, the patron saint of the Order of the Garter, were particularly emphatic. The king processed through London to St Paul's. Before him, the bishop of Chester bore a relic of considerable status: the leg of St George himself, encased in parcel gilt, a recent gift from the Emperor Maximilian. Following behind in their heavy, ermine-bordered robes of crimson velvet came the assembled members of the order, at their head 'my lord prince'. But perhaps the most significant change came in the tilt-yard itself.

In the years following Arthur's death, the summer jousts seemed to have been performed with a certain listlessness. They were, at least, unremarkable enough to go unmentioned in the chronicles that documented every event at court in meticulous detail; neither was there any sign that the king attended them at all. But by the summer of 1505, the mood had changed. Infused with new blood, the jousting set at court went about its work with renewed vigour, and at the jousts held at Richmond that July Henry was back in his accustomed role as arbiter, distributing gold rings to the combatants. For the jousters, in particular the king's spears and new Garter knights, there was somebody new to impress: the prince who, dressed in his arming clothes, ate, drank and slept chivalry.[33]

As Prince Henry settled into life in the royal household, he appeared the very model of a young prince. Charismatic, gifted, devout, he stuck dutifully to his educational programme: studying with William Hone; sitting in on meetings of his council in the rooms above the exchequer of receipt in Westminster Palace; listening deferentially to his father's disquisitions on government and statecraft. He was being moulded in his father's own image. But for a rapidly growing boy, emerging into the world and settling into his new role, it was a restricted, confined environment, one in which his movements were constantly monitored, in which he was gently but firmly told what he could not do. Conscious of all that he needed to be and, increasingly, of what he had not yet achieved, he would come to challenge his father's way of doing things. What was more, he would find the means to do so in the apparently controlled, secure world that had been built around him: that of schoolroom and tiltyard. A gap was opening up between what his father wanted him to be, and what he would become.[34]

8

Null and Void

Towards the end of summer 1504 the dean of St Paul's, Robert Sherborne, arrived in London from Rome. The man nominated by Julius II to bring to England the papal dispensation for Prince Henry's marriage to Catherine of Aragon had made the long journey over the Alps, down the Rhine, through the Netherlands and across the English Channel in terrible health. And he had come empty-handed.[1] On 28 November, the king fired off a letter whose courteous formalities could not mask his distinctly irritable tone. Despite the pope's promises – and Henry's lavish palm-greasing, which included a £4,000 donation to the 'crusade', or papal slush fund – it appeared that 'nothing at all has been done in Rome in this matter'. Actually, Henry was wrong. Julius had finally been persuaded to dispatch the bull – but to Spain, which, as one of the major players in Italy, was, after all, rather more important than England. He had sent it, 'under seal of secrecy', as a 'consolation' to Queen Isabella, who was seriously ill. What Isabella read did not improve her health. Contrary to what she had heard from Catherine's duenna, Doña Elvira, the bull clearly stated that her daughter's previous marriage had been consummated. Catherine, it proclaimed loud and clear, was no virgin.

Behind Isabella's spluttering moral indignation lay a more calculated financial objection. A payment of 100,000 scudos to Henry VII hung on the question of Catherine's virginity, and on this wording the money was his. When the final draft of the bull was prepared, there was a small but highly significant alteration, presumably to silence the mutterings emanating from Medina del Campo. Inserted into the opening sentence of the document, which stated that Catherine had contracted a marriage with Arthur 'and that this marriage had been consummated', was the word *forsan*: 'perhaps'. Julius had contrived a phrasing that would suit the interpretation of both England and Spain, and washed his hands of the affair. In the event, it was a formula that satisfied neither Henry VII nor Ferdinand. Some quarter-century later, its ambiguity would be bitterly contested as Henry VIII sought to detach himself from his wife and from the Church of Rome.[2]

Meanwhile, at a wintry Richmond, Catherine was miserable. On 26 November, she had written two letters in quick succession to her parents, and had given them to de Puebla to include in his diplomatic bag. The letters speak volumes for Catherine's sense of isolation amid the stream of dispatches flowing between England, Rome and Spain. She had, she wrote, hardly any news from them – indeed, she had not received a single message from Ferdinand 'for a whole year' – but rumours were circulating at Richmond that her mother was very ill indeed. For once, the rumours were no exaggeration. That day, the bedridden Isabella had died at Medina del Campo. Her death would change the face of Europe. It would also turn Catherine's world upside-down.[3]

With Isabella's death, the question of the Spanish succession suddenly came into sharp focus. Queen of Castile, her marriage to Ferdinand had created a united Spain; now, her demise threatened to pull it apart, and to wreck Catherine's prospects in the process. The heir to Castile was Catherine's older sister Juana, wife to the Habsburg ruler of the Low Countries, Emperor Maximilian's son Archduke Philip of Burgundy. The fruit of Philip and Juana's tempestuous marriage, their infant son Charles of Ghent, stood to inherit a sprawling empire that spanned much of eastern and central Europe, the Low Countries, Castile, and – unless Ferdinand could remarry and produce a male heir – the rest of Spain and Spanish Italy. Hearing the news of Isabella's death, Archduke Philip was determined to lay claim to Castile on his wife's behalf.[4]

A marriage alliance with Aragon, rather than with a united Spain, was a very different and far less attractive proposition. Ferdinand knew it. On the very day of Isabella's death, he sent a letter informing Henry of the 'greatest affliction' that had befallen him and emphasizing that Isabella's dying wish was that he, Ferdinand, should rule Castile on their daughter Juana's behalf. On this view, Philip of Burgundy's ambitions were on ice. But as Ferdinand probably knew, it was asking a lot to expect Henry to accept this version of events. Henry knew exactly what it was like to lose a wife on whose inheritance his dynasty and his kingdom depended, and the precariousness which resulted.[5] Moreover, he had other irons in the fire. The Habsburg family, which, with its imperial pretensions, its financial and mercantile powerhouse of the Netherlands and its potential for European expansion through its Spanish claims, looked an increasingly attractive proposition for a dynastic alliance. Besides which, the Habsburgs still controlled the earl of Suffolk.

○

Even before Isabella's death, animosity between the Castilian and Aragonese factions had always simmered. Earlier that year, the tensions had manifested themselves among Spanish diplomats at the Burgundian court over Suffolk, still kicking his heels in Aachen and waiting for Maximilian and Philip to provide him with funds and men. Ferdinand and Isabella had been trying to get hold of him – ostensibly to help Henry; in reality to get hold of a bargaining chip in their negotiations with England – and in February 1504, they had come within a hair's breadth of getting him extradited to Spanish-controlled territories in Naples. Suffolk, however, had been tipped off.

Leaving behind his younger brother Richard as surety for the debts he had piled up with the city's merchants, Suffolk fled to the nearby principality of Guelders, whose duke, ringed by hostile Habsburg-Burgundian territory, was an ally of France. Suffolk's informant, it transpired, had been none other than the Spanish ambassador resident at the court of Philip of Burgundy. Don Juan Manuel was an outstanding diplomat. He was also, if reports are to be believed, a Castilian loyalist whose allegiances stood as much with Philip – and with his wife Juana of Castile and their infant son Charles, Castile's heir – as with Ferdinand and Isabella. And Don Manuel's sister was Doña Elvira, who ran Catherine's household at Durham House on the Strand.

The effects of Catherine's cloistered upbringing had been exacerbated by her increasingly uncertain isolation in England. She remained ingenuous and her English was poor; beneath a fragile self-confidence, she remained desperate for affection. This, as de Puebla had delicately remarked to Ferdinand and Isabella, was a recipe for disaster in Catherine's disordered household. She was, he wrote, impressionable, and a soft touch, 'very liberal' with her wealth. There were plenty of people hanging around Durham House who were looking for every opportunity to 'strip her of her gold and silver'. Henry, too, was concerned. As her prospective father-in-law, he paid Catherine a monthly stipend of £100, a generous sum designed to keep her and her household in a manner befitting a future queen of England; she could, he said, keep whatever was left over after having paid her expenses. But it proved nowhere near enough. Her wardrobe keeper, Juan de Cuero, who watched over the collection of jewels and plate that formed part of her contested dowry, complained that pieces would mysteriously go missing, pawned to pay for Catherine's lavish lifestyle, or given away as gifts.

With its runaway expenditure and its servants involved in open infighting, Catherine's household was out of control – something to which the young princess seemed oblivious or was unable to do anything about. Henry wrote to her that he was sorry that the few servants she had 'cannot live in peace with one another', and urged her to put her house in order with help from her parents. Because Catherine's servants were all Spanish, he was careful to add, the problem was out of his jurisdiction. But in confusion, Henry had, as ever, seen opportunity.

Confronted with a stream of reports detailing the breakdown of order in Catherine's household, Isabella had decided a firm hand on the tiller was needed. Following Catherine's betrothal to Prince Henry, the influence of her duenna Doña Elvira had slackened. But by October 1504 Doña Elvira was back in charge and Catherine was once more on a short leash. What was more, when Catherine and her servants rejoined the royal household at Westminster that Christmas, she was kept in the 'same rule, seclusion and observance as in her own house'. Even de Puebla, who detested Doña Elvira and her latent Castilian tendencies, agreed that this increased discipline was a good idea – and Henry, he wrote, particularly approved. But the king had done more than approve the new arrangements. Behind the scenes, he had evidently been lobbying hard for Doña Elvira's reappointment. He insisted to de Puebla both that Catherine should not find out about his involvement and that the changes in the running of her household remain concealed. To reinforce the princess's public image and authority, Henry sent her a magnificent gold headdress – but there was no doubt who was pulling the strings. After Isabella's death that winter, Doña Elvira's ascendancy brought Henry further benefits. Her close ties to her brother, Don Manuel, meant that Durham House was now a useful diplomatic back-channel to the Burgundian court – and hence to Castile.[6]

Throughout the first half of 1505, Henry kept up appearances with Ferdinand. Apart from anything else, he was preoccupied with his own remarriage, and Catherine's parents had proposed a bride for him. That May, he dispatched two of his privy servants, Hugh Denys's sidekick James Braybroke and the diminutive Breton Francis Marzen, to the Aragonese court at Valencia, to look into the state of the twenty-seven-year-old Giovanna, queen of Naples. They took with them a questionnaire drawn up by the king himself, who was determined not to accept her 'if she were ugly, and not beautiful'. This meticulously compiled document covered everything from Giovanna's finances to her personal attributes: her figure, her face – including eye colour, complexion and breath – to neck, breasts and facial hair. Marzen and Braybroke studied her carefully and compiled the answers minutely. The young queen wore a mantle, concealing much of her body. She was short and plump, making her appear 'somewhat round', but vivacious and attractive, with grey-brown eyes, clear, fair skin, and 'great, full' breasts – though they could not approach close enough to find out whether she had bad breath. But if all this appealed to Henry, her financial assets were less enticing.[7]

Having sent their dispatch, Marzen and Braybroke moved on to the second part of their mission. Travelling on to Ferdinand's court, then at Segovia, ostensibly to cement the Anglo-Aragonese entente, they were to find out as much as possible about the newly precarious situation in Spain, and about the likely reception that Philip and Juana would meet with when they arrived to claim the crown of Castile.[8] Unbeknown to Ferdinand, Henry had already started making new overtures to the Habsburgs. And he was using Catherine and her fractured household to do so.

Some months before Marzen and Braybroke set off, Henry had reopened negotiations with the Habsburgs over a marriage contract between his younger daughter Mary, and Philip and Juana's infant son Charles of Ghent; and for himself, with Philip's sister, the wealthy, recently widowed Margaret of Savoy. It was a match that both Philip and Maximilian, with an eye on Henry's overflowing coffers, were quick to encourage – though the prospective bride was said to be less than keen. Later that year Henry sat for a portrait, to be sent to Margaret of Savoy.

The finished painting, which was to become Henry's most celebrated portrait, provides a snapshot of the king as he approached his fiftieth year. He wears a gown of rich crimson velvet cloth-of-gold trimmed with white fur, and – a nod to the Anglo-Habsburg entente cordiale – his collar of the Order of the Golden Fleece, Burgundy's answer to the Garter. The ubiquitous black felt cap and dark shoulder-length hair flecked with grey frame a face whose sharply defined, hollowed cheekbones suggest the illnesses he had suffered, but whose firm chin and set mouth express firmness of purpose. His long, fine hands rest lightly on the border of the painting itself: the right clasping a small bouquet of red roses, the tips of the fingers of his left perching on it, anticipatory. Rather than looking detachedly off-camera, his characteristic sidelong glance causes him to look directly out of the frame; his uneven, heavy-lidded eyes glinting, the interrogatory stare with its arched left eyebrow. This was the public Henry, regal, coolly appraising, the reader of the viewer's inmost thoughts. The reality, though, was rather different.[9]

Henry's prolonged intelligence operation against the earl of Suffolk had had its successes. Some time in 1504 Sir Robert Curzon had resurfaced in Calais. Henry's agents had worked away on the precarious loyalties of the man whose conversations with Emperor Maximilian had prepared the ground for Suffolk's flight. Having succumbed to the king's 'importunate labour' – bribery and the offer of a royal pardon – the rogue captain of Hammes had once again switched sides.[10] Curzon was now doing very well indeed out of his treachery. Drawing a hand-some annual salary of £400 from the king's chamber, he was also renting the lands of Suffolk's unfortunate steward, Thomas Killing-worth, which the king had annexed.[11] And, in Calais, he was liaising with the man who had in all probability turned him, the spymaster Sir John Wilshere. Both men continued to receive substantial quantities of cash for their intelligence operation against Suffolk. One of the men through whom they received funds was a banker from Bologna, Lodovico della Fava.

Of the cluster of Italian merchant-bankers at court who 'never stopped giving the king advices', della Fava had emerged as the king's favoured broker. For years, he had been head of the London branch of the Medici bank, following which he led the English operation of one of the firms that had filled the vacuum left by the Medici's collapse, the Florentine bank of Frescobaldi. Della Fava was involved in the usual trade in fine Italian imports – gold, silks, satins and damasks. But he had gained Henry's affections through finance: offering the king busi-ness opportunities, investing large sums of money on the international currency markets on his behalf, taking delivery of iron coffers full of coin, and preparing bankers' drafts, to be cashed at other Frescobaldi offices across Europe. In 1502 Girolamo Frescobaldi, della Fava's boss in the bank's Bruges headquarters, had overseen Henry's £10,000 pay-ment to Maximilian; indeed, he had been the only banker willing or able to arrange the transfer of 'so great a sum'. The Frescobaldi proved particularly Anglophile. The following year, the head of its Florentine branch, Francisco, welcomed an eighteen-year-old English boy into his household, training him as a clerk. His name was Thomas Cromwell.[12]

Payments to Lodovico della Fava peppered Henry's accounts. He seemed part of the furniture, submitting expenses claims 'upon his bill' to the king's chamber treasurer John Heron for all the world like one of Henry's regular privy chamber staff. Della Fava, it was clear, had the king's confidence. Not only did he handle funds from the king's French pension, but he oversaw payments to Henry's spies and key intelligence officers abroad: cash to Wilshere and Curzon at Cal-ais, letters of credit to Matthew Baker and Sir Charles Somerset in France. Della Fava was one of the vital cogs that kept Henry's infor-mation network ticking over, liberally supplied with funds.[13]

But by 1505, this formidable operation had drawn a blank as far as Suffolk was concerned. Henry's men roamed through Flanders' febrile patchwork of heavily militarized city-states, watched and listened among the expatriate merchant communities, and floated around the courts of Burgundy and France. With the flourish of a token, a handshake, or the uttering of a codename, information was filtered through the counting-houses and warehouses of Antwerp; posts galloped along the roads of the Low Countries, while dispatches streamed through Calais, and were passed off the merchant galleys arriving in London from the Flanders ports. But nobody could provide the breakthough that Henry so desperately wanted.

In one of his characteristically detailed questionnaires, encrypted and sent to his point man at the Burgundian court, Anthony Savage, Henry laid bare his concerns. After a long series of questions about Margaret of Savoy, he came to the crunch. What was likely to become of the earl of Suffolk – or, as Henry referred to him, Edmund de la Pole? Did Maximilian favour him, in words or deeds? Was Philip in cahoots with the duke of Guelders over Edmund's imprisonment there? What were the duke's plans for Edmund? Did he like him, or not? Was he keeping the earl closely guarded, or was he given freedom to move around? Apart from the obvious security value of such answers to his agents, Henry's questions betrayed his own anxieties. Henry himself, when dealing with previous pretenders, had made a point of belittling them to emphasize their low birth and insubstantiality: Simnel had been set to work as a spit-turner in the royal kitchens, while Warbeck had been kept at court as a whimsical curio, an object of amusement – until the joke had finally worn thin. But as a genuine aristocrat of the blood, Suffolk would be treated far differently by his captors. How he was being kept, moreover, would reveal just how credible they felt his prospects were.[14]

After memorizing the contents of Henry's questionnaire, Savage was to slip it to the papal representative at Philip's court: a man who Henry regarded, he wrote to Savage, as 'one of his most intimate councillors'. For all Henry's meticulous staking-out of Philip's court, it said something that the contact who he valued most was Pedro de Ayala, previously Doña Elvira's boss in England. De Ayala, who back in 1498 had offered one of the sharpest critiques of Henry and his style of government, was hardly a man of staunch English loyalties. In fact, he was a Castilian through and through – and, since Isabella's death his allegiances had been transferred lock, stock and barrel to the court of Suffolk's captor, Burgundy.

Henry tried every trick in the book. He peremptorily demanded that Maximilian extradite Suffolk's younger brother Richard, in order that he could 'make an example' of him; he bribed Archduke Philip's enemy, Guelders, brazenly denying he was doing so in the face of Philip's irritation. He continued resolutely to hold in place the economic sanctions against Flanders that had been reimposed following Suffolk's flight to Habsburg territory in 1501 – much to the chagrin of London's merchant adventurers, who were now forced to sell all their textiles through the Calais staple, and to pay its substantial duties.[15] But if all this constituted the stick, Henry was also prepared to offer the Habsburgs something besides his and his daughter's hands in marriage: money, and on a scale that beggared belief.

Bribing princes had been an integral part of Henry's strategy in dealing with Suffolk. As he watched the shifting currents of European politics, he could barely help but notice, as his first and most celebrated biographer put it, 'the necessities and shifts for money of other great Princes abroad' – particularly those who, like Maximilian, Ferdinand and Louis XII of France, were prosecuting ruinously expensive foreign wars. In April 1505, in the same week that saw the Garter procession through London, Henry's chamber treasurer John Heron recorded an astonishing transaction. In exchange for 'certain writings', a secret understanding between Henry and Archduke Philip, the king ordered delivery of £108,000 to the waiting ambassadors from Flanders – processed, very probably, by letters of credit supplied by Lodovico della Fava. A massive sum, it equated to Henry's entire ordinary annual income.[16] No other monarch in Europe could produce such quantities of hard cash. And it was not just danger money, but an irrefutable statement of the regime's wealth and ambition, against which fugitive Plantagenet claims paled into insignificance.

As well as guarantees about Suffolk's security, Henry was buying himself a seat at the dynastic high table of Europe. Archduke Philip was now the self-styled king of Castile and, as John Heron recorded in his neat secretary hand, the money was to fund Philip's 'next voyage unto Spain' to mastermind the Habsburg takeover of Castile, and the extension of the empire of which Henry was determined to be a part.[17]

The question of how Henry could lay his hands on such prodigious quantities of liquid capital is one that has long exercised historians. There was of course his substantial French pension, paid annually, while the proceeds of his financial 'aid', granted by Parliament the previous year, were siphoned directly into his chamber accounts.[18] Henry's zealous financial administrators, with Edmund Dudley at their head, had started their drive to enforce and collect on financial bonds. But there was another source of income, too, one which has gone almost completely unnoticed. It was Henry's trade in one of Europe's most precious commodities, a trade that bound England closer to the Habsburgs, and which had the king's broker, Lodovico della Fava, at its heart: alum.

○

A natural astringent and antiseptic, potassium alum was coveted for its medicinal and cosmetic properties. But in the late Middle Ages, it was used on an industrial scale in the textile industry of northern Europe as a dye-fixer, a property which made it indispensable to the functioning of the wool and cloth trades of England and the Low Countries. As a result, alum was very big business indeed. It was, in short, a mineral without which the Western economy would grind to a halt.[19]

In the Turkish-controlled eastern Mediterranean, alum was plentiful, but in Western Europe there was only one main source: the papal-owned mine complex at Tolfa, near Rome, where massive deposits of high-grade alum had been discovered back in 1462. To a perennially impecunious papacy, it was heaven-sent. Alum profits were assigned to the 'crusade', the all-encompassing term that the papacy gave for its expansionist projects under the fig-leaf of a Christian war of liberation against the Muslim Ottoman Empire. And those profits had to be maximized and protected.

In order to exploit its lucrative new resource to the full, the papacy assigned the Tolfa monopoly to a succession of banking firms, the first of which was the Medici; by 1501, it had been taken over by the Sienese bank of Agostino Chigi, who had built a reputation as the most ruthless businessman in Italy. In order to ring-fence its monopoly – an economic practice illegal in canon law and one that could only be validated by the excuse of the crusade – to restrict the supply of alum and keep prices high, the papacy operated cartels. It backed up this rigged market with the full range of spiritual threats and punishments, bulls visiting excommunication, anathema and perpetual condemnation on anybody trading alum illegally with the 'infidel' – that is, anybody who exported alum from anywhere except Tolfa.[20] In the Low Countries, these controls had, more or less, been in place for two decades when Pope Julius II arrived on the scene in late 1503 and, needing income to fund his bellicose plans to restore papal power in central Italy, immediately ramped up the price of papal alum. The combination of high price and scarcity hit hard. The ensuing economic slump in the textile trade brought outbreaks of violence in the commercial centres of Bruges and Antwerp, which threatened to escalate into something bigger. Maximilian and Philip were very worried indeed.

They convened a group of merchants from Bruges to explore possible solutions to the crisis. There was, the merchants argued, only one way out: to fly in the face of papal injunctions and increase the supply of illegal alum from the eastern Mediterranean. Maximilian and Philip agreed – but as Holy Roman Emperor, Maximilian could hardly be seen to flout papal decrees openly. Another option presented itself. The alum could go via England, where it would effectively be laundered to disguise its origin, then re-imported to the Low Countries. The middleman for this massive, illegal trade would be the Frescobaldi bank, whose European dominance and reach made it ideal – and whose representative in England was Henry's own broker, Lodovico della Fava.[21]

Henry, of course, had made conspicuous efforts to toe the papal line, assiduous in his courting of successive popes. On Julius's election in 1503 he had sent embassies and gifts, loudly proclaiming himself a faithful son of the church and expressing his desire to go on crusade, and had indulged Julius's nepotism, lavishing favour and high office on the pope's friends and relatives. Henry's loyalty, it appeared, extended to the alum trade. He had a contract with the pope's monopolist, Agostino Chigi, who imported substantial quantities of the mineral to England and whose representative, Francesco Tomasi, known popularly as 'signore della lume' – 'Mr Alum' – maintained a high profile in Austin Friars. But as he dutifully signed up for papal alum, Henry was up to his neck in the illegal alum racket. In fact, he had, it seems, been involved in it – or at the very least, had been well aware of its potential – from the very start of his reign.[22]

Back in February 1486, a Genoese merchant trading in England, Giovanni Ambrogio da Negroni, hearing of a Spanish ship en route to the Low Countries with an illegal consignment of alum, had sensed an opportunity. He hired a crew of English pirates, who waylaid the ship in the English Channel, boarded it, killed several of its crew and towed it into port in England. There, Negroni, flourishing papal legislation against illicit alum imports, had intended to appropriate the cargo on behalf of the 'Apostolic treasury' – no doubt taking a very healthy cut himself. But at this point a shadowy figure, a 'certain Florentine merchant', intervened with Henry through unnamed representatives. The merchant protested that there were no laws in England against the free trade in alum, and what Negroni had done – capturing the ship by force, without the king's consent – was wrong. The protracted case became an international incident, and the pope intervened. Henry explained that he was desperate to favour the Apostolic See, but that his hands were tied; he could hardly go against existing laws of the land, not least, he added demurely, because 'he was new to the kingdom'. Negroni and the pope lost their case; Henry, probably, was paid a large chunk of the alum proceeds by the grateful merchant.[23]

Who the 'certain Florentine merchant' was remains unknown – though it was, very possibly, della Fava himself. Whatever the case, when in 1504 della Fava came to Henry with details of the new Frescobaldi scheme, the king knew precisely what was involved and his eyes, it seems, lit up. The scheme was simple, and the potential profit margins enormous.

Through della Fava, Henry loaned capital to the Frescobaldi and licensed them ships, including his great carracks *Sovereign* and *Regent*, both of which he ordered to be overhauled in preparation.[24] Registered as Frescobaldi vessels, these ships ran the gauntlet of Julius's edicts, bringing back alum from the Ottoman world: Anatolia, Thrace, the Greek islands and, in particular, the vast mine complex at Phocaea on the Gulf of Smyrna; in London, della Fava then brokered deals onwards to the Low Countries.[25] For all parties except the pope, it was a win-win situation. Despite the re-importation charges and massive customs duties demanded by Henry, the Frescobaldi could still get an excellent price for alum – which was for the purchaser still much cheaper than the stuff that came from Tolfa. For Henry, the increased flow of cheaper alum placated English merchants and drapers, allowed him further control over the alum supply and therefore the textile industry, and in the process increased his revenues. All he had to do was to supply money to della Fava and turn a blind eye. At Henry's shoulder, helping him broker the deals, was Edmund Dudley, with his intimate knowledge of London's customs and excise.

Henry stood to make a lot of money out of the racket. Duties payable on each 'quintal' or hundredweight of alum seem to have been in the region of one mark, or 13s 4d. In one import licence alone, the merchant in question was instructed to bring in 13,000 quintals of alum, which, snapped up by industries in England and the Low Countries, would yield the king a cool £8,666 13s 4d. Another alum shipment brokered by Henry, Dudley and della Fava, the biggest single mercantile deal of the reign, was worth £15,166 13s 4d.[26]

All of which, too, added a further level of sophistication to Henry's vast £108,000 'loan' to Philip in the spring of 1505. Unwilling to get involved in foreign wars directly, Henry was nevertheless desperate to remain at the heart of European power politics. With his grasp of the financial and commodity markets, surrounded by sharp advisers and with ample funds, he knew a better way of brokering power: through investments and capital flows he could, he felt, manoeuvre the situation to his advantage, tip the scales one way or the other as it suited him. But in all this he had, quietly, determined one thing. Ferdinand had had his chance to marry Catherine off – and he had blown it. He had also failed to come up with her long-overdue dowry, and now, as far as Henry was concerned, he was at the bottom of the pile.

On 27 June 1505, the day before his fourteenth birthday, in a room on the ground floor on the eastern side of Richmond Palace, Prince Henry gathered with a small group of counsellors. In front of the

king's diplomatic mastermind, Richard Fox, bishop of Winchester, he read from a short statement that his marriage to Catherine had been contracted before he was of age. Now, as he was 'near the age of puberty', he was taking matters into his own hands. The timing was significant. Canon law considered marriages made after the age of puberty – twelve for girls, fourteen for boys – indissoluble, because they could be consummated. Child marriages, on the other hand, might be dissolved, and regularly were. Of his own free will, the prince declared, he would not ratify the marriage contract; it was, he stated, 'null and void'. He then signed the statement, followed by the other witnesses. They included the king's chamberlain and vice-chamberlain, Lord Daubeney and Sir Charles Somerset, the king's secretary Thomas Ruthal and Fox's protégé Nicholas West; also there was the prince's own chamberlain, Sir Henry Marney. With a day to spare, Prince Henry had cancelled his long-projected marriage to Catherine.[27]

It was quite clear, however, that this act of adolescent self-assertion was nothing of the sort. Rather, his renunciation was a put-up job, carefully co-ordinated by the king and a select group of counsellors headed by Fox, who as a trained canon lawyer and one of those most closely associated with the prince since his christening, was perfectly placed to advise on the matter.

Some quarter-century later, Fox, blind and seventy-nine years old, was quizzed by Henry VIII's lawyers during the tortuous preliminaries to the king's divorce from Catherine of Aragon. Casting his mind back, he could not recollect precisely the young prince's opinion of the marriage when the papal bull was obtained but, he thought, he wanted it because he loved Catherine. His memories of the prince's protest were, he regretted, similarly hazy. He remembered being in a room at Durham House when the statement was later read out in front of the anguished princess; and believed that it was made 'at the command of Henry VII', the reason being that Henry was livid at Ferdinand's refusal – or inability – to pay Catherine's marriage portion. The renunciation was never publicized; neither, Fox added, did the king object to his son 'showing signs of love' to Catherine thereafter. But the fact remained that, whatever his assertions, and whether of age or not, the prince had little say in the matter – in fact, he had about as much as Catherine herself.

As far as Henry was concerned, the secret declaration was insurance against Ferdinand's foot-dragging over the dowry. But it was, ultimately, about control. Some four years previously, the French king Louis XII, trying to prevent his wife, Anne of Brittany, from marrying off their only daughter to Philip and Juana's son, the infant Charles of Ghent, had signed a similarly clandestine document to be flourished should political circumstances change and need arise. With one eye on the changing European situation, Henry was very keen indeed to keep in reserve the hand of his eligible young son, heir to some of the deepest coffers in Christendom. For good measure, however, he sent a letter to Ferdinand days before, saying that the marriage was still on. If circumstances changed, the prince's renunciation could be flourished, and the whole thing blamed on the independent-mindedness of youth.[28]

One Friday not long after, the Spanish ambassador de Puebla was summoned to Richmond. Admitted to the privy chamber, he found it quiet: 'nobody there but the king', his secret servants hovering unobtrusively in the background. Henry exploded with rage. Breaking bilateral trade agreements contained in the Anglo-Spanish marriage treaty, Ferdinand had forbidden English ships to export goods from Spain, leaving eight hundred sailors to make their way, destitute, back to England from Seville. And still Ferdinand was promising much and delivering nothing. Where was the outstanding payment of 100,000 scudos of Catherine's marriage portion? And what about the jewels and treasure that Catherine was busy frittering away? And all the 'other things, which he had already forgotten'?

In the face of this torrent of obsessive abuse, de Puebla stood silent until the king had exhausted himself. That weekend, a messenger arrived at the ambassador's house bearing a freshly slaughtered deer, a gift from the king. The following Monday, when he returned to Richmond to thank Henry, he found him 'perfectly calm'. They conversed about affairs of state as though Friday's meeting had never occurred. In light of the prince's renunciation – an episode about which de Puebla knew nothing – there was, perhaps, something calculated, stage-managed about Henry's anger, almost as though he were preparing the ground for a decisive rupture with Ferdinand, Aragon and Catherine.[29]

As summer drifted on, the household set off on progress, down through Surrey and Sussex, into Hampshire and the New Forest. In the suburbs west of the city, the law courts were deserted; so too the riverine palaces along the Strand, occupied only by their desultory skeleton staff. But at Durham House, Catherine and her household, left behind, were still in residence. One day in early August, de Puebla walked over from his lodgings in Austin Friars to see her and, on his way in, bumped into one of her chamber attendants. Gesturing inside, the servant told him that an ambassador from Philip of Burgundy, en route to the king, had stopped off to pay his respects to the princess, and was waiting to see her. Taken aback, de Puebla went into Catherine's apartment and told her the news; she cheerfully asked him to show the ambassador in. Kneeling at Catherine's feet, the diplomat placed the services of Philip, Maximilian and Margaret of Savoy at her disposal. Then, in front of the horrified de Puebla, he and the princess launched into a full and frank conversation about diplomatic affairs, taking in the latest news about Suffolk and Henry's prospective marriage plans. The ambassador had, he said, brought portraits of Margaret of Savoy with him for Henry's inspection. Catherine, apparently oblivious to her father's plans for Henry's marriage to his niece, Queen Giovanna of Naples, asked to see them and, when they were brought in and uncovered, enthusiastically critiqued them. Not bad, she said, though in her view Michel Sittow – the Dutch master who had painted her and whose workshop had done Henry's portrait – would have done a better job.[30]

Catherine seemed transformed from the nervous, ill girl of the preceding months. The reason was clear: suddenly, she was wanted. Doña Elvira, it transpired, had been grooming the princess for a key role in Anglo-Castilian affairs, encouraging a steady stream of Habsburg diplomatic staff to Durham House, and advising Catherine to part with more expensive gifts from her dowry. To the princess, it seemed that her household had become a hub of European diplomacy, and that her role was to bring about a new political entente: an ever-closer union between her own adoptive country and the most fashionable dynasty in Europe. Under the direction of her brother, Don Manuel, Doña Elvira had proposed that Catherine herself could engineer a summit meeting between Philip, Henry and Margaret of Savoy, at

Calais – and, too, she would have her own reunion with her sister Juana.[31]

Shortly after the troubling episode with the Flanders ambassador, de Puebla was summoned back to Durham House. He entered Catherine's chamber to find her sat at her desk, radiant, surrounded by paper, quills and ink. She picked up two letters and flourished them at the ambassador. One was from Philip – written in his own hand, no less – the other from Don Manuel: both agreed to the summit. Another letter, folded and sealed, was from her to Henry, summarizing what she had done and begging him to agree. Outside Durham House, a horsebacked courier was waiting to leave for the king.

Aghast at this Castilian stitch-up, de Puebla proposed that Catherine hand over the letters to him, as Ferdinand's accredited ambassador, to deliver to Henry; Catherine, rightly suspecting that the letters would never be seen again, refused. De Puebla then hurried off to confront Doña Elvira. He knew exactly what was going on, he told her, and made her promise that the letters would not be dispatched. No sooner had he got back home and sat down to dinner than an attendant, who he had left watching the house, ran in: the courier had galloped off. Hurrying back to Durham House, de Puebla burst into Catherine's chamber in a state of high emotion; tears streaming down his cheeks, he swore the princess to secrecy before spelling out the situation. She had, he told her, been duped by Doña Elvira and Don Manuel into furthering Anglo-Habsburg diplomatic ties that would leave both her father and sister highly vulnerable. Under de Puebla's direction, Catherine scribbled another note to Henry disavowing the previous one and beseeching him to put her father's interests first. De Puebla's messenger rode off in a cloud of dust, the gouty ambassador following behind as fast as his mule could carry him, to explain everything in full.

Before he left, de Puebla told Catherine that she must pretend that nothing at all had changed – not to alter her behaviour at all. She was too open, he said; she had to learn to keep secrets. 'Dissimulation', he stressed, was the key. It was a lesson Catherine would learn well.

When Henry received the news of Catherine's amateurish backdoor diplomacy he was, reportedly, 'astonished'.[32] It seems highly unlikely, though, that he was genuinely surprised. After all, he had been calculatedly involved in Doña Elvira's reinstatement at the heart of Catherine's household – what was more, he would himself soon be using Catherine as a go-between in much the same way. More probably, he was taken aback by a situation that had got out of control. Doña Elvira, it was clear, was working not for English interests, but for those of Castile. Catherine, meanwhile, with her loyalties veering wildly between Castile and her sister, and Aragon and her father, was proving a loose cannon – and Henry, whatever his aims, was concerned to keep them secret. It would not do for him to be openly implicated in any plot against Ferdinand. Moreover, Henry already knew what Ferdinand was now telling him: that Doña Elvira's brother, Don Manuel, had been instrumental in convincing Philip to keep hold of the earl of Suffolk at all costs. Perhaps Henry's questions to his agent Anthony Savage had been spot on, and that Suffolk's custodian the duke of Guelders, far from being Philip's enemy, was in cahoots with him. That summer, rumours reached court that 6,000 armed men were massing in Guelders to help Suffolk invade England.

Whatever the case, Doña Elvira, now known to be openly intriguing against Ferdinand, could hardly remain at Durham House as the head of Catherine's household. After a vicious struggle behind the scenes – a 'horrible hour', one of Catherine's servants recalled – Doña Elvira left to join her brother in the Netherlands. She would not return.[33]

Throughout the summer of 1505 fighting in Flanders continued to flare spasmodically. In July the duchy of Guelders was captured by Philip's men, and with it the castle of Hattem, where Suffolk was held prisoner. In Antwerp, talk filled the Burgundian court of how Philip was planning to 'bridle' the king of England. Henry, meanwhile, continued to throw money at the problem. That September, in four large iron coffers bought for the purpose, the Flanders ambassadors carried away another huge non-returnable loan from the royal coffers: £30,000, lent by Henry to Philip, now 'King of Castile', for his impending voyage to claim his throne. Honour- and treaty-bound to hand Suffolk over, Philip resorted to a stratagem worthy of his father, Maximilian. Returning Suffolk to Guelderland, and having taken the money, he blandly told Henry that there was nothing he could do: Suffolk was out of his hands, and his territory. Given that Philip was now openly styling himself duke of Guelders, this was a bit rich.[34]

As 1505 drew to a close, Catherine wrote to her father from Richmond in a state of nervous anxiety. She had, she wrote, hardly a penny since her arrival in England, except for food, and she could barely keep her servants decently clothed. On the face of it, the complaint seems curious: Catherine was not – yet – financially embarrassed, and Henry continued to pay her monthly expenses. What had changed, however, was the organization of her household.

On Doña Elvira's departure, Catherine had begged de Puebla to ask the king for a new mistress of her household, somebody harmless, like an 'old English lady'. Henry, though, had other ideas. The Doña Elvira experiment having failed, he dismantled the princess's household, sacked a number of her male servants, and absorbed Catherine and her remaining staff into his own. It was a move that looked uncannily like the arrangements he had made for his own son.[35]

Unable to blame her father, or Henry, for the limbo in which she found herself, Catherine directed her ire at the one person who remained in the firing line: the ambassador Rodrigo de Puebla. With his suspiciously comprehensive knowledge of English affairs and his subtle behaviour, the corpulent, deformed lawyer was an obvious target. What was more, his daughter's recent arrest by the Seville Inquisition – a Jewish *converso* like her father, she had probably failed to display the requisite enthusiasm for her new Christian religion – only confirmed to the Spanish everything that they had suspected about de Puebla's general shiftiness and evasiveness. Despite his increasingly frantic dispatches beseeching that his daughter not be treated 'with too great rigour' – the danger she was in, he wrote pleadingly, 'deprives me of my tranquillity, my energy of mind, and my health' – no strings were pulled on his behalf. It was de Puebla, Catherine wrote to her father, who had wrecked everything, who was the cause of all her troubles. Ferdinand, she said, should send a new ambassador, somebody she could trust.[36]

Meanwhile, Henry's agents continued to circle around Suffolk, whose circumstances were dire. A virtual prisoner in Philip's fortress of

Namur, in southern Flanders, he was kept on a meagre allowance in a lodging with barred windows and six guards who doubled as attendants. His dwindling band of followers were scattered through towns in the region, some – including his brother Richard, still in Aachen – detained for non-payment of Suffolk's mounting debts. Always prone to flights of self-delusion, the earl had become manic, veering from fevered panic to flashes of grandiose optimism, still believing that he could dictate his own terms for his voluntary return to England – a belief that Henry did much to encourage.[37] Although Suffolk's conviction of his own importance was not entirely misplaced, his future remained Philip's to decide and to manipulate.

That winter of 1505, talk at the archduke's court described the earl as a 'great thorn' in Henry's eye, how 'the people of England love and long for him', and the considerable damage he could do Henry.[38] Philip knew how much the king feared the spectre of Suffolk backed by a well-equipped Burgundian army. Having banked £138,000 in danger money from Henry in that year alone, Philip was hardly about to yield up his Yorkist cash cow, whatever Suffolk wanted. In the meantime, he was focused on his impending voyage to Castile, now finally coming to fruition with the aid of Henry's funds.[39]

In his pre-Christmas dispatch to the Signoria, the Venetian ambassador to Flanders reported on Philip's preparations. It was a high-risk journey. Philip may have got Henry over a barrel as far as Suffolk was concerned, but he needed more than the English king's neutrality. An overland trip to Spain, which would have involved negotiating French territory, was impossible. Habsburg–French relations were at a new low – as the Venetian ambassador drily remarked, the mere mention of Louis XII's name caused words of a 'very evil nature to escape the king of Castile's lips'. The only alternative route, west along the English Channel between a hostile French coastline and England, and through the Bay of Biscay, was treacherous, particularly in winter; should 'fortune cast him on the shore of England', Philip wanted to make sure that Henry would not hinder his onward journey. With this in mind, he was willing to concede all Henry's swingeing trade demands; he was even, it seems, happy to facilitate some contact with Suffolk. That December, the earl was jubilant to receive a series of visits from an English contact who he referred to as 'father' – but who, unknown to him, was almost certainly one of Henry's double-agents. But still Philip was in no hurry to give the earl up, and, to add insult to injury, he made the trouble-making Don Manuel a knight of the prestigious Order of the Golden Fleece. Then, as winter deepened, where four long years of cat-and-mouse over Suffolk had failed to yield Henry any result, fortune intervened.[40]

9

This Day Came de la Pole

On the evening of 15 January 1506, icy storms raged across southern England. Funnelling up the English Channel from the Atlantic, gales hit London with such force that trees were uprooted, 'weak houses' collapsed and roofs were ripped off. Torrential rain swamped the city and surrounding countryside 'to the great hurt of sundry cattle and especially of sheep'. The bronze eagle that topped the steeple of St Paul's was ripped off its perch and flung the length of the churchyard, crashing into a nearby bookshop at the sign of the black eagle. That night, out at sea, off England's southern coast, the tempest was about to bring Henry VII an extraordinary stroke of luck.[1]

Two days later, as the winds began to abate, a man dismounted at the gates of Richmond Palace, grimy and breathless from hard riding, bringing 'word of the landing of strangers in the west country'. Shown into the king's presence, he told his news under Henry's fixed gaze, and was rewarded with a lavish tip of ten shillings. Other dispatches followed, from the south coast ports of Winchelsea and Weymouth, the abbeys of Cerne Abbas and Melton, confirming the man's story. Philip of Burgundy had been shipwrecked off the Dorset coast on his way to Spain. The earl of Suffolk's protector, the heir to the Habsburg throne in which Henry had invested so much time and money – indeed, whose very journey he had financed – had fallen into his hands. Summoning his counsellors, giving orders for relay riders to be deployed at staging-posts between Richmond and the southwest to feed him with a regular supply of intelligence, and sending a message to his mother, then in residence at her nearby palace of Croydon, Henry began to plan how he could best use this unexpected gift from God.[2]

Five days before, Philip and his wife Juana, together with a large retinue of Burgundian nobles and two thousand German mercenaries, had set sail from the Dutch port of Arnemuiden on their long-delayed journey to lay claim to the kingdom of Castile. The couple were barely on speaking terms. When Philip's early passion for her had faded to apathy, and he began to resume his bachelor lifestyle of jousting and womanizing, Juana's love turned to a neurotic jealousy, lashing out at his servants for conniving in his amorous exploits. According to the Venetian ambassador to the Burgundian court, she could barely countenance her husband 'except on those nights when he sleeps with her'.[3] When, on Isabella's death, Juana refused to sign her Castilian inheritance away to her estranged husband, things deteriorated further. Philip forged her signature and exacted a horrible revenge. He destroyed her credibility as queen, withholding her household expenses and closeting her away, all the while insisting it was for her own good. His wife, he said, was insane. By 1506, Juana's life at the Burgundian court had become a living hell. If Catherine felt that she had it bad as a prisoner in England, the situation of her older sister, manipulated, abandoned and deeply depressed, was immeasurably worse.

The twenty-eight-year-old Philip, however, had the world at his feet. A chivalric icon, archduke of Burgundy and heir to the Habsburg Empire, he was now about to lay claim to Castile. Unfortunately for him, his wife, as queen of Castile, had to come with him.

Philip had been itching to get going. After last-minute delays due to bad weather, the fleet of some forty ships weighed anchor on the morning of 10 January. The weather was fine, and that night, as the fleet passed Calais on its port side, there was a party atmosphere on board, the ships lit up with torches, trumpets blaring, cannons firing. In the following two days, they made fast progress, strong easterly winds driving them west down the Channel to where it opened out into the Atlantic; there, they were briefly becalmed. Then, the southwest hurricane roared in. The fleet was scattered and forced back towards the English coast. In pitch darkness, Philip and Juana's ship was chaos. The guns were thrown overboard; the mainsail, which collapsed, dragged the ship half underwater before it was cut free; three times, fires broke out. Towards the end of the night, the winds finally abated, and as dawn broke through a dense, freezing fog, the ship dropped anchor off the little port of Melcombe Regis on the Dorset coast.

Looking around them, they could see only two other vessels looming out of the mist, similarly wrecked. Detached from his main fleet, which had limped into the Cornish port of Falmouth some hundred miles west, and mentally and physically shattered, Philip went ashore to recuperate. He was met by a knot of curious locals and, pushing his way through the crowd, the local dignitary Sir Thomas Trenchard, who offered the archduke hospitality at his nearby home.

As the Burgundians made themselves comfortable, Trenchard sent men to secure their landing craft, and messengers with hastily scribbled notes to the king, before gently but firmly relocating Philip further inland to a place which, he said, could better accommodate him in the manner to which he was accustomed. Resigning himself to the inevitable, the archduke dispatched his own secretary to Henry who, summoned into his presence at Richmond, bowed low, and communicated his master's respects and his request that the reception be 'as brief and simple as possible'. Beneath the diplomatic language, both kings understood the situation perfectly well. Philip would be the most honoured of guests – but he was also a prisoner. He would stay in England until Henry had Suffolk firmly in his grasp; and, Henry was determined, a lot more besides. In the meantime, Henry would overwhelm the self-styled king of Castile with hospitality, and he chose the location for Philip's reception with typical care. Perched on a chalk cliff above the Thames valley, its crenellated drum keep dominating the surrounding countryside, Windsor Castle was resonant with chivalric overtones, the spiritual home of the Order of the Garter: a perfect venue, in other words, to welcome Europe's most glamorous knight.[4]

As they progressed through the wintry countryside, Philip and his weatherbeaten nobles were greeted by an advance party led by the earl of Surrey and Sir Thomas Brandon, and smothered with attention, including menus prepared by the king's clerk of the kitchen, and hawks for Philip to hunt with as he rode. At Winchester, they were received with luxuries and fine wines at the castle by its bishop, Richard Fox. The choice of Winchester, widely believed to be King Arthur's Camelot and which resonated with chivalric romance, was deliberate.

Some two decades earlier, Queen Elizabeth had given birth to Prince Arthur there, and Henry had milked the association up until his son's untimely death. Now, it would be resurrected.[5]

Supervised by Fox, Winchester would be the scene for a new chivalric encounter between England and Habsburg Burgundy. It would, too, provide a perfect setting for Prince Henry's international debut. To welcome his guest and to accompany him on the last stage of his journey to Windsor, Henry VII had sent his son.

The point at which the prince starts to emerge from his chrysalis, no longer the small carrot-haired boy but the young man whose presence and physicality would astound Europe, is difficult to pinpoint. The transformation, though, had surely begun to occur by January 1506, midway through his fifteenth year. Henry remained a master of stage-management: he would only have sent his son to a meeting of such significance if he had thought the prince could carry it off.

If he was awestruck on meeting Philip and his nobles, the flower of sophisticated Burgundian chivalry, Prince Henry hid it well. Clattering into the courtyard at the head of a glittering company, wearing a riding gown of black velvet, a cloth-of-gold doublet and scarlet hose, he dismounted and made straight for the archduke; the pair greeted each other, one of Philip's entourage noted, like old friends, or blood brothers.[6] As they dined, the prince, chatting away fluently in French, undoubtedly drew his guest's attention to the painted Round Table, which hung in the castle, inscribed with the glorious deeds of its knights. For all the prince's insouciance, Philip would make a deep impression on him.[7]

On 31 January, at around 3 p.m., the two kings met at Clewer Green, outside Windsor. Philip pushed his horse slowly forward towards Henry, down an avenue formed by horsebacked members of the king's spears, dressed in their coats of green and white cloth-of-gold. The king himself was surrounded by a thicket of nobles, all of whom had dressed to impress. Most conspicuous among Henry's attendants were the two twentysomethings on whom he had bestowed the Order of the Garter a year previously, and whom he kept close to him at court: the duke of Buckingham's younger brother Lord Henry Stafford, whose

hat of 'goldsmith's work' was encrusted with diamonds and rubies, and Richard Grey, the slack-jawed earl of Kent, dressed in a coat of cloth-of-gold and crimson velvet, together with the latter's cousin Thomas Grey, marquis of Dorset, on a horse with a large white feather fixed to its crupper. Set off against his gaudy retinue, the king was swathed in his robes of estate, a gown and hood of deep velvet; around his neck he wore the Garter collar of linked gold esses, from which suspended a figure of St George, made entirely of diamonds. Underneath a hood of purple velvet and his customary black felt hat, his face was split by a smile of welcome. For his part, Philip's party numbered barely a dozen men. Dressed almost entirely in black, their apparel, one observer noted, was markedly 'sad'.[8]

The kings embraced. Henry, it was clear, was in an exceptionally good mood. His guest was, he said, as dear to him as his own son, and he had never been so happy since the day he was crowned; he then dismissed his unaccustomed expansiveness with a brisk 'anyway, this isn't the time for a long sermon'. As the short winter afternoon faded the party processed to the nearby castle, Philip sandwiched between Prince Henry, on his left, and the king. Brass fanfares sounded as the party rode through Windsor's great gate, past the chapel of St George and the keep.[9] An elaborate game of precedence began as they climbed the stairs to the royal lodgings: Henry, it was clear, was determined to prove to his guest that English courtliness could outdo that of the sophisticated Burgundians themselves.

Inside, he had put on a spectacular show. Before them unfolded the royal apartments, a succession of four chambers, richly decorated according to Henry's own exacting directions, lined with arras and hung in cloth-of-gold, sideboards filled with gleaming plate. The centrepiece of each room was a ceremonial royal bed, its frame intricately carved and painted, richly upholstered with matching drapery: a sure statement of wealth, given that such beds were the most valuable pieces of furniture kings owned. Guiding his guest through the rooms, each filled with courtiers of greater rank than the last, Henry announced that his own newly built lodgings would be at Philip's disposal. He himself would stay in the queen's apartments, interconnected with those of his guest by a series of galleries and closets.[10]

It was Candlemas, the time of year when Henry's memories of his

wife were particularly keen. But that Candlemas, he seemed moment-
arily transformed. His procession to the chapel to hear mass was a far
cry from the usual heavily guarded remoteness, the uniformed yeomen, halberds in hand, who pushed back the crowds and made sure
that no man was 'so hardy to sue, nor to put bill, nor to approach
nigh to him during the said procession'. Instead, he lingered, milking
his triumph. It was 'long time' before the royal entourage managed to
weave its way through the crowded apartments and galleries.[11]

Among the press of people loitered men like William Makefyrr,
scribbling down details of Philip's reception for his friends the Pas-
tons, down in London from Norfolk and staying at the fashionable
George Inn on Lombard Street; Robert Plumpton's servant George
Emerson, and Conway's spy, pairs of eyes and ears hired to 'lie about
the court' and inform their employers 'how the world goeth'. One of
Lady Margaret's men sent frequent dispatches via a rider to her at
Croydon, where she waited for updates. The whole spectacle, he
wrote to her, could not be conveyed in words: the messenger bearing
his note 'can show your grace better than I can write it.'[12]

Philip, however, took some time to thaw out. Following his arrival,
he had spent as much time as possible closeted away, as he came to
terms with Henry's enforced hospitality. After mass, the king progressed to his guest's apartments for a lengthy fireside chat, pouring
on the charm, followed by an elaborate public leave-taking. Finally,
Philip said with pointed politesse: 'I see right well that I must needs
do your commandment, and to obey as reason will.' He had got the
message. If he was ever going to leave this gilded prison, it would
be on Henry's terms. And that meant, first and foremost, the surrender of Suffolk.[13]

Later that afternoon, Henry managed to entice Philip out of his
apartments for an afternoon's entertainment, hosted by Catherine –
his sister-in-law – and Henry's youngest daughter, Mary. Taking Philip
by the arm, Henry led him through a succession of galleries and rooms to
a 'dancing chamber', where the princesses and their gentlewomen were
waiting. The presence of Catherine, an uncomfortable reminder to Philip
of his own wife – who he had brusquely left behind in Hampshire – and
her family, was like a red rag to a bull. Irked by her eager efforts to get
him to dance, he refused repeatedly and with growing irritation,

finally bursting out with a curt rejection before turning back to Henry. Mortified, Catherine retreated. But the focus of the entertainments, it was clear, was not Catherine but Mary. At the centre of a new Anglo-Habsburg treaty, Henry planned, would be Mary's betrothal to Philip's son Charles, the infant Habsburg heir.

The afternoon, which Catherine's miserable anxiety and Philip's petulance had threatened to ruin, was salvaged by Mary who, it was clear, had inherited her mother's empathic gregariousness. Even at the age of eleven, Mary had a self-possession about her, an awareness of the power of her looks – alabaster skin, grey eyes and golden hair inclining to auburn – coupled with the effortless charisma she shared with her brother. That afternoon, nobody could take their eyes off Henry VII's poised daughter, first dancing, then sitting in quiet solidarity with Catherine, before playing the lute and clavichord with dexterity. Given centre stage, Mary had grasped the opportunity with both hands. She was 'of all folks there greatly praised', one of the onlookers later recorded. In everything she did 'she behaved herself so very well'.[14]

In the next days, Henry and Philip rode out into the forested royal parkland that stretched away south of the castle. Duly impressed by the five thousand acres of well-stocked game reserves – he hadn't, he said, really known 'what deer meant' before his arrival in England – Philip set to work, shooting some ten or twelve deer. Henry himself was still the keenest of huntsmen, but his ever-worsening sight made him a liability with a crossbow – on one occasion, his servants had to compensate an outraged farmer whose cockerel the king had shot, mistaking it for game. No match for Philip, instead he took the opportunity to lay on a display of military prowess, thirty green-and-white uniformed yeomen of the guard dazzling the king's guests with a co-ordinated display of archery.[15]

By the middle of the week, foul weather made further hunting impossible. The party was kept indoors, heightening the sense of intense diplomatic activity. As rain lashed at the windows, Henry was closeted away with his counsellors in a working party headed by his chief negotiators, Richard Fox and Nicholas West. The constant scurrying to and fro, the whispered lobbying and horse trading, could not disguise the fact that Henry would dictate the terms of the forth-coming treaty.[16]

In the intervening days, as the weather cleared, the outdoor enter-tainments resumed. On Saturday afternoon, after watching a horse being baited by dogs, Henry and Philip strolled over to the tennis courts opposite the royal lodgings, where Thomas marquis of Dorset was partnering Thomas lord Howard, eldest son and heir to the earl of Surrey, in a game of doubles. Henry, who followed the game com-pulsively, had installed tennis courts at all his houses, playing, betting – and usually losing – with gusto. But since his first major ill-ness six years previously he had been content to watch and lay bets, which he continued to lose. Philip, though, grew restless. Removing his cloak, hat and jacket, he asked Dorset for a game; the short, wiry Howard retired, thin-lipped. The pair played until the light started to go. Henry, meanwhile, stayed in the tapestry-lined gallery, lounging on cloth-of-gold cushions, his eyes flickering over the participants.[17]

Monday 9 February came, and with it the day for Philip to pay his bill for Henry's lavish hospitality. That morning, Henry, the prince and the Garter knights assembled in the presence chamber, dressed in the order's ermine-fringed, crimson velvet gowns, where they were joined by Philip and his knights.[18] Riding the short distance to St George's Chapel, the party dismounted, progressing through the church to the choir where Philip was to be invested with the Garter. One of Philip's attendants was overwhelmed; he had, he wrote, never seen anything like it. Burning tapers illuminated a vision of gold: gold plate, gold chains, relics in their gilt reliquaries including, at the king's elbow, a piece of the True Cross on a cushion of cloth-of-gold; uni-formed heralds-of-arms everywhere. In his capacity as master of ceremonies, Thomas Wriothesley had excelled himself. The rather overcooked opulence – 'excessive', thought the Burgundian writer – positively exuded tradition and timelessness. In fact, he added, it was the kind of thing you might have seen in a king's palace a hundred years previously. It was precisely the kind of permanence that Henry liked to convey.[19]

Following the kissing of relics and swearing of chivalric oaths, Philip was invested with the order's accoutrements, a kneeling Prince Henry buckling the garter eagerly round the archduke's leg, the king placing the heavy gold collar around his neck, murmuring 'my son' as he did so. Then came the prince's turn. Invested with the Order of the Golden Fleece, its golden gown billowing out on the floor behind him, he pronounced the oath excitedly in resounding and fluent French, and was kissed by Philip 'in sign of fraternal love'.

Sandwiched between the two investitures was the meat of the ceremonial: Henry's treaty. In his capacity as the Garter's prelate, Richard Fox, hovering at Philip's elbow, indicated wordlessly where he should sign. This mutual defence pact – which included, of course, the extradition of each other's rebels – paved the way for further agreements: Henry's betrothal to Margaret of Savoy, and a new trade agreement whose main feature was to allow English merchants to import cloth duty- and tax-free into the Low Countries, with few concessions in return. Unsurprisingly, it quickly became known in the Netherlands as the *intercursus malus*: the wicked treaty.

The treaty, however, underscored everything that Henry was now working for. With it, he turned decisively away from Ferdinand and from Aragon, and aligned England's future with the Habsburgs. Its secrecy, however – it went unmentioned in eyewitness reports heavy on the ceremonial detail – meant that the only people who knew about its terms were the negotiators themselves, although Ferdinand and the French, who had recently signed a similar treaty of their own, probably had their suspicions. Days later, Philip turned to Henry in a moment of choreographed spontaneity and, 'unasked', offered to hand over the earl of Suffolk – or, as the official chronicler dismissively called him, 'Ed. Rebel'. Henry, keeping up the charade, graciously accepted.[20]

With business concluded, Henry, Philip and the prince retreated to a 'little chamber' within Philip's apartments to dine. Flushed with success, the king was in loquacious mood. Over dinner, he expatiated on the new treaty, seeing it as the latest in a line of glorious deeds stretching back to King Arthur – whose table, he reminded Philip, he had seen hanging in the hall at Winchester. Warming to his theme, Henry said that his achievements and those of his son would be documented alongside those on the table; then, whenever people saw it, they would think of this 'true and perpetual friendship between the empire of Rome, the kingdom of Castile, Flanders, Brabant, and the kingdom of

England.' Turning to his son, Henry then embarked on a fatherly lecture of the 'watch and learn' variety.

Why, he asked the prince rhetorically, did he think he had lavished such expense on Philip? It was, he continued, solely because he wanted to recognize Philip's honour and his virtuousness – and 'absolutely not', he insisted, because he was 'looking for something from him in return'. Henry also gave voice to the thought that had been revolving incessantly in his mind since the death of Prince Arthur nearly four years before: 'My son of Wales', he told the prince, 'you see that I am old. Soon you will need your good friends.'

Prince Henry, though, needed no invitation from his father. He revelled in the thought of Philip as his 'good friend'. When the French ambassador, newly arrived at court, greeted him, the prince, noted one of Philip's retinue delightedly, barely favoured him with a glance. Struggling to come to terms with the new entente between England and Castile, the ambassador tried to make up ground; during a hunting expedition, Prince Henry brought down a buck with a clinical shot, eliciting gushing compliments from him. 'It would have been good for a Frenchman', came the whip-smart retort. As one of Philip's party was at pains to point out, the ambassador chose to misinterpret the prince: rather than complimenting French archery, he was saying that he would have preferred to be shooting Frenchmen rather than deer. The prince's barbs, it was clear, were as effortless as his shots.[21]

Queen Juana's arrival the following day could hardly have been more different from that of her husband. Philip had tried to keep Juana as far away from the English court as possible. On his arrival at Windsor he claimed that 'a small incident' had kept her from accompanying him – even his close attendants claimed not to know where she was staying – and he was keen to avoid her being accorded a reception befitting her status as Queen of Castile in her own right.[22] At his insistence Juana and her entourage entered Windsor unobtrusively, via a side gate. But Henry, his interest undoubtedly piqued by the reports of Juana's celebrated beauty, ignored Philip's repeated requests for him not to give Juana an official welcome and waited for her, together with Catherine and Princess Mary. His appraising gaze took in Juana's jet-black hair and feline eyes, and he embraced her in welcome, perhaps a little too long.[23] For both sisters, meanwhile, the reunion was heartfelt, though all too brief. Philip immediately whisked Juana off to his apartments and left her there. As far as he was concerned, Juana was at Windsor solely to add her signature to the new trade agreement. He would pack her off again the next day, when the ink was barely dry.

In marked contrast to the activity of the previous days, Henry kept to his chamber on the 11th, the anniversary of Elizabeth's death. While he contemplated his own wife, Philip could not wait to get away from his, and asked Henry if they could have dinner together in his privy chamber. As if all this were not evidence enough of Philip and Juana's estrangement, the king of Castile's attendants were at pains to emphasize quite how mad his wife was. During the storm that had shipwrecked them, they described how she had been a liability, sobbing at her husband's feet, her arms locked fast round his legs. Later, the Venetian ambassador travelling with Philip's party put it rather differently: she had, he wrote, 'evinced intrepidity throughout'. Henry concurred with the Venetian. Reports of Juana's insanity were, he later concluded, groundless. 'She seemed very well to me', he recalled. 'And although her husband and those who came with him depicted her as crazy, I did not see her as other than sane.'[24]

As a well-armed detachment, headed by the veteran diplomat Sir Henry Wyatt, left Richmond for the Low Countries to take Suffolk into custody, Henry prolonged his guest's stay with a further programme of entertainments, as he awaited news that Suffolk was safely under lock and key. Hunting parties were punctuated by a trip down the Thames to London, whose highlight included a 'wonderful peal of guns [shot] out of the Tower'. Would Philip, Henry asked, like a guided tour inside the Tower? His guest hastily declined.

The party, including Prince Henry and Princess Mary, also rode over to the nearby palace of Croydon, to pay a call on the king's mother. There, gifts were exchanged – Lady Margaret was presented with a commemorative account of 'the coming of the king of Castile' – and Philip's minstrels performed in front of the king's mother who sat, appreciative, her customary glass of malvesey to hand. Then, there was a surprise for the prince from his doting grandmother: a new horse, and with it a custom-made saddle finished with tuffets of Venetian cloth-of-gold, gold buckles and pendants, and a harness fringed with flowers of black velvet and gold. It was a well-judged gift. As Lady Margaret was well aware, the culmination of Philip's visit would be a tournament, at Richmond: Henry's jousters against Philip and his men. Probably mindful of the spectacular display of Burgundian chivalry at Calais six years before, the king was determined to show his guest that the English could compete. Prince Henry would not take part in combat – but he could show off his skills and horsemanship, anyway, on his new horse.[25]

For the king's spears, it was a rare chance to pit themselves against the best jousters in Europe, men like Philip's favourite, the cool, cultivated Henri, lord of Nassau-Breda: a member of the Golden Fleece who would joust alongside Philip then host lavish banquets and afterparties that lasted 'well nigh the whole night', and which involved dancing 'and other amusements'. During these soirées, Nassau-Breda would fold open the panels of a triptych recently commissioned from his favourite artist Hieronymus Bosch, to reveal the world of supercharged erotic anarchism contained in *The Garden of Earthly Delights*.[26] For even the most talented of the English jousters – and Henry had augmented the spears with men like the louche, athletic twenty-two-year-old Charles Brandon, nephew of his master of horse Sir Thomas – simply being in the lists against these dazzling Burgundians was an experience that they would never forget. It was a tournament that would leave an indelible impression on all who saw it, in particular the fourteen-year-old prince, watching starstruck from the stands. Henry, too, was delighted, rewarding his jousters £6 13s 8d each.[27]

Finally, Philip was ready to continue his journey onward to Spain, the first stage of which was the long ride two hundred and fifty miles southwest to Falmouth in Cornwall, 'a wild place which no human being ever visits, in the midst of a most barbarous race', where repairs were being made to the wrecked fleet that had been swept ashore, and where the majority of Philip's retinue – including the two thousand German mercenaries – had spent the last six weeks kicking their heels. As he and his entourage prepared to depart, shortly after the midday dinner on 2 March, their saddled horses waiting, Henry and the prince appeared; at first refusing to let Philip leave, they then insisted on accompanying him on the first leg of his journey. It was the kind of ponderous charade that Henry VIII, with his love of 'surprise' entrances, would later delight in.[28]

As soon as he had waved Philip off, the smile disappeared from Henry's face. Philip had pledged that Suffolk would be handed over before he embarked. Henry kept him to his word, keeping close watch on him all the way to Falmouth, in constant contact with Philip's escorts, the earl of Surrey and Thomas Brandon, through his system of posts; meanwhile, messengers rode hard between London, Calais and Flanders with updates on Suffolk. In fact, laid low by illness and then to his 'intense vexation' kept in port by spring storms, Philip's departure was further delayed; he eventually set sail on 16 April.[29]

Even before he had done so, Prince Henry had put pen to paper – remarkably, for someone who would prove a reluctant letter-writer at the best of times. Desperate to consolidate this friendship with his new-found chivalric hero, he wrote from Greenwich on 9 April asking after Philip's health, 'which I particularly and with all my heart desire to be of long continuance as I would my own', and asking him to stay in touch, to write 'from time to time' – as, he said keenly, would he.

In the way of infatuated teenagers through the ages, he had bashfully cited an excuse for getting in touch with Philip so soon after his departure. Don Pedro Manrique, Catherine's chamberlain, was planning a trip to Castile 'for certain matters' and had buttonholed Prince Henry, asking him to write to Philip 'in his favour'. And then, the prince went on to refer to Catherine, the bride who he had so resoundingly jilted at his father's direction the previous year, as *'ma chère et tres aimée compaigne, la princess ma femme'*: 'my most dear and well-beloved consort, the princess my wife'.[30]

There was, however, more to the prince's letter than his own schoolboy crush. Don Pedro Manrique was the husband of Catherine's former duenna Doña Elvira, whose pro-Habsburg intriguing the previous year had resulted in her dismissal. Catherine's household was still full of servants with Castilian sympathies, Don Pedro among them, and, as the prince's letter now revealed, it was still being used as a diplomatic back-channel to Philip and Juana's court. There was, too, no doubt that Henry's hand lay behind the letter, which was, after all, an official communication. Through his son, Henry was exploiting Catherine's household to cement the new Anglo-Habsburg entente cordiale. The prince's undoubtedly sincere protestations of love for his bride, too, masked the king's increasing indifference to her. Less than two weeks after his letter, Catherine wrote in desperation to her father: she was deep in debt, not for 'extravagant things', but just to pay her household expenses. She had written to Henry countless times, without reply, and he had waved away her pleading. Ferdinand, he stated, had failed to deliver her dowry, and that was that. Catherine begged her father to remedy the situation. In response, Ferdinand promised another date for payment: 24 June, the Feast of St John the Baptist. The date came and went, and again he failed to deliver. His belated and contradictory excuses to Henry only made things worse.[31]

Machiavelli wrote about Ferdinand that he used to talk of nothing but 'peace and good faith'. However, he continued, if Ferdinand had practised what he preached, he would have been ruined: both his credit with banks and his estates would been lost several times over. Machiavelli gave the impression that Ferdinand's way was the right one. Catherine, however, was left in limbo – and, consequently, so too was Prince Henry.[32]

That summer, too, cracks began to appear in the Anglo-Burgundian treaty. Margaret of Savoy, a committed widow, obstinately refused to contemplate marriage to Henry, despite the pleas of her brother and father, with their eyes on Henry's money. Away in Castile, Philip's triumphant arrival had descended into a prolonged squabble with Ferdinand over the succession. Then, on 25 September, he died suddenly, in mysterious circumstances; he had, according to one Italian ambassador, 'eaten something'.[33]

Henry, though, was not unduly concerned. The negotiations for marriage between his daughter Mary and the young Habsburg heir Charles of Ghent were gathering pace, and Philip's death, in fact, opened up another window of opportunity: marriage to his widow, Juana. And besides, he now had Suffolk.

On 16 March, Suffolk rode into Calais under armed guard and was delivered into the custody of the town's indefatigable comptroller and spymaster Sir John Wilshere. If he had initially come 'not altogether unwillingly', labouring under the misapprehension that Henry would welcome him back to court and restore his titles and lands, it was probably now, as he embarked with Wilshere, Sir Henry Wyatt and sixty armed soldiers of the Calais garrison, that the penny dropped. Some ten hours later, the ship docked at the port of London, from where Suffolk had fled some four and a half years previously, and where Sir Thomas Lovell now waited, grim-faced, at the head of a heavily armed reception committee. Without ceremony, Suffolk was taken through the back streets to the Tower, through its gatehouse and across its moat, into its depths. He would not come out alive.[34]

But Suffolk's associates had evaded Henry's clutches – among them his charismatic younger brother Richard de la Pole. In the last months of Suffolk's captivity, relations between the two had grown strained. From his cramped lodgings in Aachen, Richard had scribbled a pleading, anxiety-ridden letter to Suffolk. Both of them, he wrote, were dishonoured by the crippling debt they had racked up over the years – but that was the least of Richard's problems. Everywhere he went in the city's crowded, bustling streets, he had the creeping feeling of being watched. Looking over his shoulder, out of the corner of his eye, he saw figures loitering. The place was riddled with Henry's agents. Convinced he was in great personal danger, he had resolved not to go out anymore. Even the local creditors who regularly threatened him had been bought off: 'if I am killed in the street, king Henry will pay them their money.'[35] Penniless and terrified, Richard felt utterly abandoned by his brother. With Suffolk's extradition, he was completely on his own.

But Richard's luck finally turned. The new prince-bishop of Liège, whose territories bordered Aachen, was sympathetic – neither was he bound by his predecessor's extradition treaty with Henry. Paying off Richard's debts, Liège brokered his flight, across the territories of the Holy Roman Empire, to the kingdom of Ladislaus II of Bohemia and Hungary. Ladislaus, who had also been bribed by Henry, nevertheless welcomed Richard with open arms. For the next decade, until his death, Ladislaus would continue to pay an annual pension to the man who, taking up the Yorkist cause, would become known simply as 'White Rose'.[36]

At Croydon, Lady Margaret noted Suffolk's arrival neatly in the book of hours that doubled as an occasional diary: 'this day came de la Pole'. She was presented, too, with a new, fully updated account of 'the coming of the king of Castile', which contained the satisfying sequel 'and Edmund de la Pole'.[37] As he had done after Perkin Warbeck's capture eight years before, Henry went on a pilgrimage of thanksgiving through East Anglia, to the Norfolk shrine of Our Lady at Walsingham, a model of devotion amidst the relics and graven images. By mid-May, he was back at Westminster, then took barge for the Tower. There, the inquests began.

While Henry had been in Walsingham, the expert inquisitor Sir Thomas Lovell and his colleagues had embarked on a prolonged interrogation of de la Pole – 'exhaustive', as one chronicler delicately put it. By the time the king arrived, Suffolk had undoubtedly been softened up, reduced to a state of mental and physical collapse, as Warbeck had been years before. Now, the king got to work.

What now happened to Suffolk in the bowels of the Tower was, characteristically, kept under wraps – but he was almost certainly tortured. As the poet Sir Thomas Wyatt later recalled, his father, Henry VII's jewel-house keeper Henry Wyatt, had been racked on the orders of Richard III, who had sat there and watched. Whether Henry did the same with Suffolk during the course of his relentlessly insistent questioning can never be known, but although technically speaking nobles were not to be tortured, such rules were rarely observed. Besides, Suffolk, attainted – stripped of his hereditary title – was no longer a member of the nobility, merely 'Ed. Rebel'.

Whether or not Suffolk confirmed Henry's suspicions about doubtful loyalties and conspiracy at court, his capture and interrogation opened another can of worms. While Suffolk had been in Flanders, the king had moved with caution against members of the political elite. Now he was safely under lock and key, Henry let his counsellors off the leash.[38]

1. A miniature astrological world map, with the signs of the Zodiac and personifications of the four winds. This is the frontispiece of the 'Liber de optimo fato', or 'Book of Excellent Fortunes', by William Parron, the Italian astrologer who prophesied the deaths of Warbeck and Warwick. Given as a New Year's gift in January 1503, the book predicts that Queen Elizabeth would live to the age of eighty.

2. Terracotta portrait bust of Henry VII by Pietro Torrigiano.

3. Portrait of Elizabeth of York, Henry's queen.

4. (*top left*) A laughing boy, thought to be Prince Henry aged about eight, by Guido Mazzoni, *c.* 1498.

5. (*top right*) Lady Margaret Beaufort, the pious and politicking mother of Henry VII, in characteristic dress and pose.

6. (*left*) Portrait of Catherine of Aragon, aged about twenty, by Michael Sittow.

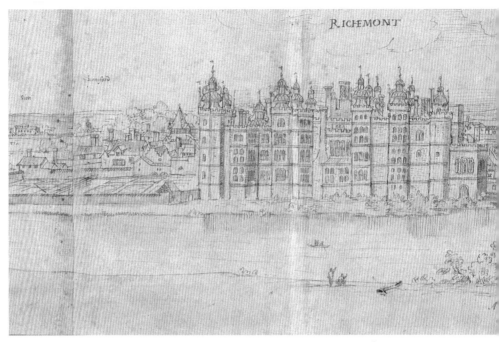

7. Richmond, 'the beauteous exemplar of all proper lodgings'. Drawing by Antonis van Wyngaerde, *c.* 1562.

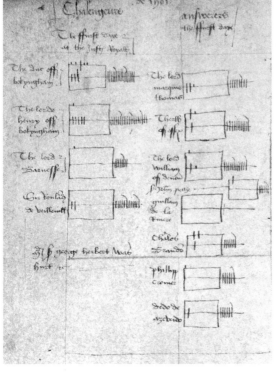

8. The 'score cheque' from the first day of the Westminster jousts of November 1501, celebrating the marriage of Prince Arthur to Catherine of Aragon. The columns represent the two teams. Each combatant's score is indicated in the box next to his name: strokes indicate blows to the head or body and, bisecting the horizontal lines, lances broken. Heading the 'challengers' team (*left*) is the duke of Buckingham; the 'answerers' team (*right*) is led by (*top*) the marquis of Dorset and includes (*second*) the earl of Essex and (*third*) Lord William Courtenay, all of whom were suspected of conspiring with Suffolk. Fifth down is a youthful Charles Brandon.

9. A group of plate-armoured jousters arrives at a tournament. These are the 'venants', or 'challengers', who take up the challenge issued on the king's behalf. On the left, ladies of court look on from the royal pavilion.

10. Informer's report by John Flamank, detailing the secret conversation among Henry VII's officials at Calais, September 1504. The officials describe the king as 'a weak man and sickly, not likely to be no long-lived man' (*line 6*) and discuss a debate among 'great personages' at court over possible heirs to the throne: 'none of them spoke of my lord prince' (*lines 12–13*).

11. 'They think he is a fox – and such is his name.' Richard Fox, Henry VII's lord privy seal and diplomatic mastermind. Portrait by Hans Corvus.

12. The death of Henry VII, 'secretly kept by the space of two days after'. Drawing by Garter king-of-arms Thomas Wriothesley.

13. From Thomas More's coronation verses, on the rainstorm that disrupted Henry VIII and Catherine of Aragon's procession through London, 23 June 1509: 'if one looks at the omen, it could not have been better. To our rulers, days of abundance are promised by Phoebus with his sunshine, and by Jove's wife with her rains.' Below, an intertwined red-and-white rose and pomegranate of Granada, flanked by a French fleur-de-lys and Beaufort portcullis, are surmounted by a crown imperial.

14. Henry VII's accounts. This page, written in the king's own hand, details monies that he himself has processed and delivered to his chamber treasurer John Heron. Items include the annual payment of Henry's French pension in 'plain crowns' and 'crowns of the soleil' (lines 6–8), 'diverse coins of gold' from the Calais treasurer (lines 13–15) and £1,133 in 'old weighty crowns' (lines 16–17).

For the hopelessly insolvent Sir Richard Guildford, things had gone from bad to worse. This once-influential loyalist was now a political deadweight, unable to maintain control in his native Kent and deep in debt: imprisoned in the Fleet, he was stripped of office early in 1506. That April, before he left for Walsingham, Henry VII issued a pardon for Guildford's embezzlement of crown funds. But with his creditors hovering, prosecution impending, and political pressure building, Guildford left court. In a well-worn method of self-imposed exile, he made his will and set off on pilgrimage to Jerusalem. He would not return.[39]

Guildford's enforced grand tour was a revelation to him, and to his chaplain, who kept a diary of the trip. Through France, Germany and the Austrian Alps into the plains of northern Italy, they marvelled at shrines and relics and, at Padua, the tomb of the Roman historian Livy. At Venice, they followed the time-honoured tourist route, taking in the Byzantine richness of St Mark's, the glass-makers at Murano, and the 'many abbeys and houses of religion that stand in the sea'. Henry's former armourer and master of ordnance, Guildford was astonished by the walled, heavily fortified Arsenal, swarming with ropemakers and engineers, its hundred battle-ready galleys, its 'wonder and strange ordinance'. The icing on the visit came on Ascension Day, with the annual ritual of Venice's symbolic wedding to the sea: the Venetian Signoria being rowed out into the lagoon in an ornate galley, trumpets rasping, the Doge proclaiming the marriage vows and dropping a gold ring into the depths. Venice had all things 'that maketh a city glorious . . . above all places that ever I saw.'

From there, Guildford and his party took ship, down the Adriatic, stopping at the Venetian city of Ragusa, or Dubrovnik – 'the strongest town that ever I saw in my life' – and out into the Aegean, journeying through Venice's marine empire: Kythira, where 'Helen the Greekish queen was born' and 'ravished by Paris in the next isle by', and Crete – 'right evil people', though they made 'great wines'. Proceeding cautiously 'for fear of the Turk' through the eastern Mediterranean and the newly colonized territories of the Ottoman Empire, they arrived at the Palestinian port of Jaffa, hired camels 'with great difficulty and at outrageous cost', and reached Jerusalem that August, five months after leaving the Sussex port of Rye. No sooner had Guildford arrived than he succumbed to fever, died, and was buried on Mount Zion. It was probably the neatest way out for all concerned.[40]

With Guildford's departure, another of the king's Bosworth companions was gone. Henry had shown a flicker of sentiment over Guildford's fate, allowing him a way out – even if it meant exile. After all, Guildford had intimate connections with Lady Margaret's household, where his widow, Lady Anne, had been brought up and was one of her closest attendants; Anne had also served Queen Elizabeth, and Henry's two daughters, Margaret and Mary. Of Sir Richard's two sons, Henry Guildford was the prince's ever-present companion, while his older half-brother Edward was one of the court's foremost jousters, idolized by the prince: part of the fabric of the regime. Indeed, they had little choice. Their father's bankruptcy had left them reliant on their court careers for income and Edward followed in Sir Richard's footsteps, taking over the running of the royal armoury in Southwark that he and his father had run together. Now, Henry turned his gaze on Suffolk's associates. One of the first he moved against was Sir Richard Guildford's rival in Kent, the man with whom the king had been forced into an understanding: Lord Bergavenny.[41]

In June 1506, an indictment was brought against Bergavenny in the court of King's Bench. It involved events of nine years previously when, back in the summer of 1497, Bergavenny, then twenty-eight years old, had been with the earl of Suffolk at his manor of Ewelme in Oxfordshire with a detachment of men, vainly attempting to slow the rapid advance of the Cornish insurgents, then at Wallingford some miles to the west. Henry had sent a dispatch rider ordering them to pull back along the Thames valley towards London, and to hold the vital bridge at Staines. At Ewelme, the rider burst in upon the pair together in bed, whereupon Bergavenny hid under the bedclothes. After the messenger had left, Suffolk turned to his partner and asked why he was hiding himself, and whether it was because he was afraid. Bergavenny replied that he didn't want the messenger to know he was there, and then said that the moment had come – whether to stick with Henry, or twist with the rebel forces nearby. 'What will you do, now it is time?' he asked Suffolk. The earl grabbed Bergavenny's shoes to prevent him going anywhere, mounted his horse and prepared to follow the king's instructions. If he had listened to Bergavenny, the indictment concluded, they would have joined the rebels.[42]

So much of the incidental detail in the indictment seems preposterous – the hiding under the bedclothes, the grabbing of shoes – but it was on such split-second decisions that the kingdom's future hinged; in 1485 William Stanley had taken the gamble at Bosworth that had won Henry a kingdom.

Henry's habit of sitting on information and persistently 'groping further' to find out as much as he could suggests that he had known about these accusations for some time but that, with the problems in Kent, and with the earl of Suffolk at large, he had continued to wait, concerned about the wider instability that any move against Bergavenny might provoke. That the indictment was lodged barely a month after his interrogation of Suffolk suggests either that Henry now felt more confident – or that Suffolk had confirmed what he already knew about Bergavenny.

Arrested, Bergavenny was brought to London and locked in the Tower.[43] So were two others alleged to have dined with Suffolk in the days before his flight in August 1501: Thomas Grey, marquis of Dorset and Sir Thomas Green. Despite his assiduous attendance at court and prominence in the tiltyard, Dorset had never shaken off the cloud that hung over him – his Yorkist blood, his father's flaky loyalties – and Henry's eyes continued to slide inquiringly over him even as he heaped honours on him. In the Tower, Green and Dorset joined William de la Pole, Suffolk's youngest brother, and William Courtenay, both of whom had already been there for four years. Bergavenny, shaken and subdued, was released after a few months after the allegations went unproven; Green, already sick when he was arrested, died in the Tower on 5 November. Dorset and Courtenay stayed. There would be no trial. The following autumn, they would be transferred to Calais Castle where, people believed, they had been sent to die.[44]

Then there was the matter of Calais. With John Flamank's report in hand, Henry had waited, gathering and sifting intelligence passed to him by the likes of Sir John Wilshere, the double-agent Sir Robert Curzon – a regular presence in the town – and by Sir Thomas Lovell, who brought information back along with the revenues that he collected and paid into Henry's coffers. In July 1506 Henry moved against the conversationalists, ordering the dismissal of 'Sir Richard Nanfan, Sir Hugh Conway and Sir Sampson Norton, knights, of such authorities and rooms as they had in our town'. Conway was soon reinstated; Norton, though, was dismissed and Nanfan, worn out and under a cloud, retired to England. The following year Lady Lucy Browne, whose manoeuvrings among the Calais garrison had caused Conway such anxiety, was fined a hundred marks on behalf of her husband, now dead, for having paid soldiers in his retinue who 'were not sworn' under oath.[45]

The biggest fish of all, however, was Giles lord Daubeney, Henry's lord chamberlain, the man whose power and influence in the Calais garrison and the royal household had been wondered at, and whose loyalty in the face of the rampant Cornishmen in 1497 had, Nanfan believed, been suspect. Towards the end of 1506, when Daubeney was alleged to have embezzled the Calais garrison's wages, Henry threw the book at him. That December, Daubeney entered into bonds for £2,100, payable in annual instalments of £100, for a pardon for his financial improprieties. The men who took the bonds on the king's behalf were Daubeney's colleagues, familiar faces in the king's inner circle: Sir Thomas Lovell, Sir Henry Wyatt, Richard Empson, Edmund Dudley. He was also forced to make over to the king his annual French pension of 2,000 crowns, gained back in 1492 after Henry's invading army had been bought off. These fines were wholly disproportionate to Daubeney's alleged crime. What lay unspoken were Henry's suspicions of his lord chamberlain's allegiance. Daubeney, the fines intimated, was being watched. In the recent past, chamberlains had a habit of being executed for their disloyalty. He would have to tread very carefully indeed.

The stakes were being raised. In summer 1506, Henry went after his Stanley step-family with renewed vigour. Two years previously, Lady Margaret's estranged husband the earl of Derby – who, as Lord Stanley, had placed the crown on Henry's head at Bosworth twenty-one years previously – had died, and his young, ingenuous son and heir was played ruthlessly, forced to enter into a series of bonds, and to purchase the obligatory 'pardon'; by the time Henry had finished, he was in debt to the tune of £10,000. In a carefully staged trial at Lancaster, Sir James Stanley was fined an exorbitant £145,000 for retaining offences, saddling much of the family and their leading men with huge debts. Something similar happened to Bergavenny. Found guilty in the court of King's Bench for illegal retaining between 1504 and 1506, he was fined £70,650 for the illegal retaining of 471 men. After some horse-trading, Henry settled for a suspended fine secured by the guarantees of twenty-six of Bergavenny's friends. Then, Bergavenny was banished from the lands in which he had been rampant, forbidden from setting foot in Kent, Surrey, Sussex and Hampshire without the king's license, on pain of another fine of 5,000 marks.[46]

These were sums that the guilty parties could never hope to pay off. And that, in a way, was the point. The schedule of payments was such that the slate would never be wiped clean: these nobles would be bound in perpetual debt to the crown, a debt that they would pass on to their children, and their children's children, until such time as the crown, at its pleasure, decided to cancel it. The suspended fines, or 'recognizances', meanwhile, were like being on permanent bail. If triggered, their victims would be ruined – and, as they knew, Henry was watching their every move. This was what Dudley had meant by the king keeping people 'in danger at his pleasure'. As well as generating astonishing amounts of income, these debts splintered traditional loyalties, binding them instead to the crown. Anybody who broke the conditions of their bonds risked not just their own financial ruin, but the ruin of those who stood surety for them – who, afraid for their own financial well-being, now looked far more closely at the behaviour of those whose debts they were forced to guarantee. It made the idea of disloyalty and rebellion not only unthinkable, but unaffordable.

All this was caught in Dudley's burgeoning account book. In it mingled the records of Daubeney's fines and bonds, his French pension (itemized by Dudley as a 'grant' to the king, as though the chamberlain had made it out of his own volition); of Bergavenny's condemnation, for which Dudley had the indictments 'having received them from the king', and fines for 'true allegiance'; of Lucy Browne's fine, and the fines for pardons issued to Nanfan and the earl of Northumberland.

These entries nestled among countless others, the fruits of Henry's increasingly implacable application of the law. What was remarkable about the book was its scope, and its reach. It confirmed what by 1506 – and, in particular, following Suffolk's extradition – was becoming glaringly evident. By this point Henry's financial and legal counsellors were not only, or not even primarily, after recalcitrant nobles. They were after anybody and everybody they could get.[47]

10

New Heaven, New Earth

In autumn 1504 Desiderius Erasmus was in Paris; as usual, he was broke. News reached him from England, where his friend John Colet, the ascetic mentor of Thomas More, had been appointed to the lucrative and influential post of dean of St Paul's Cathedral. Erasmus sensed an opportunity. Overcoming his terror of the 'ill-famed' cliffs of Dover, on which he had been 'wrecked' – the exactions of Henry's customs officers lingered in his mind, four years after they had confiscated the hard currency that he had tried to take out of the country – he decided to try his luck in England again. For Erasmus felt he had something new to offer.

His previous visit to England had jolted Erasmus out of his intellectual comfort zone. In the intervening years, his scholarship had started to blossom into maturity, his writings exhibiting the deceptively easy, colloquial eloquence that would become his trademark. He had also mastered Greek, which had opened up to him the writings of the early Church fathers, and the original language of the New Testament. Study of the classics, Erasmus had begun to believe, could reinterpret the world anew. It could reform society, strip away ingrained customs and traditions that blinded people to the evils of the world – like chivalric culture, which conferred a veneer of legitimacy and glory on the war and conquest of the military classes, and the outward rituals and observances, the indulgences and graven images that were the expressions of a church riddled with corruption. Knowledge, Erasmus believed, should be liberated from the clutches of the scholastics, with their arcane, hair-splitting debates, and, through the new technology of print, be brought out into the full light of the world and put to the service of humanity. He was, in short, becoming the complete humanist.

Nonetheless, he also remained a pragmatist. He knew how power politics worked and was perfectly happy to tailor his thinking to it. If princes were to be the true rulers of society, they should abandon their militaristic tendencies, embrace the *studia humanitatis* and rule not through the abuse of power but through wisdom. Yet as with many humanists, it was impossible to tell where his reforming zeal stopped and his self-interest began. Behind every good prince was a good educator. Erasmus needed a patron. That December, from a wintry Paris, he wrote to Colet.

His letter, he knew, had to be finely judged. Insulated by his family's phenomenal mercantile wealth and connections, Colet viewed with fastidious distaste the desperate scrabbling-after-favour of the less privileged, of networking academics and clergymen who ran, panting, after 'fat benefices and high promotions' – even when it involved his friends. Erasmus pressed all the right buttons. Heaping fulsome praise on Colet's scholarship, he said how desperate he was for someone to help him realize his 'burning zeal for sacred studies', and enclosed a copy of his new book, the *Enchiridion*, of which he knew Colet would approve: an all-purpose spiritual guide to everyday life based on a pure piety and 'true goodness' rather than relics, images, cults and convoluted ceremonial and liturgy.[1]

But Erasmus also had some awkward explaining to do. The previous year, he had written a poem in praise of Philip of Burgundy, a syrupy panegyric dripping with wheedling flattery of the worst kind. He had been reluctant to write it, he told Colet; in fact, he could not remember ever having done anything 'more unwillingly'. However, he continued, his panegyric was not just sycophancy. It was, in fact, a 'novel stratagem', something more subtle: a way of educating princes, of speaking truth to power without seeming to do so.

In telling Philip how wonderful he was, Erasmus was in fact telling him how he ought to behave. What better way to reproach a wicked ruler 'more safely, yet more severely', than by proclaiming his mildness, or 'for his greed, violence and lust, than by celebrating his generosity, self-control and chastity?' This 'pattern for goodness' became a way to 'reform bad rulers, improve the good, educate the boorish'. In Erasmus's hands, flattery had become advice, praise a policy document. A new twist to the kind of 'advice to princes' literature that had been peddled hopefully to princes for centuries, it also subtly repositioned the relationship between the intellectual and his patron. It showed that scholars were not a frivolous luxury, but essential to princes: they educated them, and they made them glorious too.[2]

Although in his letter to Colet Erasmus seemed to deprecate his panegyric to Philip, he shrewdly guessed that the picture it depicted of a glorious, learned prince was likely to prove as effective a calling-card as anything else he had written. For it was not Colet that he had in his sights, but his former pupil Lord Mountjoy – and through Mountjoy, his student Prince Henry, now heir to the English throne. Would Colet, Erasmus asked delicately, put in a discreet word on his behalf with Mountjoy? It would make sense, given their previous association – but he was terrible at petitioning for favour and could not possibly approach Mountjoy himself.[3]

Erasmus's letter worked a treat. By autumn 1505 he was back in London, boasting how Mountjoy had 'pressingly invited me to come back to England'. Settling into the comfort of Mountjoy's townhouse in Knightrider Street, he looked up old friends, Colet, Grocyn, Linacre, and Thomas More, now immersed in his legal career and in city life. Erasmus basked in their attention: 'without flattering myself', he purred, 'I do believe there is not one of them who does not pay high tribute to my talents and learning'. Fuelled by his friends' admiration, and Mountjoy's expansive predictions of rewards forthcoming from Henry VII, Erasmus was convinced that a torrent of royal favour would soon be flowing in his direction. Previous experience should have warned him not to take Mountjoy's words at face value.[4]

Erasmus was entirely ignorant of the transformation that had taken place since his last visit: that Mountjoy's conditions of office, hedged about with bonds and financial sureties, had left him rushed off his feet, constantly looking over his shoulder for royal informers eager to make money reporting alleged infractions of service; and that Prince Henry was now incubated in his father's household. As Erasmus would find, the king and his advisers had a hard-edged attitude to scholarship that was worlds away from the enquiring dilettantism of Eltham.

In seeking favour from Henry, Erasmus was treading a path already well worn by the footsteps of countless humanists who, from France,

Italy and the Low Countries, had come to England flourishing presentation manuscripts of fashionable Latin and Greek texts, which they hoped would be passports to royal favour. As his sons' tuition had shown, Henry knew the value of a cutting-edge classical education, and he loved employing foreigners. But for him intellectual brilliance was only half the equation. When he admired the erudition of foreign men-of-letters, he did so wondering how they could serve him, how they could add value and authority to his rule and his dynasty, how they could provide the access that he craved to the courts and chancelleries, trading centres and financial and commodity markets of Europe.

As Erasmus's friends would tell him, actually getting to Henry was the most difficult thing of all. It meant approaching the cluster of senior foreign policy advisers, canon lawyers with their interests in international culture and political theory who were the gatekeepers to his favour, who appraised, selected and vetted people for diplomatic service. At their head was Henry's omnipresent éminence grise, the man whom scholar after scholar had addressed hopefully as Maecenas, that epitome of classical patrons, and whose hand lay behind the royal preferment of practically every humanist during the course of Henry's rule: the privy seal and bishop of Winchester, Richard Fox.

While Erasmus had a sophisticated grasp of how humanist letters might be put to the service of power, he had little desire to enter the cut-throat world of power politics, to commit himself, like Adriano Castellesi, to be *ex toto anglicus*, English through and through. Rather, he wanted the freedom of the public intellectual, with his international network of friends, drifting from house to house, country to country, wherever there was good conversation, ample hospitality and – with any luck – funding.[5] But Erasmus and his friends would find that their attempts to gain favour with the king and his counsellors would become enmeshed in political rivalries, faction and the machinations of Henry's international affairs.

At first, all seemed well. Erasmus was 'in high favour', he felt, and spent much of his time getting reacquainted with his friend Thomas More. Recently married, More had moved into a sprawling stone-

and-timber manor house, the Old Barge, in the middle of London. In Bucklersbury, a narrow street lined with herbalists and druggists' shops, the house's name was a nod to the nearby Walbrook, the paved-over waterway which in former times brought boats up from the Thames into the heart of the city. A short walk east lay the Stocks Market and the financial district of Lombard Street; to the north, across the teeming thoroughfare of Cheapside, lay the headquarters of the Mercers' company, from whom More had rented his accommodation, and Guildhall, the centre of London's political life.

More's debate with himself about whether or not to enter this world, to test himself against its dangers and pitfalls, had found expression in his recent translation of a biography of Pico della Mirandola, the Italian thinker whose deep spirituality had a profound and formative influence on him. More's *Life of Pico* stressed the Italian's refusal to compromise his principles, his constant cheerfulness in the face of tribulation, and his eventual turning away from the world to a life of piety. Pico was a 'pattern of life' to More – not least because More, like him, was drawn irresistibly towards that public arena whose temptations and corruptibility he so feared. All this was evident in a letter that More had written to Colet, in which, describing his native London as a claustrophobic city of sin, he lingered over a description of its vices with a brilliant, lascivious relish.

The overhanging upper storeys of buildings, he wrote, leaned in on the narrow streets, seeming to block out natural light. The atmosphere choked and asphyxiated, heightening the senses: the gleam of goldsmiths' and silversmiths' shops, the fine, richly coloured silks of drapers, the tempting scents of cooking mingling with the sights and smells of decay and corruption. All this, More wrote, to produce an endless supply of 'materials for gluttony and the world, and the world's lord, the devil'.[6] This was now More's everyday life, surrounded by 'feigned love and the honeyed poisons of smooth flatterers', by 'fierce hatred and quarrels'. It was a struggle that he found intoxicating, and his vocal opposition to Henry's tax in the 1504 parliament displayed a desire to get involved at the sharp end of politics. Despite – or perhaps because of – all this, Erasmus found his friend, at the centre of a busy household surrounded by servants and the constant stream of lawyers, clients and city and royal officials that beat a path to his door, as 'cheerful as ever'.[7]

For his part, More was delighted to see Erasmus. He, too, had been working hard on his Greek, and he suggested to his friend that they translate into Latin some dialogues of Lucian, a withering classical satirist newly in vogue. This would be not just a linguistic exercise but also a political one. As an exposer of sham and pretension, a scourge of sacred and secular customs, Lucian's relevance appealed to both men – and he would, they hoped, also appeal to Henry VII's counsellors, to whom they planned to present their work.

Erasmus made new acquaintances too, among them a young Italian scholar recently arrived in England. Andrea Ammonio had made the long journey from Rome not in hope, but in expectation. The son of silk-weavers from the Tuscan city of Lucca, he had gone to Rome to seek his fortune at the papal curia, where he had joined the circle of Lucchese high in the favour of Pope Julius II. Among them was Silvestro Gigli, Henry's ambassador and bishop of Worcester, who had taken the talented young intellectual under his wing. When, having helped secure the dispensation for Prince Henry's marriage to Catherine, Gigli made his triumphant journey back to England in mid-1505, Ammonio travelled with him. Staying in the Gigli household in Coleman Street Ward, south of Lombard Street, he settled among the Italian expatriate community and quickly made friends with Mountjoy and More.[8] But the man whose acquaintance he was desperate to make was Erasmus, whom he hero-worshipped. For his part Erasmus, who always welcomed the company of charming young men, was particularly taken with Ammonio.

Like Erasmus, Ammonio would not find things in England as straightforward as he suspected. Neither would his boss, the divisive and self-aggrandizing Gigli, who brought the combustible politics of Italy and the papal curia into the heart of Henry VII's court and, via Ammonio, to the intellectuals who aimed to shape the king's son: More, Erasmus and Mountjoy.

Away in Rome, Henry's other representative at the curia, Cardinal Adriano Castellesi, had developed a persecution complex. Convinced that Julius II, with his venomous hatred of everybody and everything associated with the former regime of the Borgia pope Alexander VI, was intriguing against him, he was also sure that his place in Henry VII's favour was slipping, that the king was sidelining him for the more effective Gigli.

Castellesi's pressure valve was gossip, and he started sniping about his English employer. Inevitably, his comments reached the pope's inner circle and found their way – doubtless via his rival Gigli, now at the king's side in England – to Henry himself.[9] Julius also stoked the fire. When he received a letter from an incensed Henry, demanding to know if the rumours about Castellesi were true, Julius seemed to defend the cardinal before murmuring that yes, perhaps he had been a little indiscreet.

When news of the correspondence reached Castellesi, he was thoroughly alarmed. He fired off a letter to Henry, protesting that he was loyalty itself and that the whole thing was a smear campaign, designed to blacken his good name. He also realized that he needed to do something about Gigli. Writing to Richard Fox, the man who had done much to advance him in the king's favour over the years, Castellesi suggested he examine very closely the documentation that Gigli had brought back to England with him from Rome. Gigli, said Castellesi, was in the habit of forging documents, and he had proof: one of the papal licences appointing the diplomat Robert Sherborne to the bishopric of St Davids was a fake. Fox agreed.

An accusation of this kind was potential dynamite. For if one of the papal documents Gigli had obtained were proven to be false, the validity of others could be called into question – including the most significant document of all, which had made his English reputation: the dispensation for Catherine's remarriage to the prince. Henry may have had his son repudiate the marriage, but it had been done in secret, and was something he could always reverse if circumstances dictated. If, on the other hand, the dispensation wasn't worth the parchment it was written on, then neither was Catherine – and Henry would be deprived of one of his most significant cards at the poker-table of European power politics.

Henry was enraged. He hated his affairs being made public at the best of times, and this very conspicuous spat between two of his ambassadors did nothing for his credibility in Rome. The affair provoked an uproar among Henry's high-level diplomats. Sherborne, Gigli and their chief backer William Warham – who, as archbishop of Canterbury, perhaps felt duty-bound to back the pope's favoured representatives – were ranged against Castellesi's supporters, headed by Fox.[10] On the face of it, Fox's backing of the increasingly paranoid and gaffe-prone cardinal seems curious. Gigli was high in papal favour and Henry, lavishing gifts and offices on him, was surely grooming him to replace Castellesi as England's point man in Rome. But Fox continued to support Castellesi – and, despite his anger, Henry was content to tolerate him as well.

Castellesi, of course, had a long association with both the king and with Fox, and his largely faithful record of service probably counted for something. Henry always liked to have at least two independent lines of intelligence in any situation, so that he and his council could compare – and contrast – information that was sent them. Where Gigli was a papal loyalist, Castellesi was now a distinctly contrarian voice, increasingly disinclined to toe the papal party line. This was of particular use to Henry. Although he went out of his way to show himself a faithful son of the church, lavishing favour on the pope's friends and relatives, he was deeply concerned about what Julius II was up to.

Following his election, Julius was proving the latest in a long line of popes ambitious to transform the papacy into a secular power to be reckoned with. His predecessor, Alexander VI, had attempted much the same thing. Trying to turn the papacy into what was more or less a Borgia family empire, Alexander had constructed a succession of complex and changeable alliances with a variety of European states, from France, to Venice, Spain and the Habsburgs against France, then back to France with Venice's help, mostly under the pretext of a crusade against the Turks (whose help against France he had at one stage also unsuccessfully tried to enlist). When Alexander VI died, the inevitable happened: his allies moved in. Declaring itself 'liberator' of the rich lands in the Romagna conquered by Alexander's son Cesare Borgia, Venice annexed them.[11]

The republic of Venice irritated Julius beyond measure. Not only had it absorbed papal lands into a land and maritime empire that stretched from Bologna to Cyprus, but it had a stranglehold on eastern Mediterranean trade and, as far as the Turks were concerned, far preferred peace – and profit – to crusade, to the detriment of papal finances. One commodity that Venice continued to import in huge quantities, turning a deaf ear to Julius's increasingly strident orders to desist, was alum. Desperate to protect the value of papal alum through the papacy's cartels, Julius took a particularly dim view of Venice flooding a northern European market desperate for the mineral. If the republic would not stop, then he would put a stop to it.[12]

For Henry, Julius's belligerence was highly problematic. The pope was muscling into the Italian financial and commercial centres with which Henry did considerable business: Genoa, and the Tuscan cities of Florence and Lucca. And in the economic superpower of Venice he was targeting one of England's main trading partners, whose galleys, en route to the Low Countries, docked at Southampton loaded with luxurious commodities, and exported vast quantities of English wool and cloth for processing and reselling by the thirty thousand employees of Venice's textile industry. What was more, in agitating for his crusade, Julius had started moves to bring together the mutually antagonistic dynastic players in Italy – Spain, France and the Habsburgs – in an anti-Venetian alliance, a move that would realign Europe in a way entirely contrary to Henry's plans. If Julius could bring off such a reconciliation, it would wreck Henry's self-styled role as European power-broker. And then there was the alum, in whose illegal trade Henry was involved up to his eyeballs, brokering deals through Florentine banks, and doubtless with the co-operation of Venice, the gateway to the eastern Mediterranean.[13]

Apart from the considerable profits alum brought him, Henry understood perfectly well the political ramifications of what he was doing. By increasing the alum supply, he lowered its value and hence papal profits, something which was an effective bridle on Julius's ambitions. At the same time, it allowed him a handle on international affairs.

For his part, Julius knew exactly what Henry was doing. By 1505 he was chasing the king's carrack, the *Sovereign* – funded by the Frescobaldi bank and skippered by one of Henry's chief captains, Nicholas Waring – around the western Mediterranean, writing to princes from Portugal to Genoa promising indulgences to any who detained the ship, arrested its crew and impounded its cargo. But besides issuing irate proclamations and writing letters to Henry telling him to desist, there was not a great deal the pope could do. Julius simply did not have the muscle to back up his threats. Henry made polite, obedient noises in reply, and ignored him.

In all this, Castellesi assumed a greater significance. As the former private secretary to Alexander VI, he had a wealth of experience and contacts with Venice, the former Borgia ally. In Castellesi's unseemly spat with Gigli, Julius's man, foreign policy on a grand scale crystallized. And, as the dispute involved Henry's foremost diplomatic advisers, Fox and Warham, on either side, it also sucked in others.[14] With courtiers and counsellors aligned around the two Italians, a discernible fracture began to emerge among the intellectuals at court. In Gigli's corner, Warham was an admirer of Erasmus and sympathetic to Andrea Ammonio. Like Gigli himself, these avant-garde men-of-letters were desperate for royal favour – and envious and contemptuous of those who had it. Faction began to emerge.

One of the men in possession of such favour was Castellesi's deputy, Polydore Vergil. Arriving in England in 1502, when his boss was still in high favour with Henry, he recalled how the king was 'gracious and kind', 'attentive to visitors'; Vergil, indeed, is probably the first and only courtier to go on record as saying that Henry was 'easy of access'. Whereas the doors to royal favour remained shut fast to most, to Vergil they swung magically open.

To those in residence at the Old Barge, Vergil inspired envy and fury in equal measure. Erasmus loathed him, labouring under the mistaken belief that Vergil had stolen the idea for his *Adages*, the collection of classical proverbs and epigrams that he had published in Paris on his return from England in 1500, and which became his first international bestseller. Vergil's admittedly very similar book had in fact been published before his own, something he would later acknowledge. But Erasmus's grudge was fuelled not only by envy of Vergil's success and wealth but also by his friend Ammonio, whose resentment of Vergil took on a political edge: Vergil and Ammonio eyeballed each other with mutual suspicion, Castellesi's man against Gigli's.[15] There was, however, another Italian at court who attracted the ire of everybody in Erasmus's circle: Henry's Latin secretary, Pietro Carmeliano. Not only was Carmeliano close to the king, at the nerve centre of his foreign policy, and very rich to boot, he was also a Venetian agent.

A native of the Lombard city of Brescia in Venetian territory, Carmeliano had been an unobtrusive presence at Henry's side since the start of the reign, when he had transferred his loyalties easily and effortlessly from Richard III. His literary skills attracted scorn from Erasmus and his friends – but as a tireless, well-connected diplomat and spy he had proved himself exceptional. As a royal chaplain, Carmeliano was a familiar face in the king's private apartments, where he and Henry discussed confidential foreign affairs. He was inconspicuous, a man who stayed in the shadows, going largely unnoticed by English courtiers. Foreigners and diplomatic staff, however, watched his movements like hawks. When he disappeared from public view, they reasoned, it generally meant that something was up: back in 1500, when last-minute doubts surfaced over Prince Arthur's marriage to Catherine, de Puebla had got particularly jumpy at the Italian's absence, thinking that he was involved in negotiations to marry Arthur off to somebody else. Close to Henry, Carmeliano had quietly accumulated massive wealth. One year, his New Year's gift to Henry of £50 trumped that of Sir Thomas Lovell, one of Henry's richest counsellors, by a cool £30.

Somehow, Carmeliano had maintained loyalties to both Henry and to Venice for two decades. His influence reached behind the marble façade of the Doge's palace, to the heart of its government, the Signoria, to whom he was known simply as 'the friend'. As he stood demurely at the king's side, writing and performing diplomatic orations, penning official letters, and tiptoeing about the privy apartments, Carmeliano was also a go-between, Venice's man in the king's secret chamber. And, as papal sabre-rattling against the republic grew ever louder, so his role as Henry's foreign-policy adviser became increasingly significant. From his privileged vantage point, Carmeliano eyed the manoeuvrings of Julius's favourite Silvestro Gigli, watched him circling ever closer to the king's counsellors.[16] He would have been perturbed when Henry appointed Gigli to the small coterie of royal chaplains that doubled as high-level diplomats, papal intriguer and Venetian agent sizing each other up as they discussed international affairs with the king. And neither was he particularly well disposed to Gigli's protégé Ammonio, who, he rightly suspected, was after his job.

By the end of 1505, Erasmus had finished the first of his dialogues. He aimed high. On 1 January 1506, he sent a presentation manuscript to Richard Fox, prefaced by a typically arch, self-abasing dedication that begged him to accept the 'trivial' New Year's gift, and hoped that he would continue to 'cherish, succour and help Erasmus, as you have done for so long'. In fact, there was no indication that Fox had ever helped Erasmus. Nor was he about to.[17]

Erasmus's timing could not have been worse. At the turn of that year, Henry's counsellors were working frantically to prise the earl of Suffolk from Philip of Burgundy's stronghold of Namur; barely two weeks after Erasmus's manuscript landed on Fox's desk Philip was shipwrecked on the Dorset coast. Fox, the arch-diplomat, was at the forefront of the reception committee and the ensuing negotiations for Suffolk's extradition. He was up to his ears in work, and petitioners of all kinds were getting short shrift: the archdeacon of Wells found Fox, as he delicately put it, 'somewhat rough' at a meeting, though he had recovered his silky demeanour the following day. Worse still, with Henry mobilizing all available resources in his extended charm offensive, Lord Mountjoy was also co-opted, dancing attendance on the volatile Queen Juana. Erasmus's impeccably turned phrases fell on deaf ears.[18]

He tried other avenues. On the 24th he and William Grocyn wandered down the teeming Thamesside streets to the river, where they took a boat west to the archbishop of Canterbury's palace at Lambeth. There, William Warham received Erasmus's literary gift with enthusiasm but, as Erasmus acidly pointed out to his friend as they were rowed back to London, bestowed only a meagre tip by way of reward. With a twinkle in his eye, Grocyn replied that the archbishop suspected Erasmus got full value from his works by dedicating them to a number of different patrons at once.[19] Erasmus, characteristically, bridled. Grocyn, however, had hit the nail on the head: if Erasmus was to attain substantial favour, he would have to make real demonstrations of his commitment and loyalty.

Months passed. In the first days of April Erasmus wrote exasperatedly and with typical self-absorption that Philip of Burgundy, who was still in England, had distracted Henry from delivering on the benefice that – Mountjoy had assured Erasmus – he had promised, and that his English stay was now costing him 'a pretty penny'. But through all Erasmus's correspondence at this time, the name notable by its absence was that of the prince.

If Erasmus managed to catch any glimpse of Prince Henry during this time, it seems to have been fleeting. A crashing name-dropper, he would have been sure to mention any prolonged meeting with the prince in his letters. Not only was access to the prince restricted but Erasmus's avenue to him, Lord Mountjoy, had his hands full, running around at court after Philip and Juana – and 'at his own expense', Erasmus reported, no doubt echoing Mountjoy's own grumbles – not to mention his responsibilities at Hammes. The prince, meanwhile, was fully absorbed with Philip and his knights, revelling in the war-like chivalric culture by which Erasmus was so appalled. But though Erasmus may have been out of sight, he was not wholly out of mind. Later, commenting on Henry VIII's letter-writing, he would remark that it was 'no wonder the prince had a pleasing style' since Mountjoy, Erasmus's own protégé, had encouraged him to read Erasmus's works.[20]

As spring drew on, Erasmus was fast running out of cash, patience and literary gifts. He sent another dialogue to Richard Whitford, the Cambridge academic who had accompanied Mountjoy on his study trip to France years before, and who was now chaplain to Richard Fox; yet another went to the powerful, highly influential secretary to Henry himself, Fox's associate Thomas Ruthall. In his dedications to both men, Erasmus featured Thomas More's name prominently, reminding Whitford how he used to describe Erasmus and More as two peas in a pod, so similar in outlook that 'no pair of twins on earth could be more alike', and telling Ruthall that he had written to him on More's advice. Not only did More's name carry weight, it was clear that he was the guiding spirit behind Erasmus's programme of dedications.

Later, when the Lucianic dialogues were printed – they became bestsellers, running through at least fourteen editions – More dedicated his own part in the dialogues solely to Ruthall, and compared to

Erasmus's, More's letter was altogether more focused. He highlighted Lucian's scourging of ecclesiastical privilege, something that would have pressed the right buttons with a man who knew how noxious Henry found the church's ability to override the king's law. Praising Ruthall's learning, his skill in diplomacy and loyalty – 'without complete confidence in these qualities of yours our wise monarch would never have chosen you as his secretary' – More offered the dialogues as a token of 'my willingness to serve you'. Unlike Erasmus, More sensed instinctively how to go about seeking favour.

Erasmus's dedications in the first months of 1506 failed to secure him any meaningful recognition. Swallowing his pride, he approached Henry's historiographer, Bernard André, for help, but the instincts of the blind Augustinian canon remained sharp. Erasmus thought André a 'backbiter' for having turned the king against his friend Thomas Linacre years earlier; now, it seemed, André led Erasmus a similarly merry dance. Erasmus recollected how he had followed a 'blind guide . . . And so, being blind myself and having chosen a blind man to lead me, the result was that we both fell into the ditch.'

He had better results with Carmeliano who, in return for a gift of money, received the loose change of Erasmus's flattery: Carmeliano, he wrote, was the 'high prince of elegance', a 'prince of letters'. In fact, Erasmus thought him nothing of the sort. Back at the Old Barge, he, More and Ammonio bitched about the Latin secretary's uninspired and ungrammatical Latin. As Erasmus later wrote to Richard Whitford, there were plenty at the English court who claimed to be steeped in the most eloquent authors – which was surprising, given there were 'so few who do not seem totally inarticulate' when called upon to deliver an official speech.[21] All this, of course, was born out of feelings of resentment and insecurity, as much as intellectual superiority. And to the chagrin of Erasmus and Ammonio, somebody else was getting ahead at court, someone whose scholarly credentials could not be impugned: Polydore Vergil.

As Philip of Burgundy finally left that April, Henry, with the ink still wet on the new Anglo-Habsburg treaty, and with his conversations with Philip fresh in his mind, was thinking of new ways to cement his legacy. As Erasmus had noted, Henry 'especially regarded' the study of history. Now, he wanted a new history of England, one which underscored his family and its achievements, and written in fashionable humanist Latin for international consumption.

Vergil was perfectly placed to write it. Since his arrival in England four years previously, he had immersed himself in his adopted country's history, keeping a journal in which he jotted down his thoughts and ideas. While he delighted in some native historians – the muscular Latin of the sixth-century Gildas, and the worldly erudition of the twelfth-century monk William of Malmesbury – he could barely disguise his contempt for the most popular chronicle of them all: Geoffrey of Monmouth's bestselling *History of the Kings of England*, which had given new impetus and credibility to the founding myth of King Arthur in British history. Monmouth's twelfth-century work, in Vergil's eyes, was barely history at all. It was 'fable', he spat; he could barely mention it without 'extreme distaste'.

Vergil could learn about the traumatic events of England's recent past from those who had been intimately involved in it. A number of those people were his diplomatic colleagues, sources 'worthy of credit' like Richard Fox. It was very probably Fox – who Vergil would write prominently into his account as a man of 'excellent wit' – that suggested Vergil's name to Henry. Summoned to the king's presence, Vergil was commissioned to write an official history of England, which would encompass, as Henry put it, 'the deeds of his people . . . from early times to the present day' – with his family as the latest and most glorious instalment.[22]

The result, Vergil's *Anglica Historia*, would be years in the writing, and Henry would not live to see the result. First completed in 1513, it was finally printed in 1534 in a form substantially revised to suit the convulsive politics of those years. From prehistory to Vergil's present, it would be England's first modern history: a continuous narrative structured around the lives of kings, and containing analysis – 'digressions', Vergil called them – on everything from his source material to the country's political development.[23] And while Vergil's account, with its sustained assault on the Arthurian 'British history' tradition, was vilified in some quarters, it was astonishingly influential. In his *Chronicle* of 1548 the lawyer Edmund Hall paid it the ultimate compliment, translating it and passing copious undigested chunks of it off as his own work. By the end of the sixteenth century, the *Anglica Historia* had become the accepted national story, as Shakespeare recognized: the plots of his history plays, *Richard II*, the two parts of *Henry IV*, *Henry V* and *Richard III*, are pure Vergil.[24] The Italian, in fact, might be said to be one of the most influential English historians of them all – and Fox, one of the architects of Henry's reign, was the man who spotted his potential.

In mid-1506 Erasmus finally got his break. It came in the unexpected form of Giovanni Battista Boerio, a member of London's affluent Genoese community and, as one of Henry VII's physicians and diplomats, a man with regular access to the king. Boerio asked Erasmus to accompany his two sons to Italy and supervise their education; Erasmus, who had been dreaming of a trip to Italy for decades, leaped at the chance. By the start of June, he was en route with his two young charges. After an appalling, four-day-long Channel crossing, he recovered for some days with Mountjoy in Hammes Castle, from where he dispatched the last of his Lucianic dialogues and a series of valedictory letters to his friends in England: More, and Ammonio, for whom things at court had failed to improve, and whose mood was darkened still further by the departure of his intellectual mentor. Far from home, disillusioned and short of cash, Ammonio was appalled by London's noise and grime – 'the dirt of these people is altogether hateful to me', he sniffed fastidiously in a letter to Erasmus. His only refuge, it seemed, was the Old Barge, where he spent an increasing amount of time.[25]

As Erasmus made his way to Italy in the summer of 1506, Pope Julius II was on the warpath. Agitating for a new Holy League, a grand coalition to confront the Turkish armies rampant in southeast Europe and the eastern Mediterranean, he announced the latest in a long line of papal calls for a crusade. But whether or not the Ottoman Empire was his ultimate end in view, his immediate aim was Venice: to reconquer the papal states it had annexed and, ultimately, to bring the republic to its knees. To fund his military adventures, Julius knew he had to protect his revenues. On 17 May, he launched his most forceful and wide-ranging papal proclamation to date against the illegal alum trade. The first of its kind to be printed, it was addressed to 'all persons secular or ecclesiastical, of whatever state or condition they might be'. It inveighed against iniquitous dealers and brokers involved in the trade, and forbade, under pain of anathema, all Christian princes and their subjects to have anything to do with any other alum than that which came from the Tolfa mines, whose alum was 'reserved and consecrated to the preparations for a great crusade against the Sultan of Constantinople'.

Throughout the financial centres of northern Europe, from the Low Countries to London, papal representatives marched into banking houses and served the bull on merchants, together with covering letters stating that dealings with certain alum speculators, who were 'the source of a pernicious contagion to the souls of the faithful', were certain to be harmful to the spiritual health of those faithful to Christ. In Bruges, the papal commissioner's letter included a list of the dealers to be avoided. Among the seven principal names were 'Nicolas Vuaringh', or Nicholas Waring, the skipper of Henry's ship the *Sovereign*; the head of the Frescobaldi company Jerome, or Girolamo, da Frescobaldi; and Louis – or Lodovico – della Fava, Henry's own broker.[26]

In the Low Countries, publication of the bull provoked enough consternation to make Margaret of Savoy, Henry's hoped-for bride, summon her council for an urgent discussion of the situation. But in London, the pronouncement appeared to have no effect at all. Julius had dispatched a new commissioner, Pietro Griffo, to remind Henry of his responsibilities and to persuade him to join the crusade.[27] Henry was unmoved. Having previously contributed funds both to the pope and to the knights of St John of Jerusalem – earlier that year, he had received the rare title of 'protector' to the knights' garrison at Rhodes – he was perfectly enthusiastic for the idea of a crusade; just not Julius's war against Venice.

That autumn, at the head of an army of Swiss mercenaries and French soldiers, Julius cut an all-conquering swath through the Romagna, the Venetian armies in headlong retreat. As he entered Bologna in triumph on 11 November, away in Richmond Lodovico della Fava came to Henry with a new business proposition. He offered the king the opportunity to invest in a consignment of 7,000 hundredweight of alum worth £10,000 – a huge deal, by any standards. Henry would pay in two tranches, 60 per cent up front. As usual, as well as this cheap consignment of high-grade alum, he would receive from della Fava and the Frescobaldi company customs duties payable on the imports, and a large fee for the lease of the vessel in which the consignment would be shipped. Edmund Dudley, who helped broker the deal, was also present, itemizing everything in his account book, which was signed, as ever, by the king. The combined sum owing to Henry on customs duties and lease of his 4-masted, 600-ton, 225-cannon carrack *Regent* – the perfect way to transport such a precious cargo – was £5,100. And on 18 December, the chamber treasurer John Heron signed off the first instalment of £6,000 to della Fava, who drew up bills of exchange to send to the Frescobaldi branch in Florence.[28] Henry had effectively ripped up Julius's papal bull and thrown it in his face.

Livid, Julius recalled Pietro Griffo, ordering him to fix copies of the papal censure to every English church door he passed on his way to Dover. Little did Julius know, but during his stay at the English court Griffo had succumbed to temptation. Whatever his conversation with Henry had been, the outcome was glaringly evident in an entry in Dudley's account book: 'Pope's orator Peter de Griffo for licence and custom of 1,300 kintals [hundredweight] of alum to come in by assent of Lodovico della Fava £433 6s 8d by obligation.' Sent by Julius to persuade Henry to give up his illegal alum racket, Griffo had come in on it instead. Even for the pope's own commissioner, the lure of alum had proved too great to resist.[29]

Money, of course, was not the only motivating factor. Julius's efforts to form an anti-Venetian coalition in the form of a Holy League were bearing fruit, and with it, a growing threat to Henry. If Julius really could reconcile the French king Louis XII, Maximilian and Ferdinand, it would throw a spanner in the fine mechanism of Henry's balance-of-power diplomacy, and might well destroy his vision for an Anglo-Habsburg-dominated Europe into the bargain. In fact, Henry had pursued his own, apparently genuine initiatives to broker a crusade coalition involving England, Castile and Portugal. The following year, he wrote with apparent ingenuousness to Julius, to urge peace between Christian princes in order to co-ordinate a crusade against the Turks, with the implication that the pope should lay off Venice.

Henry had the welfare of Christendom at heart – but he saw no reason why he should not make a tidy profit at the same time.[30]

○

Lodovico della Fava's contact at the Italian end of the alum deal, Giovanni Cavalcanti, was from a prestigious Florentine family. Leaving the city following the fall of the Medici in 1494, he had gone into business, working as a broker in the Frescobaldis' Rome offices.[31] Coupling a sharp business mind with a sophisticated taste in antiquities, in early 1506 he had been in Rome during one of the defining discoveries of the Renaissance, the unearthing of the 1,500-year-old statue of the Trojan priest Laocoön and his two sons being strangled by sea serpents: Cavalcanti wrote of the 'miracle' that had kept intact the sculpture's tortured, writhing complexity. But he was also an enthusiastic patron of contemporary arts. Among the artists he favoured were Michelangelo Buonarroti, the pre-eminent Florentine sculptor of the age, and Michelangelo's childhood friend and rival, Pietro Torrigiano. Torrigiano was a sculptor of great talent; he was also a liability.

Glowering and hot-headed, Torrigiano revelled in the chaos of early sixteenth-century Italy, filling in between jobs as a mercenary in the ravening army of Cesare Borgia. And he fell out spectacularly with Michelangelo, whose success had put him firmly in the shade, and who had a habit of getting under his skin. Once, when Michelangelo had been winding him up, Torrigiano smashed his nose in. 'I felt bone and cartilage go down like biscuit beneath my knuckles', he recalled proudly, adding that his friend would carry that mark 'to the grave' – as indeed he did.[32]

It was very probably the man involved in Henry's alum deal, Cavalcanti, who suggested to the frustrated sculptor that he try his luck in England. There, he would be free of Michelangelo's oppressive shadow and besides, the English king's keen interest in sculpture was well known. In their dusty studios Florentine artists chiselled busily away at portrait busts of 'Enrico VII', orders brought back from England by merchants doing business with Henry. The dispatch of Torrigiano, a Florentine artist of the first order, was the perfect way to flatter

Henry, to add a dash of fashionable Tuscan glamour to his court – and to cement the Frescobaldi company's ever-closer ties with it.[33]

Indeed, Henry's thoughts of his legacy were increasingly Italian-inflected. Years before, the Florentine merchant Francesco Portinari had, at his request, sent him the statutes for Florence's hospital of Santa Maria Nuova, Europe's pre-eminent medical institution. Poring over them, Henry set his sights on a foundation to rival it. He fixed on a site on the south side of London's Strand, sloping down to the Thames: his ancestor John of Gaunt's palace of the Savoy. Sacked over a century previously by Kentish commoners marauding through London in the Peasants' Revolt of 1381, it had since stood derelict. In 1505, as Erasmus arrived in England, Henry set the wheels in motion for a major new charitable project. Just as Richmond had rivalled the great palaces of Burgundy, the Savoy Hospital would aim to outdo Florence's 'first hospital among Christians'. Founded on Portinari's plans, and taking almost a decade to build, it would be the first great architectural expression of the Italian Renaissance in England – rendered in English Gothic.[34]

Meanwhile, the outline of Henry's new chapel at Westminster Abbey was beginning to emerge from under its forest of scaffolding. It would be his family's mausoleum, housing Queen Elizabeth's tomb and, alongside it, his own. Henry had been thinking about the tomb for some time, procuring an estimate and design by the Modenese sculptor Guido Mazzoni. Mazzoni, who had previously carved out a glittering career at the French court, had been in England for almost a decade, during which time his work had included the finely observed bust of the laughing boy now widely assumed to be Prince Henry. In 1507, however, he had returned to France. Whether he had been dismissed from the project, or whether he had left voluntarily, is unclear – but it left an opportunity for someone else.[35]

Around the same time, Pietro Torrigiano arrived in London. Lodging with della Fava at the opulent Frescobaldi company mansion on Botolph Lane, south of the Italian enclave of Lombard Street and Austin Friars, he set out to find work. With della Fava to take up his cause, Torrigiano had what the likes of Erasmus and Ammonio lacked, a passport to Henry VII's court, through the people that mattered: his financiers. Henry's Italian business contacts had brought him the

Savoy hospital, the first architectural flowering of the English Renaissance; now, his alum deals would bring him its sculpture in the form
of Torrigiano. Soon, Giovanni Cavalcanti himself would arrive in
London and take over the reins from della Fava at the Frescobaldi
company offices, where he would be one of Torrigiano's chief sponsors. Torrigiano, meanwhile, would take over the work for Henry
VII's tomb. His impact on English art would be spectacular.[36]

By November 1506 a disillusioned Erasmus was finding that Italy was
not all it was cracked up to be. He beat a hasty retreat to Florence
from a newly 'liberated' Bologna, having been horrified by the spectacle of a warlike Pope Julius, at the head of his conquering army of
mercenaries and French troops, marching into the city. There, news
reached him of the death of Philip of Burgundy. Recalling the seemingly interminable months of feasting and entertainment that had
accompanied Philip's arrival in England earlier that year, Erasmus's
mind turned to the young English prince, some 1,500 miles away, and
he put pen to paper. Nobody in Bologna, he wrote to Prince Henry in
a letter of extravagant regret, could believe the sad reports of Philip's
demise, but they were 'too persistent to appear altogether unfounded'.
Whatever contact Erasmus had had with the prince during his recent
stay in England, he had evidently been all too aware of his infatuation
with Philip. Two months later, the prince wrote back.[37]

Composed in elegant Ciceronian Latin, Prince Henry's letter was a
small masterpiece in epistolary form. In it, he spoke of his 'great
unhappiness' at the death of Philip, his 'deeply, deeply regretted
brother' – indeed, he continued, he had not had such terrible news
since the death of his beloved mother, four years previously: 'I was',
he wrote, 'less enchanted with this part of your letter than its marvellous elegance deserved, for it seemed to re-open a wound which time
had healed.' Effusive in his praise of Erasmus's eloquence, the prince
urged him to continue the correspondence, and asked for updates on
Italian affairs.[38]

Heartfelt the letter may have been, but it was, too, a typical humanist schoolroom exercise, laboriously composed by a fifteen-year-old
boy with his teacher standing over him. Erasmus was impressed. Years

later, he wrote how he had tackled Mountjoy on the letter, asking him whether he had written it himself, for the prince to copy out. No, Mountjoy replied, producing drafts of the letter in the prince's hand, complete with crossings-out and corrections, it had all been his pupil's own work. There were, of course, subtexts to all this. In recounting the episode, Erasmus wanted to show off his own connections with nobility and royalty, all the while flattering Mountjoy's teaching skills – despite Mountjoy's protests to the contrary, it was as much his letter as the prince's.[39]

The letter also said something else: here was a young prince who knew the value of a humanist education, for whom intellectual culture was not simply a by-product of international diplomacy, trade or the currency markets, but something that was intrinsic, fundamental to the way he saw the world. Or, to put it another way, the letter showed Erasmus that Prince Henry, as king, would be a ruler who understood the importance of scholars – and who would reward them accordingly. Prince Henry may have been brought up to resemble the perfect knight, but to intellectuals like Erasmus, Ammonio and More he was beginning to look like the perfect, disinterested patron of learning, who would recognize the true talents of those excluded from favour under his father. At least, that was what they hoped.

The man who, more than anyone else, had brought together these two worlds was Lord Mountjoy, who, as Erasmus put it with his characteristically elegant flattery, was 'the most noble of scholars, most scholarly of noblemen, and in both classes the best'. There was, as Erasmus had acknowledged, a fundamental tension between the aims and ambitions of humanists, and those of noble ruling elites, a circle that he had tried to square in his *Panegyric*. It was a tension that Mountjoy himself embodied. When, some years later, Andrea Ammonio was about to send a new book of his verses to the printing press, he planned to include a fulsome dedication to Mountjoy that combined sycophantic praise with a scathing attack on the boorish ignorance of the nobility in general. Mountjoy, alarmed, had a quiet word with Erasmus, who wrote to his friend to tone it down. Mountjoy, he wrote, feared 'opprobrium' if the dedication were published: it would look as if he 'were glad to have men of his rank censured.'[40] In the final analysis, the classically educated, intellectually curious

Mountjoy identified himself first and foremost with the ranks of the king's 'natural counsellors', and with the traditions and values of the ranks from which he came. But as the reign reached its final terrifying stages, these brittle, divisive contradictions were submerged beneath a shared fear and loathing of Henry VII, and of those occupying positions of power around the increasingly remote king.

PART THREE

A State of Avarice

'For bleeding inwards and shut vapours strangle soonest and oppress most.'

Francis Bacon, Henry VII

'Right mighty prince & redoubted sovereign
From whom descendeth by the rightful line
Noble prince Henry to succeed the crown
That in his youth doth so clearly shine
In every virtue casting the vice adown
He shall of fame attain the high renown.'

Stephen Hawes, Pastime of Pleasure

11

Extraordinary Justice

According to the London chronicler, it was around the autumn of 1506 that things started to get really bad, when 'much sorrow' spread 'throughout the land'. Elaborating, he described how many 'unlawful and forgotten laws', some of them hundreds of years old, were reactivated to the 'great inquietness' of the king's subjects. This was something that had been going on for a while, he added, but recently, 'and especially since Empson and Dudley were set in authority', the situation had rapidly deteriorated.[1]

Two years had passed since Henry had given Empson the duchy of Lancaster seals, and with them the informal presidency of the council learned in the law. He had been impressed with the assiduity with which Empson worked, pursuing the king's rights with a ruthlessness of which Bray himself would have been proud, and had confirmed him in his post, appointing him chancellor of the duchy.[2] Under Empson, the council learned was becoming even more systematic, or rather, more indiscriminate. It pursued any and every case that was brought in front of it, irrespective of the reliability of the informers – often 'simple persons of small reputation and little credence', who were just out for what they could get, 'for to have a bribe' – who were motivated as much as anything else by personal animosity or personal gain.[3]

When hauled in front of the king's counsellors, people were presented with one option: to 'fall to agreement', which invariably meant paying fines and accepting financial bonds. Many, in order to mitigate their own financial punishment, agreed to turn informer themselves.[4] They had no choice. The council learned's ubiquitous 'letting and stopping of justice' and use of bonds meant that once people had been informed against to the king and his counsellors, they had stepped outside a world governed by recognized judicial processes into one of nightmarish contingency, from which there was no escape: where the law was the king's will, expressed by mutable committees that coalesced and fragmented, and in which paper trails vanished into thin air, into the duchy of Lancaster's offices, into the boxes in Henry's secret chamber – or into Edmund Dudley's house.

Since his appointment two years previously, Dudley had become the king's go-to man for legal and financial matters, from the dredging up of old debts and managing bonds to brokering Henry's investments. Theirs was a curiously intimate relationship, one defined entirely by their mutual absorption with the law, and by Dudley's ability to distort and twist it into baroque patterns. The evidence of their private discussions lies in Dudley's account book – page after page of fines and payments for every conceivable offence and opportunity: the sale of export licences, wards, marriages, lucrative crown lands and 'temporalities', the sinecures that accompanied religious office; the king's favour in everything from royal appointments to court cases; and, throughout, the sale of justice, fees for royal pardons for offences from illegal wool-trading and customs infringements to murder. At the bottom of each page, the king signed his monogram, the imprimatur to their decisions. One entry in Dudley's book seems to sum up their relationship: a note about the 'great book of jura regalia which I had of his highness'.[5] In order to help his protégé in his work, Henry had lent the counsellor his own book of sovereign rights. Of all Henry's counsellors, Dudley understood his system best – he even talked of knowing the king's 'inward mind' on the subject.

In 1506, Henry appointed Dudley president of the king's council. Two years after becoming a royal counsellor, and still only an esquire, he was the first layman ever to be appointed to a post traditionally held by one of the great lords spiritual. Now in his mid-forties, he had reached the very top. Dudley's promotion spoke volumes for Henry's priorities, and for his own effectiveness. Since the reshuffle that had followed Bray's death, the number of people in debt to the crown had soared, increasing by hundreds each year; the amounts owed on bonds and fines had also risen steeply and was rapidly climbing. For the calendar year of 1506 alone, debt due to the crown from financial sureties of one kind or another came to an unprecedented £106,382, a sum that, if all those debts were to be called in, would more than double the king's annual income.[6]

Something else had changed, too. It said something about the current atmosphere that even the days of Sir Reynold Bray had acquired a rosy glow. Bray, wrote the London chronicler, might have been 'rough' and intimidating, but at least he would never accept gifts, only food and drink. This, of course, was nonsense – Bray had made himself extremely rich through graft in the king's name, as indeed the chronicler, immediately contradicting himself, pointed out. But although Bray did take gifts, 'the giver was sure of a friend and a special solicitor in the matter'. Ultimately, the chronicler was saying, you had known where you stood with Bray: despite his harshness, he adhered to an accepted culture of lobbying, petitioning and palm-greasing, the sense of quid pro quo, favours bestowed for service rendered. Empson and Dudley, on the other hand, didn't.

Like all royal servants, their own interests blurred indistinctly with those of the crown. Showered with bribes, cash and land in exchange for 'secret labour' with the king, they took every opportunity that came their way – and proved particularly adept at doing so. Empson took bribes and fat ecclesiastical sinecures as danger money, for 'avoiding of his displeasure'; people paid him lobbying fees to further their legal cases, only to discover that he was also accepting money from the other side. When the Sussex gentleman Roger Lewknor was imprisoned for murder, Dudley sold him a pardon in return for the title deeds to his estates.[7]

These were men, the chronicler continued, who 'spoke pleasantly', in the smooth officialese that most of Henry's counsellors were accustomed to deploy, but 'did overthwartly'. In pushing the law to its limits, they lured people into making compromising statements and provoked them into seeking extra-legal ways of solving their problems, then accused them of breaking the law. Then, they sold their victims justice on the king's behalf. It was all, said one of Dudley's victims, Sir William Clopton, 'contrary to the right and order of the law'. Clopton's own case illustrated the point. Dudley had halted a private suit which Clopton was on the point of winning, then let it proceed after

Clopton offered the king half the 'profits': two hundred marks, a sum for which he sought the counsellor's approval. Dudley then invited him and his lawyer in for a chat. In Dudley's eyes, the agreed settlement was too low. Evidently thinking he could do better, he offered Clopton fifty marks to 'go his way', he proposed to take on the case himself, on the king's behalf, at which point Clopton's lawyer – himself a royal counsellor, as it happened – intervened, mildly pointing out the blatant irregularity: this was a private case and the king had 'no right' in it anyway. Dudley exploded. 'Are you of the king's council and yet would argue against the king's advantage?' What happened next had an air of inevitability about it. Dudley took the case on and won, receiving damages of three hundred marks, which disappeared into the king's coffers; Clopton received 'not one penny thereof'.[8] If this behaviour – the probing inquisition, the pleasant, reasoned benevolence combined with violent anger – seemed familiar, it was. Dudley was behaving rather like Henry himself.

As the London chronicler bitterly observed of Dudley, the greatest lords in England were 'glad to be in his favour, and were fain to sue to him for many urgent causes'. In an echo of Robert Plumpton's comment about Empson, he noted that it was easier to approach and speak to 'the best duke in the land' than to Dudley, a mere esquire, a man who flaunted his title of 'counsellor to our sovereign lord the king' as though it were a noble title.[9] A deep-rooted sense of betrayal underscored Londoners' criticisms of Dudley – after all, the city had nurtured him, helped make him what he had become. It was, above all, in the economic honeypot of London, through its wharves and warehouses loaded high with luxury goods, its whorehouses and taverns, townhouses, marketplaces and Guildhall that Dudley's shadow was spreading inexorably.

Despite Henry's sporadic trade embargoes with the Netherlands and his interference in city politics, business in London was booming. Although in meetings of the common council, self-censorship was the norm – minute books often revealed large gaps where full and frank discussions about the king's attentions had presumably taken place – and the city inveighed against Henry's preference for foreign merchants – 'we the king's subjects' merchants no thing in regard to them', noted the mercers grimly – the truth was more complex. City merchants and London's alien communities worked hand in hand in illegal exchanges and import/export rackets, while with the increase in trade came endless 'new ways or deceits' to avoid the crown's attentions.[10] But where there were offences, Henry's lawyers saw opportunities to extract wealth, and to extend royal control over the city's government. For those who knew where to look, and how to use the law, the dark underbelly of finance and commerce represented almost limitless opportunities for threats, intimidation and extortion. Edmund Dudley did, and Henry gave him open season.

In Dudley's hands, Henry's tactics against the city reached fruition. He knew exactly how much the Corporation would be prepared to pay for renewal of its charters of self-government and trade privileges, and how much he could squeeze out of London's merchants in customs duties and the sale of export licences. He knew, too, how to exploit the city's pressure points, meddling in its politics and preying on the grudges and jealousies between its guilds, privileging certain companies over others and interfering in city elections. As various London politicians pointed out uneasily, the king was riding roughshod over due process, changing procedures when he had 'none authority' to do so. In the municipal elections of autumn 1506, the city rejected the king's preferred candidate for sheriff, the merchant taylor Sir William Fitzwilliam. Dudley walked into Guildhall, annulled the results and called a new election, which Fitzwilliam duly won – paying Henry £100 for the king's 'gracious favour for being sheriff'. The London chronicler noted acidly how city elections were now fairly academic anyway – it didn't much matter who Londoners voted in because 'whosoever had the sword borne before him, Dudley was mayor, and whatever his pleasure was, was done'.[11] The real centre of power was, as the chronicler intimated, not to be found in Guildhall, but a short walk east and south from there in Dudley's own house in Candlewick Street.

One of the city's main commercial thoroughfares, running east to west parallel with the river, Candlewick Street was the centre of the city's textile trade, lined with wealthy drapers' warehouses. With the financial centre of Lombard Street a few minutes' walk north, and the port of London to the south, Dudley's house was perfectly positioned, an island of royal power in the city's commercial heart.

Despite a two-storey frontage extending 180 feet along the street, the house's exterior was unassuming enough. Like many merchants' townhouses with their small windows and plain façades that to one unimpressed Venetian 'do not seem very large from the outside', it gave little sense of the extent within. But once inside, such houses – living spaces, offices and warehouses rolled into one – seemed to expand to an extraordinary degree in a proliferation of chambers, parlours, corridors and closets. As the same visitor discovered, to his surprise, 'they contain a great number of rooms and garrets and are quite considerable'.[12]

So it was with Candlewick Street. In its warren of rooms, fashionable touches of interior design – 'rich arras' lining the walls, fine inlaid furniture and exotic glassware of 'beyond sea making' – vied for space with the luxury goods and textiles in which Dudley dabbled, and the endless coffers and boxes crammed with financial and legal paperwork, 'bills, obligations, evidences and other writings'. At the back, its double-storeyed gallery gave onto a fine garden. The nerve centre of his operations, Candlewick Street was incessantly in motion. Apart from its domestic staff, the house admitted a constant flow of clerks, messengers, city representatives, guild- and company-men, royal officials and counsellors and, above all, Dudley's victims. People came to plead their innocence, arrange their schedule of payments, or to pay an instalment of their debt, received and logged by one of his clerks: the smaller of the two parlours where he conducted his interviews incorporated a counting-house. Or, like Sir William Clopton, they came to progress matters in which Dudley had taken a hand, and left defrauded or bound over to the king.

Among the regular faces in Candlewick Street were Dudley's eyes and ears in the city, those who supplied the fuel for Henry's fiscal machine. Many of them worked in the world of economic crime where, in the way of informers more generally, they were allowed a cut of the possessions of those they managed to convict, and where the pickings were particularly rich. People had a special name for them: promoters. Royal promoters had long been at work in the city, several of them familiar and hated faces; now, working with Dudley and his sidekick and enforcer Richard Page, their activities acquired a new virulence and impunity.[13]

As warden of the exchanges, Henry Toft was part of the regulatory machine that attempted to control London's rampantly corrupt money markets. Toft was a regular presence in Lombard Street, at the new currency exchange at Leadenhall market, and at Westminster, where he paid into the exchequer the crown's profits from financial dealings in the city. 'Affectionate' – or manipulative – and 'covetous', Toft regularly abused his authority and, in Londoners' eyes, was a man to be avoided as far as possible. Involved in inummerable prosecutions, his biggest catch had come in May 1496, when he successfully sued the then mayor, the prominent draper William Capel, for financial irregularities. Capel was fined the sum of £2,763. Toft, though, had not been operating alone. The man who supplied him with the evidence for Capel's prosecution was a man who was to become the doyen of promoters, Empson and Dudley's 'worst disciple': Giovanni Battista Grimaldi, or, as he was more commonly known, 'John Baptist' or 'Grumbold'.[14]

Grimaldi, a broker, was head of the London branch of the eponymous Genoese banking house which his father, Lodovico, had opened decades previously. The Genoese were the largest of the Italian merchant 'nations' or communities that clustered around the traditional Italian quarter of Lombard Street, and the Grimaldi one of the foremost families, their names featuring prominently in the lists of licensed alien brokers approved by the Corporation of London. The Genoese were a byword for sharp practice and corruption – perhaps unsurprisingly, given that they were Europe's finest financiers – and it was a stereotype to which John Baptist fully adhered. Even where illegalism was the norm, he stood out, his career littered with examples of extortion, bribery and intimidation. In 1488, he was imprisoned for racketeering, and it may well have been then that he agreed with the royal authorities to turn informer.[15]

Suffering from an acute skin condition, erysipelas, Grimaldi stood out from the crowd with his swollen 'blobby face' and 'cankered complexion'. He had the invaluable ability to engage people in conversation, to 'feel and tempt' them, make them speak out of turn and betray confidences. His rancour towards London's notoriously xenophobic mercantile community only made him more driven. Styling himself a member of the royal household, Grimaldi shuttled around the city picking up gossip, sifting information and bringing cases to the attention of the king's counsellors. He drifted into the exchequer offices at Westminster with impunity. Treating its staff with a casual familiarity, he had much 'privileging' there – though no formal royal position – riffling through official documents and peering over clerks' shoulders as they enrolled debts. In his previous career as under-sheriff, Dudley would have known of Grimaldi's activities, and would have crossed paths with him on many occasions; now, Grimaldi's financial acumen, his knowledge of London's demi-monde and his utter lack of scruple made him particularly useful.[16]

For the city bourgeoisie, another alarming sign of Dudley's dominance after 1504 was the rise to power of John Camby. A member of the grocers' guild and a sheriff's sergeant – a key position in city law-enforcement – Camby moved easily between London's mercantile and political communities and the shadier world that he was supposed to police. Keeping a 'stew' or brothel in London's Thamesside red-light district, Camby was heavily involved in the prostitution trade. This in itself was hardly unusual: after all, the biggest stews in the country, in Southwark, outside the city limits, were owned by the bishop of Winchester – none other than Henry's close adviser Richard Fox. Nevertheless, in a city in which, as one Venetian merchant was at pains to point out, it was dangerous merely to step outdoors after dark, London's prostitution trade had long been the focus for crime of all kinds, from robbery to homicide.[17] It was a world in which Camby loomed large, and from which he had made a lot of money. According to his contemporaries, he lived a 'wayward life' and was associated with a litany of offences from bribery to gross bodily harm; somehow, though, he had escaped being dismissed from office. As well as a liberal way with bribes, Camby evidently had a way of getting out of tight corners, a gift of the gab. And he realized early on that Dudley was destined for great things.[18]

Flattering Dudley and showering him with gifts, Camby quickly became one of his closest associates. In November 1505 Dudley appointed him to the highly profitable office of weigher of wools in the port of London's custom house, whose stone bulk stood out among the mass of wharves just west of the Tower. Posts like these were often filled by members of the royal household – in particular, by servants in the wardrobe, who could bring to bear their expertise in textiles and accounting in sniffing out sharp practice. Camby brought other kinds of expertise: an intimate knowledge of London's political and criminal worlds, his own network of informers, and an appetite for extortion with menaces.

The city was dismayed at his appointment, but worse was to come. Camby was given the keepership of one of the two Counter prisons, in Poultry Yard off Cheapside, traditionally run by London's sheriffs, where many convicted of offences in the city courts were held – in particular, of offences relating to the prostitution industry in which Camby had such a considerable stake. London's politicians were aghast. Dudley's preferment of Camby was the latest, and most egregious, example of the overturning of the natural order of things, of royal interference in the way London regulated itself. Given a free hand, Camby used it with gusto. Universally feared, he was 'far in authority above any of the Sheriffs to whom of right he ought to have been subject and servant'.[19]

That Henry knew much of what was going on is all too clear. It was he who agreed the fines with Dudley – as Dudley had pointed out to Clopton, it was the king who 'bade me offer you fifty marks' to take over his court case. Toft, meanwhile, was rewarded personally by the king; so too was Grimaldi, who Henry used in a variety of financial activities.[20]

Through London's teeming port and customs house, its warehouses, taverns, guildhalls and exchanges, everywhere where business was transacted, the promoters moved. Suspicion seeped through the city. Using the information they provided, Dudley and his colleagues on the council learned in the law prosecuted aggressively, arresting and detaining indefinitely without trial, the accused coerced into 'agreeing' with the king for whatever sums the counsellors, Dudley at the forefront, deemed suitable and, always, being forced into further financial bonds.

In the council learned's minute books, and in Dudley's accounts, the names mounted up, a litany of victims: men like the mercer Richard Gittins, 'long in prison and paid much money upon a light surmise';

to James Yarford, who paid a hundred marks for release from a false indictment for felony; to the London haberdasher Robert Hawkyns, convicted and imprisoned for murder on flaky testimony – 'the surmise of a lewd fellow' – who paid 100 marks and entered into a bond for the same amount for his future good behaviour.[21] In one of the most egregious cases, Thomas Kneseworth, the former mayor, was pulled up for trading offences allegedly committed under his mayoralty, together with his two sheriffs, Shore and Grove. All three were imprisoned indefinitely in the Marshalsea until they agreed to exorbitant penalties for their release. Their pardons came to another £1,133 6s 8d, as much as possible paid cash down, the rest to be paid in instalments. They were, as Dudley later acknowledged, convicted on a 'light cause', a technicality.[22] London's citizens were terrorized. But if they felt things could get no worse, they were mistaken.

In southern England, the winter of 1506–7 was unseasonably warm. Frost scarcely lingered on the ground, no snow fell and – unlike the previous winter, which had dealt Henry such an extraordinary stroke of luck with the shipwrecking of Philip of Burgundy – there were no storms. At the end of January, the royal household left Greenwich, its flotilla of barges moving up the Thames through London to Richmond, where Henry again fell ill with a recurrence of the quinsy that had prostrated him following Elizabeth's death three years previously. Despite the mildness of the winter, it was always the time of year that he was most susceptible, when despite the fires banked high and the thick arras-lined walls, the damp still seeped into the riverine houses along the Thames and, at high tide, the river itself trickled into cellars, undercrofts and kitchens. At Candlemas, in mid-February, Henry was able to take barge to Westminster to observe the anniversary of Elizabeth's death, but shortly after, he fell into a steep decline. By early March it was becoming clear that his illness – tuberculosis, complicated by asthma – was life-threatening. The moment of crisis, it seemed, had arrived. Its harbinger was Lady Margaret Beaufort, who that month descended on Richmond with her household and immediately took charge.[23]

In recent years, Lady Margaret had stayed closer to her son, moving in 1505 from Collyweston to her Hertfordshire manor of Hatfield, a day's ride from her London house of Coldharbour and the Thameside royal palaces. That March, she organized with her customary zeal, taking over the supervision of Henry's domestic servants, diet and physicians, and ordering a consignment of improving tomes of spiritual consolation: the fashionable *Shepherds' Calendar*, a mixture of medical advice, prognostication and religious consolation, and a copy of the German mystic Henry Suso's *Horologium Sapientiae*, with a life of St Benedict bound 'in the same book'.[24] But Lady Margaret's presence at Richmond was, as ever, about more than her son's physical and spiritual well-being: it was to ensure Prince Henry's smooth succession to the throne. As she made payments to the king's privy servants – constantly about him as he lay prostrate, unable to swallow food or water, fighting for air – the king's mother was, as ever, alert to the slightest changes in atmosphere, to anything out of place.[25]

By mid-March, Henry was close to death. Lady Margaret directed operations, paying Garter herald Thomas Wriothesley twenty shillings for 'making of a book of mourning clothes', and a substantial quantity of 'black material' – £57 6s 8d-worth – was bought to manufacture them with. She sent riders to alert her confessor John Fisher, bishop of Rochester and, in his East Anglian estates, the earl of Oxford, whose role as constable of the Tower would be paramount in any crisis. As the king weakened, he found enough strength to command two of his chaplains to order 7,209 sung masses as intercessions for his soul, and another thousand masses from his favoured Friars Observant at Greenwich. One of the chaplains, hovering by Henry's bedside, was a sleek cleric in his mid-thirties, a 'Master Wolsey'.[26]

After an academic career in theology at Oxford, Thomas Wolsey had gained a foothold in court circles as tutor to the marquis of Dorset's children. He had transferred to the service of Henry Deane, the short-lived archbishop of Canterbury, standing at the archbishop's graveside after his untimely death, a week after Queen Elizabeth's, in February 1503. Then, amid the security alerts and household reshuffles, he headed for Calais as chaplain to its deputy governor Sir Richard Nanfan, a position of trust which would have undoubtedly seen him involved in the troubled conversations over the king's illness and the succession. When, in late 1506, the ailing Nanfan returned to

England and retired to his Buckinghamshire estates, he recommended Wolsey's abilities and energy to the king in glowing terms. Henry took him on.

Wolsey's new position as royal chaplain gave him considerable personal access to the king's privy chamber. Ministering to Henry's private devotions, he was in constant attendance: 'in present sight of the king daily by reason he attended and said mass before his grace in his privy closet'.[27] As the king's spiritual needs intensified along with his physical decline, the attentive Wolsey was perfectly placed to observe the political manoeuvrings being played out.

He was well aware of the value of his position. Never one to let the grass grow under his feet, he had started to ingratiate himself with his fellow chaplains, in particular Silvestro Gigli, and to cultivate the great men at court, making a beeline for Richard Fox and Thomas Lovell. Both counsellors quickly realized that Wolsey, sharp and energetic, would make a very useful apprentice indeed, a 'meet and an apt person to be preferred to witty affairs', affairs that might range from diplomatic missions to rather more informal requests, such as keeping a close eye on the goings-on around the ailing king's bed. A discreet, watchful presence, Wolsey registered who controlled admission, who let people in and rebuffed others, who stayed longest. He saw, too, how the secret chamber, an arrangement designed by the king to control access, might have its weak points, how in certain conditions – when the king was in extreme ill-health, perhaps – it might seem as if those closest to Henry were controlling him, rather than the other way round.[28]

Particularly notable were the number of servants with close connections to Empson and Dudley. William Smith, Henry's groom of the wardrobe of robes and a financial enforcer for the council learned, was a close colleague of Empson's; then there was the groom of the stool Hugh Denys, the man in charge of the running of the secret chamber. Responsible for the king's everyday necessities, Denys was handling increasing quantities of cash, while fines for certain common-law offences were being siphoned off to him. He got on well with Dudley, with whom he shared business interests in finance and real estate. What was perhaps Denys's most remarkable acquisition had come the previous year, when he and a syndicate of 'feoffees' or trustees had bought Edmund Dudley's alma mater, Gray's Inn: astonishingly, the owner of one of the four legal inns of court was now the king's closest personal servant.

That March, too, the sudden appearance in the king's chamber accounts of one of Denys's fellow Gray's Inn trustees, a 'Master Lupton', seems to confirm what was happening. Roger Lupton, a canon lawyer and provost of Eton College, was another of the coterie of royal chaplains around the king's bedside. But now, for the first time, Lupton was invested with considerable financial responsibility. Like Denys and William Smith, he made payments, arranging for alms to be distributed and money disbursed to redeem debtors from London's prisons in the customary acts of contrition, a sure sign that the king was nearing his end. But there was a particular reason for Lupton's rise to prominence: he was an associate of Dudley's.[29]

Men like Denys, Smith and Lupton were faithful, trusted servants of the king, people who could be relied upon in the most serious of crises. But they were also Empson and Dudley's friends, and their pre-eminence around the dying king revealed which way the wind of royal favour was blowing.

On 19 March, a clerk was paid forty shillings to draw up the king's will, copying meticulously from an earlier draft and incorporating new provisions. Added to the list of the twelve key executors, Henry's most intimate and trustworthy advisers that included Fox, Lovell and the vice-chamberlain Sir Charles Somerset, were two new names: Sir Richard Empson and, at the bottom, 'Edmund Dudley, esquire'. Both men had proved themselves indispensable. Now, they were among those few brokers charged with arranging the transfer of power from Henry VII to his son, who would be responsible not just for the first proper dynastic succession for a hundred years, but who, guiding the new, young king, would help determine what kind of regime it would be.

Downriver from Richmond, the London chronicler remarked on a renewed air of optimism. With a warm, early spring – in March, 'buds were as far out this year as some year they be, by the latter end of April' – came an atmosphere of détente. From Camby's Counter prison in the Poultry to the Fleet prison, from the Marshalsea, the

King's Bench gaol run by Sir Thomas Brandon across the river in Southwark, to the fetid dungeon under Ludgate, cell doors swung open and debtors were released.[30]

Henry's act of contrition seemed to work. Towards the end of the month, he was out of danger. On 31 March, Wednesday of Holy Week, Rodrigo de Puebla was admitted to the king's presence; sidling into the privy chamber, he found Henry convalescing and still, as he reported with a certain self-importance, not seeing many people. Asked to return the following week, de Puebla spent time locked in discussions with the king, counsellors occasionally flitting in and out.[31] But as Henry recovered, so the brief thaw dissipated. Empson, Dudley and their men went about their work with renewed vigour.

London's prisons started to fill again. The city chronicler described a daily stream of men from all regions of England through the city gates, hauled before Henry's learned counsellors and committed to the Tower or one or other of London's prisons 'where they remained to their displeasures long after'. Victims were subject to the now ubiquitous process: summary imprisonment until they agreed to pay large fines for their supposed crimes, more fines for pardons, and yet more fines for agreeing not to break the law in the future. Anybody who approached members of the judiciary for advice or representation was told with a shrug of the shoulders to 'fall to agreement'. There was no way that any lawyer was about to represent a case against the king's counsellors, while few people were brave or stupid enough to stand witness.[32]

Following the crisis of spring 1507, Empson and Dudley had emerged even more prominent among the king's inner circle; they seemed, too, to be working more closely together, their access to the king more exclusive. Following his arrival at the king's bedside, business now kept Empson increasingly in the environs of court. That summer, he took a lease on a large house next to the duchy offices at Bridewell, south of Fleet Street on the city's western edge. 'Le Parsonage' was surrounded by orchards running down to the Thames, and was within easy reach of the inns of court and the London houses of the nobility, which extended around the curve of the river towards Westminster.[33]

In April 1507, as Henry recovered, a man mingling among the crowds of petitioners and lawyers in Westminster Hall could be heard telling anybody who would listen an appalling story. It concerned the London haberdasher Thomas Sunnyff – a prosperous, respectable man – and his wife, Alice. They had murdered a newborn child, then dumped the tiny body in the Thames. Even by the standards of the myriad malicious 'informations' lodged with the king's counsellors it was a truly horrible allegation. What made things even worse was the fact that it was entirely false. The rumour-monger was a servant of Dudley's promoter, John Camby, who had fabricated the entire case in order to force Sunnyff into paying a fine of £500 that was apparently owing to the king.[34]

The 'fine', though, was nothing of the sort. It was an old, run-of-the-mill bond to keep the peace – a bond whose conditions Sunnyff had now, according to Camby, broken in the most horrific way. Helpfully, Camby supplied evidence: the testimony of a prostitute, Alice Damston, whose child it seems to have been. Probably a prisoner of Camby's, given that the Counter prisons were where those convicted of prostitution offences ended up, Damston had been forced to testify against the Sunnyffs. Undoubtedly, she had no choice in the matter. With his information lodged, and his evidence in hand, Camby arrested the bewildered haberdasher and frogmarched him to Empson's house for a hearing. What happened next was a terrifying example of how Empson and Dudley's roles increasingly interlocked in pursuit of the king's rights, and of the impunity with which they and their promoters moved through London.

After Camby had repeated his trumped-up case, Empson ordered Sunnyff to settle his 'fine' of £500. When the haberdasher refused, he was carted off to the Fleet prison and locked up.[35] Six weeks went by, and with Sunnyff still refusing to pay, Camby decided to try another avenue. Extracting his victim from the Fleet, the pair went downriver to Greenwich, where the king was in residence. Leaving the nervous Sunnyff under guard, Camby wandered off to find Dudley; after a while, the pair returned. Dudley said, shortly, 'Sunnyff, agree with the king or else you must go to the Tower.' When the draper refused to 'agree', Camby rowed him back to London, taking him not to the Tower but to his own prison, where he locked Sunnyff up and embarked on a campaign of psychological intimidation. The king, he said, wanted his £500 and what the king wanted, the king got. He gave Sunnyff an example. When Henry had coveted Wanstead manor, he had victimized its owner, Sir Ralph Hastings, until Hastings sold it to him. Hastings had died of the stress: the implication was that Sunnyff would, too. But again, the draper was resolute, demanding a proper trial. In an unconscious echo of William Cornish's plea from the Fleet three years previously, he retorted: 'if the king's good grace knew the truth of my matter he would not take a penny from me'.

When Sunnyff's case was, finally, brought in front of the court of King's Bench in Westminster Hall, another of the king's judicial cabal, the attorney-general James Hobart, told the judges not to grant him bail. Committing Sunnyff to the Marshalsea, the judges ruled that they had to obey the king's commandment because Hobart said so: 'in so much that Camby had brought with him the king's attorney.' With Sunnyff back in prison and still refusing to pay up, Dudley, Camby and Richard Page broke into his house in Bower Row, in the north of the city, on 26 June and helped themselves to goods worth the required amount – vastly undervaluing the goods as they did so.[36]

Having been moved between royal prisons, beyond the city's jurisdiction, for over three months, subjected to a rigged trial, and with no prospect of release, Sunnyff broke. He agreed to the fine, fearing that he 'should have died in prison'. On 21 July, Dudley entered in his account book Sunnyff's £500 fine in exchange for a pardon 'for the murdering of the child'. But still he was not released until well into November, when the fine had, unaccountably, increased by another £100, and Sunnyff had been forced to sign another bond for his future good behaviour – which might, in the hands of Camby and his cohorts, be triggered again.[37]

Whether or not Henry knew the truth of Sunnyff's matter – or of the slew of other manipulated cases – he was unconcerned to find out. He approved Sunnyff's fine and signed his pardon; all the money was paid into the hands of John Heron in the king's chamber treasury.[38] Sunnyff and his wife had spent six and a half months in separate prisons, on trumped-up charges, without trial, had their names dragged through the mud, their house ransacked and goods stolen, and had been mulcted of £600 into the bargain. Little did he know it, but Sunnyff's Kafkaesque ordeal, even then, was still not over.

○

When Thomas More had written to his friend John Colet describing London as a city of sharp eyes, silver tongues and barely suppressed violence, his letter had not been mere literary conceit. This, after all, was a city that felt itself infiltrated, besieged by royal informers; where the knocks on the door, the arbitrary summons to court, were becoming ever more frequent; where merchants like Sunnyff were imprisoned at random, their houses broken into and their goods confiscated; and where people died of stress after months of harassment at the hands of the king's promoters. The shadow of More's near neighbour and fellow-lawyer Edmund Dudley, whose house lay a brief walk from the Old Barge, down Walbrook, also fell across his family and friends and, it seems, More himself.

One friend was Mountjoy who, as he never failed to remind everyone, was up to his ears in debt – not only his own, but the financial bonds of at least twenty-one others, for whom he stood surety. Mountjoy's father-in-law, Sir William Say, a close friend of the More family, was also in desperate trouble. As well as being embroiled in a lawsuit with his son-in-law, he was in bond to the king for £1,666, as Dudley recorded in his account book. Another name that Dudley had written down was that of Thomas More's father, Sir John.[39]

As a sergeant-at-law, Sir John More was a member of the elite group of common lawyers from whom the king chose his judges. Whatever he thought of the promoters' excesses, Sir John was part of the establishment, a legal adviser who had been chosen to uphold the king's law. He was hardly likely to start pleading against the king's causes; rather, he would have been among those lawyers who, when approached by defendants desperately seeking legal advice, would say that the best counsel they could give was to 'fall to agreement' with the king. But even sergeants-at-law were not safe. One of Sir John's colleagues, Sir William Cutler, had recently nipped in the bud a plot to forge a treasonous letter in his own hand, and 'the same letter to have been cast into the king's chamber' – at which point, as his defence simply but eloquently put it, Cutler would have 'stood at his own jeopardy'. According to Thomas More's son-in-law William Roper, Sir John himself fell victim to the king's promoters, imprisoned in the Tower until he stumped up a fine of £100.[40] And then, according to Roper, Thomas More himself was targeted.

After More's vocal part in the 1504 parliament, things seemed to go quiet. Then, one day, More had gone to see Richard Fox on a 'suit', possibly legal matters relating to the city. After official business was concluded Fox drew More aside and, 'pretending great favour', advised him to 'confess his offence against the king'. Henry, Fox implied, was distinctly ill-disposed towards the young lawyer, and a full confession would immediately restore him to the king's good books. More evidently said he would think about it. Coming away from the meeting, he fell into conversation with Richard Whitford, who was well placed to give an opinion: this close friend of Mountjoy, Erasmus and More was also Fox's chaplain. Whitford's advice was emphatic. 'In no wise', he said, should More confess to anything at all – particularly to Fox. What More had to understand, Whitford continued, was that Fox would do anything to serve the king; why, he would even sign his own father's death warrant. According to custom, in which members of Parliament in formal session were allowed to oppose the king, provided they did so with the requisite deference, More had done nothing wrong. If he confessed to a crime, however, that was a different matter entirely. He would have been condemned out of his own mouth.[41]

In Roper's hagiographical biography of Thomas More, these two episodes formed part of a systematic campaign of intimidation waged against More and his father by Henry VII, the result of More's speaking truth to power in the 1504 parliament. As ever, Roper tried to claim particular privilege for the Mores' suffering. Although the possibility remains that Henry harboured specific ill-feeling towards Thomas More, both father and son were more likely to have been victims not of special treatment, but quite the reverse: the indiscriminate and terrifying opportunism of Henry's lawyer-counsellors. Sir John More was arrested on a 'causeless quarrel', probably a legal technicality of the kind Dudley's promoters delighted in spotting; the £100 he paid for his release – while, very probably, entering into further financial bonds – was precisely the kind of 'agreement' with the king that so many were forced to make. Likewise, in implying that Thomas More had somehow incurred Henry VII's wrath, Fox was trying the same tactic, intimidating him into admitting some unspecified offence – a confession that could only end in More and his family being snared in the king's financial web.

From that time on, More viewed Fox with unease. Erasmus noted how, for More, Fox was the malign genius behind Henry's novel methods of taxation commonly known as 'Morton's Fork'. Erasmus, too, talking to the garrulous Andrea Ammonio some years later, would warn him to be particularly careful about what he said in front of Fox – an opinion that seemed to come straight out of the Old Barge. Indeed, it was a view shared by the young Henry VIII himself: 'Here in England', he later informed the Spanish ambassador, 'they think he is a fox – and such is his name.'[42]

Sometime in late 1507 or early the following year, More left England for a period of study leave at the universities of Paris and Louvain. Perhaps the timing was a coincidence – or perhaps, as people often did at such times, he had thought it best to remove himself from the tense atmosphere of city and court, to let things cool down a bit. At that stage in his life, he may have thought discretion the better part of valour.[43]

Even as Henry's other counsellors worked with Empson and Dudley at the task of enforcing bonds, collecting fines, imprisoning and asset-stripping their victims, they looked askance at the two men whose pre-eminence had been emphatically asserted during the recent crisis of the king's illness, as they and their friends clustered around his bedside. Henry, increasingly, seemed to go directly to them, over the heads of other members of his inner circle. In a series of memos on a variety of matters to the chancellor, Archbishop Warham, the king told him simply to take Dudley's advice and follow his instructions; one such command told Warham to get Richard Fox to draw up writs preventing people from leaving the kingdom, 'after [such] manner, form and effect as our trusty councillor Edmund Dudley shall show unto you.' To veteran advisers like Fox and Warham, being lectured by the king's keen new protégé must have been deeply irritating. So, too, it seems, were Dudley's views on religion.

On the face of it, Dudley's disapproving attitude towards the church – a vast, wealthy corporation that was answerable in the final analysis to Rome rather than the king of England – was no more than the robust orthodoxy of the time. In the eyes of many, the church was simply too political, too worldly, too powerful. Ecclesiastical abuses were endemic: absenteeism and pluralism – being away from one's flock and holding more than one holy office – went hand in hand with simony, paying for holy office: 'temporalities', the lands and incomes that came with church livings, were often highly attractive. All this was frowned upon. The role of priests and bishops was to provide a moral and spiritual example to the realm, not to sully themselves in the world of politics. And above all, privileges like sanctuary and benefit of clergy – where clerics were allowed to opt for favourable trials in church courts, rather than submitting themselves to the king's justice – allowed people to get away, literally, with murder. Appealing legal cases to Rome, effectively in contempt of the king's law, was even worse.[44]

Plenty of people, men like Fox and John Colet – a friend of Dudley's, as it happened – believed to some degree or other, and for differing reasons, that the church's practices, or abuses, or organization, needed sorting out. Neither did they see their own devotion to the church as remotely inconsistent with pursuing the regime's vested interests and their own: Lady Margaret Beaufort, with her intense piety and vigorous deployment of her son's lawyers – Empson and Dudley included – in pursuit of her various business and legal matters being a case in point. But Dudley, Empson and the other common lawyers among Henry's counsellors had a particularly aggressive attitude towards the church. They were, after all, the self-styled 'high priests' of the common law, and it was their job, and in their interests, to tighten the king's hold over the church, to close the legal loopholes – and, in the process, bleed the ecclesiastical cash cow for as much money as they could get, on the king's behalf. Inevitably, their assault on the church became another focus for resentment. Among the spiritual, religious concerns mingled with corporate solidarity: churchmen stuck together. In the likes of Lady Margaret, Fox and Warham, this fused with a feeling that they had, somehow, been displaced from the king's side.[45]

All this came together in the person of Christopher Urswick, Henry's former almoner. Urswick had been friendly with Bray and Archbishop Morton; he was close to Fox and Lady Margaret, whose confessor he had been, and with the intensely spiritual John Fisher, the cleric whom Henry had appointed bishop of Rochester as a salve to his conscience. He was, too, a friend of Erasmus and More. Way back in 1484 it was Urswick whose decisive, perilous journey from Flanders to Brittany, to warn Henry that he was about to be extradited, had saved his skin. Now, the otherwise mild-mannered Urswick – who, it seems, had gradually been sidelined for his conservative religious views – bristled against Henry's lawyers, 'opponents of ecclesiastical liberty', and the 'detestable rapacity, nay rather sacrilege' that they exhibited. His friend and colleague Richard Nykke was so enraged that he denounced Henry's attorney-general James Hobart as 'an enemy of God and his church'.[46]

Occasionally, these resentments reached Henry's ears. As concerned as the next man about the state of his soul, he even listened occasionally. In July 1507, the ungodly Hobart was forcibly retired, and fined £500 into the bargain. As it turned out, however, the action was little more than a sop to both the church and to Henry's spiritual conscience. Hobart's replacement as attorney-general was John Ernley, an unexceptional lawyer who had one thing in his favour: he was a friend and business partner of Edmund Dudley, and he took up with renewed vigour where Hobart had left off.[47]

Even as Henry's counsellors tightened the financial screws, the more seasoned among them were undeniably aware of the burgeoning resentments: from the church, the nobles, the merchants. Both Fox and Thomas Lovell, honorary members respectively of London's mercers' and grocers' guilds, could not help but notice the atmosphere of sullen anxiety that had settled on the city, the preachers shouting fire and brimstone against the king's counsellors at St Paul's Cross, stories of the many 'murmerous and grudging' reactions to the king's commissioners throughout the country reaching their ears.[48] As Lovell enforced the duke of Buckingham's latest set of fines, he would have detected the simmering rancour of a nobleman who, he knew, detested him. In Henry's secret chamber, Fox and Lovell's man, Richard Weston, passed them information even as he smilingly offered to stand surety for the earl of Northumberland's debts. As loyal servants to the king, these old-established counsellors, architects of the regime from which they derived their power, were hardly about to express even the slightest murmur against Henry's promotion of Empson and Dudley, the two men who had carried his policies to a new level. But experience told them that there would, eventually, be a reckoning – and when it came, they had to be ready.

There was a story that did the rounds at court, about the king's pet monkey. Goaded by one of Henry's privy chamber servants, it snatched up an account book that Henry had left lying around, and ripped it 'all to pieces', a tale that apparently spread through the court like wildfire, to the amusement of those that 'liked not those pensive accounts'. It was a brief moment of levity in an intensifying sequence of prosecutions, fines and imprisonment. But it also showed how contingent was the whole system that Henry had built: reliant on the mass of data kept and maintained privately by his financial administrators, and, ultimately, on his own personal authority.[49]

With Suffolk out of the picture, and with the likes of Buckingham under close scrutiny, any overt threat to the regime had been stifled and suppressed. Bound and divided, people were sullen and resentful – but they were also scared. There were, as Buckingham later said, many nobles resentful at having been 'so unkindly handled', and they could have 'done something' if they had dared talk to each other, 'but they were afraid to speak'.[50] As people had been for years, they were waiting for Henry to die for normal service to be resumed, for the return of the status quo, the redressing of wrongs and the reassertion of vested interests. It was something that Empson, Dudley and their colleagues had perhaps sensed as they had moved around what they had thought was the king's deathbed in March 1507, as close as possible to the source of power. The ground was shifting. Opposition to Henry and his counsellors now was not so much about the struggle for the dynasty – though that lurked, ever-present, under the surface. It was about the struggle for its soul.

12

Courage to Be Bold

Despite his increasing, carefully controlled, public appearances, Prince Henry continued to live in his father's pocket, incubated within the royal household. The king liked to talk about himself and the prince in the same breath, as being of one mind – 'my son and I' – and funded projects in both their names, like the completion of the fan-vaulted ceiling of St George's Chapel in Windsor Castle. If the king's aim was to mould his son in his own image, he seemed to be succeeding: foreign ambassadors reported that the prince was 'prudent', like his father. The pair walked together, Henry talking in his precise way about politics and government, the prince listening quietly. Late one summer evening in July 1506, around 11 o'clock, they were pacing one of the newly built private galleries at Richmond when, suddenly, the floor caved in, almost – but not quite – beneath their feet. It was a narrow escape. But to those who believed in portents, it perhaps said something else. The king could keep his son as close as he liked, but dangers still lurked, right under his nose.[1]

In the balmy early spring of 1507, a jousts royal was proclaimed. The May jousts were a longstanding tradition, but that year there seemed a particular energy and purpose about their organization. Henry may have been disinclined to take England into war, but he remained constantly suspicious of France's expansionist ambitions and, with the belligerent Pope Julius II attempting to unite Europe's warring dynasties – Habsburg, Valois, Trastamara – in a coalition to crusade against the Turks, was keen to show that he, too, remained a major player on the European stage. A glittering display of chivalric martial arts was a perfect and risk-free way to show off England's military readiness.

Another impulse underlay the jousts, too. They would showcase the new generation of courtiers in a display of carefully choreographed loyalty to the emerging dynasty: to Princess Mary, Henry's poised younger daughter, and to the prince, who would turn sixteen that June.

Unusually for a king who pored obsessively over every minute detail of court ceremonial, Henry had almost nothing to do with the jousts' organization. Still weak and recovering from the illness that had almost killed him, he waved through the plans, perfectly happy to delegate them to the prince and his friends, who were all too keen to oversee the preparations – which was very probably why things turned out the way they did.

Two miles south of London Bridge, the royal manor of Kennington had seen better times. Henry VII barely, if ever, visited it, preferring the Thamesside houses that he had had rebuilt at great expense, and between which he shuttled in the royal barge. But Kennington, down at heel and dilapidated, nevertheless had a historic lustre of its own, as well as a longstanding association with the prince of Wales. In the mid-fourteenth century, it had been rebuilt by the Black Prince, the son of Edward III who had defeated the French in the great battles of the Hundred Years War, at Crécy and Poitiers. A short ride from London and Westminster, equidistant from Greenwich and Richmond, it was the perfect base for the prince and his friends, and for their endless, obsessive practice of martial arts.

By spring 1507, the prince seemed to have undergone a transformation. There had been hints of his emergence at court in the various heralds' reports and diplomatic dispatches written during Philip of Burgundy's stay: his astonishingly accurate marksmanship in the hunt, his barbed comments to the French ambassador. There had, though, been few comments on his appearance. But, as he approached his sixteenth birthday, the prince's physical development was glaringly obvious. Ruddy-cheeked, and with a sensual cupid's-bow mouth, he had, admirers noted, a soft, feminine complexion – all of which served to make his massive, athletic frame all the more astonishing. Later that year, de Puebla would report to Ferdinand in awestruck tones that there was 'no finer a youth in the world'. He was impressively, intimidatingly 'gigantic'. Standing next to his ill, consumptive father, the prince dwarfed him.[2]

Now, the prince had the power and physique to go with his undoubted martial skills. In the tiltyard, his companions felt the juddering impact of his sword-blows and saw the muscled precision of his archery and his tilting at the quintain. The prince, it was clear, wanted to hit harder, shoot and joust better than anyone else.

The tournament's organization had its roots in Philip's enforced stay in England the previous year. The impact of Philip and his knights of the Golden Fleece had been plain to see in a tournament put on at Greenwich in the spring of 1506, only a matter of weeks after he had finally left for Spain. Held in the tiltyard that ran behind and at right angles to the main apartments that fronted onto the river, these games reflected a court still bathing in the lustrous afterglow of Philip's visit. Following the latest Burgundian fashions, they had been framed by a dramatic tableau, the first of its kind in England. Introducing the tournament, Lady May, the servant of Dame Summer, breathlessly recounted how she had heard tell of a recent joust honouring her 'great enemy' Lady Winter and her servant Dame February – a direct reference to the tournament at Richmond put on in Philip's honour three months previously.[3] This, then, was more about keeping up with chivalric fashions; or, rather, it showed how they mixed with international power-politics, underscoring the new special relationship between England and the Habsburgs that had been concluded during Philip's stay: Henry's own projected marriage to Philip's sister, Margaret of Savoy, and that of Princess Mary to Philip and Juana's young son Charles, heir to the Habsburg lands – including Castile. The focal point of these jousts, too, had been the eleven-year-old Mary herself. As the games opened, Lady May, curtseying deeply, petitioned her to 'licence my poor servants' to defend her honour 'in exercise of chivalry'. The jousts seemed to go down very well indeed.

So when, in spring 1507, Henry lay convalescing, it was only natural that he should leave the tournament plans in the hands of the prince and his friends. That year there would be two tournaments, in May and June. Both would take place at the prince's manor of Kennington, and they would highlight the group of jousters who had featured in the previous year's tournaments in honour of Philip and the new Anglo-Habsburg entente cordiale.[4]

As the prince grew and began to present that focus for loyalties that Henry had hoped he would, courtiers and counsellors placed their sons where they could best impress him: in the tiltyard. Younger sons of the nobility like the belligerent Sir Edward Howard, Henry Stafford and Sir Edward Neville – a man with an uncanny physical resemblance to the prince – jostled for favour with the offspring of Henry's financial advisers and diplomats. There were, inevitably, tensions. Personal rivalries and political faction compounded nobles' dim view of the pushy lower orders muscling their way up the social order via the tiltyard. Sir Edward Neville, son of the Kentish nobleman Lord Bergavenny, was a talented improviser of 'merry songs' and apparently had a taste for ripe political ballads about knaves being put down and lords reigning.[5] This tangled skein of interests was evident in the team of challengers chosen for the May jousts to take on all comers: William Hussey, Giles Capel, a newcomer called Thomas Knyvet, and the man who seemed the tournament's guiding spirit, Charles Brandon.

William Hussey was the son of the royal counsellor Sir John, who as the king's master of the wards was intimately associated with the king's financial exactions. Sir John had bought himself into the nobility, marrying the sister of Richard Grey, earl of Kent, and had married William off to Ursula Lovell, the niece of Sir Thomas. Marriage had also provided Knyvet, an athletic twenty-one-year-old and superb horseman, with his big break: in July 1506, his wedding to the earl of Surrey's daughter brought him into the fold of the most influential noble clan in Henry's court and council. Capel's father, meanwhile, was Sir William, the rich, influential London draper and former mayor who was fighting a running battle with the king's informers, in particular his nemesis John Baptist Grimaldi.[6]

Like most aspiring courtiers, Giles Capel had been packed off to be educated in a noble household, to serve and learn manners. As befitted the son of one of London's most affluent businessmen, he had been sent to the best: the household of Henry Bourchier, earl of Essex, which had an unrivalled reputation as a chivalric finishing school, and whose London house was in Knightrider Street, a short walk from Lord Mountjoy's.[7] In November 1501, Essex's men, with their fancy horsemanship and fabulous costumes, had wowed the crowds during Catherine of Aragon's procession through London. But by that point Essex was already a watched man. Of all the guests at Suffolk's fateful supper in Warwick Lane, he had been the only one to escape Henry's wrath. Essex, though, had had the good sense to keep his head down and demonstrate his unswerving loyalty to the regime. He stayed at court, cultivated his friends close to the king, like Arthur Plantagenet, and supplied to the royal household a steady stream of gentlemen trained in 'feats of arms' – including Capel, who became a member of the king's spears. Another familiar face in Essex's house-hold was Charles Brandon.

Brandon had an impeccable pedigree as far as Henry VII was con-cerned. Back in 1484, his father, William, and his uncle Thomas had fled to join Henry in France after an abortive uprising against Richard III in their native East Anglia; later that year they had spearheaded the special-forces-style raid on Hammes that had liberated the earl of Oxford. Henry's standard-bearer at Bosworth, William Brandon had become one of the regime's first martyrs. Thomas had gone on to become one of the king's intimates: royal counsellor, master of the horse, and a trusted diplomat. His nephew Charles, meanwhile, had grown up in the royal household, working as a sewer, or waiter. A job in which you needed to have your wits about you – 'full cunning' and 'diligence' – it involved descending into the 'veritable hell' of the royal kitchens to liaise with cooks, taste the innumerable dishes, and super-vise their presentation. It was also a role that needed an awareness of the minutiae of precedence, as well as 'courtesy' – impeccable manners, charm and good looks: attributes that Charles Brandon had in spades. In his spare time, he had ready access to the royal stables through his uncle and had, evidently, become an exceptional horseman.[8] By the age of seventeen, when he jousted at Arthur and Catherine's wedding, Brandon was already the consummate courtier; in 1505, around the time he became one of the king's spears, he landed the prestigious post of Essex's master of horse. Seven years older than the prince, Brandon was frequently around him at court, in the tiltyard and, probably, his own small household, where Brandon's uncle was the prince's treasurer.

Brandon, though, had inherited a distinctly unchivalrous approach to women. His father's own behaviour made contemporaries wince: on one occasion, William Brandon had raped an 'old gentlewoman' and, 'not therewith eased', moved on to her older daughter and was only narrowly prevented from doing the same to the younger. Charles, it seemed, was a chip off the old block – though his behaviour was altogether more calculating. Some time around 1503, he confided to a friend and fellow servant that he was in love with one of Queen Elizabeth's gentlewomen, Anne Browne – the daughter of Sir Anthony Browne of Calais Castle and the troublesome Lady Lucy – to whose company he 'much resorted'. His resorting was so enthusiastic that she was soon pregnant. In the ensuing scandal, Brandon was hauled in front of the earl of Essex's council, where he pledged to marry her. Shortly after, though, he broke off the engagement, instead marrying Anne's aunt Dame Margaret Mortimer, twenty years older than him, a shock which apparently induced Anne to miscarry their child. Charles, however, only wanted to get his hands on Dame Margaret's assets. Selling off his wife's portfolio of property, he pocketed the proceeds to fund his extravagant life at court – clothes, horses and, undoubtedly, the organization for the spring 1507 jousts, into which the participants ploughed their own funds.[9]

For all its fancy ritual and style, jousting remained an extreme sport. It was one that called for a cool head and precision, particularly when executing the flashy techniques which Brandon, Knyvet and their friends performed, and which they were teaching the prince. Even with blunted lances and filed-down or 'rebated' blades, grave injury and death were all too frequent, and tended to 'disturb the cheerfulness of such events', as a contemporary Spanish herald understatedly put it. Edmund Dudley echoed the prevailing opinion at Henry VII's court: 'beware of dangerous sports, for casualties that might fall', he later wrote, emphasizing that in his son's 'only person dependeth the whole wealth and honour of this your realm.'[10] So, although the prince's skills were obvious to all who had seen him in practice, he would not be given the chance to show them off in public. While his friends charged each other in plate armour either side of the wooden tilt, and fought on foot with axes and swords across knee-high barriers, he would sit and watch.

None of this was intended to belittle the prince – in fact, quite the opposite. As Henry increasingly preferred to shun the limelight, so he thrust his son into it, as the visible face of the regime. An enthusiastic sponsor of her grandson's chivalric pretensions, Lady Margaret Beaufort paid for 'a saddle making and harness' for his appearance in the accompanying ceremonies. Ultimately, though, the prince was not where he wanted to be, in the tiltyard, but in the stands, presiding over the jousters – he was playing not his own role, but his father's. In the May jousts, moreover, he was not even the main focus of attention. Rather, the jousts were all about his younger sister Mary.[11]

On each Sunday and Thursday in May, as late spring shaded into summer, people flocked to the tournament from all over the country. Among the crowds filing into Kennington was Lady Margaret's cultivated young cupbearer, Henry Parker, to whom she had given expenses to travel down to London for the occasion.[12] Above the din of anticipation, the food- and drink-hawkers shouting their wares, and the musicians – lutenists, flutes and the dry percussive crack of taborins – trumpet fanfares heralded the start and conclusion of each round of jousting. From two in the afternoon until church bells struck six, charging plate-armour-clad horses raised clouds of dust. The action was so vivid that to one observer, it was as though it happened in slow-motion: 'it seemed to a man's eye/ That they would have hanged still in the sky'. Presiding over the jousts in a flower-strewn pavilion, alongside a blossoming hawthorn tree festooned with coats of arms and, at their centre, a shield quartered with the Tudor green and white – 'which colours be comfortable and pleasant for all seasons' – sat the prince and Princess Mary. The king, it appeared, was absent: still recovering from illness or, perhaps, just disinclined to be seen in public.[13]

Two months previously, Mary's marriage contract with the Habsburg heir Charles of Castile had been drawn up. Now, appropriately enough, she played the lead role in the dramatic tableau that introduced the tournament's theme: that of new love, of Venus and Cupid, symbolized by the colour green. In a green dress entwined with spring flowers, surrounded by green-clad servants, Mary herself played the Lady May, 'this lady sovereign', presiding over the contest and awarding prizes. Her challengers fought wearing her favours: green badges fixed at their throats. Now thirteen years old, Mary clearly had the presence to carry off the lead in this game of courtly love. As the reporter swooned, she 'had such beauty/ It would a heart constrain to serve her.'[14]

All this was the currency of courtly love, and seemed decorous enough. But a souvenir account, in rhyme, published to commemorate the games – the author remained anonymous – hinted at an undertow of discontent. Some people, it appeared, had not been happy with what they had witnessed. Not only that, but there had clearly been none-too-complimentary whisperings in some quarters against those involved with the tournament. 'Some reprehend', the versifier wrote, before politely telling the detractors to be quiet: 'God them amend/ And grace them send/ Not to offend more/ Till they die.' In the following month's jousts, the tensions came to the surface in spectacular fashion.

The two men given star billing in the June jousts were Brandon and another ubiquitous presence in the tiltyard, Richard Grey, earl of Kent. One of Queen Elizabeth's Woodville relatives, Kent, in his late twenties, was a contemporary of Northumberland and Buckingham. Like them, he spent plenty of time and money acting as a glorified clothes-horse in royal ceremonials, with little visible return by way of political responsibility or power. And he was a disaster waiting to happen.

Since inheriting his earldom and estates in December 1503, Kent had done his best to uphold his father's gloomy deathbed prediction that his son would 'not thrive but be a waster'. Profligate and chaotic, he squandered prodigious amounts of money at the gambling tables of the Lombard Street inns – situated conveniently near his own London base, the sign of the George, a familiar haunt of rackety jousting types – where he also found a supply of brokers ready to extend him credit, many of them Italian moneylenders. He also found willing creditors among the most practised and manipulative of Henry VII's counsellors. Proving a corrupt and astonishingly inept businessman, 'as unmeet to govern his estates as a natural born idiot', Kent walked straight into their clutches.

Those who took full advantage of Kent, a 'prey set open to the spoil of all men', were the same royal counsellors that shook their heads meaningfully at his lack of education and self-control. Foremost among them were Giles lord Daubeney and the vice-chamberlain Sir Charles Somerset, the king's jewel-house keeper Sir Henry Wyatt, Sir John Hussey and, inevitably, Empson and Dudley.[15]

Trying to ingratiate himself with the king's inner circle, and to pay off his crippling debts, Kent mortgaged and sold off tracts of his Bedfordshire estates at knockdown prices. Some of them he practically gave away: Lord Daubeney apparently bought one of his manors for two pieces of cloth and a horse with its harness on.[16] Desperately casting around for sources of cash, Kent abducted an heiress whose lucrative wardship had been left to his half-brother and, in the ensuing tug-of-war over the young girl, the inevitable happened. The king intervened, confiscated the disputed wardship and imposed on him a series of punishing fines. The man who took care of business for the crown was Kent's new brother-in-law, Sir John Hussey – who had paid the earl two thousand marks to marry his sister.

By early 1507 the hapless Kent had mortgaged the greater part of the family estates. He had tried to play the property game, to buy influence and mix it as a sophisticate at court and with the king's counsellors, but he had failed. More than that, he was being ruined and humiliated into the bargain. Something, it was clear, had to give and, as court geared up for the spring jousts, it did so.

On 6 May, when Kent defaulted on his programme of repayments to the king, Henry's ruthless, opportunistic response was masked by a veneer of concern for the earl's financial state. As the suave legalese put it, given that Kent had neither the wherewithal – nor, it added, the inclination – to pay up, the king, 'of his gracious and benign mercy and pity' agreed to step in, to call his counsellors to heel, and to help Kent work out how to meet his debts. In part-payment Henry agreed to accept the income from two of the earl's prime estates in north Wales – which added to the portfolio of lands, including the Bedfordshire manor of Ampthill, that the king had already annexed from him. But this was no act of mercy. Henry had long had his eye on Kent's Welsh estates. The earl had blundered into a trap. And the men who had stitched him up on the king's behalf were the lawyers whom he had retained as informal financial advisers: Empson and Dudley.[17]

Having placed considerable faith in the 'loving' advice of the pair, Kent had been lured into a false sense of security over his repayment deadlines. The counsellors had seemed perfectly relaxed, telling him that the paperwork 'should not require so great haste', and assuring him that he 'should incur no indemnity for non-payment thereof at the said time appointed'. The day after the deadline passed, they swung into action, hitting Kent with a royal summons demanding immediate payment on the king's behalf – and, because he had defaulted, payment in full. Kent had fallen for the cheapest of confidence tricks. As people at court sniggered behind their hands, it had finally begun to dawn on the earl that he was being played.

Bewildered, angry and utterly unable to protest, he had nowhere to turn. By the time of the June jousts, weeks later, he was still simmering with a pent-up sense of injustice. Having been systematically asset-stripped by the king's counsellors, and by extension by Henry himself, Kent had come to realize that, politically marginalized and with no way out of his financial entanglements, he would not get any change out of the current regime. He was not alone. The jousts of June seemed to mark a change in the atmosphere, a palpable shift of focus. Although the king, now fully recovered from illness, was attending the spectacle, there was little doubt who the participants wanted to impress the most. The same anonymous author that had written the account of the May jousts picked up on it, too: 'Every man of them was the more ready/ Perceiving that our Prince Henry should it behold.'[18]

That June, instead of a refined demonstration of chivalric loyalty, the protagonists tore up the rule book and lashed out. Pieces of body armour were sheared off; swords splintered and broke as the combatants hacked away at each other. Most of the contestants were injured to some extent or other – 'none of the lusty sort/ Escaped free' – and one of them, not mentioned by name, was 'hurt in deed' and had to retire. Maybe the combatants were simply bad technicians, but this seems improbable: the likes of Brandon, Kent and Sir Edward Howard had years of experience jousting in the spotlight of royal tournaments, while Knyvet was by all accounts a shimmering talent. Rather, for one reason or another, it seems as though they were deliberately pushing the sport to its boundaries in a thrilling, violent spectacle.

For Henry and his counsellors it was all highly troubling. There was something brash and warlike about it, something uncontainable. There was, of course, a prominent strand of intellectual opinion about the king that disliked chivalric culture and the way it gave precedence to the military classes – who were bad enough as it was – and the warmongering it led to. Men like Richard Fox had spent decades masterminding Henry's diplomacy, an approach designed to avoid war at all costs and – in Dudley's words – they saw war as pointless and a 'great consumer of treasure and riches'. In fact, this went for the majority of Henry's lawyer-counsellors, who, of course, were echoing the king's own mind.[19]

Now, profligate, louche and belligerent men like Brandon, Kent and Sir Edward Howard – 'by whose wanton means', it was later noted disapprovingly, the young Henry VIII 'spendeth much money, and is more disposed to war than to peace' – had put on a display that was 'fondly', or foolishly, undertaken. In fact, some seemed to suggest, the jousts' violence was no accident, but deliberately subversive, a mailed fist in the face of Henry VII's kingship. People connected with the tournament were, it was insinuated, 'most busy' spreading 'evil', 'false tongues' were 'slandering' Henry and his counsellors. Certain people around the king clearly felt threatened – not least, because the prince loved it.[20]

So unlike his father in other respects, the prince had nevertheless inherited his singleminded focus – though the objects of his desires would prove rather different. In years to come, his obsessiveness would manifest itself most obviously in his pursuit of love. 'So ardent was he when he had begun to form an attachment', said one observer, 'that he could give himself no rest.' Martial arts, though, always competed with women for his affections and, that June, his all-consuming absorption in the tournament was evident.[21]

Ruddy with excitement, the prince sat massively alongside his father, fidgeting with passion. Caught up in each splintering of lances, and each grinding clash of the heavy double-handed swords that plate-armoured knights wielded at the barriers, he seemed to forget everything – including himself – in the process. People noticed that he was so hungry to 'speak of arms and other defence' that he eagerly welcomed 'gentlemen of low degree' into his presence, talking animatedly about the technical aspects of the martial arts he saw enacted before him.[22] In sharp contrast to his father's carefully cultivated role as a remote, detached arbiter of tournaments, Prince Henry's artlessness resembled that of his Plantagenet relatives: his mother, whose effortless openness had been so carefully monitored by Lady Margaret, and his ingenuous uncle Arthur. And for those old enough to remember, there was another, more significant comparison to hand.

With his burgeoning physicality and relaxed informality, the prince was his maternal grandfather reincarnate. Edward IV had been a man 'easy of access to his friends and to others, even the least notable', frequently summoning 'complete strangers' to his presence. This apparent spontaneity and bonhomie, of course, had its own art. But Edward went so far out of his way to present himself as a king with the popular touch that his counsellors had become deeply concerned. Such familiarity, they said, was dangerous. It risked demeaning 'the honour of his majesty' – the authority of the crown and of the king himself – and laid him open to all kinds of influence. Now, the prince was behaving not like his remote, distant father, but like his grandfather. To the king and his counsellors, none of this seemed particularly prudent. The prince clearly had appetites that had to be 'repressed'.[23]

The jousts' organizers evidently realized that they had overstepped the mark very badly indeed. An account of the tournament by the same author, the 'Jousts of the Moneth of June', was little more than a glorified damage-limitation exercise, one evidently written with the jousters' backing – or in expectation of their approval. Stressing how the jousters had been practising for months to put on a good show for the king, it gave the tiltyard mayhem a romantic gloss. This, it said, was the very stuff of King Arthur and his knights of the round table – those who sneered at it were the kind of critics who would find fault even with that perfect jouster, Lancelot of the Lake. The point was, the account continued, that everybody had liked it, especially the prince. In fact, it was the prince who had given the jousters 'courage to be bold', and whose support for them was 'comfort manifold'. The jousters would rather have his backing than 'all the treasure and gold of the world'. Like the prince whose favour they sought, they valued honour and glory above riches – unlike, it did not say but which readers could hardly help inferring, the king and his counsellors.

But, as the author went on to protest, these jousts royal had been done in the name of the king and the regime. The challengers had deliberately worn the colour of fidelity: emerging from their pavilions in gleaming, blue-enamelled plate armour, they rode horses caparisoned in blue sarcenet. Violent it may have been, but the action was hardly the stuff of subversion or treason. People could whisper and spread rumour, but no overt accusations of disloyalty could be laid against the jousters. Henry and his counsellors may have been alarmed, but they could only wait, and watch.[24]

One of the 'gentlemen of low degree' who hung around the royal children was the chamber servant and poet Stephen Hawes. By 1507 he had been in royal service for four years or more, and his star was rising. Wynkyn de Worde continued to publish him enthusiastically, and people loved his *Pastime of Pleasure*, whose allegorical storyline – the quest of a chivalric hero, Grande Amour, for his love, La Belle Pucelle – was larded with hackneyed platitudes on the importance of education, in particular rhetoric, 'The noble science which, after poverty,/ May bring a man again to dignity.' On Twelfth Night 1506, days before Philip of Burgundy's unscheduled arrival in England, Hawes had his biggest break to date, performing a 'ballet', a heavily ornamented song of courtly love, in front of Henry VII himself, receiving a ten-shilling tip from the king by way of reward.[25]

But Hawes, it seems, spent much more of his time in the company of the prince and his friends, and Mary and her gentlewomen. Reflecting the renewed atmosphere of courtly love and violence, his verses praised the prince's emboldening effect on combatants, 'encouraging your hearts with courage chivalrous'. He proved, too, an incurable romantic, 'sighing full oft': in his dealings with Mary, if his poems are anything to go by, the line between formulaic courtly love and overt eroticism wore very thin indeed. Like the accounts of the 1507 jousts, his poems' thinly veiled allegory depicted the young princess, who seems to have possessed the qualities of a Lolita, as an alluring, unattainable maiden. He cast himself as the chivalric lead.

On closer inspection, moreover, the verses of the jousts, with their robust defence of the combatants' behaviour, bear uncanny echoes of Hawes' poems, punning on their titles and incorporating phrases from them. If Hawes wasn't their author, he certainly shared their sentiments.[26] Naïve, giddy with success and the exalted company he was keeping, and in contravention of the terms of his employment, which required him to steer clear of any faction, 'bands, quarrels and debates', Hawes, it seems, allowed his writings to become the mouthpiece for certain political elements at court – very probably, the group of up-and-coming young courtiers around the prince.

As he later recounted in a poem, *The Comfort of Lovers*, in which his personal experiences at court ruptured what was otherwise a straightforwardly allegorical love-story, the climate in the royal household was one of febrile uncertainty, in which courtiers 'full privily' tried to outmanoeuvre each other 'by craft and subtleness'. Somehow, Hawes had become privy to a conversation in which he was shaken to discover that the speakers 'did little love' Henry VII. As a chamber servant, he was of course required immediately to report 'any treason or thing prejudicial compassed, accounted, or imagined' against the king or his family. Hawes did so, repeating the 'truth' he had discovered in no uncertain terms: 'I did dispraise to know [tell of] their cruelty.' In other words, he denounced them publicly – probably in verses that he circulated around court. If all this had echoes of William Cornish's brush with Empson, so did what followed.

Hawes' allegations, whatever they were, were dismissed as the work of a troublemaker seeking favour. Shortly after, he was set upon and beaten so badly that his life was 'near spent', a traumatic experience that left him constantly 'in fear of death', looking over his shoulder for would-be assailants. As he put it, simply but arrestingly, 'from my brows for fear the drops down did sweat'. While Cornish, well-connected, had been able to pull strings, Hawes was less influential: people, he found, fell away from him and avoided his company. Caught up by those who aimed to, as he put it, 'sweep the house clean' of awkward, dissenting voices, he was thrown out of the royal household, never to return.

With Hawes' abrupt departure, the literature of court, the satirical songs and ballads that served as a pressure-valve for frustrations and tensions, seemed to dry up. People had seen what happened to poets whose work cut too close to the bone, or into which subversion could be read. Skelton had been politely retired – or jumped before he was pushed; a chastened Cornish survived by toeing the line; Hawes was beaten to within an inch of his life. Others, jobbing rhymers like the yeoman usher and sometime lord of misrule William Ryngeley, and Henry Glasebury, the marshal of the king's minstrels, probably kept within the strict limits of what was permissible. Or perhaps they followed Hawes' subsequent efforts at self-preservation. 'Three years ago', Hawes wrote in 1510, in a vain attempt to get noticed by the new young king, 'my right hand I did bind.' He simply stopped writing.[27]

In June, as usual, the 'gests' for the summer progress were published at court. For six weeks from the second half of July, Henry's route would take him northeast of London into East Anglia, before turning west, aiming for the Thames Valley and his Oxfordshire manor of Woodstock. It was an ambitious schedule, but by now the king had recovered his health, and with it his energy. On the way, he would stay at the usual assortment of houses best able to accommodate the riding household: sprawling monasteries, bishops' palaces and courtiers' residences. It may have been a rare privilege to put up the royal household but it was, too, an onerous expense and a logistical nightmare – for which reason, such stays tended to be short. Five days in one house tended to be the upper limit, for those courtiers who were in special favour, and who could afford it.[28]

Leaving Greenwich on 16 July, Henry's riding household, together with that of the prince and Lady Margaret, travelled north, to Sir Thomas Lovell's Middlesex manor of Elsings. Henry liked staying there. With its fine interior décor peppered with red roses and Garter badges, its library of French romances, and its auditor's chamber and counting-house, it must have felt like a home from home: Lovell, always an excellent entertainer, had had a suite of six rooms especially constructed for the king.[29] From there, they progressed into East Anglia, stopping off at Cambridge, where they were treated to a number of orations praising the munificence of Henry, and in particular his mother, towards the university. While there, Henry took note of the half-completed shell of King's College Chapel, which 'resteth as yet unperfected and unfinished, little or nothing wrought or done thereupon' since the death of his uncle Henry VI a half-century previously.[30]

The household then turned southwest, towards the earl of Kent's Bedfordshire manor of Ampthill, which it reached by 15 August. 'Standing stately upon an hill', Ampthill's generously proportioned inner court contained '4 or 5 fair towers of stone'; outside its large gatehouse, a sprawling courtyard was formed from a range of lodgings and stabling. With its well-stocked wooded parkland and noted 'cleanness of air', Ampthill was the ideal hunting place for the tubercular king.[31]

Henry, in fact, seemed in better health than he had been for years – indeed, he had 'grown fat'. In marked contrast with the painful progresses of recent years, where he had lingered, bedridden, in the same house for weeks on end, he was now constantly in motion, 'going from one hunting place to another' with a vigorous, almost manic energy. Not only were messengers and ambassadors, shuttling to and from the itinerant household, left trailing in his wake, they couldn't find him half the time. His evasiveness, indeed, seemed almost deliberate. Catherine, marooned in London at Durham House, complained that he stayed nowhere long enough to get down to business – by which she meant dealing with the matter of her dowry.[32]

But between the incessant hawking and hunting, Henry was, as usual, constantly involved in business. Surrounded by his coterie of administrators and counsellors, he continued to read correspondence, receive diplomats, sign accounts and hear lawsuits. Among the matters he tied up at Ampthill was that of the earl of Kent.[33]

Earlier that summer, Henry had summoned to him all those who had been involved in real-estate dealings with the hapless earl, and told them to detail their transactions in full. Then, 'in discharge of their conscience', he presented them with two options. Either the estates they had purchased would be confiscated by the crown – or they could pay the king large sums of money to keep them. Sir John Hussey, who had obviously driven a sensational bargain with Kent, opted for the latter, paying the king £66 13s 4d for permission to hold on to his newly acquired lands in Northamptonshire.

Henry had had his cake and eaten it. He had allowed his counsellors free rein to exploit the earl; then, when they had done so, he moved in and did the same to them. At the same time, he had assumed the moral high ground. Kent was obviously incapable of looking after his own property, so Henry, 'perceiving and knowing the danger that would be the confusion and utter undoing of the said earl of Kent', acted as custodian. Income from Kent's lands would flood into the royal coffers, and lucrative estate-manager jobs would be sold to the highest bidders. There would be no chance of the impecunious earl buying them back. As ever, the king's sense of timing was vicious. On 14 August, the day before he arrived at Ampthill, he ordered Kent to sign indentures making it over to the crown.

For Kent, insult followed injury. Five days later, Henry imposed on him a number of draconian conditions, including a personal control order that stipulated that he had to 'be seen daily once in the day within the king's house', and was not to leave court without written authorization. Kent was effectively gated. To encourage him to keep his word, Henry made him sign a bond for £10,000.[34]

By 22 August, the royal household had moved on to Easton Neston in Northamptonshire. This was Empson's manor: he had been born and brought up in the nearby market town of Towcester, on Watling Street, the Roman road that ran arrow-straight between London and the east midlands. In 1499, Empson had obtained a licence from Henry to create a park around his house. He enclosed four hundred acres, including all the former common lands of the adjacent village; the village itself was destroyed and its inhabitants turfed out. His aspirations did not end there. He transformed Easton Neston into a lordly mansion, with a crenellated gatehouse (built across a public right-of-way), twenty-two chambers, two kitchens and a profusion of up-to-the-minute architectural features, glazed windows and tiled floors.[35] The result was a house and park fit for a king.

Henry's stay at Easton Neston that summer – his first visit there – was another benchmark in Empson's rise. With Lovell, the king had stayed three days: with Empson, it was five. As the royal hunting party moved through Empson's cultivated parkland, shooting its way through flocks and herds of game, which Henry distributed to local notables, the counsellor's smooth easiness in the king's presence – at the king's side, no less – was noted. Typically, though, Henry missed no opportunity to take him down a peg or two. When, the following month, Empson petitioned him for a grant of 'certain manors', Henry paused, crossed out the clause that read 'for term of life', and scribbled in the margin, 'at pleasure'. It was a reminder to Empson, if he needed it, that what the king gave he could also take away.[36]

By late August, Henry had arrived at Woodstock. One of the royal standing houses, it was big enough to accommodate not just the itinerant household but the whole circus of court. Earlier in the reign, it had been one of Henry's favourite places to hunt, and he had frequented it often, making extensive improvements and upgrades: a vaulted conduit for running water, a new gatehouse and two new courts, refurbished apartments for him and for Elizabeth. The location of Prince Arthur's first proxy marriage, Woodstock had held fond memories – memories which, with Arthur's death, had become unbearable. Henry hadn't been there for years. Now, he would be based there for a fortnight, allowing the various envoys and diplomats to catch up with him. Among them was the ailing Rodrigo de Puebla, whose gout was giving him such pain that he had to be carried in a litter from his cramped, overpriced rooms in the nearby village. There, too, Catherine finally joined the party.[37]

For Catherine, things had got desperate. Now twenty-two, she had been in England for six years, and was part of the furniture. But she was oddly out of place. There seemed no room for her in Henry's vision for a Europe dominated by an Anglo-Habsburg alliance. In April 1507, Ferdinand had compounded the problem. Missing yet another deadline for payment of Catherine's dowry, he had written to Henry asking for an extension until the end of September. Henry had agreed.

On hearing of this latest setback, Catherine wrote a desperate letter to her father, painting a melodramatic picture of her destitution. Her servants, she wrote, walked about in rags. She had been forced to sell quantities of her jewels and plate in order to maintain her household in some semblance of dignity. Worse still, Henry now treated her not with the loving respect of a father-in-law, but with polite indifference.

She was, too, refused access to the prince, 'even though', as she wrote, 'he lived in the same house as her'. Indeed, she had not had so much as a glimpse of him for four months. But, she wrote proudly, she followed her father's orders, always conducting herself as though her betrothal remained an established fact, 'as though God alone could undo what has been done'. It was an attitude that these difficult years would ingrain in her for the rest of her life.

Catherine, though, was beginning to learn the lesson that de Puebla had impressed upon her, following her disastrous attempt to try and mix it in Anglo-Spanish diplomacy almost two years previously. 'Dissimulate', he had said. That spring, she tried to do exactly that. One source of this new-found worldliness, it seems, was a recent arrival in her household: her confessor, a young friar called Father Diego Fernández.

Quite where Father Diego had come from, or when he had materialized, is uncertain – a member of Henry's favoured order of Observant Franciscans, he may well have been resident at the friary at Greenwich – but one thing was clear: Ferdinand had not sent him. In April 1507, writing in response to her father's concern for the state of her soul, Catherine reassured him that she already had a confessor who was 'competent'. In fact, Father Diego quickly proved more than competent. In the way of spiritual mentors, he quickly came to exercise what some viewed as an unhealthy hold over the young princess. And, somehow, he had imbued in her a renewed sense of purpose. Lamenting the 'insufficiency' and 'incompetence' of ambassadors – she meant de Puebla – Catherine wrote to her father asking for the keys to the Spanish diplomatic cipher. She had taught herself to read code, and had indeed written to him in it, but perhaps she had done so incorrectly, perhaps he had not understood her clearly. She wanted to be able to write confidentially to Ferdinand about her marriage – and to be absolutely sure that he got the message.[38]

There was one thing that, she knew, might yet swing matters in her favour. Henry was still keen to remarry. Philip of Burgundy's unexpected death in September 1506 had got him thinking again about Catherine's older sister Juana, whose pale, isolated beauty he had admired at Richmond the previous year, and who was now Philip's widow. In recent years Henry had of course been pursuing Philip's sister, Margaret of Savoy – rich, Habsburg, and aunt to Philip and Juana's son Charles of Castile, who was due to be betrothed to Henry's daughter Mary. Marriage to Margaret of Savoy would, Henry told Catherine, suit him 'perfectly well', but marriage to Juana would be 'still better'. In fact Juana, queen of Castile, could provide him with a direct route on to the European stage. By the spring of 1507, Henry had begun to fixate: both on Juana herself, and on the possibilities for European domination that she represented. Behind the scenes, he had started to agitate hard for the marriage. Catherine realized that as Juana's sister and a way to her ear, she now had value. If she could help Henry achieve his desire, she could also help herself.

In mid-July Catherine wrote to Ferdinand having successfully deciphered her father's dispatches, something that left her in 'unearthly spirits' of jubilation. Finally, she felt able to do something decisive. Her latest letters, though, were not those of the inscrutable Gioconda she now felt herself to be, but of a young girl utterly at the mercy of events. She told her father about a recent exchange with Henry, just before his departure on progress that summer, in which she had passed on Ferdinand's latest positive dispatch to the king and 'explained the ciphers to him'. Henry – unsurprisingly – had shown himself 'much gratified', and had made positive noises to the effect that obstacles to Catherine's wedding would be soon overcome. But, he mentioned offhandedly, there was just one thing. He had heard that the king of France, Louis XII, was interested in concluding a new alliance with Spain: at the heart of it would be a marriage between Juana and Louis' nephew, the count of Foix, something which would, he told Catherine, cause 'much discord'. He wasn't, he added, telling her this by way of 'warning or advice', he just thought he would mention it, as a matter in which she was 'personally interested'.[39]

A new Franco-Spanish treaty would threaten England, wreck Henry's marriage plans – and, he implied gently, Catherine's own. She took the hint. Writing breathlessly to her father, she begged Ferdinand not to marry her sister off to Louis XII's nephew but, she implied, to Henry. If Catherine had set out to act as her father's agent, she was, wittingly or not, rapidly turning into an English mouthpiece. Ferdinand, who had clearly not been telling his daughter anything like the whole story – and who had evidently only sent her ciphers that she

could safely 'explain' to the English king without any detriment to
Spanish diplomacy – had seen this coming.

Late in August, Catherine journeyed up the Thames valley to join
Henry and his son in a state of nervous anticipation about the payment of her marriage portion. She arrived at Woodstock to find that
her father had postponed the payments yet again, by another six
months. Finally cornering Henry, she asked how the latest delay left
her prospects. Welcoming her with the air of a benevolent uncle,
Henry told her that he was perfectly happy to accept the postpone-
ment. As far as he was concerned, the equation remained the same.
Neither he nor his son was bound by any marriage commitment, and
until Ferdinand put his money where his mouth was, he had no intention of reassessing the situation. 'My son and I', he told Catherine, 'are
free.' Indeed, Henry added, almost as an afterthought, he had heard
from a reliable source at the French court that Ferdinand's ambassador had recently told Louis XII that he did not believe Catherine's
marriage would ever take place.[40] If that were the case, Henry said,
Ferdinand would be most welcome to start lining up other prospective suitors for Catherine if he so wished. For all Catherine's new-found
resourcefulness, this latest exchange was shattering.

It also confirmed what had begun to dawn on her: that Henry was
perfectly happy to keep rescheduling the payments, although, as she
wrote to her father in her latest letter, 'he would make us believe the
reverse'. Henry's words were kind; his deeds, though, 'were as bad as
ever'. But doubts over her father's behaviour had also begun to seed
themselves in her mind. Surely, she asked Ferdinand, it couldn't really
be that he had told her one thing about her marriage and the French
king something entirely different?

Ferdinand's procrastinating seems to have been as much about
disorganization as deception. On progress around Spain, he tended
to dump large chests and coffers full of paperwork at whatever house
he happened to be at. This was no kind of filing system, as he discovered the following year when unsuccessfully scrabbling around
for the Treaty of Medina del Campo, the first marriage agreement
between England and Spain that had been signed almost twenty years

previously.[41] But there was no doubt that Henry's two-pronged efforts to marry into Spain had complicated the picture. Already thoroughly alarmed by Princess Mary's impending betrothal to his grandson Charles of Castile, the idea of Henry marrying Juana filled him with horror.

In a fulsome letter to Ferdinand, Henry had painted a glorious vision of the benefits a new Anglo-Spanish entente would bring. His marriage to Juana would profit not just their two countries, but Christendom itself. Not only would Henry be prepared to make the long journey to Spain in person, but he would even go to war on Ferdinand's behalf – something Ferdinand had been trying to make him do for the best part of two decades. He would go on crusade to North Africa, against the infidel Moors, or, if Ferdinand preferred, against the Turks in Hungary. Henry's offer, as ever, was not as straightforward as it looked, given that he was trying to prise Ferdinand away from Pope Julius's anti-Venetian alliance. But there was no doubting his obsession with Juana.

Henry pursued every possible diplomatic avenue, marshalling his own ambassador to the Spanish court and lobbying influential opinion-formers such as Ferdinand's close adviser, the fiercely intellectual Cardinal Jiménez de Cisneros. As ever, he leaned on the obliging de Puebla, whose dispatches to Ferdinand described a similarly rose-tinted view of the prospective marriage, while adding a few choice details of his own. Henry, de Puebla told Ferdinand, had an 'incredible love' for Juana, and was desperate to marry her even if she were indeed a stranger to reason. Frankly, he added, Henry would want the match 'even if worse things were said of the daughter of your Highness'. He would be a much better husband to her than Philip had ever been, and in his loving company she would quickly recover her sanity – besides which, any mental derangement would hardly affect Juana's ability to procreate. Catherine, too, added to the barrage of correspondence.[42]

Writing to her father – in cipher, of course – Catherine described proudly how she had suddenly become useful to the English. She told Ferdinand how she 'baited' Henry with apparently ingenuous talk of her sister, all the while maintaining her demure, innocent façade. Henry and his counsellors, she said, 'fancy I have no more in me than appears outwardly'. But as much as Catherine tried to play this new, dissimulating role, it was one that she found impossible to sustain. The tone of her correspondence veered wildly from desperate self-assertion to panic about her own situation, which she begged her father to resolve, 'since it is in [your] power to alter the state of things', stating that she would 'rather die in England' than give up her marriage to the prince.[43] Catherine saw her future inextricably linked to England's and, she probably felt, her fate now hinged on the king's marriage with Juana. If she could help cement it, her own wedding to Prince Henry would surely follow.

Catherine's new-found boldness with her father masked that she was, in fact, prepared to do whatever Henry asked of her. Not only did the letters she wrote separately to Juana that autumn urge her to marry Henry, their phrasing seemed to come straight out of the English diplomatic handbook. Henry was, she told her sister, 'a very passionate king', 'very wise' and 'endowed with the greatest virtues'. The phrasing was such that Henry might as well have been standing over her, dictating while she wrote.[44]

Ferdinand replied to Catherine and to Henry in much the same way. He was not sure if Juana could be persuaded to remarry – Philip's death had left her horribly bereaved – but, if so, Henry would of course be first in the queue. In truth, Ferdinand, now undisputed regent of Castile, had no intention whatsoever of relinquishing Juana: the prospect of Henry inheriting the kingdom of Castile in her name, and of Juana giving birth to a brood of Anglo-Spanish heirs, was unthinkable. It was just as well, he gave out, that he had gone to Castile when he did, for he had arrived to find a country in a mess, 'in great upheaval and scandal before my return'. Although Juana was 'serene', she was, he implied, plainly incapable of governing in her own right. Soon, stories emanated from Spain of how, insane with grief for her late husband, she rebuffed all attempts to persuade her to bury him; instead, she careened around the country with his coffined corpse in her baggage train. Highly resentful of Ferdinand's duplicity over the years, Henry suspected that he was now playing up his daughter's madness in order to hold on to her throne. It only added fuel to the fire.[45]

Meanwhile, de Puebla was doing his best to push forward Catherine's own prospects. As Henry embarked on his intensive round of

Juana-related diplomacy, so the ambassador sensed that Ferdinand might, finally, be prepared to pay Catherine's marriage portion. Trying to smooth the path, de Puebla wrote with advice on financial practicalities, proposing suitable merchant-banking firms in Spain who could draw up bills of exchange 'for the whole sum of the marriage portion to be accepted in London'. Among the most suitable brokers, he opined, were the Genoese Grimaldi, whose London agent John Baptist 'enjoys great credit' and was 'well known to the King of England'.⁴⁶

For de Puebla, a great player of the long game, Catherine's marriage had become his life's work, a project he had progressed inch by inch, patiently rebuilding it after each collapse. But Catherine, panicky and miserable – hers was 'always the worst part', she wrote to her father – had had enough. As ever, she took it out on de Puebla. For years she had been asking Ferdinand to recall him; now, she rehearsed all the old arguments again. Low-born, deceitful and wheedling, he did no honour to Spain, nor to her. The English, she said, found him contemptible, saying that he only came to court to take advantage of the free meals, and he had become a laughing-stock – even Henry found the jokes funny. He had gone native, and was in Henry's pay; he had done more than anybody else to block her marriage; and he was, besides, old, ill, and 'nearer death than life'.⁴⁷ Catherine wanted somebody else: somebody who was fine, upstanding, aristocratic, trustworthy and – not to put too fine a point on it – a good Christian. She was to regret not having been more careful about what she wished for.

Late in September, as the hunting season drew to a close, the royal household moved back down the Thames valley towards London, in slow stages. It stopped at the spacious brick-built manor house at Ewelme, which Henry had confiscated from the earl of Suffolk, at Reading Abbey, and at Woking, a spacious house set in orchards and parkland that had formerly been owned by his mother – much to Lady Margaret's chagrin, he had forced her to swap it for the rather less agreeable manor of Hunsdon in Hertfordshire.⁴⁸ Towards the end of October, Henry arrived at the most recent addition to his property portfolio.

He had chosen Hanworth with studied care. Within easy riding distance of Richmond, a few miles to the east, it was a bolt-hole from court – much like Wanstead on the other side of London, whose keeper was Hugh Denys, Henry's groom of the stool and head of his secret chamber. It was an appointment that spoke volumes for how Henry regarded the secluded manors at which he increasingly spent much of his time. Denys, the man who oversaw Henry's private world, was perfectly placed to make security and domestic arrangements when the king was ill, or when the privy apartments were not enough of a refuge. When at Richmond, Richard Fox recollected, Henry would leave the court behind and ride the few miles south, crossing the Thames to the bishop of Winchester's palace at Esher, where Fox – the bishop in question – would provide him with an atmosphere of monastic calm. Esher had been, Fox said, Henry's 'cell to Richmond'.[49] Now, in Hanworth, equidistant from both Richmond and Esher and sited conveniently near the Benedictine monastery of Chertsey, which Henry favoured, the king had found his own 'cell' where, heavily guarded by his yeomen and secret servants, he could be alone with his thoughts – and with his accounts.

On acquiring Hanworth – another compulsory purchase, this time from his administrator Sir John Hussey – Henry had immediately set about transforming it. By the time he arrived that October, a hunting park had been enclosed and the grounds emptied of detritus. Now, with typical attention to detail, he planned a pleasure garden, with sunken beds, a hunting lodge and an aviary.[50]

Henry's studied distance, exacerbated by conspiracy and illness, had become acute. Increasingly, and even when in the best of health, he seemed not to want to be seen: during his energetic progress that summer, even though his itinerary had been detailed in the published 'gests', he had been impossible to pin down. He paid lip-service to the rhythms and rituals of court, but this was a king whose will operated through his counsellors. The contrast with the vital son whom he pushed into the ceremonial limelight on every occasion was there for all to see. So, too, was the confined, powerless life that the prince led.

13

Savage Harshness Made Complete

Through the late summer and autumn of 1507, the carts and carriages of the royal household rumbled slowly along the Thames valley from house to house, the sixteen-year-old prince and his servants trailing along in their wake. He shadowed his father's progress, a swift gallop away in the event of any emergency, or a recurrence of Henry's ill-health – or in case of anything untoward in his own retinue. On occasions when space for both households was lacking, the prince might lodge at a separate house – while the king was at Woking on 11 October he spent the night at Easthampstead, from where his brother had set out eagerly to meet Catherine six years before. But ultimately, where Henry went, the prince went too. At his side, through the whole progress, '*per totum itinerum*', were Lord Mountjoy and the man who appears to have been the prince's head of security, Sir John Rainsford.[1]

Rainsford was one of the king's household knights. A link in the crown's chain of command in his native Essex, where he had ties with the earl of Oxford, he had got his job with the prince through his chamberlain Sir Henry Marney, a neighbour and in-law. Rainsford seems to have been a security chief of the shoot-first-and-ask-afterwards variety. He passed his violent disposition on to his son, John junior, 'a very dangerous man of his hands and one that delighteth much in beating, mayheming and evil entreating the king's subjects'. Such violence, of course, came in handy when maintaining a ring of steel around the prince – if properly controlled.[2]

The sixteen-year-old Henry seemed a model prince: magnificent in ceremonial, chivalrous in the tiltyard, and pious in prayer. But even if the impulse took him, he knew that any aberrant behaviour would be likely to get back to his father through Sir Henry Marney, or one or other of the servants who doubled as members of the royal household. On progress, there seemed little opportunity for the kind of teenaged rampaging up and down the Thames valley that his ancestor Edward I had indulged in when barely a year older: waylaying passers-by, assaulting them and making off with their horses, carts and provisions.

Within this closely controlled environment, however, there were already hints of the extravagant carelessness to come. That August, hunting at Langley, the prince had contrived to lose a number of jewels, among them a ruby ring given him years before by his mother, and a red-and-black enamelled diamond ring, a present from Edmund Dudley. The sloppiness was catching: the keeper of the prince's jewels, Ralph Pudsey, mislaid a delicate gold chain of the prince's – 'and', wrote the king's jewel-house keeper Sir Henry Wyatt grimly, 'the king knoweth of it'.[3] The prince had men around him who, like all good servants, were keen to bend themselves to his will, to have 'good wait to come to him if he do call them, or make any countenance to them, to do him service or message'. Servants rode up and down the Thames valley, to London and back *pro negociis suis*, on his business or on shopping trips for necessaries and luxuries – musical instruments, perhaps, to add to the prince's growing collection, or books of 'ballets' such as the voguish ballad 'A Gest of Robin Hood', in which the outlaw roamed through the countryside, bow at the ready, looking for random targets or 'rovers' to fire at. The prince particularly liked to think of himself as Robin, and he was, of course, a crack shot. Maybe he danced late into the evening with his companions and select female company, 'in his shirt and without shoes', as he would do in his first years as king: 'he does wonders and leaps like a stag', said the Milanese ambassador admiringly.[4]

One servant to whom the prince was becoming particularly attached was William Compton. Now in his mid-twenties, Compton's life had been defined and shaped by the royal household in which he had made his way since the age of eleven. Performing his domestic duties, he watched how men gained power and wealth: the swagger of Empson and Dudley; the discreet, submissive confidence with which privy servants like Denys, William Smith and Richard Weston moved in the king's presence. Slowly, Compton was making himself similarly indispensable to the prince, becoming his confidant and fixer, prized for his 'wisdom and fidelity' and wordlessly anticipating his every desire: shortly after Henry VIII became king, Compton would be arranging his sexual liaisons.[5] A servant-companion of a different calibre was Henry Guildford, son of Sir Richard, who had been a constant presence at the prince's side for almost a decade. Stocky, a head shorter and two years older than him, Guildford was an imaginative, exuberant influence who had inherited his father's love of court entertainments. An enthusiastic master of the revels under Henry VIII, he would dress up as one of the merry men to the king's Robin. Together with his half-brother Sir Edward, Henry Guildford was a fully paid-up member of the jousting set.

Both Compton and Guildford, in their different ways, were vital conduits to the world from which the prince was, by and large, insulated, bringing the news and gossip he craved. The talk of the town, more often than not, was Charles Brandon.

Brandon's behaviour had gone from bad to worse. Having jettisoned the pregnant Anne Browne to marry her aunt Dame Margaret Mortimer, Brandon, flush with the proceeds from the sale of Dame Margaret's lands, had annulled his marriage on grounds of consanguinity and transferred his attentions back to the more fragrant Anne. As the inevitable court case ensued, late in 1507 he rode into Essex, where Anne was living in traumatized seclusion, and whisked her away. The witnesses to their shotgun marriage in Stepney church early the following year included Brandon's partners-in-crime, Sir Edward Guildford and the earl of Surrey's belligerent second son, Sir Edward Howard.[6]

With his limited freedom, the prince probably viewed the dashing Brandon's liaisons with something like a scandalized and envious admiration. But there was – and always would be – a strong romantic idealism in him. Brandon's grubby, exploitative behaviour may well have acquired a chivalric lustre in the retelling, an adventure story in which he swooped to carry off his damsel-in-distress, heedless of the consequences. This, after all, was the way that the prince's own parents' love-story had been portrayed in verse, with the dashing Henry Tudor, 'banished full bare ... in Brittany behind the sea', coming to

rescue his golden-haired bride from her lecherous uncle Richard III –
a story Lady Margaret had bought into with her commission from
Caxton of the romance of *Blanchardin and Eglantine*, the exiled
knight returning to claim his amour. Either way, the prince clearly
hankered after the life of chivalrous passion and adventure that his
jousting friends were already pursuing. Some two decades later, his
own love-match would have cataclysmic repercussions.[7]

The prince, moreover, had his own damsel-in-distress at hand.
Although he and Catherine spent little time in each other's company,
she seems to have exercised a strong hold on his imagination. During
the gift-giving on New Year's Day 1508 at Richmond, the prince
bestowed presents on those closest to him, including Lord Mountjoy
and Sir Henry Marney. To Catherine he gave a 'fair rose of rubies set
in a rose white and green'. As a token of his esteem, its significance
was unmistakeable: it was a gift that symbolized himself, a jewelled
Tudor rose.

There was another connection, too. During Philip of Burgundy's
enforced stay in England, Mountjoy – who evidently had some knowledge of Spanish customs – had been deputed to look after Juana and
her household after they had been abandoned by her husband and
his entourage. After that, he had become a regular presence in Durham House; soon, he was wooing one of Catherine's gentlewomen,
Inéz de Venegas. Mountjoy, then, was perfectly placed to advise the
prince on the courtship of the princess that he still believed to be his
betrothed, and to act as a line of communication between them. When
the mood took him, the prince was more than capable of well-turned
expressions of courtly love in his excellent French, as he had
already proved. As he would later show in his passionate correspondence with another woman, Anne Boleyn, he tended to express himself
most eloquently when the object of his desire was long distant or
unattainable. And Catherine, at the time, was most certainly out of
reach.

◉

In December 1507, Richard Fox returned from Calais bearing the
new treaty of 'perpetual peace' with the Emperor Maximilian. Ratify-
ing the Anglo-Habsburg mutual defence pact signed at Windsor

almost two years previously, the treaty had at its heart the marriage contract between Maximilian's grandson Charles of Castile, now nine years old, and Princess Mary, whose proxy marriage was now slated to take place the following Easter. Up to his neck in debt, Maximilian could not process the paperwork fast enough. As he admitted to his daughter Margaret of Savoy, in whose care he had placed his grandson – and who he was still trying to persuade to accept Henry's own offer of marriage – the main reason that he had agreed to betroth Charles to Mary was to get a 'good sum of money' from Henry, his prospective in-law. Maximilian's investment would soon start to yield returns. In mid-January 1508, Henry transferred to him another huge sum of money, £38,000, probably via della Fava and the Frescobaldi bank, 'upon a loan' – which, as both kings knew from long experience, was non-returnable.[8] Years before, Henry had castigated Maximilian for his unreliability; now, it seemed, they were the best of friends, the futures of their dynasties intertwined.

At Richmond that Christmas, Henry's 'high contentment' infused the festivities. In towns as far away as Dover and Shrewsbury, bells were rung and bonfires lit in celebration; in London, Henry ordered an official celebration – at the city's expense, naturally. Nine large bonfires were constructed in the streets, and hogsheads of wine laid on, 'free for all men to fetch and drink of, while it lasted', the better to make 'evidently known what gladness and rejoicing is generally taken and made' by the announcement of the betrothal, as Henry explained in a letter to London's officials. With the new treaty, he boasted, he had built a 'wall of brass' around his kingdom. Invoking God's words to Jeremiah following the unpopular prophet's persecution, Henry may have intended them to have a similar resonance: his subjects may not have liked him, but he had made the country safe. At Guildhall, the king's letter probably prompted thin smiles among the city's merchant-politicians – after all, it was their brass Henry was using.

Henry's aims were, as usual, far more ambitious and complex than mere defence. As his colossal payments to Philip of Burgundy had been, this most recent loan was for a specific purpose: Maximilian's 'business towards Rome at his voyage', as the chamber treasurer John Heron noted neatly in his account book. The 'business' in question was Maximilian's coronation as Holy Roman Emperor, a title which, although emperor-elect since 1493, he had been unable to use for the last fifteen years because he couldn't foot the bill for a trip to Rome to be crowned by the pope. Now, Europe's biggest summit meeting could finally take place – thanks to the financial backing of Henry, the most solvent king in Christendom. With it, he evidently hoped, would come not only influence with Maximilian, but a more direct line to papal policy.[9]

This was Henry the diplomatic puppet-master, as he saw himself, able to pull the strings of international affairs, of ambassadors and princes through huge transfers of capital. As a foreign policy, however, it had assumed a baroque complexity – and its outcomes were often unpredictable. In spring 1508, Maximilian would go to Italy. But he would do so at the head of a large army, across the Alps and down into the plains of the Veneto. On the pretext of picking up his imperial crown, Maximilian would invade Venice's territories, with Pope Julius's blessing – and with an army funded by the extortions of Henry's counsellors.

In London, the information-gathering and persecution, the arrests and financial penalties continued unabated. As Polydore Vergil noted grimly, daily, in the halls of Empson's and Dudley's houses, you could see 'a host of convicted persons awaiting sentence'. In response to their requests for a fair trial, defendants were given 'wretchedly evasive replies' by the counsellors and their colleagues. People were, he reported, so intimidated, so 'exhausted by the duration of their anxiety', that they voluntarily gave up their money. 'For many preferred to do this, rather than remain longer in that sort of agony.'[10]

Vergil would have seen the queues himself, people summoned by privy seal or letter, or waiting to pay instalments of their fines, as he went down past Candlewick Street towards the Thames from his house in St Paul's Churchyard, to catch a boat towards one of the royal palaces; or as he rode out over the Fleet bridge towards Westminster, past Empson's 'Le Parsonage' and the duchy of Lancaster's offices. The cases were legion: Thomas Baynard, a king's commissioner, imprisoned on unspecified charges before 'agreeing with the king's grace' for £120; the London mercer Christopher Hawes, who died of 'an unkind thought' – stress, perhaps, or a heart attack – brought on by prolonged harassment from Dudley's promoters; another, Sir George Talboys, paid £500 to avoid being declared a certified lunatic and having his lands confiscated as a ward of the crown. No stone went unturned. As the London chronicler put it, 'By one mean and other almost no-one that anything had was without trouble in these days.'[11]

While England's merchants went in fear and trembling, Candlewick Street grew grander. In September 1507, Dudley had written a suave letter to London's council, asking for permission to run a private 'current of water' off the Standard, the conduit in Cheapside, to his own house – permission which the council had of course readily granted. Emulating the Italian palazzi he so admired, with their hot-and-cold running water, Dudley had decided to install a mains supply himself, off one of the city's public water supplies. That autumn, workmen dug up city streets, piles of lead piping lying by, turning his house into the lap of continental luxury. He and his fellow financial counsellors, it seemed, could do what they liked.[12]

In October 1507 de Puebla had written to Ferdinand with his latest thoughts on how to establish some sort of line of influence to Henry. Ten years previously, diplomats had identified a small cluster of people – Morton, Bray, Lovell, Fox – who had the king's ear. Now, according to de Puebla, the king had 'no confidential advisers' at all, nobody whose opinion he trusted or who was privy to his innermost thoughts.

Henry, of course, still had people about him, the small clusters of counsellors through whom he ran things. But it was the nature of Henry's relationship with his advisers, de Puebla was saying, that had changed. A decade before, ambassadors had noted how Henry had wanted to 'throw off' his council: now, it seems, he had done so. Implicit in de Puebla's observation was the sense that counsellors no longer performed their traditional roles: even those few men formerly intimate with the king, to whom he had occasionally opened his mind, were shut out. Francis Bacon, Henry's first biographer, summed it up: nobody, he wrote, was permitted 'any near or full approach, either to his power or to his secrets.'[13]

Even the king's relationship with his oldest and closest supporters was measured not in trust but money. Richard Fox paid £2,000 for a pardon for retaining offences; Archbishop William Warham appeared in Dudley's book, bound for £1,600 for prisoners escaped from episcopal gaols; so too did the king's mother herself, paying her son 700 marks for an abbey and benefice.[14] The sense of bewildered, aggrieved alienation was summed up by Giles lord Daubeney, Henry's chamberlain, over whom a cloud had hung for the past two years. When, in May 1508, Daubeney died at his manor of Hampton Court, he made extensive provision in his will for the paying-off of his debts to the king. Even though it had 'pleased the king's highness' to charge him a recognisance of £2,000 and to confiscate his French pension he had, he protested, been the king's true servant 'these xxvi years and above'.[15]

In the chill damp of the new year, Henry's tuberculosis returned. His public appearances, always infrequent, were now fleeting. For most of February, he was holed up in the privy apartments at Richmond, where access to him was even more constrained than usual. Reports of his physical condition leaked out. He was breathing with difficulty, unable to eat, and had again grown weak and emaciated. An arthritic condition left his hip joints swollen and inflamed. At Candlemas, on the anniversary of Elizabeth's death, unable to move, he dispatched Daubeney to attend her memorial service at Westminster Abbey, and to make the customary offerings.

For many, Henry seemed a name only, a cipher for the activities of his agents. Rarely visible, he seemed not to want to be seen. For people who caught a glimpse of him, hollow-cheeked, blue eyes burning fiercely, he seemed more dead than alive. Illness seemed to provoke even further his fierce obsession with control and obedience: in between fits of choking and arthritic pain, with his army of physicians on hand, he continued to pursue his subjects with an intensity even more savage than before, almost as if he was afraid that he might lose people's loyalty. In the midst of all this, he tipped lavishly – as he had always done – small acts of service and kindness, such as the twenty shillings given to the sergeant-at-arms who brought a bottle of mead for his ravaged throat. There were days, too, when he could haul himself to his feet and give unfortunate petitioners a dressing-down.[16] But, more often that not, he was incapacitated. The annotated names in John Heron's chamber accounts reveal the identity of the men in charge, making payments and sending an incessant stream of privy seals and letters on the king's behalf: the master of the wards Sir John Hussey, Empson's, Dudley's and Denys's associate Roger Lupton, and Dudley himself.[17]

In a sure sign of the gravity of the situation, Lady Margaret Beaufort had again descended on Richmond. With lodgings constructed for her household servants, she settled in for the duration with her retinue and chief advisers, including her confessor, John Fisher, bishop of Rochester, and fired off a volley of letters and commissions, ordering – a typical maternal reaction to the quality of her son's furniture – new beds, and dispatching a servant upriver to London for a barrel of muscadel.[18]

Towards the end of February, a new ambassador from Aragon arrived, and with him, renewed hope for Catherine. Finally giving in to his daughter's carping about de Puebla, Ferdinand had sent a man who was the very antithesis of the subtle, low-born, disabled Jew: Don Gutierre Gómez de Fuensalida.[19] A stiff-necked aristocrat and ex-military man, Fuensalida may have ticked the right social boxes but his diplomacy had all the subtlety of a sergeant-major on parade. He had won his ambassadorial spurs at the Burgundian court, where he developed an idiosyncratic approach to tricky negotiations. As he told Ferdinand in one dispatch, there was only one way to deal with scheming foreigners, and that was to show them who was boss – 'they're only humble when they're badly treated' – a strategy which inevitably failed with both the Burgundians and his diplomatic colleagues. Why Ferdinand thought Fuensalida was the man to improve Anglo-Spanish relations is a mystery. Unsurprisingly, he didn't.

Ferdinand had given his new ambassador two letters, both addressed to de Puebla: one confirming him in his post as resident ambassador, the other dismissing him from his duties. After sizing up exactly where de Puebla's loyalties lay – with Henry and England, Ferdinand strongly suspected – Fuensalida could use whichever he saw fit. What was more, Fuensalida had not travelled alone. With him came a representative of the Aragonese branch of the Grimaldi bank. Francesco Grimaldi, cousin of Dudley's sidekick John Baptist, was carrying the bills of exchange for Catherine's marriage portion. Finally, Ferdinand had stumped up, and, despite sidelining de Puebla, had used his recommended broker to do so. Catherine's purgatory seemingly was almost at an end. But appearances, as ever, were to prove deceptive.

While his father remained in the seclusion of Richmond, Prince Henry and his companions had again retreated to Kennington. There, throughout February, they practised for the early March jousts, in honour of the arrival of the latest embassy from Maximilian, to be held downriver at Greenwich.

Two days before the festivities, the king staggered to his barge. Thick with carpets and cushions under its canopy, the barge nosed down the Thames to the bishop of Bath and Wells's luxuriously appointed palace on the Strand, which the king had recently confiscated from Adriano Castellesi. Arriving at Greenwich, Henry made a brief appearance before the assembled ambassadors in a forced display of familial unity. Taking his daughter Mary by the hand, and gripping Catherine with the other, he discussed his prospective daughter-in-law with the ambassadors. He and his son talked often about Catherine, Henry said to Fuensalida, and the prince thought her 'a beautiful creature'.[20] But whatever the prince thought, as Fuensalida was to discover, was neither here nor there.

The prince looked on enviously at his companions-in-arms, Buckingham's brother Henry Stafford and Richard earl of Kent, as they fought 'fiercely backwards and forwards'. After the jousts, the king retreated to his privy apartments, ill, reluctant to be seen, closeted away. He was worsening: all the telltale signs were there. Masses were ordered: two thousand to be sung by the Friars Observant at Chertsey, eight thousand at Oxford and Cambridge, at sixpence the mass. Diversions of every kind were tried – in a boat on the Thames, mariners 'rowed up and down singing', music drifting into the royal apartments. Outside, in the public rooms of the palace, the entertainments continued. On 15 March, in the presence chamber, the prince dined 'with certain lords, as was customary'. Served by his father's waiters, presided over by his gentleman-ushers, he sat 'in place of the king'.[21]

Easter came and went, and still Henry was withdrawn. Physically, he had begun to recover, but he was rarely seen. Bernard André, for once, seemed to put his finger on it: the king was, he said, 'depressed', exhausted and thin. As the prince practised incessantly in the tiltyard at Greenwich, Henry remained shut away, absorbed in his worlds of finance and diplomacy, distracted intermittently by minstrels, new chess sets and dice, and by tempting offerings from his French pastry chef.[22]

Disregarding the advice of de Puebla, and of Catherine, whom he dismissed as little more than a girl, Fuensalida plunged into the negotiations. In an interview headed by Henry's crack diplomats – Fox, Nicholas West, Surrey and Charles Somerset, Lord Herbert – the entente quickly unravelled. Although Fuensalida had brought the bankers' drafts, there was a major catch: they only covered two-thirds of the dowry. The balance would be paid in Catherine's jewels and plate. The problem was, as Fox and West blandly outlined, the treasure was not Catherine's to pay. When she had married Arthur, it became his; and when he died, it reverted not to her, but to the king. Henry had, of course, graciously allowed her to keep it – but since then, she had sold nearly half of it. If Ferdinand really wanted his daughter's marriage to the prince to go ahead, he would have to pay the whole dowry upfront, in cash.

Fox and his colleagues ran legal rings around Fuensalida, and the more sweetly reasonable they were, the more irascible the ambassador became. His requests to see Henry were batted away by Fox, who would emerge from the privy apartments, the door closing quietly behind him, shaking his head: the king, regretfully, was indisposed, and could not be seen. Fuensalida had got precisely nowhere. Ultimately, though, the underlying problem was not the money.

With his daughter's Habsburg marriage in the bag, and obsessed with his balance-of-power policy, Henry wanted, it seems, to continue manoeuvring his son around the European marriage market as long as he could: the prince could marry another Habsburg, perhaps; even Louis XII's daughter Margaret of Angoulême was mooted. Although Catherine remained, in theory, a reasonable option, Henry by now found the idea of an alliance with her father utterly noxious. Over the years Ferdinand had slighted him with his constant procrastinations over the marriage portion, accompanied by barely believable excuses. He had played fast and loose with Henry's protestations of love for Juana. He had refused to countenance Mary's betrothal to his grandson Charles. In short, he had behaved with much the same calculated suspicion as Henry himself.[23]

Ferdinand understood all too well that Henry was, as his secretary of state Almazan put it, 'not his friend'. Having reached a dead end with the king, he urged Fuensalida to try another tack: the ambassador must get as close as possible to the prince, and get him onside. Prince Henry, Ferdinand was sure, wanted to marry Catherine. What was more, with his chivalric bravado the prince had the air of somebody who might be far more amenable to the kind of foreign adventures that Ferdinand had tried so long, and so unsuccessfully, to get his father embroiled in.

Fuensalida had little luck this way either. The prince was kept apart from the rest of court, he wrote acidly, in seclusion, 'like a girl'. At Richmond, his chamber could only be reached by way of the king's apartments, which were themselves inaccessible. When exiting the palace – to joust, perhaps, or hunt – the prince was hustled out of a side door into a private park, presumably the privy gardens adjoining Richmond, and surrounded only by those people expressly appointed to accompany him: his chamber companions and security advisers. Nobody, Fuensalida continued, would dare approach the prince for fear of their life, a message undoubtedly driven home by the presence of the bruising Rainsford. What was more, when the prince appeared in public alongside his father, he was subdued, speaking quietly and only when spoken to: 'so subjected', said the ambassador, 'that he doesn't say a word except in response to what the king asks him'.[24]

In observing the English king and his son, the Aragonese, it was clear, had sensed a pressure point, a fissure in the relationship between the two. It was a tension, they felt, caused not only by Henry's sense of his son's youthful vulnerability and his susceptibility to factional influence, but by the potency of this imposing sixteen-year-old bursting with vitality and energy. As Almazan later remarked, King Henry was 'beset by the fear that his son might obtain too much power by his connexion with the house of Spain'.[25]

Recent history provided examples of the destructive tensions between kings and their sons – and Henry and his son, both keen students of the lives of their predecessors, would have been uncomfortably aware of one in particular. In the last days of the suspicious, diseased Lancastrian King Henry IV, the king and his son Prince Hal were at loggerheads over various issues, in particular foreign policy. Relations between them had deteriorated to such an alarming extent that Prince Hal had been forced publicly to vigorously deny widespread rumours that he was 'affected with a bloody desire for the crown of England', that he 'was planning an unbelievably horrible crime' and 'would rise up against my own father at the head of a popular outbreak of violence', and that he would 'seize his sceptre and other royal insignia on the grounds that my father and liege lord was living a life to which he had no proper title and which relied on tyrannical persuasion'. In short, that he was plotting to usurp his own father.

Having identified with Henry V himself in various ways – in his abortive invasion of France sixteen years before, and in the designs for his tomb – Henry VII had always tried to associate himself with the glorious Lancastrian forebear from whom he was not, quite, descended. But by the last years of the reign his caricature had come to resemble far more closely that of Henry IV, who himself had gained a kingdom by usurping his cousin Richard II, and who in his last years, ill and paranoid, had retreated into his shell. The prince, by contrast, modelled himself on Henry V: indeed, in his first years as king, he would commission a biography of the triumphant conqueror of France to commemorate his own plans for an invasion, one designed to emulate Henry V's deeds.[26] There is no suggestion, of course, that Prince Henry was contemplating the overthrow of his father. But it was becoming increasingly clear that as king, surrounded by his chivalrous friends, he would pursue a very different path, one of visible, aggressive, glorious kingship – if given the chance.

All of which was obvious in the summer tournaments that year, held at Greenwich in mid-June and at Richmond the following month, in which the prince competed for the first time. Competed – but not in armed combat. Rather, he was restricted to the sport known as 'running at the ring': charging at a suspended hoop and spearing it with the point of a lance. An exercise that demanded skill and considerable hand–eye co-ordination, it was a recognized part of any tournament. Later, people even wrote songs about Henry VIII's prowess: 'My sovereign lord for my poor sake/ Six courses at the ring did make/ Of which four times he did it take/ Wherefore my heart I him bequest . . .' But, crucially, 'running at the ring' was a non-contact form of jousting. The prince was on view – but he was still not allowed to pit himself against his peers.[27]

As the crowds and his appraising companions looked on, he ran through the whole repertoire of flashy techniques, including the jouster's favoured way of disguising the intended blow until the last minute: carrying his lance vertically and only lowering it into its rest as his plate-armoured charger thundered down on its target. It was the kind of showy brilliance that the likes of Kent, Stafford and Brandon favoured, and Prince Henry executed everything perfectly. Six feet two inches, with flaming auburn hair, this was the prince who transfixed Thomas More: 'There is fiery power in his eyes, beauty in his cheeks as is typical of roses.' Prince Henry, it was clear, impressed everybody else as well. Fired with grandmotherly pride and crusading zeal, Lady Margaret sent him a handsome tip of twenty marks for his 'running at the ring'; another admirer sent a new horse. But for all his brilliance, the prince was restricted to glorified target practice, kept in cotton wool while his companions-in-arms duelled under the midsummer sun.[28]

Away from public view, however, the prince was proving himself as aggressive as the men who had overseen his martial education. Towards the end of the month, Richard earl of Kent broke his arm in training, 'while fighting with the prince'.[29] Whatever the king's advisers thought, the prince had grown up.

That June, in one of the walled orchards abutting the tiltyard, Henry spent three hours quizzing Margaret of Savoy's ambassador: the king on horseback, the diplomat trotting beside him, Sancho-Panza-like, looking up from his mule as he tried to keep pace. Earlier that month, in north-eastern Italy, the army on which Maximilian had squandered Henry's money had been massacred by Venetian forces in the floodplains of Friuli; now, both the emperor and his daughter Margaret, the unwilling target of Henry's own marital plans, were desperate for English money and intervention in the Low Countries against France. In the meantime, they had failed to dispatch the ambassadors who were supposed to enact the proxy marriage that would legally wed Henry's daughter Mary into the house of Habsburg. It was the same old story. As their horses ambled slowly between the cherry trees, Henry talked, in his mind pushing the counters across Europe's dynastic map. France's aggression had to be limited, he agreed, but there was no point in plunging the Low Countries yet again into war – particularly when all the Habsburgs had to do was to go and lay claim to Castile on behalf of the young Charles, his future son-in-law. This, after all, was the imperial project into which he had poured so much time and money, and into which he planned to marry his daughter – and, possibly, himself and his son. It would be sweet revenge on Ferdinand, currently ruling Castile on behalf of his daughter Juana. And besides, Henry still did not want to see these great dynasties ganging up on Venice.[30]

Behind Henry's words, perhaps, lay the delicate advice of Carmeliano, the 'friend' of the Venetian Signoria. There were others, too. Back in October 1507, convinced that he was about to be assassinated by Pope Julius's agents, the jittery Castellesi had fled Rome and headed southeast across Italy to the Adriatic seaport of Trani, then under Venetian control, where he threw in his lot with the republic. All the while continuing to send dispatches to Henry, the following April he had arrived in a Venice increasingly alarmed by Julius's military and diplomatic offensive. Castellesi had, he told the Signoria, an inside line to Henry, 'an agent at the English court, by name Polydore Vergil'. The Venetian ambassador in London should talk to Vergil and 'make use' of him, to try and dissuade Henry from joining Pope Julius's Holy League.[31]

But then, in the Greenwich orchard, Henry paused, changed the subject, and stared down at Margaret's ambassador. One of his counsellors, he said, had recently given the ambassador a list – did he remember? – of names, 'rebel subjects and others who daily do him blame and dishonour', still at large in Europe: men like the self-styled 'white rose', Suffolk's brother Richard de la Pole, a refugee in far-distant Hungary; and Sir George Neville, still skulking around the Netherlands. As Henry talked, a change came over him, the calm, statesmanlike tones modulating into savage vehemence. The Habsburgs – and in particular Margaret – were not doing enough for him. He wanted those rebels, who were his subjects, taken alive, so that he could punish them himself. The rest, he said, should have justice visited upon them, pre-emptively, without 'warning by which they might save themselves'. They should be taken out.

As he recalled Henry's speech, the ambassador's dispatch to Margaret of Savoy grew shocked, bewildered as he tried to put into words 'what things he said to me about it'. Nothing he could say to Henry would calm him: 'I should never have imagined he had the matter so much at heart.' Eventually, he gave up. 'I have too heavy a heart to write to you what I have heard, so shall make an end.' On that late June day, in the walled garden at Greenwich, the ambassador had glimpsed the king's soul, and what he saw had scared him witless. He did not want to get involved, he wrote; he just wanted to be somewhere, anywhere, else.[32]

Soon, though, the ambassador was writing again, frantically, to Margaret. Henry was getting tired of waiting for the Habsburg embassy that was due to perform his daughter's proxy marriage. He was already withholding further loans he had promised and, the ambassador warned, unless Margaret sent the embassy quickly, Henry would call the whole thing off and do a deal with the king of France instead: he had, the ambassador concluded, a habit of backing the winning side.[33]

After the midsummer celebrations at Greenwich, the court moved upriver, the king's oarsmen propelling the royal barge fast through London. At Richmond, as Bernard André noted, Henry's mind had cleared, for the first time in months it seemed. He rewarded fishermen who drew their nets for him on the banks of the Thames, ordered a consignment of books from the printer Richard Pynson, and attended the July jousts, watching his son run at the ring. He hawked – from nearby Esher, Richard Fox sent a servant with a hobby, which Henry received enthusiastically – and hunted, sending a present of freshly slaughtered deer to Princess Mary. But most of the time he was away from court in the seclusion of Hanworth, out of view and out of reach.[34]

○

That May, Edmund Dudley had completed the book of accounts that he had started nearly four years previously. Since that time, through the endlessly complex proliferation of fines that he had ferreted out on the king's behalf, Dudley had accrued a staggering £219,316 6s 11d, singlehandedly increasing the crown's yearly income by 50 per cent. And that was in just one of his account books. As Dudley himself noted, there were several more besides, such as the book of £31,000-worth of old debts that the king had handed over to him to sniff out. Another telling statistic showed the rampant effectiveness of Henry's administrators and promoters. In the first fifteen years of the reign, some 870 people had been bound in debt; in the last seven – from around the time of Suffolk's flight and Arthur's death – it was 3,500.[35] And that July, another building block was put in place.

The latest in the production line of ruthless royal officials, Edward Belknap was cut from Dudley's cloth, a 'mini-me' of the most obnoxious variety. John Fisher, bishop of Rochester, would complain that Belknap's zealous 'straight handling' was far worse than the man who he had previously been forced to deal with, the king's chief auditor Sir Robert Southwell. That July, Belknap was appointed 'surveyor of the king's prerogative', a newly created office that gave formal expression to much of the nebulous work that Empson, Dudley and their colleagues had been doing. But where, four years before, Dudley had simply been told by Henry what he wanted doing, Belknap's job description was drawn up in minute detail.[36]

The surveyor would shine the spotlight of the king's prerogative into the darkest, most obscure recesses of the realm. He was to create a national network of deputies, who were to investigate all possible instances where the king's rights might be applied to his financial advantage, where bonds could be imposed and fines taken. He and his men would be furnished with search warrants on request – no questions asked – and as usual, their work would not be salaried, but incentivized: they would receive a cut of the profits they made for the king. In paying in these funds, Belknap was to bypass even the chamber treasury, the shadow financial system run by John Heron. He was to remit them straight to the closest man to the king, his groom of the stool Hugh Denys; Belknap's accounts, moreover, were to be audited personally by Henry.

Never legalized, the office of surveyor was the fullest expression of Henry's government, of what Dudley described as exactions of 'set plan', the elastic policy which had emerged from the king's piecemeal attempts to provide a rapid, decisive response to the emergencies of his reign, run by the financial and legal specialists – 'fiscal judges', Polydore Vergil called them – who were accountable to him, and to him only. The surveyor formalized all this: the undermining of the common law courts, the dismembering of the body politic, the compact by which the king was bound to listen and respond to his subjects, and the discernible outline of a very different kind of rule – a French one, in fact: absolutism.[37]

On 1 July 1508, Edward Belknap signed indentures for his new role with Sir Thomas Lovell, Sir Henry Wyatt, Empson and Dudley. Three days later, he gave financial guarantees, bonds of a thousand marks, for the good performing of his role. The men who took the money, who oversaw his work, and to whom he was accountable – indeed, the men who had very probably devised his role in the first place – were Empson and Dudley.[38] 'Thus', as Vergil said, 'through the agency of these two men, who behaved as if they were plotting to snatch all lay and ecclesiastical wealth, the most savage harshness was made complete.'

By the end of July, as the grass season approached, Henry was strong enough to go out, north and east of the city, on progress. But underlying the leisurely stages was a new panic. In the hot, stagnant summer, the sweating sickness had settled over London. People collapsed in the streets, slumped in doorways playing with their children, tumbled off horses as they rode. They ate dinner at 11 a.m. with every appearance of health and were dead by suppertime. They died 'everywhere in this city', wrote Bernard André. Carts rolled through the deserted streets and lanes, carrying away bodies; bells tolled; occasional fervent gatherings of people praying, mourning. Prayers were said daily in St Paul's, at the cross, whispered in thousands of houses throughout the city.

And the sweat seemed to follow the royal family, a constant, invisible presence, first in Greenwich and Eltham, burrowing into the households of the prince, and of the king himself. It was no use running away, said André, for death conquered all: '*mors omnia vincit*'.

That August, the stately progress north of London, from Thomas Lovell's house at Enfield to Lady Margaret's at Hatfield, and east through Essex became a frantic dance: bags, coffers and trunks hastily packed at the first sign of pestilence; servants quarantined, harbingers riding ahead with particular vigilance. Three of the prince's chamber servants died; by mid-August, at Wanstead, disease had wormed its way into the king's privy chamber. Hugh Denys, the groom of the stool, was struck down. So too were Richard Fox, and the man who had replaced Lord Daubeney as chamberlain, the trusted Charles Somerset, now lord Herbert. Henry, anxious, issued an edict. Nobody travelling from London was to be admitted to the household precincts, and nobody was to go to the city on business or pleasure, except for medical staff – physicians and apothecaries.[39]

In the infected city, nothing seemed to stop the promoters. John Baptist Grimaldi's vendetta against Sir William Capel re-ignited, the Genoese informing Empson and Dudley of coinage offences that the merchant had failed to prosecute during his mayoralty. Found guilty by a jury packed with men 'fast bound to the girdles of Empson and Dudley', Capel was ordered to pay £2,000. When he refused, Camby locked him up. London's prisons were bursting.[40]

The atmosphere of impunity took curious turns. At Old Ford, near the king's disease-ridden manor of Wanstead, the prince's bodyguard Sir John Rainsford turned highwayman. Holding up a convoy of Italian merchants travelling into London, he found to his delight a consignment of furniture of exquisite manufacture, which he pillaged. Rainsford, though, had put his foot in it: the consignment, it turned out, was an order placed by Henry himself for Mary's betrothal ceremonies. Rainsford was given a dressing-down – possibly escaping harsher punishment in the general panic over the sweating sickness, possibly through the quick intervention of Sir Henry Marney, or even the prince himself. But maybe, too, this was not such an isolated incident. The only reason it was recorded was that it concerned the king's goods: the ensuing investigation, and presumably Rainsford's abject self-abasement in front of the king, had come to Bernard André's attention. Perhaps the prince's household, with the thuggish Rainsford, pranksters like Henry Guildford, and the sly, streetwise Compton, was more like the rampaging youthful Edward I's than people cared to admit.[41]

By the end of August, the disease had disappeared as quickly as it came. The king's household had had a remarkable escape. Both Fox and Lord Herbert recovered; so too, eventually, did Denys. With the end of summer, the king arrived back at Greenwich, and the travelling household folded smoothly back into the larger, standing household. With a renewed, almost manic determination, Henry set about putting the final pieces of his daughter's marriage treaty into place.[42]

As one of Henry's coterie of chaplains, Thomas Wolsey's diplomatic career was progressing fast. Close to his mentors Fox and Lovell, and ingratiating himself with up-and-coming ambassadors like Silvestro Gigli and his literary protégé Andrea Ammonio, he was increasingly entrusted with important diplomatic missions. Indeed, he had already proved himself to the king in a spectacular feat of diplomacy, one that he later recalled for the benefit of his admiring biographer, George Cavendish. Henry had sent Wolsey on embassy to Maximilian in the Low Countries, a mission he accomplished with superhuman speed. Leaving Richmond around noon, he arrived back three and a half days later in the dead of night; slipping into his surplice, he was waiting demurely in the king's closet when Henry arrived for early-morning mass. As he debriefed his chaplain, the king's scepticism – had Wolsey actually been away at all, he wondered – turned to amazement, 'a great confuse and wonder of his hasty speed'. Fox and Lovell rejoiced 'not a little': their man was another confirmed route to the king.[43]

That autumn, Wolsey was an unctuous presence at Margaret of Savoy's court at Malines, sending back studious, detailed dispatches, and drawing on a handsome expense account set up by della Fava with the local Frescobaldi branch.[44] Finally, the Habsburg diplomatic wheels were turning. In early December, after another ratification of the treaty at Calais overseen by Richard Fox and Thomas Howard earl of Surrey, the imperial ambassadors crossed the Channel and rode through Kent, the bare winter landscape punctuated by lavish receptions, handsome gifts of wine, wax and spices, along the route. Lord Bergavenny and his unruly retainers were long gone. The lone big man in the county, whose retinues now accompanied the ambassadors, was Sir Edward Poynings, the renowned military commander whose loyalties had been constant since Henry's exile, through Bosworth and the many battles, clashes and emergencies of the reign. In the fields outside Dartford, the bishop of Worcester, Silvestro Gigli, rode towards them at the head of a reception committee, and 150 horsemen, followed by Archbishop Warham and the earl of Oxford. Escorted through the town to the nearby Thames, the ambassadors were rowed upriver by barge to Greenwich, where Henry and the prince, surrounded by the anxious Spanish ambassador Fuensalida, 'twelve or thirteen' bishops and an array of nobles, made them welcome. It was true, Henry said to the head of the embassy, the Anglophile lord of Bergen, that he had felt 'some unpleasantness' at the delay – but no matter; the cloud passed.[45]

The festivities for Mary's proxy wedding would rival those of Catherine and Prince Arthur's marriage seven years previously. Over the past months Henry had overseen the preparations with his characteristic eye for detail. He vetted the furnishings for the guests and for his daughter's lodgings, writing minute corrections to the hierarchy of interior décor, from a bedchamber saturated in cloth-of-gold and crimson velvet and adorned with Mary's badges, to a fourth chamber more simply hung with 'good and fine' arras. No detail was missed: even Phip, Henry's favourite fool, had a new gown, ordered by his head of the wardrobe of robes William Smith.[46] Mary herself had sat, still and collected, for Pietro Torrigiano, who modelled a portrait bust of her: the likeness of 'Madam Marie d'Angleterre' was carefully packed and shipped across the Channel to her betrothed, Charles of Castile. It impressed Henry so much that he also ordered a model of himself.[47]

The entertainments, too, would rival those overseen by William Cornish at Westminster in November 1501.[48] In London, the pageant designer Harry Wentworth set to work with a team of craftsmen, leasing a large townhouse in the shadow of the crane at Vintry wharf, and given the run of 'certain houses' in the bishop of Hereford's nearby palace complex. The gates swung open daily to admit deliverymen with wagonloads of timber, canvas, linen, pullies and cogs; carpenters and joiners, scene painters, tailors and embroiderers, and the 'grinders of colours' who mixed up the vivid pinks, greens and reds of brasil-wood, verdigris and *sanguis draconys*, dragon's blood. As the days shortened, the pageants took shape in flickering fire- and candlelight, massive timber structures finished with intricate ironwork depicting hawthorn leaves, roses and marigolds, and swathed in painted cloth. Finally, three months later, the pageants – a castle, a tree, and the ubi-quitous rich mount – were carefully wheeled down Thames Street to secure storage in the nearby prince's wardrobe. Heaving two packing-cases and two great coffers into a barge at nearby Vintry stairs, Wentworth set off upriver to Richmond 'so that the king might see the disguising stuff', waited for a day while the king inspected it minutely, then packed everything up again and shipped it back down-stream to London.[49]

That November, as the wedding plans neared completion, at the house of the unfortunate London haberdasher Thomas Sunnyff, there was a knock at the door. Ushered in was a messenger from Dudley's sidekick John Camby, telling Sunnyff to come and 'speak with Master Dudley in all haste'. Sunnyff was perplexed: he had only just got back from Dudley's house, 'even now, from his place', maybe to pay an instalment on his fine. The haberdasher was told to go, not to Candle-wick Street, but to a pub in nearby Fish Street, the Boar's Head – later immortalized as Falstaff's and Prince Hal's hostelry of choice. When he got there, there was no Dudley, but a reception committee: Camby, the lieutenant of the Tower and a number of armed retainers. Sunnyff was taken off to the Tower 'by the arm with one of his servants as Camby had commanded', and locked up.[50]

A little before midday on Sunday 17 December, in front of a press of courtiers in Richmond's presence chamber, Princess Mary was betrothed to Charles of Castile through his proxy, the lord of Bergen.[51] The fourteen-year-old Mary clasped Bergen's hand, her grey eyes fixed on those of the ambassador, and recited the long matrimonial speech from memory, 'perfectly and distinctly in the French tongue', without any hesitation, pause or 'bashing of countenance'. Then, after marriage contracts had been signed and exchanged, Bergen kissed her 'reverently', placing a gold ring on her wedding finger. The ensuing entertainments, the feasting, dancing and jousting, all went off spectacularly, including Wentworth's entertainments – though he had a narrow escape, a horseman having to ride 'in haste' back to London to fetch a costume that somebody had forgotten to pack. Richard Pynson, now the king's printer, had published a souvenir account of the occasion. The actors and dancers, it noted, performed in clothes and on stages 'made and appareilled in the best and richest manner'.

The pioneer of a new Tudor–Habsburg alliance, one made in the best Habsburg traditions – making weddings not war, as its motto proclaimed: *Tu, felix Austria, nube* – Mary was to be queen of an empire that spanned Christendom, stretching from the southern tip of Spain to the borders of Poland and Hungary, from Naples to the Netherlands. As Pynson's account put it, she would carry the Tudors into a new age of dynastic glory: 'Thy flourishing red roses be so planted and spread in the highest imperial gardens and houses of power and honour', that by such 'buds and branches as by God's grace shall proceed to them, all Christian regions shall hereafter by united and allied unto thee, which honour till now thou could never attain.'[52]

Throughout the fortnight-long entertainments, Prince Henry and his on-off bride-to-be were the wallflowers, their long-mooted marriage no nearer to a resolution. Mary had bypassed them both, and their participation must have been tinged with envy. For Catherine, her friend's wedding was another nail in the coffin of her own prospects. Fuensalida had in his inimitable way ordered her not to attend the festivities at all, given that Ferdinand had withheld his consent to the match; she ignored him. The prince, meanwhile, knew that his younger sister was the focus of spectacular ceremonies that, thanks to his father's diplomatic machinations, he had never enjoyed.

Away in the city of Cambrai, representatives of Maximilian – emperor, as he could now style himself – and Louis XII of France met under papal mediation, to resolve their longstanding quarrel over the province of Guelders. An independent bishopric embedded in

Habsburg territory, and close to France's north-eastern border, Cambrai was a constant focus for diplomatic intrigue.[53] Now, Henry's ambassador Sir Edward Wingfield travelled there with secret instructions to forward another proposed marriage alliance: this time for the prince's marriage to Louis's daughter, Margaret of Angoulême. Through such a match, Henry hoped, he could tear Louis away from his alliance with Aragon, and leave Ferdinand exposed and isolated. Catherine would be left high and dry as well.

But when Wingfield arrived in Cambrai, he learned the real purpose of the summit. Involving not only Maximilian, Louis and the pope, but Ferdinand too, it was to conclude the Holy League against Venice, whose land territories were to be partitioned among the treaty's signatories. Julius had succeeded in his grand coalition – and Ferdinand, joining it, had outflanked Henry's attempts to sideline him. Undeterred, Henry kept playing the game, confident in the hand he held. Not only did he refuse to join the league of Cambrai, he tried to break it up. Sending warning to Venice, telling the Signoria what the summit had in fact been all about, he offered to broker a separate pact between the republic and Maximilian. He continued, too, to make Maximilian loans: £10,000, on the security of a 'jewel called the rich fleur-de-lys'. After all, Maximilian was now part of the family.[54]

Back in London from his period of self-imposed study leave in the Netherlands, Thomas More flicked through a copy of an account, in Latin, of Mary's betrothal – an expanded companion edition that Pynson had published for the international market, authored by Pietro Carmeliano. More shook his head in disbelief. Trying to compare Henry VII and the mythical hero Aeneas, Carmeliano had echoed a line from Virgil's *Aeneid*. In doing so, he had unwittingly put Henry at the bottom of the pile. As More pointed out, *princeps cui nemo secundus* didn't mean, as Carmeliano thought, a king beyond compare. Rather, it meant the converse: a king 'to whom no one is second'.[55]

Luckily for Henry's Latin secretary, there were few at court qualified to spot his sloppy scholarship; fewer still cared as much as More and his friends. Carmeliano, after all, had rather more important business on Henry's behalf. At the Spanish court at Valladolid, moreover, his poem had its desired effect. Henry's ambassador there, John Stile, wrote to Henry how he had presented a copy to Ferdinand, then stepped back and watched the reaction: 'your grace may be right well ensured that it is much more displeasure to the king [Ferdinand] and all his affinity than comfort for to hear of the said noble marriage.'

Away to the east, bonfires were lit throughout London, flames licking the night sky hungrily, 'with other demonstrations and signs of joy and gladness'. But behind the junketing, the mood in the city was grim. In the Tower and gaols across the city, Sunnyff and his fellow-prisoners marked time. At the Old Barge, Thomas More and his friends waited expectantly; so too, around the prince, did Mountjoy and Compton. At court, the likes of Buckingham, Northumberland and Kent brooded. And those at the centre of power, who had risen with the regime and profited from it, wondered how they were going to secure the dynasty, to preserve the king's legacy, and themselves.[56]

14

The Art of Dying

The imperial ambassadors left in the depths of January. With them, the energy of the past months dissipated, and a miasma of ill-health seemed to settle over Richmond. Ordering plentiful supplies of medicine, devotional literature and alcohol, Lady Margaret had retreated to her chamber, surrounded by attentive apothecaries, members of the king's privy chamber, and her dutiful grandchildren. When in the middle of the month she departed with her household, so too did Henry, retreating to the seclusion of nearby Hanworth. There he settled back into his routine of paperwork and looked over the improvements: newly laid ornamental gardens, together with espaliered apple trees and an aviary; and, in the surrounding parkland, a hunting lodge. But then, in the winter damp and cold, he fell ill again.[1] The symptoms were all too familiar: tuberculosis, combined with the suffocating quinsy. He fought on but, as he had done before, he sensed death approaching.

Henry's preparations for death, modified and developed over the ten years since his illnesses had started, had always been meticulous and to the letter. In his devotion to the sacraments, to the Virgin Mary and the saints, in his good works and religious foundations – the chapel at Westminster Abbey, sightseers already admiring its soaring fan vaulting; the Savoy hospital, on which work had just commenced – the strength of his piety was evident.[2] In all this, Henry mirrored the attitudes of the age. People were terrified by the idea of death coming suddenly and unexpectedly. To prepare yourself for death – a battleground for the human soul between God and the devil – was the stuff of life itself: 'Learn to die', so one authority stated, 'and thou shall learn to live.' It was, too, an art. The countless cheap printed editions of *Ars Moriendi*, or *Craft of Dying* offered

333

guides to the penitence, restitution of wrongs, contrition and unswerving concentration on the hereafter that enabled people to prepare themselves to meet the judgment of Christ, and to give them the best chance of salvation from the horrors of purgatory.[3] But for Henry, these preparations had an earthbound significance, too: they were intended for his son's smooth succession as much as for the eternal well-being of his soul.

In early February Henry paid a visit to the Benedictine abbey of Chertsey, returning a few days later. On his way back to Hanworth, there was a slight but unusual adjustment to his itinerary. Henry rarely travelled on a Sunday. This time, however, he did, journeying south and east to the bishop of Winchester's palace at Esher, Henry's 'cell to Richmond', the home of Richard Fox. What the king was doing there can never be known for sure, but it seems likely that he and Fox, the man who had been close to him for over twenty-five years, mulled over the possible outcomes and dangers that would face the dynasty on his death.[4]

There remained the possibility of a challenge for the throne. The earl of Suffolk was still in the Tower, while his brother Richard continued to float around Europe. Then, too, there was Buckingham, who gave the impression of wanting nothing more than the heads of Henry's counsellors on the block and the crown on his own. Those resentful at their exclusion from favour or at their ill-treatment, from the earls of Northumberland and Kent to London's merchants, had no lack of figureheads from which to choose; neither did foreign powers, such as France or Spain, which would sense an opportunity to manipulate things in their favour. On the other hand, Henry's death would bring about regime change anyway. Prince Henry had given little indication of wanting to continue the system that his father had sustained – he was, it seemed, far more interested in the glory of kingship. Everybody, from his jousting friends, to nobles, churchmen and men of business, looked to him to provide reform: to restore the political order that his father's reign had twisted out of shape – in their favour, naturally. The king's regime would, it was clear, die with him; or it would have to give every impression of doing so. The question now, for both Henry VII and those close to him, was how to smooth his son's path to the throne while preserving the status quo. In order for things to remain the same, it was clear that they would have to change.[5]

Candlemas came and went. Again, Henry was unable to make the short barge journey to Westminster, but Elizabeth seemed to linger in his thoughts as he ordered money to be given to a 'woman that lay in childbed'.[6] Shortly after that time, people around him started to notice the familiar signs of death.

On the first Sunday in Lent, 25 February, John Fisher, bishop of Rochester, preached before the king at Hanworth. Even by the standards of the age, Lady Margaret's confessor had a morbid fixation: when saying mass, 'he always accustomed to set upon one end of the altar a dead man's skull', and would also place the same skull before him 'when he dined or supped' – a habit which undoubtedly caused the table talk to evaporate. Fisher, who had been at hand during the king's illnesses, knew death when he saw it. By the beginning of Lent, he recollected, the king had 'clearly recognized that he was going to die'. While there was probably some dramatic license involved in the timing – nothing, after all, could become the king's preparation for death so much as its coinciding with the season of penitence – he had probably spotted what others saw, too: the mental deterioration that accompanied Henry's physical decline.

So when at the end of February the royal household moved the few miles downriver to Richmond, it was evident that Henry was going there to die.

Few glimpsed Henry from then on. In the presence chamber, courtiers and servants alike did obeisance to the empty throne under its cloth of estate. The king's health remained a closely guarded secret and Fuensalida reported how, inaccessible behind the firmly shut door to his privy apartments, he would 'not allow himself to be seen'.[7] As the ambassador acknowledged ruefully, this was hardly surprising on his own account: Henry had blackballed him three months previously, since when he had had no access to the king whatsoever. But it was impossible to conceal from the wider court that all was not well. When ambassadors from Maximilian and Margaret of Savoy arrived on 6 March to consolidate the new treaty, Henry would not even admit them. Instead, they were received and handsomely entertained by the prince. But around the same time the king, hankering after young female company, sent for his daughter Mary and also for Catherine, then at nearby Windsor.

Following the frustrations of Mary's proxy wedding, Catherine had gained a new boldness. Determined to get to the root of the problems over her dowry, she demanded to inspect the original treaty of her marriage to Arthur. Ill, angry, Henry turned the air blue – or, as Catherine delicately put it in a letter to Ferdinand, 'permitted himself to be led so far as to say things which are not fit to be written to your highness'. But Catherine, Fuensalida implied in his latest, prurient, dispatch to Spain, was out of control, her assertiveness encouraged by the only man who she would now listen to: her Rasputin-like confessor Friar Diego, who preyed on her extreme devotion and was a bad influence on her, in more ways than one. In fact, Diego's influence caused Catherine to commit 'many faults'.

Fuensalida did not list these faults – except, that was, for her spreading malicious gossip about him – but, he said, the blame lay at Diego's door: he was 'scandalous in an extreme manner'. Skirting delicately around the subject, Fuensalida finally got to the point. The king and his advisers, he said, could not bear to see the lubricious friar 'so continually about the palace and amongst the women'. He let the insinuations about Diego and Catherine hang in the air.[8]

For Catherine, on the other hand, Fuensalida was proving even worse than de Puebla. Apart from treating her like a child, and his utter lack of diplomatic finesse, he had introduced her months before to the Genoese banker who had come with him from Spain: Francesco Grimaldi, cousin to Edmund Dudley's sidekick John Baptist. At first, Francesco had seemed too good to be true. Not only had he brought with him the letters of credit for Catherine's dowry, but he was more than happy to accommodate her desperate need for cash.

On the advice of Friar Diego – now, apparently, her financial adviser as well as everything else – Catherine borrowed substantial funds from the bank of Grimaldi. Meanwhile, Francesco proceeded to make himself thoroughly at home in her household, seducing her lady-in-waiting Francesca de Caceres. When Catherine dismissed her in a fit of petulance, Fuensalida acted as guardian angel, employing Francesca himself and encouraging her to marry her suitor. For his part Grimaldi, put out by Catherine's wilfulness, now wanted his money back – with menaces. If she refused to pay her debts, he said, he would leave England, and would take the letters of credit with him.

Early that March, when Catherine – who had been sick much of the night – emerged to join Mary on the short ride from Windsor to Richmond, she found Friar Diego blocking her path with a quiet 'You shall not go today.' Not having seen the king for over three weeks and desperate to remain in his good books, Catherine protested. Her confessor was insistent. After two hours, Mary's party eventually rode off, leaving Catherine behind. On his sickbed, Henry was reportedly 'very much vexed' at Catherine's absence, but, to Fuensalida's astonishment, he let the episode pass. 'That the king allows these things', the ambassador pondered, 'is not considered a good sign by those who know him.'[9]

When Catherine eventually arrived at Richmond with her down-at-heel entourage, Fuensalida's fears were confirmed. Henry, it appeared, could barely be bothered with her any more. It was not, the king told her, his job to keep her shoddy household in order and subsidize its expenses, but 'the love he bore her would not allow him to do otherwise'. Imagine, Catherine wrote to her father in miserable indignation, the state she was in: to be told that she was dependent on the king's goodwill even for her food, which 'is given me almost as alms'. The situation, it seemed, was hopeless, and Catherine began to think the unthinkable: after over seven years in England, and now twenty-three years old, she would have to return to Spain.[10] But while the king's lassitude reflected his almost total indifference towards Catherine as a bride for his son, it was also a sign of something else. Whether or not Fuensalida suspected it, Henry was, by degrees, losing control. As he declined, faction stirred at the heart of power: in the king's privy chamber. Barely detectable, it revealed itself, almost inevitably, in his account books.

Over the years, the name of Hugh Denys, the groom of the stool and head of the privy chamber, had been a constant in the accounts of chamber treasurer John Heron, with whom he had an open-ended expense account on the king's behalf. In recent times, the informal 'privy purse' that Denys kept to meet Henry's personal payments had been supplemented by other forms of income, in particular the profits of justice: fines siphoned off from various courts of law. The latest of these were the fines generated by the efforts of Edward Belknap, which were assessed by Henry himself and paid straight into Denys's hands. Belknap, who had barely been in his role for six months, was already proving a highly effective fundraiser – which may have been why, from 14 January 1509, Denys's name ceased to appear in the king's chamber accounts: he no longer needed to take his chits and receipts to Heron now that he had a ready supply of cash on tap. But then, that February, Henry stopped signing Belknap's books – and from the end of the month, Denys's name vanished from them, too.[11]

Why this should have been remains a mystery. Illness is one possibility. Although Denys had survived the sweating sickness the previous summer, it had, perhaps, left him weak and unable to fulfil his duties. There is, though, a more likely explanation: that Denys's influence was fading along with the king, with whom his fortunes were inextricably entwined. Quietly, with no outward change in status, he had relinquished his leading role; others, equally quietly, were stepping into his shoes. None of this was formalized, and to anybody outside the privy chamber, it was undetectable. But for those familiar with the delicate web of relationships that knitted together the king's close counsellors and servants, it was a warning sign.

Richard Weston was one of Denys's longstanding colleagues in the privy chamber, and he had profited greatly from his intimacy with the king. Like Denys, he had become closely acquainted with the circle around Edmund Dudley, taking debts with his colleagues on the king's behalf. But while Denys's association with Dudley was particularly close, Weston's friends were different.[12] Years before, Queen Elizabeth had favoured him with particular commissions; Prince Henry, too, liked his air of agreeable urbanity. In recent years, Weston had gone out of his way to express quiet solidarity with certain prominent nobles, standing surety for the earl of Northumberland's extortionate debts and receiving a grant from him in return. And he was linked, in particular, with two of Henry's greatest counsellors. Back in 1503, in his battle with Sir Richard Empson, the Yorkshire knight Sir Robert Plumpton had remarked that Weston was a man who could be trusted – along with his friends, the bishop of Winchester Richard Fox and Sir Thomas Lovell.[13] Over the next weeks, Hugh Denys, Dudley's line of information into the privy chamber, would be replaced by Fox and Lovell's man, Weston. It would prove crucial to what followed.

By the end of March, the king was close to death. Henry's spiritual officers ordered thousands of masses to be sung on his behalf, among them, padding around, the now-ubiquitous Thomas Wolsey. In early April, Lady Margaret's retinues arrived at Richmond and quantities of 'kitchen stuff' were rowed downstream from her London house of Coldharbour, along with her favourite bed. Shortly after, the familiar slight, wimpled figure descended from her litter.[14]

Unable to eat and struggling for breath, Henry's mind was fixated on the hereafter. On Easter Sunday, 8 April, emaciated and in intense pain, he staggered into his privy closet, where he dropped to his knees and crawled to receive the sacrament. Chief among those who guided the king through his preparations for death was John Fisher. Close to both Lady Margaret and Richard Fox, the intense Fisher was one of those clerics who quietly detested the rapacity of Henry's common lawyers, and their aggression against the privileges and liberties of the church. As he interrogated Henry relentlessly, in the way that priests did in order to bring the dying to a 'wholesome fear and dread' of their sinful condition, Fisher apparently worked away at one particular aspect of the king's sinfulness.

Pervading the carefully worded penitential formulas, Fisher later noted, was a sense that the king acknowledged and truly repented the depredations of his regime. As Henry lay amid mounds of pillows, cushions and bolsters, throat rattling, gasping for breath, he mumbled again and again to the clerics, doctors and secret servants around him – indeed, 'freely', to anyone within the close confines of the privy chamber – that 'if it pleased God to send him life they should find him a new changed man'.[15] This was all fairly customary. Contemporary treatises stipulated that the dying man, appealing to the 'good lord Jesus Christ', was to 'acknowledge that I have sinned grievously, and by thy grace I will gladly amend me if I should live'. But the king's promises, Fisher said, took very specific form. If he lived, Henry promised a 'true reformation of all them that were officers and ministers of his laws'.[16]

All of which caused deep disquiet among all those associated with the reign. In the face of widespread resentments, they had to prepare for a transfer of power that was fraught with uncertainty; to show, in other words, that they were part of the brave new dispensation, rather than the old.

The air of tension and repentance masked something else, too – a sense of things fragmenting and falling apart. It was evident in the latest version of Henry's will, drawn up on 31 March. This was the ultimate expression of his legacy, spiritual and earthly, a document drafted years before and revised constantly. Much of it was formulaic, even the carefully turned words of penitence and the provision for the most faithful of servants, who had put themselves 'in extreme jeopardy of their lives' in his service; there were also blanks for dates to be filled in. There was, however, no doubting the genuine contrition with which the king exhorted his executors to implement the conditions of the will with meticulous care, and to ensure 'restitutions and satisfactions for wrongs' were made. The king's path through purgatory depended on his will being carried out properly; so, too, did the regime's continuance and the executors' place in it. But the will also, inadvertently, betrayed that the king's mind was slipping away.[17]

Uncharacteristically for Henry's micro-management, the will was riddled with copyist's errors that went uncorrected: he had even failed to fill in a space left blank for the date of his recent dynastic triumph, Mary's proxy marriage to Charles of Castile. What was more, treading quietly around the bedridden king, his servants were already starting to implement the terms of the will, and to prepare for the succession.[18]

Amid the public signs of the king's decline – the releasing of prisoners, copious distribution of alms, profusions of paid masses – a general pardon was proclaimed on 16 April. In recent years, people had become accustomed to the brief window of opportunity afforded them by these displays of royal contrition, before the king recovered and his counsellors started again. Now, they scrambled to avail themselves of the opportunity, filing into the chancery offices off Westminster Hall, where scribes enrolled their names and issued pardons – in return, naturally, for a fee.[19]

By the evening of the 20th, Henry was fading. Still, Fisher recalled, he hung on with fierce determination, 'abiding the sharp assaults of death' for 'no short while, but by long continuance by the space of 27 hours together'. Henry made an exemplary death: eyes fixed intently on the crucifix held out before him, lifting his head up feebly towards it, reaching out and enfolding it in his thin arms, kissing it fervently, beating it repeatedly against his chest. Finally, as his life vanished and death drew on, the king's grey-habited confessor urged him to speak, if he could: '*In manus tuas Domine commendo spiritum meum. In nomine patris et filii et spiritus sancti. Amen.*' Then, administering the *commendatio*, the confessor placed a taper in Henry's limp hand, lighting the departed soul's path to God.[20]

The servants standing around the royal bed raised their bowed heads, dried their ritual tears and met each other's eyes. It was 11 o'clock at night on Saturday, 21 April 1509. Henry VII had dragged the kingdom to the brink of dynastic succession. Almost, but not quite.

Outside the privy chamber the palace slept; life continued as before. The scene around the dead king's canopied bed, his eyelids being closed by one of the servants bending over the body, was later depicted by Garter herald Thomas Wriothesley in a detailed pen-and-ink drawing. In the flickering candlelight fourteen figures clustered around. Three, including Henry's chief physician Giovanni Battista Boerio, were doctors clutching flasks; two, as indicated by their tonsures, were clerics – the king's confessor and, perhaps, Thomas Wolsey. The identities of the nine others we know, because Wriothesley painstakingly painted in their coats-of-arms above their heads. They included the bruising Sir Matthew Baker, who had accompanied Henry on his escape from Brittany into France some quarter-century before; and the gentleman ushers John Sharp and William Tyler, who had reported to the king Thomas More's insubordination in the parliament of 1504. Then there was Hugh Denys and the new, de facto head of the secret chamber, Richard Weston. And at the head of the royal bed, on its left-hand side, was the bishop of Winchester and lord privy seal, Richard Fox.[21]

Fox, a key architect of Henry's regime, the man who had been privy to his inmost anxieties in exile, who had fought for him, who had masterminded his foreign affairs and conducted espionage on his behalf, whose palace had been the king's refuge, and who had watched as, in recent years, Dudley and Empson had moved closer and closer to the king, was at the heart of what followed. This time, the two lawyers were nowhere near Henry's bedside, but away in London. The only people who knew of his death were those present in the privy chamber. Fox and his fellow-counsellors now had a brief window of opportunity to order the succession to their advantage, to position themselves around the new, young king. It was what Henry VII would have wanted – and it would ensure their own survival.

There would be no announcement of the king's death, no general summons to court. Rather, the news would be, as Wriothesley put it, 'secretly kept'. For, as it turned out, the timing of Henry's death was almost perfect: in two days' time, one of the ceremonies of the ritual year would bring to court 'the substance of the lords', among them the great men of the regime.[22]

St George's Day, 23 April, was the feast of the Order of the Garter. Among the order's members were many of Henry's named executors: Fox himself, as the Garter's prelate, and his close colleague Sir Thomas Lovell; the two chief military commanders, the earls of Oxford and Surrey, and the chamberlain Charles Somerset, Lord Herbert. Those hoping for election included Thomas lord Darcy, and the prince's chamberlain, Sir Henry Marney. Also present, and a member of the order, was Lady Margaret Beaufort, who numbered the likes of Fox, Lovell, Herbert and Marney among her own executors. Just as significant, however, would be the absentees. Buckingham and Northumberland were both Garter knights, but both, perhaps in fits of independent-minded petulance, had made their excuses and stayed away. Dudley and Empson, meanwhile, had nothing to do with the Garter at all.[23]

In the last weeks of Henry's life, the workload of both men had intensified as his faculties diminished. Their eyes and ears at court kept them in touch with developments at the king's bedside – but unknown to them, the information that continued to flow through their usual channels in the privy chamber was being filtered. They were, though, sharply aware of the mounting tensions in London that, simmering for years, were coming to the surface as rumours spread of the king's impending death; foreign merchants scurried for cover, securing their valuable goods in safe storage.[24] It was, very probably, this potential for widespread disorder – or worse – that had kept Empson and Dudley in the city. If anybody could be trusted to ferret out information on planned riots and conspiracies against the regime, it was the two counsellors and their network of informers.

Around the time the general pardon was proclaimed on 16 April, unusual movements of men and materiel had been noticed around Le Parsonage, Empson's house on the city's western edge, and in Dudley's parish of St Swithin. Clearly anticipating trouble, both men were assembling armed retinues. Empson sent dispatches into his home county of Northamptonshire, mustering 'as many persons . . . whom he could firmly and secretly retain, to be ready in defence'. By mid-April, several had slipped through the city gates; others were making their way 'by separate companies'.[25] On the 22nd, as the king's body grew cold and rumours of his death filtered into Candlewick Street, Dudley scribbled separate orders to his sidekick Richard Page to take to nine men, including the household knight and jouster Sir Edward Darrell. The notes required them urgently to muster groups of armed retainers 'arrayed in manner of war', and to join Dudley in the city, where they were to await his further command. Meanwhile, he checked the well-stocked armoury in his house: quantities of plate armour and mail; sixty spiked, bladed bills; over a hundred and fifty bows – longbows and crossbows; thirty-five sheaves of arrows.[26]

Watchful, tense, both counsellors were acting on behalf of the regime's security. But there was, perhaps, more to it than that. In marshalling these private armies, Empson and Dudley were also positioning themselves for a potential struggle for influence over the young king. But, so accustomed to wielding power and to the king's confidence, both men evidently felt secure in the friendships of influential fellow-counsellors such as Fox, Lovell, Herbert and Oxford, and of Lady Margaret, who had recently sent the two lawyers a gift of fresh fish in reward for a lawsuit of hers they were prosecuting, as she passed through the city to Richmond. Empson and Dudley had failed to understand how resented and isolated their rapidly acquired power now made them, and how exposed they now were. Consequently, they failed to watch their backs.[27]

On the morning of St George's Day, the presence chamber at Richmond was packed. Garter herald Wriothesley presided over the ceremonies with a punctilious eye. By this point, he too had very probably been told the truth: he had the heralds cry Henry VII's largesse quite deliberately, in order that all those at court 'should have less suspicion of his death'. At noon, the assembled lords dined in the presence chamber, headed by Prince Henry, who was 'named and served as prince and not as king'. Surveying proceedings, pacing up and down the chamber with their staves of office, were the four gentleman ushers, three of whom – Sharp, Tyler and William Fitzwilliam – had been present at the dead king's bedside some thirty-six hours previously.[28] Then, after dinner, a slight movement fixed everybody's attention: the oak door leading to the privy apartments was opened from the inside.

Emerging with a 'smiling countenance', Richard Weston walked unhurriedly over to Archbishop Warham and told him and 'certain other lords' – almost certainly the likes of Oxford, Surrey and Herbert – that the king, Henry VII, wished them to attend on him. Following Weston back through the door, the small group of nobles stayed in the privy apartments 'a good pause' before emerging unconcernedly, 'with good countenance . . . as though the king had not been dead, showing no great manner of mourning that men might perceive'.[29]

But Warham and the most senior of Henry VII's counsellors now knew that the king was dead. The timing of their summons, moreover, had been deliberate. Shortly after, the prince – in place of the king – would progress with the assembled company to evensong in the Chapel Royal: it would provide the perfect cover for the counsellors to brief him on what was to be done. As was customary, the prince would hear mass in the holyday closet – sumptuously furnished with cushions, carpets, relics and its own altar – on the first floor of the ante-chapel. From there, when occasion demanded, he could descend via a private staircase to the main body of the chapel, to take part in the focal points of the service. But most of the time, the privacy of the closet allowed its occupants to catch up on business and discuss confidential matters undisturbed while the mass proceeded. This, very probably, was precisely what happened during that St George's Day evensong.[30]

Towering above the pack of counsellors and nobles clustering around him, Prince Henry, swathed in his hood and cloak of the Garter, passed through the crowded galleries leading to the Chapel Royal, his way lined on both sides by the guard in quartered white-and-green, halberds gleaming. He and a select few counsellors were ushered into the holyday closet, and the doors were shut on the jostling petitioners and courtiers outside. As the voices of the choristers and the sonorous notes of the chapel organ drifted up from the main body of the chapel below, Archbishop Warham and the 'other lords' that had emerged from the privy chamber hours earlier briefed the prince on what they believed should happen.[31]

After evensong, the prince returned to the presence chamber for the ceremonial Garter supper, 'all which time he was served and named as prince and not as king'. Finally, after supper, Henry VII's death was announced.

At this point, Wriothesley's account of proceedings gives no sense of any triumphant acclamation of Henry VIII. In fact, he fails to mention the seventeen-year-old king at all. The sense, rather, is of a small group of counsellors taking control, 'over seen by the mother of the said late king'. Far into the night, this coterie, headed by Lady Margaret and Archbishop Warham, and including Richard Fox, John Fisher, Thomas Howard earl of Surrey and the chamberlain Lord Herbert, discussed what was to be done. In all this, Henry VIII was deferred to: he, after all, was king. But he was, too, young and remarkably inexperienced – and he was now dealing directly with the powerful inner circle of his father's counsellors, men who were now suggesting to him in their thoughtful, measured way a certain course of action that was entirely necessary for the regime's security and his own. The impressionable seventeen-year-old, now finally the focus of a fast-moving, unstable and undeniably exciting sequence of events, and made to feel as though he was very much in charge, undoubtedly agreed to everything that was proposed.[32]

The following day, the 'prince called king' would be transferred to the Tower, now in the control of Henry VII's seasoned military commander the earl of Oxford, 'for the surety of his person'. Accompanied by members of his own household – the likes of Marney, Mountjoy, Compton, and the brutish Rainsford – he would stay there while the situation was monitored and until his father was buried. Henry VII's executors, Lady Margaret and Warham chief among them, would stay upriver at Richmond to implement the terms of his will. But first, they had to send out an emphatic statement that the new regime would not be like the old.

Polydore Vergil, in attendance on Lady Margaret at Richmond during these uncertain days, later summed it up. Empson and Dudley were, he wrote, singled out by a 'politic mean'. In the sun of Henry VII's favour they had risen far and fast, but now he was dead – and they were intimately associated with the repressive activities of his regime. For the old king's veteran counsellors, it was a chance to get rid of two men who might, potentially, build a close relationship with the new king, and to offer them up as scapegoats in the process. Empson and Dudley had to go.[33]

Early on 24 April, the round-ups started. At court the duke of Buckingham's brother and the marquis of Dorset's stepfather, Henry Stafford, identified as a potential troublemaker, was arrested. Meanwhile Dudley's associate Richard Page had been intercepted, and the letters he was carrying ripped open. As dawn rose over the city, bodies of armed guards – ferried downriver from Richmond, or let in through the city gates – slipped through the empty streets and quietly surrounded Empson's and Dudley's slumbering houses. Then came the hammering on doors, with bleary-eyed household servants sliding back bolts and lifting latches. Whatever moves the counsellors might have made were nipped in the bud. They were taken away to the Tower.[34]

In London later that morning, Henry VII's death was announced and the succession proclaimed. In the afternoon, the 'prince called king' rode through a city crawling with royal soldiers, to the Tower. On the following day, the 25th, Henry VIII set his signature, a painstaking 'Henry R', to his first piece of legislation: a new general pardon, superseding the one issued just over a week before in his father's name. Probably drawn up following the intensive discussions on that evening of the 23rd, it was carefully, deliberately worded, its expansive tone indicating what people could expect in the new dispensation – and in doing so, distinguishing it emphatically from the old.

Exhorting the king's subjects to peace, the pardon stressed that normal judicial service had been resumed, 'according to the old true course of his letters'. Justice would henceforth be 'freely, righteously and indifferently' applied – and the king would be as subject to the law as anybody: his judges would see to it that there would be no privileging of any kind. What was more, all merchants, 'clothiers, artificers and folks in all manner of mysteries and occupations' could now work and trade 'freely, quietly and peaceably', with no fear of 'untrue informations'. There would be no more informers or prying royal agents, no 'persons calling themselves promoters'. The new king would provide 'reformation of the rigour wherewith they [his subjects] have been vexed'. Neither was there to be any violent settling of scores: nobody, of whatever rank, was to take the opportunity to revenge his or anybody else's quarrel 'by way of fight'. The crown, it was implied, would take care of that.[35]

A copy of the pardon was dispatched to the king's printer Richard Pynson at his print-shop by Temple Bar on Fleet Street. He and his assistants set to work with concentrated precision and speed, the compositors setting and securing the type in place, then passing it to the printers, who inked it up, swung the frame of taut paper over it, slid the whole into the press and forced the press-plate down, removed the freshly printed sheet and began the process of inking again: a copy every twenty seconds.[36] By the morning of the 26th, thousands of copies were in circulation, to be posted on church doors from St Paul's to the remotest parish in the land, and proclaimed aloud at crosses and marketplaces, 'that every man thereof might have knowledge'.

In the city, a mood of retribution was in the air. Among the flood of prisoners emerging from the Tower and cells across London were the three former mayors, Kneseworth, Aylmer and Capel, all bent on revenge. When, days later, the pardon roll marking the start of the new reign was published, a number of names had been excluded.[37] John Camby was arrested, along with the financier Henry Toft and several who had sat on Empson and Dudley's carefully packed juries. Forcibly entering Camby's home to recover the fruits of his 'vice and polling', city officials expressed astonishment at the quantity of fine textiles stashed neatly away in a room that was 'more like a mercer or draper's shop than a man's chamber'. But the man they particularly wanted, the counsellors' 'worst disciple', had disappeared into thin air. Like his bosses, John Baptist Grimaldi had sensed the changing mood as Henry lay dying; unlike them, he had found an escape route. Securing his possessions out of reach of the crown's officers, he had fled beyond the reach of royal justice to the precincts of Westminster Abbey, where he claimed sanctuary.[38]

By 27 April, Fuensalida was writing in dispatches of the gaoling of the two most prominent of the old king's 'ministers of the briberies and tyrannies which used to be'. Empson and Dudley were, he stressed, the 'two principal men . . . who gathered all the riches'. It was a story that all the others involved in the 'briberies and tyrannies' were only too happy to run with. Fuelling the atmosphere of moral indignation were a slew of hastily composed 'opprobrious and shameful rhymes and tales': scrawled down, printed, passed from hand to hand, sniggered and frowned over, pinned up and read out in public places. Pouring out all the pent-up frustration of the previous years, they documented in lurid terms the abuses of the disgraced counsellors and their promoters.[39]

The London chronicler, who had heard and seen an assortment of these 'opprobrious rhymes' sung in taverns and posted on walls and doors, faithfully copied down two of them for posterity. One of the poems was a 'detestable legend' of John Baptist Grimaldi – so 'vile' a subject, the anonymous rhymester declared, that one could hardly expect poets of the calibre of John Skelton, Thomas More or William Cornish to sully themselves by writing about him. The other poem written out by the chronicler, a 'Ballad of Empson', consisted of a litany of the wrongs perpetrated under Henry VII, blame for which was placed squarely at the door of the gaoled counsellor. This, however, was very probably composed by Cornish, who had suffered abuse at Empson's hands. What was more, it had been commissioned or 'caused' by Richard earl of Kent, desperate for Empson's comeuppance. The new regime's efforts to 'shift the noise' onto Empson and Dudley, 'for to satisfy and appease the people', was bearing fruit. Meanwhile, in the Tower, one of Henry VIII's first actions was to command the head of the clerk of works to construct a tilt: as the young king waited, he jousted.[40]

At Richmond, as the dead king's body, washed, anointed and embalmed, lay in state, a 'right sumptuous household' was kept.[41] But beneath the enforced jollity, there was a palpable anxiety among those implicated with the old regime and with the two counsellors. Men kept their heads down, or tried to make themselves indispensable, or both. The head of the great wardrobe Sir Andrew Windsor, Dudley's brother-in-law, and Sir John Cutt busied themselves with the funeral arrangements. For them, the danger passed. Others were not so lucky. Dudley's fellow-counsellor Sir John Hussey was omitted from the accession pardon and arrested; so too was William Smith, groom of Henry VII's personal wardrobe and sometime factotum of Empson's, who was stripped of office and carted off to the Tower.

On 9 May, late in the afternoon, Henry VII's funeral cortège reached the southern entrance to London Bridge, and processed through the city's streets, following the time-honoured route to St Paul's. Amid the heralds, the chanting monks and friars, the black-clad household servants, the nobles, prelates, knights and officials, rolled a carriage containing the king's coffin, drawn by five coursers draped in black velvet and decorated with heraldic banners and flags depicting Henry's titles and dominions. On top of the coffin, reposing on cloth-of-gold cushions, was a life-size effigy, its head worked uncannily after the king's death mask, dressed – as perceptive observers might have noted with some irony – in the parliament robes he had barely had occasion to wear in the last twelve years, its right hand gripping his sceptre and its left an orb of gold. At the cathedral's west door, twelve yeomen of the guard carried the coffin and effigy to the high altar, staggering under its weight. There the *placebo*, the office for the dead, was sung, and a vigil kept throughout the night. The following morning, after mass, John Fisher climbed the pulpit stairs, placed his skull in front of him, and preached a funeral sermon.

Ranging over the achievements of Henry's reign, Fisher described the king's last days: his illness and piety, his exemplary death, his promises for reform. Henry, he said, had had 'full little pleasure' from this 'wretched world', but 'much displeasure and sorrow'. As Fisher urged his listeners to mourn and pray for the dead king, he seemed to interrupt himself in full flow. 'Ah king Henry, king Henry', he declaimed ruefully, 'if thou were alive again, many a one that is here present now would pretend a full great pity and tenderness upon thee.'[42] The enforcers of Henry VII's regime, bent on preserving a system of power and their place in it, had already succeeded in disassociating themselves from their late master, who had died just a fortnight before.

That afternoon, the cortège resumed its journey, down Fleet Street, past Charing Cross to Westminster. Henry's body was borne into the abbey and placed in its hearse, a multi-storeyed stage hung with banners, standards and lit with 'the most costly and curious light possibly to be made by man's hand'.[43]

It was already light when, at six the following morning, 11 May, nobles, clergy and heralds reassembled in the abbey to bury Henry VII. After three masses had been sung, the last of them a requiem led by Archbishop Warham, the earl of Surrey's second son Sir Edward, dressed in the late king's plate armour and bearing his shield and poleaxe, rode a warhorse through the west doors of the abbey and up to the altar. Dismounting, he was stripped of the weapons and armour, which were offered up 'with great reverence' by the duke of Buckingham and the earl of Northumberland. Then, Henry VII's corpse was lowered into the vault, buried, as his will stipulated, alongside 'our dearest late wife the queen', whose body awaited his.[44]

After Warham had cast earth into the open tomb, the old king's household officers broke their staves of office and threw them in. The heralds, taking off their emblazoned coats, shouted in French, 'The noble king Henry the Seventh is dead.' As the words' echo dissolved in the silence of the abbey, they put their coats of arms back on and cried 'Vive le noble Roy Henry le VIIIth' – which as the herald's account of the funeral helpfully explained, 'is to say in English tongue, "God send the noble king Henry the eight long life."'

These shouts of acclamation – 'long live the king' – were familiar enough. But for Henry VII's funeral, his counsellors had made two crucial changes. The cries 'the king is dead; long live the king' were run together in a way that was new in England, though it had been done before in France, after the death of Charles VIII in 1498. And, for the first time, the names of the king and his heir were included. Kingship was perpetual: the king himself may have died, but the institution, the 'dignity', had not, because it was automatically transferred to his heir. Now, Henry VII's counsellors, the men who had transferred their loyalties seamlessly to the new king, had given full expression to this crucial concept – and in doing so, they confirmed the association of one family's name with the crown of England. The Tudor dynasty had begun.[45]

15

Rich, Ferocious, Thirsting for Glory

In mid-May 1509, after his father's funeral, the seventeen-year-old king and his court left the Tower for the riverside tranquillity of Greenwich. Here, in his mother's favourite house and the place of his birth, the new reign began to unfurl. Even those who knew him seemed taken aback by the transformation of a teenager who had been so subdued in his father's company. 'However dutiful he was before', Thomas More observed, the new king has 'a character which deserves to rule.' Henry VIII was magnificent, liberal and bullish. As the Venetian ambassador delightedly reported back to the Signoria, the new king had announced that the first thing he planned to do, as soon as he was crowned, was make war on France. And, as everybody was aware, his father had left him a fortune – which he fully intended to spend. Machiavelli, whose pithy character sketches were rarely wide of the mark, got the new king in a nutshell: *'ricco, feroce, cupido di gloria'*.[1]

The old king's opaque accounting methods meant that nobody, not even his closest advisers, knew quite how much he had salted away in money, jewels and gold and silver plate, in the Tower, Westminster, Calais, and other 'secret places' under his own personal control. This, however, only fuelled the myth. The Venetian ambassador's estimate reflected the kind of conversations and calculations that were taking place at court and in the city: Henry VII, he wrote, had 'accumulated so much gold that he is supposed to have more than well nigh all the other kings in Christendom'.[2] This, coupled with the fact that the new king seemed eager to dispel the dark last years of his father's reign, seemed to make up for everything that people had endured. Nobles like Buckingham and Northumberland felt they would now regain their rightful place as the king's natural counsellors, with their confiscated lands restored to them; churchmen and merchants alike anticipated the rolling-back of aggressive royal legislation against their privileges and liberties. And everybody whose names had found their way into the account books of the old king and his counsellors fully expected them to be erased.[3] Henry VIII, in other words, would be all things to all men – and an easy touch into the bargain.

In the warm sun of the new king's favour, the scramble for lucrative grants of office and land began. All his father's counsellors, from the earl of Oxford, to Sir Thomas Lovell, to the jewel-house keeper Sir Henry Wyatt, were rewarded; Lady Margaret Beaufort, meanwhile, was quick to reclaim the palace of Woking, which her son had annexed from her six years previously. Fittingly, Richard Weston was awarded the keepership of Hanworth, whose muted corridors he had patrolled in the last weeks of Henry VII's reign. Also recognized were the new king's tiltyard friends: the likes of Sir Edward Howard, Thomas Knyvet and, of course, Charles Brandon. These were men whose stylish aggression he admired – and who could now egg on his desire for warlike glory and his easy way with money without fear of censure.[4]

One of those who rose fastest and furthest was Sir Henry Marney. Mirroring the role he had played in the prince's household, he was appointed captain of the guard – head of security – and vice-chamberlain, two posts which tended to come together. Among a raft of other offices given him was the chancellorship of the duchy of Lancaster, previously held by the disgraced Empson. Marney's pre-eminence was evident in the new reign's first meeting of the Order of the Garter, which the young king called with alacrity for 18 May – and for which occasion he had bought himself a Lancastrian collar of esses, in emulation of his hero Henry V. Put forward for election to the order, Marney was unanimously voted in.[5]

In its way, William Compton's advancement was no less meteoric. In the first days of the reign, the man who had been the prince's closest servant had emerged as first among equals in the new king's privy chamber; soon, he would be groom of the stool. Like Hugh Denys before him, Compton looked after the king's goods and personal affairs, which would be rather different from those of his father. He would handle industrial quantities of money on Henry VIII's behalf:

in the first year of the reign, Compton received some £2,328 to spend; four years later, it would rise to £17,517. One of the first to recognize the importance of his intimacy with the king was, predictably enough, Richard Fox.[6]

◉

On 27 May, Lord Mountjoy, intoxicated by the air of the new reign, signed a breathless letter to Erasmus.[7] Still in Italy, Erasmus's woes had deepened. He had failed to gain regular funding and he was, as he had emphasized in a stream of unanswered letters to England, sick and depressed. Now, Mountjoy apologized for being a terrible correspondent: 'many distractions' had prevented him from writing, including – he hinted darkly at the events surrounding the old king's death – 'certain reasons which I did not venture to set down on paper'. Then, with his customary breeziness, he told Erasmus to cheer up, for his former pupil had ascended the throne and 'all were congratulating themselves on their prince's greatness'.

The new reign, Mountjoy said, was the Promised Land. 'Heaven smiles, earth rejoices; all is milk and honey and nectar' – and if only Erasmus could see the scenes, he would weep for joy. The young king could not be more different from his father: 'Tight-fistedness is well and truly banished. Generosity scatters wealth with unstinting hand.' This was a monarch for whom gold and jewels were nothing compared with virtue and eternal renown. Why, only days before, the king had told Mountjoy how he longed to be a better scholar. Thinking quickly, Mountjoy had assured him that nobody expected him to be an intellectual – but he was expected to 'foster and encourage' men of learning. 'Of course,' replied the king, 'for without them we should scarcely exist.' Henry VIII, the implication went, had learned his lessons well.

Then, Mountjoy got to the point. He had 'never pressed' Erasmus to go to Italy in the first place. Everybody in England was reading the new, expanded edition of his *Adages* with admiration – Archbishop Warham, no less, was 'praising it to the skies'. Erasmus must come back to England. As if to settle the matter, Mountjoy enclosed a bill of exchange for ten pounds: five from him and five from Warham. This was not, he added, a gift – there would be plenty of gifts forthcoming when he arrived – but to cover his travel expenses, 'to speed your journey to us'. Moreover, he added, Warham promised Erasmus a benefice if he came back.

If Mountjoy laid the flattery on thick, it was hardly surprising. Erasmus had fallen for the blasé optimism of his former pupil before – twice before, in fact – and both times, expansive promises of rewards and benefices had added up to precisely nothing. It was all very well for Mountjoy to say he had never told Erasmus to go to Italy, but given the complete lack of opportunity in England back in 1506, he had had little choice. Which was why, while Mountjoy's letter was fulsome, it was artful too. After reminding Erasmus pointedly of his destitute conditions in Italy – he was sorry to hear Erasmus was sick, but then, he supposed, one had to suffer for one's art, fame being 'worth the price of hunger, poverty and illness, even death itself' – Mountjoy offered hard cash. If Erasmus wanted creature comforts along with fame, England could now provide him with both.

Behind all this was an ulterior motive, one that struck at the heart of Erasmus's principles of intellectual independence. The new England wanted a monopoly on Europe's finest mind. It wanted him as its mouthpiece, amplifying its virtues to the world: where once he had written verses extolling the superhuman qualities of the king's boyhood hero Philip of Burgundy, he could now do the same for Henry VIII. The new regime, with its glorious young monarch, didn't want second-rate poets like Pietro Carmeliano or Bernard André – but it did want Erasmus to demonstrate his loyalty, to be *ex toto Anglicus*.

All of which was evident in a letter from Warham, which was probably enclosed with Mountjoy's. Warham had a high regard for Erasmus's abilities, but thoroughly disapproved of his flightiness. Now he offered Erasmus a deal, an exclusive contract with the English crown. As soon as Erasmus arrived in England, Warham promised, he would receive a golden handshake of 150 nobles 'from me', and a job for life. The condition was simple: that 'you agree to spend the rest of your life in England' – though he would be allowed trips to the Netherlands to see family and friends, 'on suitable occasions'.[8]

It was this, undoubtedly, that gave Erasmus pause for thought. His dilemma was voiced by an Italian friend, Jacobo Piso, who wrote congratulating him on his 'offer from England', before warning him to beware of the dangers of such jobs: 'Look into your heart', he wrote, 'but do not lose your head. It is certainly pleasant to be rich, but still more pleasant to be free.' Erasmus, too, knew that another hand lay behind the skilled rhetoric of Mountjoy's letter: that of his new secretary, Erasmus's Lucchese friend Andrea Ammonio, who after years spent in the shadow of the old king's Italian favourites, now found himself in a new world of opportunity. Indeed, the name of 'Andreas Ammonius' was written at the top of the letter. Erasmus, who always liked to feel he had friends in high places, crossed it out and wrote 'Guilhelmus Montioius' instead. As he knew perfectly well, though, this first, glowing picture of Henry VIII's reign, one that would become the blueprint for similar images to follow, was written not by Mountjoy but by a jobbing Italian humanist with an axe to grind.[9]

Nevertheless, Mountjoy/Ammonio's letter hit its mark. Being free, hungry, poor and ill in war-torn Italy for the sake of one's principles was ghastly. By July, Erasmus was on his way back to England. A decade later he would still be vainly invoking Philip of Burgundy's name in the hope of something more substantial than fair words.[10]

The most extraordinary transformation in fortunes came for Catherine. Fuensalida's first dispatch of the new reign had been couched in his now-accustomed gloom. Francesco Grimaldi, he wrote, had already transferred fifty thousand crowns of Catherine's dowry back out of England to Bruges, and it was just as well. On 24 April, as news of Henry VII's death was proclaimed, Fuensalida had learned from his sources that the dying king had repeated the same old mantra to his son: he was free to marry whoever he wanted. That bride, Fuensalida was further informed, would not be Catherine, for it was known that the new king would find it a burden to his conscience to marry his brother's widow.[11]

Days later, Fuensalida was summoned to Greenwich by the new king's advisers – who, consisting of Fox and his colleagues, looked much like the old. Accordingly, the ambassador launched into a long-winded defence of his actions and of the non-payment of the dowry. Then a side door opened, and secretary Thomas Ruthall swept in from an adjoining chamber, where he had been locked in private discussions with Henry VIII. Cutting through the ambassador's speech, he accepted all Fuensalida's assurances. The king, he said briskly, was utterly unconcerned about all the red tape; he was sure the dowry would be paid, and just wanted to get on with his marriage, as soon as possible. What was more, it was about time England and Spain joined forces against France: together, the two countries would be at the heart of a pan-European coalition against their common enemy.

Fox then spelled it out in black and white to Fuensalida who, for once, was dumbstruck. 'You must remember now, the king is king, and not prince', he said. 'One must speak in a different way in this matter than when he was prince. Until now, things were discussed with his father, and now one must treat with him who is king.'

With his customary elegance Fox had got to the heart of the matter. People needed to adapt, and fast, to the new king's ambitions and ways of doing things. It meant, suddenly, having to fulfil the desires of a monarch who would far rather spend his time and money in the quest for 'virtue, glory and immortality' than micro-managing government. What the king really wanted to do, apart from invade France, was to marry Catherine, as quickly as possible. His counsellors, who had spent the last years thinking up new ways of preventing precisely this turn of events, thoroughly approved.[12]

It was hardly surprising that Fuensalida was struggling to keep up. Now, Henry VIII was telling the world that his father's dying wish had been that he should marry Catherine, a wish which he was bound to respect. But as he wrote to Margaret of Savoy that July, even if he had been free to choose, it was Catherine who he would have chosen for his bride 'before all other'. Quite what provoked this sea change remains unclear, but there seems little doubt that Henry VIII liked the idea of Catherine, and – with his parents' example at the back of his mind – he liked the idea of marriage. And now he was king, he could do what he liked. Having endured endless tales of the exploits of Charles Brandon and his friends, and followed Lord Mountjoy's wooing of Inéz de Venegas, he wanted to make up for lost time. Besides which, Spain would prove an invaluable ally in the military adventures he was planning.[13]

Talking in confidence to Fuensalida, Fox said he would urge the new king to marry quickly, before other people started trying to persuade him against the match. He suggested that the ambassador advise Ferdinand to take advantage of this window of opportunity while the king's council was favourably disposed to help push things forward.

For his part, Ferdinand was frantic to secure the marriage. Although, as he wrote to Fuensalida, Henry VII had been 'a bad friend and ally', Catherine's father had high hopes of the new king – particularly of his desire to fight the French. This was a marriage of 'great political importance', he stressed. He knew perfectly well that time was key, since – echoing Fox's words – 'the French, as well as others' would do everything they could to prevent it happening. Fuensalida, he instructed, was to pull out all the stops to make sure it went ahead, 'without delay'. There should be no obstacles: the marriage was perfectly lawful, as the pope had provided a dispensation for it; Ferdinand would pay the dowry punctually; and he was even prepared to acknowledge Princess Mary's betrothal to his grandson, Charles of Castile, into the bargain. In what was presumably an unconscious revealing of his real motives, he intended, he said, to look after the interests of the new king of England 'as though they were his own'.

Ferdinand's letters to Catherine, meanwhile, were fulsome. More than anything else on earth, he had her welfare and her marriage at heart. He apologized for Fuensalida, he wrote, who had been sent to England with the best of intentions and who had evidently 'acted from ignorance'. But, he insisted, Catherine had to be nice to the ambassador, and also to Francesco Grimaldi: after all, he was 'to pay her dower'.[14]

Fox had been given a straightforward hand to play, but he did so consummately. By mid-May, the negotiations had been wrapped up, and a guarantee extracted from Ferdinand that the dowry would be paid 'at once' – which it duly was. Fox's manoeuvrings would prove a high-water mark in the management of the king's marital affairs: his successors, Thomas Wolsey and Thomas Cromwell, would lose their lives trying to achieve similar success. What was more, Fox's playing hard-to-get with Fuensalida evidently had its material benefits. Should the ambassador think it expedient 'to corrupt some of the most influential counsellors of the king', Ferdinand told him, he was to 'offer them money'.[15]

Henry VIII's marriage to Catherine took place with astonishing speed. On 11 June, three days after he had rushed through the marriage licence, Archbishop Warham wed the pair in a private ceremony in the queen's closet in Greenwich. There was nothing deliberately furtive about it. The king wanted a wife, her dowry, and her father's support against France. Unlike his own father's marriage, delayed until after he had been crowned king in his own right, for Henry VIII there were no such concerns.

○

At 4 p.m. on Saturday, 23 June, the eve of the coronation, the royal procession set out on the familiar route from the Tower, through London's densely packed streets and lanes, to Westminster. With his parliament robe of crimson velvet draped over a cloth-of-gold jacket encrusted with jewels, the king rode under a canopy borne by four high-ranking officers. Catherine, of course, had been this way before. She sat dressed entirely in white, in a canopied litter of cloth-of-gold, her auburn hair let down, on her head a gold circlet set with pearls. As the procession went down Cornhill, its houses draped with brightly coloured cloths and tapestries, and up Cheapside, storm clouds gathered ominously. The procession had just passed the Cardinal's Hat tavern when the heavens opened. The flimsy canopies were little protection: soaked through, Catherine had to take refuge in a nearby draper's stall. People sought to make light of it, though the London chronicler's grumblings about the 'no little damage' done to the expensive textiles by the 'foresaid shower' suggested otherwise – 'as little while it endured', he added hastily.[16]

Among the onlookers, as he had been back in 1501, was Thomas More, who later recorded the scenes in a poem celebrating the coronation, part of a deluge of verse written in praise of the new regime. Henry VIII's coming, he wrote, represented 'the limit of our slavery, the beginning of our freedom, the end of sadness, the source of joy'. More's poem praised the king's physicality, his strength, brilliance and bravery in arms, his pre-eminence among his war-band of nobles. It waxed lyrical about the sensitive, feminine beauty of his face, which, radiating the excellence of his mind, shone with virtue and wisdom. His justice, meanwhile, could be seen in the faces of his happy subjects. Already, More said, the young king had achieved an astonishing amount. He had restored the rule of law – which, all but suspended in the previous reign, had now regained its 'proper authority' – and the natural order, the 'ancient rights' of the nobility; he had also repealed taxes and dues on merchants, who could now trade freely again. The shadow of repression and terror had vanished: 'Now, it is a delight to ignore informers. Only ex-informers fear informers now.' People could emerge into the sunlight of the king's goodness: 'Hence it is that, while other kings have been feared by their subjects, this king is loved.'[17]

More, of course, was speaking from first-hand experience of the last years of Henry VII's reign. But he was also deliberately reflecting the general tone, lifting phrases directly from the new king's pardon and echoing the sentiments of Mountjoy and Ammonio's letter to Erasmus. And, he also borrowed directly from Erasmus himself, the man who was a master at this kind of rhetoric, of advice and admonition dressed up as flattery. In fact, More was praising the new king in exactly the same way that, years before, Erasmus had praised Philip of Burgundy – a panegyric which he had sent to England in the hope that it might get him a job. In endowing Henry VIII with all these attributes, More was telling the king everything he should and would be able to achieve because of the marvellous liberal education he had received.[18] Nowhere, of course, did this apply more than in the favour shown by the discerning monarch to 'learned men', who 'by a happy reversal of circumstances', now received the privileges that 'ignoramuses carried off in the past'. Indeed, contributions from the 'ignoramuses' – Carmeliano, André and their friends – were noticeably absent. They probably wrote verses to the young king; equally probably, they were ignored.

When he heard of his former pupil's accession, John Skelton rushed to London from his Norfolk parish of Diss. He wrote a coronation poem for the festivities, to be painted out on boards or copied onto parchment, framed and hung on display. The poem evidently made it as far as the planning stage: a wardrobe official folded up Skelton's original draft and left it in a book of accounts for jousts and revels. The unfortunate Stephen Hawes tried to write his way back into royal favour with a 'Joyful Meditation to all England', printed as a souvenir edition by Wynkyn de Worde. Andrea Ammonio's elegy for Henry VII *'et felice successione Henrici Octavi'*, meanwhile, killed two birds with one stone.[19]

All the poems stressed the evils of the old reign, and the restoring of the natural order. Hawes, understandably the most cautious, hedged his bets, though even he wrote of people's opinion that Henry VII was inclined to avarice. Skelton talked of the wolves and bears 'That wrought have much care/ And brought England in woe'; no longer would people be scared of their extortion and treachery. And all the poets, in their various ways, used the Platonic idea of the Golden Age, which writers through the ages had used to celebrate the birth of a new regime. History, More explained, repeated itself. 'As spring is banished and returns', and in the same way that 'winter at regular intervals returns as it was before', so after 'many revolutions' all things will come again. For there to be a time of rebirth, moreover, there had to be a dark age, an 'age of iron', before it. Back in 1485, the likes of Carmeliano and André had drawn on precisely the same images in praising Henry VII – but then, they had been celebrating England's deliverance from the rule of a usurper, Richard III. Twenty-four years later, the new king's poets were using the same idea to commemorate a peaceful dynastic succession, albeit one in which a son was delivering the country from his own father's tyranny. The alacrity with which they did so suggests that the new king and his counsellors thoroughly approved.

Henry VII had worked tirelessly to disassociate his reign from the civil wars out of which it had emerged. Now, it was shoved together with them into a century of upheaval and instability: a 'hundred years', Skelton wrote, in which 'a man could not espy/ That right dwelt us among'. In the hands of Henry VIII's court poets, the age of rebirth started not in 1485, but in 1509.[20]

'The rose both white and red/ In one rose now doth grow', declaimed Skelton. Thomas More said the same. A white rose, he wrote, had grown near a red one, and each had tried to crowd out the other. But now, both had combined to become a single flower, a rose with the qualities of both; and so, 'the contest ends the only way it can'. If, wrote More, 'anyone loved either one of these roses, let him love this one in which is found whatever he loved'. Henry VIII's coronation, in other words, was the end of a particular history: the wars of the roses were over.[21]

The coronation took place on Sunday 24 June, Midsummer's Day, exactly five years after Prince Henry had left Eltham for his father's court. At 8 a.m., the procession, headed by twenty-eight bishops, set off from Westminster Hall down a carpet of blue cloth that stretched across the palace yard and through King Street gate, past the shell of Henry VII's near-complete chapel and along the lane that bounded the abbey sanctuary. As the royal party disappeared into the abbey, the crowd descended on the cloth, hacking and ripping up the costly fabric for souvenirs and relics.[22]

Enthroned alongside his queen on a high stage, Henry VIII took the traditional oaths to defend the laws of the land, and 'especially of the laws, customs and liberties' of the church. But the ceremonies also underscored an idea that his father had drawn on to bolster his power and authority, that of imperial kingship – which trumped royal power, because it claimed sovereignty over all other authorities in its lands, including the church. Henry VII had favoured the arched, closed imperial crown, which had also appeared on the gold coins to which he had given the name 'sovereigns', and he had found the idea a useful prop to his lawyers' aggressive and highly lucrative attacks on church liberties and jurisdictions. At his coronation, Henry VIII wore vestments like a bishop's, stressing his sacred as well as his temporal power; in the celebratory jousts that followed, a 'great crown imperial' topped the royal pavilion. As the likes of Erasmus and More had shown, ideas of a supreme Christian king devoted to justice and the common good were much in vogue – but then, that midsummer morning, as the new king vowed to uphold and protect the church and its rights, few could have foreseen Henry VIII's later obsession with his God-given supremacy, which alone could give him what Rome would deny him: a divorce.[23]

The coronation was celebrated with an extravagant feast in

Westminster Hall, presided over by the chief steward, the duke of Buckingham, pacing the length of the hall on a horse. It was all too much for Lady Margaret Beaufort.[24] Earlier that day, she had had 'full great joy' at her grandson's coronation – though, in her devout way, she took care to remind everyone that 'some adversity would follow'. It did, and rather quicker than even she might have anticipated. Though still ordering various 'waters and powders' for the illnesses that had laid her low, the tempting delicacies on offer tested even her legendary abstemiousness. Banqueting rather too well – it was, apparently, 'eating a cygnet' that did it – she was taken back to her suite of rooms above the gatehouse to the abbey cloisters, where she declined rapidly. On 29 June, barely two months after her son's death, she too passed away. The young king had lost the two controlling influences on his life in rapid succession. As Lady Margaret lay dying she might have heard, carried on the air, the faint sounds of chaos from the tiltyard nearby.[25]

Back in November 1501, Catherine's first wedding tournament had taken place under leaden skies and the penetrating gaze of the old king, and against the uncertain backdrop of the earl of Suffolk's defection; squalls of freezing rain had had everybody running for cover. Now, the sun blazed in a midsummer sky. The 'fresh young gallants' of the new regime, the tiltyard companions whom the king had grown up with – Charles Brandon, Sir Edward Howard, Thomas Knyvet and the rest – slipped the leash. Under Henry VII, their behaviour in the tiltyard had seemed a threat, a challenge to the regime. Now, they would revel in the young king's favour.

As the two teams of combatants made their bombastic entrances into the tiltyard, the newly crowned couple looked on from a gallery constructed to resemble a battlemented castle, panelled with green-and-white bricks, in each of which was painted a rose, Catherine's pomegranate emblem, or the happy couple's entwined initials. Rolling out of Westminster Hall came the challengers' pageant: a mountain, pulled by a lion made of 'glittering gold'. Grinding to a halt, its sides swung open and out thundered two horsebacked, plate-armoured knights. Through the gate on the other side of the yard appeared the defenders' pageant, a castle topped by a pomegranate tree – Castile and Aragon combined – drawn by a 'lioness'. Then, in the form that the prince's companions had been perfecting in the last years of the old reign, the games were placed in the context of a dramatic narrative. Both teams lined up and eyeballed each other, the jousters in enamelled plate armour: Tudor green-and-white, black paled with gold, all red, all green. Charles Brandon's armour was gold, from helmet to spurs. Then, the jousts' scenario was acted out, and the trouble started.[26]

The defenders, the Scholars, would joust on behalf of the goddess of wisdom, Dame Pallas; the challengers, for Love of Ladies.[27] The challengers' representative, a bellicose horsebacked Cupid clothed in a jacket of blue velvet and clutching his golden dart of love, sneeringly suggested to Dame Pallas that her scholars clearly didn't know whether they were there to give a lesson in jousting, or to be taught one – the implication being the latter.

The rivalry between the teams simmered all through the first day of the jousts, and exploded on the second. On 28 June, Henry VIII's eighteenth birthday, a huge, stylized arcadia – an enclosed forest on wheels, with fretworked trees, bushes and ferns – was wheeled into the palace yard. Its doors were pulled open and live deer released, pursued and savaged to death by mastiffs: the bloodied corpses were presented to Catherine. In the ensuing jousts, sparks flew – 'the fire sprang out of their helmets' – to such an extent that the king brought the combatants to a halt, perceiving some 'grudge and displeasure' between them. He then imposed rules restricting each side to a certain number of sword strokes; rules which, in the melee that followed, were completely ignored. In the pandemonium, with the tournament marshals unable to exert any control, the king 'cried out to his guard', who waded in, but even the robust yeomen were unable to separate the teams without 'great pain'. The rest of the games were called off: 'and so these jousts broke up', as one observer lamely put it.[28]

Thomas More's epigram on the occasion was up to his recent artful standards. 'All the tournaments kings have held until now', he wrote, gesturing expansively towards history, 'have been marked by some sad mishap or by disaster.' Knights had been mortally wounded; commoners had been skewered by stray lances or trampled by maddened horses; sometimes, stands had collapsed under the weight of cheering spectators jumping up and down. But not this time: 'this tournament of yours, sire, the most beautiful we have ever seen, is disfigured by no misfortune.'

In concluding that the coronation games had been 'conspicuous for such freedom from trouble as is appropriate to your character', either More was becoming as blind or as supine as Bernard André, the poet on whom both he and Erasmus had poured scorn, or he was daring to suggest something rather different: that the violence of the prematurely abandoned games reflected something in the nature of the king himself. Or, in More's typical fashion, perhaps he was saying both.

Over the following months, the late king's financial grip over a number of prominent nobles was relaxed. A series of bonds was cancelled, including those of Buckingham, Northumberland, Bergavenny and Mountjoy. Squashed onto the bottom of a page of accounts, almost as an afterthought, was a payment of £1,000 for Catherine's longstanding debts. Henry VII's political prisoners, too, were released: in Calais, Thomas Grey marquis of Dorset was freed by a smiling Sir Thomas Lovell; William Courtenay, in prison for some seven years, followed soon after. The new king, after all, was the rose both red and white. Unlike his father, he seemed perfectly comfortable with having his Yorkist relatives at large – and, as everybody was telling him, he was magnanimous to boot. But even for him, the line had to be drawn at some point. The earl of Suffolk remained in the Tower. And others found that the milk, honey and nectar flowed rather less freely than they had anticipated.[29]

During the coronation preparations, Buckingham had been restored to the post of constable of England, a title that he, like his father, believed was his by hereditary right. Henry VIII had, accordingly, restored it to him – but for a single day: 'the 23rd June only, viz., the day preceding the coronation'.[30] Buckingham's brother-in-law, the earl of Northumberland, was similarly irritated. Many of the estates and offices in the northeast that he regarded as rightfully his had, following his minority, never been returned to him, but had been held on behalf of the king by Thomas lord Darcy, one of Henry VII's household men; now, Darcy had all his posts confirmed, and received more, for good measure.[31] To Buckingham and Northumberland it could only mean one thing: that the king was being got at, by his father's old counsellors.

That August, Darcy wrote to Richard Fox from Yorkshire with news of local talk that had been circulating since Henry VIII's coronation. Northumberland's servants were bragging that England would be carved up between their master and the duke of Buckingham, who had his eye on the protectorship of England. Northumberland, meanwhile, aimed for what he regarded as his hereditary overlordship of all England north of the River Trent, the traditional boundary between the north and south of the country. If the king failed to grant them these offices, all 'should not long be well'.

There was more, Darcy added. As usual, merchants coming north from London brought gossip, and Richard Fox's ambitions were, apparently, the talk of the town. He had, it was said, failed to dominate the new king, and in the process to exclude from royal favour a tight-knit group of counsellors including the earl of Surrey, Sir Henry Marney and Thomas Ruthall. Now, 'it was the saying of every market man from London' that Fox was trying a different approach: to create a clique with Buckingham and Northumberland, and to rule the king that way.

'My lord', Darcy urged Fox, 'good it is to have a good eye, though much be but sayings.' Darcy concluded by saying that he would keep his ear to the ground, and would continue to supply Fox, Ruthall and Marney with information. Meanwhile, he would try to round up the rumour-mongers.[32]

All this may have been 'sayings', but it indicated something else about the new climate. Nobody ever talked about people 'ruling' Henry VII. In fact, people rarely talked openly at all – and when they did, out of turn, they soon learned not to. In the expansive glory of the new young king, however, people felt they detected a distinct susceptibility to influence. Where his father had kept even his closest counsellors at a distance, and by the end of the reign had given the impression of having no confidential advisers at all, this kind of talk indicated that people thought quite the opposite about Henry VIII.[33]

On 8 July, the king appointed a number of high-profile commissions, because, as he said, it had come to his attention that his laws had been subverted, along with the good governance of his realm. These panels of nobles, judges and counsellors were empowered to determine and punish the full spectrum of criminal offences, from trespass to treason. In particular, they were to look into all possible violations of 'the Statute of Magna Carta, concerning the liberties of England', the compact between the king and his noble subjects that, people believed, had been torn up by Henry VII and his administrators. This slate-cleaning exercise had, however, been stipulated in his will, which had instructed his executors to carry out such investigations within three months of his death. Now, the old king's counsellors were instrumental in setting up a commission empowered to investigate the abuses in which they themselves had been involved.[34]

Inevitably, any detailed inquest into grievances concerning the abuses of the old regime would raise uncomfortable questions about who had been responsible for them – not only the counsellors, but Henry VII himself. The vague remit of the commission, though, neatly precluded any genuine inquiry.[35] Besides which, there were two scapegoats conveniently to hand. The problem facing the commissioners concerning Empson's and Dudley's indictments was how to make the mud stick without incriminating anybody else. They soon found a solution.

Four days after the commissions were appointed, Edmund Dudley was hauled out of the Tower and brought before a panel of judges at London's Guildhall. Richard Empson was indicted soon after, and taken into his native Northamptonshire to be tried. Notably, there was no mention of any financial and legal offences committed under Henry VII; this, after all, was territory that the new regime wanted to avoid. Instead, scraps of circumstantial evidence were distorted into highly speculative charges of treason. As Henry VII lay dying, the charge sheets read, Empson and Dudley had conspired 'with a great force of men and armed power' to manipulate the succession to their own ends. Here, the letters Dudley had written ordering knights and their retinues to London were flourished, and the whispered pledges of allegiance between Empson's retainers cited: 'Will you be the same men that you were?' 'We will keep our promise . . .' This, it was now claimed, was evidence of the most heinous crime of all. The pair had plotted to take control of the young king, to deprive him of his liberty and to rule through him. Should the king and his rightful counsellors – his nobles and knights – have put up any resistance, Empson and Dudley would simply have destroyed them.[36]

Under the gaze of Buckingham, Northumberland and former colleagues like Lovell and Sir John Hussey, rapidly restored to grace after having been left out of Henry VIII's first pardon, Dudley pleaded not guilty; so too did Empson. Each man tried to argue his case on different grounds, attempting to excuse and justify his conduct under the late king. But nobody really wanted to listen, and given that this was a treason trial, it was a pointless defence. There was an air of inevitability about the whole thing. Both were found guilty, sentenced to the traitors' death of hanging, drawing and quartering, and taken back to the Tower.[37]

As he awaited his fate in the weeks that followed, Dudley was permitted access to his account books. Poring through them, he took a small, blank sixteen-page pamphlet and began to write, drawing up a list of victims – ranging from 'poor men' and merchants to lords 'spiritual and temporal' – who had been dealt with 'much more sorer than the causes required'. These were people who had been 'evilly' or 'sore treated', had been 'long in prison' and who had paid 'great sums' in debt on 'small causes', 'light' or 'lewd surmises', 'untrue matters', 'malicious grounds', without any 'due proof'. Dudley also wrote separately to some of the victims he had listed. One of them was the London haberdasher Thomas Sunnyff. 'Sunnyff, I cry you and your wife mercy', he stated simply. If, he continued, Sunnyff failed to gain recompense from the king's executors, then 'for truth' Dudley would reimburse him – if, that was, 'I have anything left at my liberty' – 'for there is no matter I have more remorse in.'[38]

While Dudley may still have had lingering hopes of pardon, he outlined his situation plainly in the letter or 'petition' accompanying his list. He was, he knew, 'a dead man by the king's laws' and, 'abiding life or death at the high pleasure of my sovereign lord', his life hung in the balance. Dudley may have felt that he was writing for his life – but he was also writing to ease Henry VII's path through purgatory and to ensure, as had been the late king's dying wish, 'that restitution be made to all persons by his grace wronged contrary to the order of his laws'. And Dudley was still trying to explain himself.

He had, he said emphatically, never committed treason or anything like it against the new king. As for his work for Henry VII, he had merely been doing what was asked of him. If people had been wronged, it was at the 'pleasure and mind of the king's grace', and not on his own initiative. He had bound countless people in debt on the king's behalf – so, he added meaningfully, had others – but it was the king 'that would have them so made'. It was, though, against both reason and good conscience to interpret these bonds as genuine debts. Indeed, he was sure that the king had never intended to call them in. They had, rather, been tools of political control.

Dudley addressed his petition to two of the late king's executors, men who would have known precisely what he was talking about. They were, he wrote, people in whom Henry VII had had 'as much confidence and trust as any living man', and they were bound to see justice done, for the health of the late king's soul. They were Richard Fox – 'my lord of Winchester' – and 'Mr Lovell'.

Buried within Dudley's petition, then, was a veiled 'j'accuse'. Fox and Lovell had had just as much to do with the late king's system of bonds and informers as he had; clearly, too, he felt that they had framed him, and abandoned him to his fate. As lieutenant of the Tower, Lovell was now Dudley's gaoler, and had been among the commissioners who had issued the writ for his indictment. Fox's behaviour, if anything, was even worse. If anybody could put things right with the new king, Fox could, and Dudley had been desperately trying to make contact with him since his arrest, about 'the matters contained in these books'. He never got a reply.[39]

If Dudley had expected to jog the counsellors' consciences, it was a vain hope. Fox and Lovell were happy to have his list of victims, which they made use of – indeed, Dudley, who had drawn it up 'that it may please them', had perhaps done it at their request – but less so the explanatory petition. It was copied, then filed away securely and kept secret, remaining undiscovered for the best part of five hundred years. Details of the workings of the late king's reign coming to light would, after all, do nobody any good.[40]

On 17 August, as Dudley was writing his petition, a team of royal officials led by the veteran household knight Sir John Digby – himself a victim of Henry VII's administrators – entered his Candlewick Street house on the king's command, in order to strip it, inventory the goods, and hand them over to Sir Henry Marney for the king's use. Moving through the warren of galleries and chambers, the officials worked with a thoroughness of which Dudley himself would have been proud. Everything was noted, from the detritus of a domestic life interrupted – a toasting fork and fire rake, wooden bowls, an old nightgown furred with fox – to the luxuries: the exotic furniture, silverware and glassware, gold cutlery and cups, and flagons chased with Dudley's coat-of-arms, fine tapestry and carpets, upholstery and bed-linen and quilts of crimson velvet. They noted Dudley's clothes, his fur-lined gowns of crimson and black damask, black satin doublets and velvet jackets; the fine fabrics – silk, sarsenet, camlet – folded and stored in neat piles. And then they found the writings.

At first, they started to note down the names on the slips of paper they found: a little bag with three bills and £8 in gold; an old purse containing a written obligation. Then they realized the futility of it. In wardrobes and closets they found trunks packed with 'diverse obligations concerning the king' as well as a coffer crammed with 'bills and writings'. Outside, in the gallery adjoining the garden, they lifted the lids of chests and coffers to find more of the same: 'bills and other writings' and, wearily, 'evidences, as they say'.

Also there was a cartload of old lead – left over, perhaps, from the water conduit Dudley had had installed the year before – and signs of Dudley's own business interests: stacked broadcloths, white cloths and cotton, twenty-one bags of pepper and, finally, forty-six bags of alum.

The same month, Empson's well-appointed manor of Le Parsonage, with its fine Thamesside orchards, was appropriated in much the same way. It was regranted to one of the new faces of the regime, a man now basking in the favour of Richard Fox and the young king: Thomas Wolsey.[41]

Early that October, the commissions reported back. In the way to which it was becoming accustomed, Henry VIII's council ordered their findings to be drawn up in a 'clear book', in a format to suit the royal attention span: it was to be made 'in short parcels to be shown to his highness'. Then, on the king's behalf, the council got down to business.

Transparency, it seemed, was the order of the day. In two meetings that autumn, the council swept away the remnants of Henry VII's nebulous committees: the courts of wards and surveyors, the council learned in the law. These tribunals had been a 'great abusion, vexation and trouble' to the people of England, who had been harassed 'contrary to the king's laws and to their utter undoing', and who had often ended up not even getting a proper acknowledgement at law that they had settled their debts with the crown. Now, out of the highest legal and spiritual considerations, the new king's regime would abolish the tribunals in their entirety. The underlying motive, however, was made plain in the council minutes: the reforms were not so much about abolishing a system as consolidating it.

Because Henry VII's committees had been extrajudicial, many of the prerogative rights that they had established and enforced on the crown's behalf would, in time, lapse – unless, that is, they were legally defined. The cancellations of bonds were, of course, politically necessary, in high-profile, individual cases – but the new regime was not about to reverse the overwhelming gains in extending royal authority made under the old king. Now, all the debts or claims on the crown's behalf that had not been explicitly cancelled by the recent commissions were grounded firmly in law, in order to ensure against any 'great losses to our sovereign lord of such profits as should grow to his highness'.[42]

Back in the crisis-ridden years of the mid-fifteenth century, the lawyer John Fortescue had outlined how it should be done. After the king had made successful claims to property and land, Fortescue advised, he should then legally establish this new 'livelihood' as the crown's property in perpetuity, its ownership only able to be transferred away by act of parliament.[43] This, effectively, was what Henry VIII's council now did. What was more, although his father's tribunals were abolished, their practices and personnel – with the exception of the two disgraced counsellors – continued more or less unchanged.

Early in 1510, the first parliament of the new reign confirmed John Heron in his post of general receiver of the king's revenues. Under Henry VII, he had presided over the workings of the chamber treasury, the private system of finance and surveillance that, under the old king's obsessive gaze, had assumed primacy over the labyrinthine but legally constituted exchequer. Now, Heron's role was made official, if, in theory, more accountable; so, too, were those of the old king's coterie of auditors and surveyors, including Sir Robert Southwell and Edward Belknap, whose powers were now established in law – and expanded in the process. Beneath the rhetoric of liberty and glory, meanwhile, the taking, prosecuting and collecting of bonds had continued with barely a break, apart from the superficial signs of *glasnost*.

Moreover, while parliament succeeded in rolling back certain 'unjust laws' and 'past errors', rather more remained in place. Writing in the Tower, Edmund Dudley had urged the abolition of the practice that had been the stock-in-trade of Henry VII's tribunals: the summons by privy seal or letter, circumventing and halting the process of common law – or what he called 'stopping of justice'. Parliament, indeed, proposed a bill doing away with this practice which, it stated, was contrary both to law and to Magna Carta. It also tried to pass a bill confirming the church's liberties, and its legal independence from the crown. The king vetoed them both.[44]

Finally, of course, the 'reforms' were about Henry VIII himself. Although he tried to follow – and did – his father's practice of signing everything personally, and could display a familiar obsession with detail when the mood took him, he was impatient with the minutiae of government, preferring to leave it to others, and his participation in it was fitful. After all, he had to concentrate on the pursuit of virtue, glory and immortality. The fearsome thoroughness and power of Henry VII's extrajudicial tribunals had depended on the king's tight personal control. They would hardly have the same effectiveness under a monarch who could, quite evidently, not be bothered with them half the time, and who needed his reports in easily digestible 'short parcels'.[45]

○

In December 1509, twelve royal informers, imprisoned without trial during the round-ups the previous spring, were released on bail. Among them were the notorious Henry Toft, and the wardrobe servant William Smith, who had been 'in good favour with our sovereign lord Henry VII', and who had been convicted as a promoter days after Dudley. The following February, John Baptist Grimaldi was pardoned, to nobody's surprise: after all, the bank of Grimaldi had processed Catherine's dowry, while his cousin Francesco, now married to the queen's lady-in-waiting Francesca de Caceres, was once more back in favour. The furious reaction among London's politicians and merchants, though, probably helped set the seal on the fate of Empson and Dudley.[46]

As the two men perhaps realized, they had no one left to speak for them. After a failed bid to escape from the Tower – the plans were leaked by his two accomplices – Dudley tried other avenues, his cousin Richard offering Thomas lord Darcy £200 to put in a word for him with the king. Darcy refused.[47]

Their end came in summer 1510. On progress through Surrey, Hampshire and into the west country, the king's hawking and hunting were apparently interrupted by a succession of disgruntled locals, petitioning him with 'grievous bills and complaints' against Empson and Dudley. However, the fact that the only mention of this rather vague episode comes in the London chronicle – and, at that, nearly a year after the royal commission had reported back – suggests that it may have been a cover for concerted pressure brought to bear on the king by city politicians. Whatever the case, Henry VIII had had enough. In what was to become a familiar reaction to knotty political problems, he sent a warrant to the earl of Oxford, constable of the Tower, ordering that the pair should immediately be 'put to execution'.[48]

On 18 August, Henry VII's former counsellors were brought through cat-calling, jeering crowds to the public scaffold on Tower Hill, where they were to be beheaded. Also present, inevitably, was

Thomas More. According to one of his early biographers, the condemned Dudley stopped to exchange words with More, telling him he had done well not to confess to any wrongdoing over his role in thwarting the late king back in 1504. Had More done so, Dudley told him, Henry VII would have undoubtedly had him executed.

The encounter may well have occurred, but the details of the story are apocryphal: Henry VII's preferred method of punishment, after all, was death by a thousand financial cuts. But, as the biographer – Thomas Stapleton, a Catholic who fled the Protestant England of Henry VII's granddaughter Elizabeth with an armful of source material, including quantities of More's correspondence – undoubtedly intended, the exchange foreshadowed More's own martyrdom.[49]

Two weeks later, More would be appointed to the post Dudley had once held, of under-sheriff of the city of London; in his case, too, the job would be a stepping-stone to royal service, whose allure and glory he would be unable to resist. More's career, of course, far outstripped Dudley's in its brilliance. But like Henry VII's notorious administrator, he too would be framed by the Tudor regime whose sovereignty he had worked with zealous ruthlessness to enforce.

In the quarter-century separating the two executions, however, the boundaries of royal power would change in ways that even Dudley and his colleagues, with their relentless drive to enforce the king's laws and their slavish 'obedience to our sovereign lord the king', could scarcely have imagined. Thomas More would die denying the supreme jurisdiction of the crown, not over its own laws and its subjects, but over the laws of God and the church. What Henry VII would have made of it can only be guessed at. He might have been appalled by his son's single-minded, and ultimately cataclysmic, efforts to find himself a wife who could provide him with an heir and thereby secure another dynastic succession, and his equally destructive efforts to augment his income. He might also have seen him as a chip off the old block.[50]

Epilogue

As he sat in the Tower of London awaiting his death, Edmund Dudley set to work on a book, a treatise of advice on government, his last gesture to the young Henry VIII and his counsellors. The result, *The Tree of Commonwealth*, is the only full-length expression of the way one of Henry VII's ministers thought. Using the metaphor of society as a tree, Dudley laid out a vision of an organized society divided into ranks and estates, church, nobility, commons: everything in its right place, with the king at the top, the fount of justice, order and morality. Not so subtly, Dudley repudiated the abuses of the late king's reign, in which he had played an integral role – its unaccountability, its 'extraordinary justice', its 'insatiable' avarice. But other than that, the picture that he painted was one that had been refined and sharpened over the previous quarter-century, and one to which people had gradually become inured: that the well-being and 'prosperous estate' of England, and of even its most exalted subjects, depended on loyalty and service to the crown. *The Tree of Commonwealth* presented a vision of Tudor sovereignty, Dudley's blueprint for the reign to come.[1]

The counsellors on whom Henry VIII relied to push through his megalomaniac schemes in the following decades were formed in his father's reign. The creation of his mentors Richard Fox and Thomas Lovell, Thomas Wolsey soon shouldered them aside. After his fall in 1529 Wolsey was succeeded by Thomas More – who in turn was displaced by Wolsey's own protégé Thomas Cromwell, a man in whom the spirit of Henry VII's administrators seems distilled. Cromwell incorporated Reynold Bray's financial acumen and aggression, the consummate political skill and European vision of Richard Fox and the forensic zeal of Dudley, qualities honed by an apprenticeship

375

on the battlefields and in the counting-houses of Italy – notably at the Florentine branch of Henry VII's favoured bankers, the Frescobaldi. Under Cromwell, Henry VII's council learned in the law would be reborn in devastating fashion in the notorious Court of Augmentations, the committee that oversaw the destruction of the monasteries and the siphoning of huge quantities of ecclesiastical cash into the coffers of a spendthrift crown.[2]

Beneath the magnificent, insouciant exterior, Henry VIII was to prove himself his father's son in his ingrained suspicion of the house of York and of those with royal blood. Before leaving England in 1513 for his first war against France, he had the earl of Suffolk, still in the Tower, beheaded; eight years later the duke of Buckingham, who never stopped grumbling about the indignities done him and his family, met the same fate, convicted of treason on evidence supplied by his own household servants. But the idea of York persisted. In 1514, rumours of a planned invasion by de la Pole's younger brother Richard – backed, of course, by France – was one of the motives for a hastily concocted Anglo-French peace, at its centre a marriage between the ageing French king Louis XII and Henry VIII's younger sister, Princess Mary.[3] Mary's long-awaited wedding with Charles of Castile – or Emperor Charles V, as he would become – never had taken place; now, Henry VIII abruptly called off the engagement, and with it, his father's grandiose visions of pan-European Anglo-Habsburg dominance. Mary's marriage to Louis, though, was short-lived. Having 'danced him to death', as contemporaries delicately put it, she returned to England in the company of the king's sparring partner Charles Brandon, recently given the former de la Pole title of duke of Suffolk. As it turned out, Brandon was the man Mary had had eyes for all along. Initially livid at their secret wedding, Henry VIII eventually forgave them both.

William Cornish continued to flourish, his triumphant performance at the epic Anglo-French summit of the Field of the Cloth-of-Gold in 1520 confirming him as the age's greatest musical and dramatic impresario. John Skelton too returned to court: part visionary seer, part laughing-stock for a younger generation. In the mid-1520s he fled to the sanctuary of Westminster Abbey after a vicious satirical attack on Thomas Wolsey, before turning his fire on religious radicals at Wolsey's behest. Skelton died in 1529, a year before Wolsey, as the seismic religious debates sweeping Europe were lending a new edge to the king's increasingly desperate search for his way out of a marriage that was, he was now convinced, sinful in the eyes of God.

The bickering and infighting between the Italian humanists continued. Andrea Ammonio landed his coveted post of Latin secretary to the king. His boss Silvestro Gigli stopped at nothing to get his hands on the top English diplomatic job in Rome, poisoning his English rival, Cardinal Bainbridge, in 1514. Protected by Thomas Wolsey from reprisals, Gigli repaid the favour handsomely, his intriguing bringing Wolsey a cardinal's hat. All three men worked tirelessly to sideline their rivals, Adriano Castellesi and Polydore Vergil, with varying degrees of success. Vergil, who detested Gigli, exacted a historian's revenge. In the various editions of his *Anglica Historia*, Gigli's name is nowhere to be found.[4]

Business in England boomed for the Italian merchant-banks of Frescobaldi and Cavalcanti. Their favoured sculptor, Pietro Torrigiano, had more commissions than he knew what to do with. In October 1512, he finally signed a contract to make Henry VII's tomb; seven years later, it was finished, a vision in marble and gilt bronze, inscribed with verses by John Skelton. The finely moulded effigies of Henry and Elizabeth of York still lie side by side where he left them, under the soaring fan vaulting of Henry VII's completed chapel. The location of the tomb, though, was not quite where Henry had planned. His son moved it behind the altar, reserving the more prominent space for his own tomb and that of Catherine of Aragon which, also designed by Torrigiano, was intended to trump his father's. The plans never came to fruition; neither did subsequent, ever more colossal projects. Where Henry VII is buried at the heart of Westminster in his own, meticulously planned monument to his dynasty, his son lies in St George's Chapel at Windsor under an unadorned slab of black marble.[5]

On 8 October 1621, Henry VII's first biographer presented his just-completed *The History of the Reign of Henry VII* to James I, the Stuart king who became the first monarch to rule over England, Scotland and Ireland. In his dedication, Sir Francis Bacon came up with a

fanciful conceit. Not only was Henry VII James's ancestor – his great-great-grandfather – but he was also a unifying king: after all, his reign had united the warring roses. As such, he was a touchstone for this new idea of Great Britain, 'the kingdoms by him begun', now embodied in James. Henry VII, Bacon wrote, was a wise man and an excellent king, in times that were rough 'and full of mutations and rare accidents'. Then, in the self-deprecating way of writers presenting manuscripts, Bacon excused himself and his work, noting that of course James had other, more immediate and equally good examples of kingship at hand. But, after all, he concluded, 'it is not amiss for you also to see one of these ancient pieces'.[6]

Notes

ABBREVIATIONS

AR	*Antiquarian Repertory*
BL	British Library
CCR	*Calendar of Close Rolls*
CLRO	City of London Records Office
CPR	*Calendar of Patent Rolls*
CSPM	*Calendar of State Papers, Milan*
CSPS	*Calendar of State Papers, Spain*, vol. I
CSPS, II	*Calendar of State Papers, Spain*, vol. II
CSPS Supp	*Calendar of State Papers, Spain*, Supplement to vols. I and II
CSPV	*Calendar of State Papers, Venice*
CWE	*Collected Works of Erasmus*
CWM	*Collected Works of Thomas More*
EETS	Early English Text Society
GC	*Great Chronicle of London*
HKW	*History of the King's Works*
LP HVIII	*Letters and Papers, Henry VIII*
LP RIII/HVII	*Letters and Papers, Richard III and Henry VII*
ODNB	*Oxford Dictionary of National Biography*
PPE Elizabeth	*Privy Purse Expenses of Elizabeth of York*
PROME	*Parliament Rolls of Medieval England*
SJC	St John's College, Cambridge
TNA	The National Archives
TRP	*Tudor Royal Proclamations*
WAM	Westminster Abbey Muniments

PROLOGUE

1. Bennett, *Battle of Bosworth*, p. 75; Davies, 'The Wars of the Roses in European Context', pp. 177, 244.

2. *Three Books of Polydore Vergil's English History*, p. 216.

3. Ross, *Edward IV*, pp. 36–41.

4. Ross, *Edward IV*, pp. 84–101, esp. pp. 86, 97–8.

5. Ross, *Edward IV*, pp. 175–6.

6. Jones and Underwood, *The King's Mother*, p. 58; *Memorials*, pp. 15–16.

7. *Three Books of Polydore Vergil's English History*, pp. 184–6.

8. Horrox, *Richard III*, p. 112.

9. Gransden, *Historical Writing in England*, pp. 315–16, 470–71.

10. Davies, 'Bishop John Morton', pp. 4–6.

11. *GC*, pp. 236–7; 'The Most Pleasant Song of the Lady Bessy', p. 33; Jones, '"For my lord of Richmond, a pourpoint . . . and a palfrey"', *passim*.

12. Arthurson and Kingwell, 'The Proclamation of Henry Tudor as King of England, 3 November 1483', *passim*.

13. Anglo, 'The British History in Early Tudor Propaganda', *passim*; Jones, 'The Myth of 1485', p. 95; Horrox, 'Henry Tudor's Letters to England during Richard III's Reign', pp. 155–8; Griffiths and Thomas, *The Making of the Tudor Dynasty*, pp. 125–6.

14. Commynes, *Memoirs*, pp. 354–5, 397–8; see also Griffiths and Thomas, *The Making of the Tudor Dynasty*, pp. 153–4.

15. Jones, 'The Myth of 1485', pp. 85–93.

16. Bennett, *Battle of Bosworth*, pp. 205–7; *GC*, p. 238; Entwistle, 'A Spanish Account of the Battle of Bosworth', p. 35.

17. Vergil, *Anglica Historia*, pp. 2–5.

18. Ross, *Richard III*, p. 225.

19. Davies, 'Information, Disinformation, and Political Knowledge under Henry VII and Early Henry VIII', *passim*; *Crowland Chronicle Continuations*, p. 185.

20. Horrox, 'Introduction', in Horrox, ed., *Fifteenth-Century Attitudes*, pp. 7–8; Anglo, 'Foundation of the Tudor Dynasty', pp. 3–11; Jones and Underwood, *The King's Mother*, p. 68; Watts, *Henry VI*, p. 29.

21. *The English Works of John Fisher*, I, pp. 305–6.

1. NOT A DROP OF DOUBTFUL ROYAL BLOOD

1. Braudel, *Civilization and Capitalism*, I, p. 428.

2. *CSPV*, nos. 740, 741; *CSPM*, no. 525; Mattingly, *Renaissance Diplomacy*, p. 137.

3. *CSPV*, no. 748; *CSPM*, no. 530.

4. *CSPV*, nos. 743, 747, 748; *CSPM*, no. 530.

5. *CSPV*, nos. 750, 754; *CSPM*, nos. 536–8.

6. *CSPV*, no. 754; *CSPM*, no. 539.

7. *CSPV*, no. 754; *CSPM*, no. 539.

8. Arthurson, 'The Rising of 1497', *passim*; *CSPV*, no. 755; *CSPM*, no. 541.

9. Jones and Underwood, *The King's Mother*, p. 66; Thurley, *Royal Palaces*, p. 102.

10. *Crowland Chronicle Continuations*, p. 195; *PROME*, XV, 1485 November, item 5.

11. *Memorials*, p. 39.

12. Gunn and Monckton, 'Introduction', in Gunn and Monckton, eds., *Arthur Tudor, Prince of Wales*, p. 1.

13. Leland, *Collectanea*, IV, p. 204; Stevens, *Music and Poetry in the Early Tudor Court*, pp. 364–5.

14. *Chronicles of London*, p. 193; *The Chronicle of John Harding*, p. 550; *Plumpton Correspondence*, p. 49.

15. *Crowland Chronicle Continuations*, p. 189.

16. Bennett, *Lambert Simnel*, pp. 7, 33–40.

17. Vergil, *Anglica Historia*, pp. 26–7.

18. *The Reign of Henry VII*, I, p. 185.

19. Currin, 'To Traffic with War', pp. 106–31.

20. Mattingly, *Renaissance Diplomacy*, p. 134.

21. Currin, 'To Traffic with War', pp. 106–31; Cavill, *The English Parliaments of Henry VII*, p. 67.

22. Sutton, *Mercery*, pp. 325–6; Wroe, *Perkin Warbeck*, p. 190.

23. TNA E 404/81/1, 1 September 1491; Leland, *Collectanea*, IV, pp. 179–84.

24. *LP RIII/HVII*, I, pp. 388–404; Hayward, *Dress at the Court of Henry VII*, p. 90.

25. Gunn, 'The Courtiers of Henry VII', pp. 23–4.

26. Cunningham, *Henry VII*, pp. 77–9; TNA E 154/2/5, p. 26.

27. Arthurson, *The Perkin Warbeck Conspiracy*, p. 112; Wroe, *Perkin Warbeck*, pp. 117–18.

28. *GC*, p. 274; *PROME*, XVI, 1497 January, items 12, 13; Cavill, *The English Parliaments of Henry VII*, pp. 68–70.

29. Arthurson, *The Perkin Warbeck Conspiracy*, pp. 162–7.

30. *TRP*, pp. 39–40; Arthurson, 'The Rising of 1497', pp. 1–18.

31. *CSPV*, no. 751; *CSPM*, nos. 548, 550.

32. *CSPM*, no. 540; *CSPS*, no. 210; Gunn, 'The Courtiers of Henry VII', pp. 36–8; Thurley, *Royal Palaces*, pp. 102–11.

33. *CSPM*, nos. 550, 552–3; Jones, 'Alwyn Ruddock: John Cabot and the Discovery of America', pp. 231–4; Jones, 'Henry VII and the Bristol Expeditions', p. 11; *GC*, p. 283; *Chronicles of London*, p. 219.

34. *CSPM*, no. 553.

35. *CSPS*, no. 210.

36. *AR*, I, p. 188; Starkey, 'The King's Privy Chamber', pp. 18–29; *The Household of Edward IV*, pp. 14, 106.

37. Starkey, 'The King's Privy Chamber', pp. 25–6.

38. Gunn, '"New Men"'; *CSPS*, no. 239.

39. *CSPV*, no. 743; *CSPS*, no. 210.

40. Arthurson, 'The Rising of 1497', pp. 1–18.

41. Fortescue, *On the laws and governance of England*, pp. 49–53.

42. Arthurson, 'A Question of Loyalty', p. 408.

43. Thurley, *Royal Palaces*, pp. 75, 139; for Braybroke, see Starkey, 'The King's Privy Chamber', pp. 52–3; *CSPM*, no. 571; *CSPV*, no. 768.

44. *CSPS*, no. 221; Arthurson, *The Perkin Warbeck Conspiracy*, p. 196; Wroe, *Perkin Warbeck*, pp. 393–4; Vergil, *Anglica Historia*, p. 7; *A Relation of the Island of England*, p. 105.

45. Bentley, *Excerpta Historica*, pp. 120, 121, 123; *The Book of Quinte Essence*, pp. 17–19; Armstrong, 'An Italian Astrologer', pp. 157–78.

46. Arthurson, 'A Question of Loyalty', *passim*; Condon, 'A Kaleidoscope of Treason', *passim*.

47. Gatrell, *The Hanging Tree*, p. 51. I am grateful to Rosemary Horrox for this reference.

48. *Chronicles of London*, pp. 226–9; *Chronicle of the Grey Friars of London*, p. 26.

49. *CSPS*, no. 249.

2. RICHMOND

1. Lobel, *The City of London*, p. 49; Mancini, *Usurpation*, pp. 100–104.

2. Home, *Old London Bridge*, p. 84.

3. Currin, 'Henry VII, France and the Holy League of Venice', p. 532; Currin, 'England's International Relations', p. 31.

4. Kipling, *Triumph of Honour*, p. 173; *AR*, I, p. 62.

5. Kisby, 'Kingship and the Royal Itinerary', pp. 30–32.

6. Sutton, *Mercery*, pp. 323–8.

7. Gunn, 'Sir Thomas Lovell', p. 143; Barron, *London in the Later Middle Ages*, pp. 9–10.

8. Kipling, *Triumph of Honour*, pp. 74, 173–4; Anglo, *Spectacle*, pp. 57–8; CLRO, *Repertories*, ff. 62, 61v; CLRO, *Journals*, x, 235r, 267v.

9. Barron, 'Political Culture in Medieval London', p. 117; *English Historical Documents*, p. 189; *Receyt*, p. 9.

10. BL Cotton MS Vitellius C xi, f. 126r.

11. *Crowland Chronicle Continuations*, p. 149.

12. *CSPM*, no. 539.

13. STC no. 4814; Anglo, 'London Pageants', p. 54, n. 6.

14. *LP RIII/HVII*, II, pp. 87–9; *Chronicle of Calais*, pp. 3–4.

15. *Chronicle of Calais*, p. 49, *CSPS*, nos. 268, 282.

16. *LP RIII/HVII*, II, pp. 87–9.

17. *PROME*, XVI, 1495 October, Introduction, p. 138, item 13.

18. Ross, *Richard III*, p. 41; *LP RIII/HVII*, I, pp. 397, 400–401.

19. Gunn, 'The Court of Henry VII', p. 133 n. 6; Gunn, 'Courtiers of Henry VII', p. 43.

20. *LP RIII/HVII*, I, pp. 129–34; Mattingly, *Renaissance Diplomacy*, p. 41.

21. *Receyt*, p. 103; BL MS Add. 46455, ff. 4r–6r; *CSPS*, no. 278.

22. *The Reign of Henry VII*, I, pp. 215–16; Creighton, *A History of Epidemics in Britain*, pp. 286–91; *Chronicle of the Grey Friars of London*, p. 183; Vergil, *Anglica Historia*, p. 119.

23. Davies, 'Bishop John Morton', pp. 29–30; Condon, 'Ruling Elites', pp. 121, 128; Chrimes, *Henry VII*, pp. 105–6.

24. *CSPS*, no. 292.

25. *CSPS*, nos. 268, 293.

26. *CSPS*, nos. 296, 299, 300, 302.

27. *HKW*, III, p. 97; Thurley, *Royal Palaces*, pp. 35–6; *Original Letters*, 1st series, I, xxi, pp. 45–6.

28. Cunningham, *Henry VII*, pp. 188–9.

29. Cunningham, 'The Establishment of the Tudor Regime', pp. 217–19; MacCulloch, *Suffolk and the Tudors*, p. 54; *PROME*, XVI, 1495 October, item 13; *CSPV*, no. 794.

30. Watts, *Henry VI*, pp. 34–6; Morgan, '"Those were the days": A Yorkist Pedigree Roll', pp. 112–16; Archer, 'A Skeleton in the de la Pole Closet?' pp. 12–26.

31. Vergil, *Anglica Historia*, p. 125.

32. Gunn, 'Henry Bourchier', p. 136; Lander, 'Bonds, Coercion and Fear', p. 287; Pugh, 'Henry VII and the English Nobility', p. 63.

33. *GC*, pp. 251–2; *Receyt*, pp. xxii–xxiii.

34. Anglo, 'William Cornish', p. 352; Jones and Underwood, *The King's Mother*, p. 77.

35. *Receyt*, pp. 6–8.

36. *Receyt*, p. 12.

37. *Receyt*, pp. 12–13.

38. *Receyt*, pp. 9–10; Hall, *Chronicle*, p. 493; *English Historical Documents*, no. 11.

39. *Receyt*, pp. 15–18; Cunningham, *Henry VII*, p. 102.

40. *A Relation of the Island of England*, pp. 42–3; *GC*, pp. 304–5; *Receyt*, pp. 20–21, 26–7; Barron, in Lobel, *The City of London*, p. 53; Mancini, *Usurpation of Richard III*, Ch. 8 *passim*.

41. *The Reign of Henry VII*, I, pp. 137, 204.

42. *The Reign of Henry VII*, I, pp. 175–6.

43. Stow, *Survey of London*, pp. 240–41.

44. *Receyt*, pp. 10, 30–33.

45. *AR*, II, p. 257; *GC*, p. 309; Leland, *Collectanea*, IV, pp. 271–2; *Receyt*, p. 31.

46. *St Thomas More, Selected Letters*, pp. 2–3.

47. *Receyt*, pp. 28–9.

48. Barron, 'Centres of Conspicuous Consumption', p. 8.

49. Stow, *Survey of London*, pp. 61–2.

50. *Receyt*, pp. 37–8.

51. *GC*, pp. 310–11; TNA E 101/415/7, no. 56.

52. BL MS Cotton Vespasian C XIV, ff. 100–101; Kipling, *Triumph of Honour*, pp. 68–70.

53. *Receyt*, p. 39.

54. *Receyt*, pp. 43–5; *GC*, p. 310.

55. *AR*, I, pp. 301–2; *AR*, II, pp. 291–2.

56. *LP HVIII*, IV (iii), 5774/ 2/3.

57. *LP RIII/HVII*, I, pp. 405–6; Vergil, *Anglica Historia*, pp. 145–7; Anglo, *Spectacle*, p. 100.

58. *Receyt*, p. 53; Gunn, 'Court of Henry VII', pp. 141–2, citing *Minutes of the Parliament of the Middle Temple*, ed. C. T. Martin, 4 vols. (London, 1904), I, pp. 12, 35–6; *HKW*, IV, p. 287; Young, *Tudor and Jacobean Tournaments*, pp. 74–81.

59. *Receyt*, p. 54; *GC*, pp. 310–11.

60. College of Arms MS M 3, ff. 24v–26v; Payne, 'Sir Thomas Wriothesley and His Heraldic Artists', pp. 151–2.

61. *Receyt*, pp. xxix, xxv, 62, 65; BL Harleian MS 69, ff. 28v–32; Young, *Tudor and Jacobean Tournaments*, pp. 14, 92.

62. Kipling, *Triumph of Honour*, p. 109.

63. *Receyt*, pp. 56–8; Thurley, *Royal Palaces*, p. 73.

64. *Receyt*, pp. 68–70.

65. Kipling, *Triumph of Honour*, pp. 5–8.

66. *Receyt*, pp. 77–8.

67. *CSPS*, no. 280.

3. HE SEEKS IN ALL PLACES TO DESTROY ME

1. E. Bridson, 'The English "Sweate" (Sudor Anglicus) and Hantavirus Pulmonary Syndrome', *British Journal of Biomedical Science*, 58 (1), 2001, pp. 1–6.

2. BL Add. MS 45131, ff. 37–37v; *AR*, II, pp. 322–31; Leland, *Collectanea*, V, pp. 373–81.

3. *Receyt*, pp. 80–81.

4. *A Fifteenth Century School Book*, p. 17.

5. Machiavelli, *The Prince*, p. 81; *CSPS*, no. 585.

6. Hampton, 'White Rose, Part 2', p. 465.

7. Hampton, 'White Rose, Part 1', pp. 415–16; Hall, *Chronicle*, p. 463; Arthurson, *Perkin Warbeck*, pp. 87–92; *CPR 1495–1509*, pp. 131, 236, 243; Leadam, 'An Unknown Conspiracy against Henry VII', *passim*.

8. TNA C 255/8/5, no. 100i; Cunningham, 'The Establishment of the Tudor Regime', pp. 86–8.

9. Arthurson, *Perkin Warbeck*, pp. 62, 74, 88, 196, 199; Grummitt, '"For the Surety of the Towne and Marches"', *passim*.

10. *Materials*, I, p. 270.

11. Cunningham, 'The Establishment of the Tudor Regime', pp. 215–16; BL Add. MS 21480, f. 61v; Grummitt, '"For the Surety of the Towne and Marches"', p. 199.

12. Hampton, 'White Rose, Part 1', p. 418 n. 48; Bentley, *Excerpta Historica*, p. 98.

13. Wroe, *Perkin Warbeck*, p. 511.

14. *LP RIII/HVII*, I, pp. 168–77.

15. WAM 16030.

16. Cunningham, 'The Establishment of the Tudor Regime', pp. 125–6.

17. Arthurson, 'Espionage and Intelligence', p. 143; TNA C 54/376 mm. 1–6, discussed in Cunningham 'Loyalty and the Usurper', p. 475; TNA C 54/376 m. 31, discussed in ibid., p. 478; Horowitz, 'Policy and Prosecution', pp. 437–8, 441–2, 446–7; *CPR 1495–1509*, p. 287; *CCR 1485–1500*, no. 1199.

18. Nicolas, 'Instructions Given by Henry VIII to John Becket the Usher, and John Wrothe the Sewer of His Chamber', pp. 20–25; *CSPM*, no. 626.

19. *CPR 1495–1509*, pp. 501–2; *LP RIII/HVII*, I, pp. 225–9.

20. *LP RIII/HVII*, I, pp. 225–9.

21. *LP RIII/HVII*, I, p. 226.

22. Hanham, 'Edmund de la Pole, Defector', p. 249 n. 59; Hanham, 'Edmund de la Pole and the Spies', p. 106 n. 14.

23. TNA DL 28/2/6, f. 47v, quoted in Grummitt, '"For the Surety of the

Towne and the Marches"', p. 197; Arthurson, 'Espionage and Intelligence', pp. 140–41; Gunn, 'Sir Thomas Lovell', *passim*.

24. *LP RIII/HVII*, I, p. 181.

25. WAM 16057; Arthurson, 'Espionage and Intelligence', p. 141; Bellamy, *Tudor Law of Treason*, pp. 94–5, 104–6, 108–10.

26. *LP RIII/HVII*, I, p. 180; *CPR 1485–1494*, p. 17; *CPR 1495–1509*, p. 27; Bentley, *Excerpta Historica*, p. 120; Arthurson, *Perkin Warbeck*, pp. 75, 167.

27. *CSPV*, no. 822; *CPR 1495–1509*, p. 240.

28. *GC*, p. 318.

29. More, *The History of King Richard III*, ed. R. S. Sylvester, *CWM*, 2 (New Haven, 1963).

30. *GC*, pp. 318–19.

31. BL Add. MS 59899, f. 3; BL Harleian MS 283, f. 123v.

32. *CPR 1495–1509*, p. 279; *LP RIII/HVII*, I, pp. 139, 177–89.

33. BL Add. MS 45131, ff. 38v–39; *Receyt*, p. 87; Houlbrooke, 'Prince Arthur's Funeral', p. 72.

34. *Receyt*, pp. 81–5; TNA LC 2/1, ff. 24–35.

35. *Receyt*, pp. 92–3.

36. *LP RIII/HVII*, I, pp. 183–5.

37. *CCR 1500–1509*, no. 161; Grummitt, 'Calais 1485–1547', p. 114.

38. *LP RIII/HVII*, I, pp. 220–25; TNA E 101/413/2/3, p. 74.

39. Jonathan Hughes, 'Somerset [formerly Beaufort], Charles, first earl of Worcester (c.1460–1526)', *ODNB*; *LP RIII/HVII*, I, pp. 220–25.

40. Hanham, 'Edmund de la Pole and the Spies', p. 109 n. 32; Starkey, *Six Wives*, p. 79.

41. *CSPS*, no. 322; *PPE Elizabeth*, pp. xc, 14, 103; Emery, *Greater Medieval Houses of England and Wales*, III, pp. 329–33.

42. *CSPS*, nos. 321, 323–5, 343.

43. *CSPS*, no. 327.

44. *CSPS*, nos. 325, 327, 333.

45. *CSPS*, no. 315.

46. *CSPS*, no. 334.

4. NOW MUST YOU SUPPLY THE MOTHER'S PART ALSO

1. Kisby, 'The Royal Household Chapel', pp. 151–202; TNA E 101/414/16, ff. 47, 50v; BL Add. MS 71009, f. 15v; Leland, *Collectanea*, IV, p. 234; *PPE Elizabeth*, p. 83.

2. Anglo, *Spectacle*, pp. 309–10.
3. TNA E 101/413/2/3, f. 33; BL MS Add. 59899, ff. 9v–10.
4. BL MS Royal 12 B vi, quoted in Armstrong, 'An Italian Astrologer', pp. 175–6.
5. Leland, *Collectanea*, IV, pp. 179–84; *AR*, I, pp. 304–5; Laynesmith, *The Last Medieval Queens*, pp. 111–15; Thurley, *Royal Palaces*, pp. 140–41.
6. Duffy, *Stripping of the Altars*, pp. 15–22; *GC*, pp. 320–21.
7. Leland, *Collectanea*, IV, p. 249.
8. *AR*, IV, pp. 654–63; BL Add. MS 45131, ff. 43–7; BL Add. MS 45133, f. 141v; Jones and Underwood, *The King's Mother*, p. 78.
9. *GC*, p. 321; St John Hope and Robinson, 'Funeral Effigies', pp. 550–51; Duffy, *Stripping of the Altars*, p. 362.
10. *The English Works of John Fisher*, pp. 292–3.
11. *CSPS*, no. 205; Jones and Underwood, *The King's Mother*, pp. 67–70, 73–4, 86, 148, 255.
12. *CSPS*, no. 202.
13. *Memorials*, p. 37.
14. *PPE Elizabeth*, pp. 17, 111.
15. *PPE Elizabeth*, p. 84.
16. *PPE Elizabeth*, p. 100; *Lisle Letters*, I, pp. 13–21, 145–6; TNA LC 2/1, f. 63.
17. *HKW*, II, pp. 936–7; *HKW*, IV, pp. 78–9.
18. TNA E 101/414/8, f.27; *PPE Elizabeth*, pp. 88, 99; Starkey, *Henry*, pp. 67–8.
19. Orme, *From Childhood to Chivalry*, p. 23.
20. Gunn, 'Prince Arthur's Preparation for Kingship', p. 7.
21. Orme, 'The Education of Edward V'; Gunn, 'Henry VII in Context', pp. 312–13; Emden, *Biographical Register*, III, 1555.
22. Caxton, *Prologues*, no. xxxii, p. 109.
23. Orme, *From Childhood to Chivalry*, pp. 68, 144–5.
24. MacCulloch, *Reformation*, p. 79.
25. Salter, 'Skelton's *Speculum Principis*', pp. 25–37.
26. Nelson, *John Skelton*, pp. 75–6; 'The Latin Writings of John Skelton', VIII.
27. Skelton, *Complete English Poems*, p. 61.
28. *Household of Edward IV*, p. 126; Chartier, *Curial*, pp. 1–2.
29. *CWE*, I, ep. 118.
30. Jones and Underwood, *The King's Mother*, pp. 142, 144, 245.
31. *CWE*, I, ep. 118; MacCulloch, *Reformation*, pp. 76–7.
32. *CWE*, I, ep. 118; Maddison, Pelling and Webster, *Linacre Studies*, pp. xvii, xix, 20; *CWM*, 12, p. 121.
33. *Correspondence of Thomas More*, pp. 7, 9; Ackroyd, *Thomas More*, p. 81.

34. *CWE*, I, ep. 118.
35. *CWE*, I, ep. 104.
36. *CWE*, I, ep. 108.
37. *CWE*, I, eps. 106–11.
38. N. Orme, 'Holt, John (d. 1504)', *ODNB*.
39. *CWM*, I, pp. xxi–xxiv.
40. *CWM*, I, pp. xxi–xxiv; *HKW*, III, pp. 210–11.
41. For Henry's illnesses see *CSPV*, nos. 520, 939–41; *CSPS*, no. 511; *The Reign of Henry VII*, III, pp. 187–9; *LP RIII/HVII*, I, p. 238.
42. SJC D91.20, pp. 83–5.
43. TNA E 101/415/7, nos. 129, 135, 139, 140, 251–2.
44. *The Reign of Henry VII*, III, pp. 75–8.
45. *CSPS*, no. 360.
46. Kelly, *Matrimonial Trials*, p. 70 n. 23.
47. Starkey, *Six Wives*, pp. 70–71, 88; Mattingly, *Catherine of Aragon*, pp. 52–3; BL Add. MS 59899, f. 18; *CSPS*, no. 364.
48. *CSPS*, no. 364; *LPHVIII*, IV (iii), 5774/3.
49. Machiavelli, *The Prince*, p. 61.
50. Davies, 'Bishop John Morton', p. 22; Cunningham, *Henry VII*, pp. 226–7.
51. *CSPV*, nos. 538, 542; Underwood, 'The Pope, the Queen and the King's Mother', p. 67; Chambers, *Popes, Cardinals and War*, p. 76; Hall, *Chronicle*, p. 448; Burchard, *At the Court of the Borgia*, p. 150.
52. Wilkie, *The Cardinal Protectors of England*, pp. 28–34; Mallett, *The Borgias*, pp. 233-42; Brady, *Anglo-Roman Papers*, pp. 14–15, cited in Underwood, 'The Pope, the Queen and the King's Mother', pp. 75–6.
53. Burchard, *At the Court of the Borgia*, pp. 219–26.
54. Chambers, *Popes, Cardinals and War*, pp. 75–6.
55. Chrimes, *Henry VII*, p. 286.
56. *CSPS*, nos. 370, 372, 375, 380.

5. NO SURE WAY

1. *GC*, p. 325; BL Add. MS 21480, f. 101v.
2. All references are to the transcript provided in Leadam, 'An Unknown Conspiracy', pp. 152–8; Gairdner, 'A Supposed Conspiracy', pp. 157–94.
3. Cunningham, *Henry VII*, pp. 209–21.
4. Leadam, 'An Unknown Conspiracy', pp. 152–8.
5. Duffy, *Stripping of the Altars*, pp. 136–9.
6. Leadam, 'An Unknown Conspiracy', pp. 152–8.

7. BL, Add. MS 21480, f. 101v; Cunningham, 'The Establishment of the Tudor Regime', pp. 277–8, 300.

8. Hammond, *Barnet and Tewkesbury*, pp. 43–5; Harvey, *Jack Cade's Rebellion*, pp. 80–101; Cunningham, 'The Establishment of the Tudor Regime', pp. 230–97; Cunningham, *Henry VII*, pp. 174–80.

9. I am grateful to Sean Cunningham for his perceptive thoughts on Henry's attitude to the young Lord Bergavenny.

10. Horrox, 'Service', pp. 66–8.

11. Cunningham, 'The Establishment of the Tudor Regime', pp. 288, 290, 292–3.

12. Ross, 'Sedition and the King "Beyond the See"'.

13. R. W. Hoyle, 'Percy, Henry Algernon, fifth earl of Northumberland (1478–1527)', *ODNB*; C. S. L. Davies, 'Stafford, Edward, third duke of Buckingham (1478–1521)', *ODNB*.

14. Hicks, 'Dynastic Change and Northern Society', pp. 78–80.

15. James, 'A Tudor Magnate', pp. 71–5.

16. Dudley, *Tree of Commonwealth*, p. 57.

17. Rawcliffe, *The Staffords*, pp. 1, 36–7.

18. Harris, *Edward Stafford*, p. 43.

19. Hayward, *Rich Apparel*, pp. 171–2, 184.

20. Rawcliffe, *The Staffords*, pp. 35–6, 93, 138; Horrox, *Richard III*, pp. 84–5, 134; *LP HVIII*, III, (i), p. cxxx.

21. Hoyle, 'The Earl, the Archbishop and the Council', pp. 240–41; Condon, 'Ruling Elites', pp. 117–18.

22. Leland, *Collectanea*, IV, pp. 271–2.

23. TNA STAC 2/24/79, quoted in Hoyle, 'The Earl, the Archbishop and the Council', p. 242 n. 13; James, 'A Tudor Magnate', pp. 18–19.

24. S. J. Gunn, 'Thomas Savage, archbishop of York', *ODNB*; Gunn, 'Courtiers of Henry VII', p. 43; Cameron, 'The Giving of Livery', pp. 21–22; Hoyle, 'The Earl, the Archbishop and the Council', pp. 242–5 n. 15; James, 'A Tudor Magnate', p. 49.

25. Hoyle, 'The Earl, the Archbishop and the Council', pp. 246–52.

26. *Select Cases in the Council of Henry VII*, pp. 41–4.

27. Lander, 'Bonds, Coercion and Fear', p. 283; Hoyle, 'The Earl, the Archbishop and the Council', pp. 254–6.

28. Grummitt, 'Calais 1485–1547', p. 148.

29. *CCR 1500–1509*, no. 226; Lander, 'Bonds, Coercion and Fear', p. 284.

30. TNA SC 1/58/57-8, printed in *LP RIII/HVII*, I, pp. 231–40; Grummitt, '"For the Surety of the Towne and the Marches"', pp. 198–200.

31. *LP RIII/HVII*, I, pp. 231–2.

32. Luckett, 'Crown Patronage and Political Morality', pp. 579–81.
33. Horrox, *Richard III*, p. 171 n. 119; S. Cunningham, 'Sir Richard Guild-ford', *ODNB*; L. L. Ford, 'Vaux, Nicholas, first Baron Vaux (*c*.1460–1523)', *ODNB*.
34. Fortescue, *On the laws and governance of England*, p. 5.
35. *LP RIII/HVII*, I, pp. 231–40.
36. Skelton, *Complete English Poems*, V, pp. 46–61.
37. Machiavelli, *The Prince*, pp. 57–9; 'The Petition of Edmund Dudley', p. 86.

6. COUNCIL LEARNED

1. Jones and Underwood, *The King's Mother*, pp. 74, 84–5, 158–9, 291–2; Jones, 'Collyweston – an Early Tudor Palace', p. 129.
2. Leland, *Collectanea*, IV, pp. 258–301; BL Harleian MS 78, f. 31; Jones, *Bosworth 1485*, pp. 177–8, 245.
3. WAM 16042; Gunn, 'Court of Henry VII', p. 137.
4. WAM 16047.
5. Condon, 'From Caitiff and Villain to Pater Patriae', *passim*; Gunn, '"New Men"', pp. 159–61.
6. S. Cunningham, 'Henry VII's Council Learned in the Law (active *c*.1499–1509)', *ODNB* (I am grateful to the author for an early look at this article); Condon, 'Ruling Elites', *passim*; Somerville, 'Henry VII's Council Learned', *passim*.
7. For which, see TNA DL 5/2, 5/4, *passim*.
8. TNA DL 5/4, f. 101v.
9. Condon, 'Ruling Elites', pp. 132–4; Somerville, 'Henry VII's Council Learned', pp. 430–31; Horowitz, 'Policy and Prosecution', pp. 420–23.
10. TNA E 101/413/2/3, ff. 45, 84v, 99; McGlynn, '"Of good name and fame in the countrey"', p. 549; Horowitz, 'Policy and Prosecution', p. 426.
11. TNA E405/79, f. 3v; Horowitz, 'Policy and Prosecution', pp. 439–40; Hayward, *Dress at the Court of Henry VII*, pp. 143–4.
12. Skelton, *Complete English Poems*, V, p. 58; Gunn, 'Structures of Politics', pp. 79–80.
13. M. M. Condon, 'Empson, Sir Richard (*c*.1450–1510)', *ODNB*; *Plumpton Correspondence*, pp. 120–22.
14. *Plumpton Letters*, pp. 145–6, 186–7.
15. Grummitt, 'Household, Politics and Political Morality', p. 408; *Plumpton Correspondence*, pp. 177–8.
16. TNA E 101/413/2/3, pp. 1–3.

17. WAM 16073.

18. TNA C 54/376, mm. 36–7. I am grateful to Sean Cunningham for bringing this reference to my attention.

19. Guy, 'A Conciliar Court of Audit', pp. 289–95; Cunningham, *Henry VII*, p. 136; R. W. Hoyle, 'Hussey, John, Baron Hussey', *ODNB*.

20. Gunn, '"New Men"'; S. J. Gunn, 'Dudley, Edmund (*c*.1462–1510)', *ODNB*.

21. Bratchel, 'Alien Merchant Communities', pp. 170–201; Sicca, 'Pawns of International Finance and Politics', pp. 8–17; Schofield, *Medieval London Houses*, nos. 178, 225; Dudley, *Tree of Commonwealth*, p. 2; Brodie, 'Edmund Dudley', pp. 136–8; Barron, *London in the Later Middle Ages*, p. 15.

22. Hayward, *Dress at the Court of Henry VII*, pp. 25–39.

23. Dudley, *Tree of Commonwealth*, p. 45.

24. Cavill, *English Parliaments*, pp. 28, 137–8; Brodie, 'Edmund Dudley', p. 148.

25. *PROME*, XVI, 1504 January, The opening of parliament; Fortescue, *On the laws and governance of England*, p. 10.

26. Cavill, 'Debate and Dissent', pp. 166–8; Cavill, *English Parliaments*, p. 201; *Reign of Henry VII*, I, p. 151.

27. *PROME*, XVI, 1504 January, item 11; Cavill, *English Parliaments*, pp. 210–11.

28. Roper, *The Lyfe of Sir Thomas Moore, Knighte*, p. 7; Guy, *Thomas More*, pp. 43–4.

29. *PROME*, XVI, 1504 January, Introduction (p. 316), item 5; TNA E 413/2/3, f. 120; Gunn, *Early Tudor Government*, pp. 103–4, 109–11, 126–7; Cavill, 'Debate and Dissent', pp. 168–72.

30. GC, p. 325; Dyer, *Standards of Living*, p. 263; Lander, *Government and Community*, p. 10; Hoskins, 'Harvest Fluctuations and English Economic History', *passim*.

31. *TRP*, no. 11, pp. 12–13; BL Royal MS 18 D ii, ff. 163–4.

32. Skelton, *Complete English Poems*, XVIII, p. 236.

33. TNA C 244/153, no. 136.

34. *TRP*, p. xxiv.

35. *TRP*, no. 50, p. 62; *CPR 1495–1509*, p. 380.

36. Thompson, 'The Bishop in His Diocese', p. 69; Gunn, 'Edmund Dudley and the Church', pp. 513–14; Elton, 'Henry VII: A Restatement', p. 5.

37. 'Petition of Edmund Dudley', pp. 86–7.

38. TNA E 101/516/17; TNA E 101/517/11, f. 3.

39. Dudley, *Tree of Commonwealth*, p. 50.

40. TNA E 404/81/4, 17 August 1495.

41. Dudley, *Tree of Commonwealth*, p. 37.

42. Condon, 'Ruling Elites', p. 134; Cunningham, 'Loyalty and the Usurper', pp. 462–3, 469–72; Dudley, *Tree of Commonwealth*, p. 36.

7. OUR SECOND TREASURE

1. Davidson, *Festivals and Plays in Late Medieval Britain*, p. 38; Hutton, *Stations of the Sun*, pp. 312–15; Kisby, 'The Royal Household Chapel', pp. 153–4.

2. BL Add. MS 59899, f. 58; Orme, *From Childhood to Chivalry*, pp. 6–7.

3. Gunn, 'Prince Arthur's Preparation for Kingship', p. 10; TNA E 101/414/8, f. 27; *PPE Elizabeth*, pp. 88, 99; SJC D91.20, f. 126.

4. TNA E 101/415/7, no. 124.

5. BL MS Add. 59899, ff. 21v, 26v; TNA E 101/415/11; Bernard, 'The Rise of Sir William Compton', p. 754.

6. Pierce, 'The King's Cousin', pp. 187–225; BL Add. MS 59899, ff. 45, 92; *PROME*, XVI, 1504 January, Introduction (pp. 315–16), items 2, 10; Anglo, 'Court Festivals', p. 39.

7. BL Add. MS 59899, f. 59.

8. More, *The History of King Richard III*, ed. R. S. Sylvester, CWM, vol. 2 (New Haven, 1963), p. 81, quoted in Gunn, 'The Court of Henry VII', p. 132.

9. Jones and Underwood, *The King's Mother*, p. 174.

10. E. Charlton, 'Roll of Prayers Formerly Belonging to Henry VIII when Prince', *Archaeologia Aeliana*, n.s. 2 (1858), pp. 41–5; Thomas, *Religion and the Decline of Magic*, pp. 47–9.

11. Thurley, *Royal Palaces*, p. 67.

12. Kisby, 'The Royal Household Chapel', p. 319; *CPR 1495–1509*, p. 343; *Select Cases in the Council of Henry VII*, p. 37; Cunningham, *Henry VII*, p. 178; Samman, 'The Progresses of Henry VIII', pp. 59–74.

13. *LP RIII/HVII*, II, pp. 112–23.

14. *CSPS*, no. 396; *LP RIII/HVII*, II, pp. 112–23; Clough, 'The Relations between the English and Urbino Courts', p. 213; Vergil, *Anglica Historia*, pp. 140–41.

15. Thurley, *Royal Palaces*, p. 130; *CSPS*, nos. 397, 398.

16. *CSPS*, no. 398.

17. Orme, 'The Education of Edward V', p. 182; BL Sloane MS 3479, ff. 53v–58; Ross, *Edward IV*, p. 14.

18. *A Fifteenth Century School Book*, pp. 13–14; see also Orme, *From Childhood to Chivalry*, pp. 32–4.

19. N. Orme, 'Holt, John (d. 1504)', *ODNB*; Carlson, *English Humanist Books*, pp. 271–8; Penn, 'Literary Service', pp. 77–9; STC 13604.

20. Orme, *From Childhood to Chivalry*, pp. 24, 155.

21. Penn, 'Literary Service', pp. 37–9; Fleming, 'The Hautes and their Circle', p. 93.

22. TNA E 101/414/6, ff. 62, 81; Backhouse, 'Founders of the Royal Library', pp. 36–7, n. 55; Penn, 'Literary Service', pp. 128–31.

23. TNA LC 2/1, f. 73v; BL Add. MS 59899, ff. 48, 68v and *passim*; TNA E 36/214, f. 4 and *passim*; Carlson, 'Royal Tutors', pp. 273–4.

24. *Household of Edward IV*, pp. 120–21, 127; *Collection of Ordinances*, p. 166.

25. Hawes, *Minor Poems*, pp. 1–71, at pp. 52, 70.

26. TNA LC 2/1, f. 73v.

27. Orme, *From Childhood to Chivalry*, pp. 28–32; Anglo, *The Martial Arts of Renaissance Europe*, p. 231.

28. Jones and Underwood, *The King's Mother*, p. 191; *The English Works of John Fisher*, p. 308; SJC D91.20, p. 21.

29. Arthurson, 'The King's Voyage into Scotland', pp. 8–9; A. Ailes, 'Machado, Roger [Ruy] (d. 1510)', *ODNB*.

30. Wagner, *Heralds and Heraldry*, pp. 84–6.

31. A. Ailes, 'Writhe, John (d. 1504)', *ODNB*; R. Yorke, 'Wriothesley (formerly Writhe), Sir Thomas (d. 1534)', *ODNB*; I am indebted to Adrian Ailes' observations on Machado, Writhe and Wriothesley. *Register of the Most Noble Order of the Garter*, I, p. 367; Wagner, *Heralds and Heraldry*, p. 84.

32. TNA LC 9/50, ff. 230-1.

33. *GC*, pp. 328–9, 331; *Register of the Most Noble Order of the Garter*, I, pp. 558, 562; Young, 'A Calendar of Tudor and Jacobean Tournaments', in Young, *Tudor and Jacobean Tournaments*, p. 197; BL Add. MS 21480, f. 21; BL Add. MS 59899, f. 94v.

34. *LP HVIII*, IV (iii), 5774 (9); Jones and Underwood, *The King's Mother*, pp. 165–6; BL Add. MS 59899, ff. 63v, 64; BL Cotton MS Titus A XIII, ff. 186, 189–190v; Gunn, 'Chivalry', pp. 116–17; SJC D91.20, p. 162.

8. NULL AND VOID

1. *CSPS*, nos. 401, 405, 420.

2. Kelly, *Matrimonial Trials*, p. 72; *Memorials*, pp. 416–17; Starkey, *Six Wives*, pp. 221–5.

3. Penn, 'Literary Service', p. 23. *CSPS*, nos. 412, 413.

4. Aram, *Juana the Mad*, p. 76.

5. *CSPS*, no. 409.

6. *CSPS*, nos. 401, 420; BL Add. MS 59899, f. 85v.

7. *CSPS*, nos. 419, 436.

8. Gunn, 'Courtiers of Henry VII', p. 41; *Memorials*, pp. 101, 223–39; *CSPS*, no. 437.

9. Hepburn, 'The 1505 Portrait of Henry VII', pp. 222–57.

10. *CPR 1495–1509*, p. 427; TNA E 36/214, f. 16; BL Lansdowne MS 127, f. 52v; Cunningham, 'Loyalty and the Usurper', p. 466 n. 25; Gunn, 'Structures of Politics', p. 72 n. 58.

11. TNA E 36/214, f. 16.

12. *LP RIII/HVII*, II, p. 112.

13. Bratchel, 'Alien Merchant Communities', pp. 196–7. For della Fava payments, see BL Add. MS 59899, ff. 4, 27v, 44, 49, 55v, 57v, 60, 61v, 62v, 63v, 64v, 69, 71, 77v; TNA E 36/214, ff. 11v, 15, 34v, 51v, 58v, 66, 92, 92v, 107, 119, 119v, 125v, 144, 146, 151, 158v.

14. *CSPS*, no. 429; Wroe, *Perkin Warbeck*, p. 382; Arthurson, 'Espionage and Intelligence', pp. 146–9.

15. Chrimes, *Henry VII*, p. 234; *Foedera*, XIII, p. 105; *CSPV*, no. 846.

16. Wolffe, 'Land Revenues', pp. 217, 223; Grummitt, 'Henry VII, Chamber Finance and the "New Monarchy"', p. 237.

17. *CSPV*, nos. 846, 853; BL Add. MS 59899, f. 85; Arthurson, 'Espionage and Intelligence', pp. 140–41; Horowitz, 'Henry Tudor's Treasure', pp. 560, 564 n. 13.

18. TNA E 101/413/2/3, p. 237.

19. De Roover, *The Rise and Decline of the Medici Bank*, p. 153.

20. De Roover, *The Rise and Decline of the Medici Bank*, pp. 152–64.

21. Finot, 'Le commerce de l'alun dans les pays-bas', pp. 422–3.

22. Singer, *The Earliest Chemical Industry*, p. 159.

23. *CSPV*, no. 509; *Materials*, I, pp. 299–300. Thanks to Samantha Harper for bringing this case to my attention. See also TNA E 114 (unsorted box) for more royal activities concerning alum.

24. BL Add. MS 59899, f. 64.

25. Setton, *The Papacy and the Levant, 1204–1571*, III, pp. 239, 324.

26. Finot, 'Le commerce d'alun dans les pays-bas', pp. 424–5.

27. Orme, *From Childhood to Chivalry*, pp. 7, 36–8; Knecht, *Rise and Fall of Renaissance France*, pp. 53–4.

28. *CSPS*, no. 435; Kelly, *Matrimonial Trials*, pp. 126–7.

29. *CSPS*, nos. 404, 438.

30. *CSPS*, no. 439. Frederick Hepburn argues persuasively against Sittow's

personal authorship of Henry's 1505 portrait: Hepburn, 'The 1505 Portrait of Henry VII', pp. 248–9.

31. *CSPS*, no. 439; *CSPV*, no. 850.
32. *CSPS*, no. 439.
33. *CSPS*, no.539; *CSPV* no. 860.
34. BL Add. MS 59899, ff. 96v–99, 101; *CSPS*, no. 439; *CSPV*, nos. 850, 858.
35. *Letters of Royal and Illustrious Ladies*, I, pp. 131–4.
36. *CSPS*, nos. 410, 411; Starkey, *Six Wives*, pp. 94–5.
37. *LP RIII/HVII*, I, pp. 280–85; Hanham, 'Edmund de la Pole, Defector', pp. 247–8.
38. *CSPV*, no. 861.
39. Pugh, 'Henry VII and the English Nobility', p. 64 n. 42; *LP RIII/HVII*, I, p. 282.
40. *CSPV*, no. 860; BL Add. MS 59899, f. 101.

9. THIS DAY CAME DE LA POLE

1. *GC*, p. 330; Vergil, *Anglica Historia*, pp. 137–9.
2. TNA E 36/214, f. 16.
3. *CSPV*, no. 881.
4. *CSPV*, nos. 864, 865; Gachard, *Collection des voyages*, pp. 408–10, 418.
5. TNA E 36/214, ff. 16–17; SJC D91.21, p. 93.
6. TNA E 101/416/3, f. 10v.
7. Gachard, *Collection des voyages*, p. 422; Vergil, *Anglica Historia*, pp. 138–9.
8. *The Reign of Henry VII*, I, p. 263.
9. *Memorials*, pp. 283–4; Gachard, *Collection des voyages*, pp. 422–3.
10. Thurley, *Royal Palaces*, pp. 207, 234–5; *HKW*, II, p. 879.
11. *AR*, II, pp. 193, 325–6; Kisby, 'The Royal Household Chapel', pp. 140–41 and n. 40.
12. SJC D105.162, f. 2v.
13. *Memorials*, p. 287.
14. *Chronicle of Calais*, p. 55.
15. SJC D105.162, f. 2v; *HKW*, IV, p. 5; Jones and Underwood, *The King's Mother*, p. 73.
16. Hampton, 'White Rose, Part 2', p. 474 n. 92; *Memorials*, p. 292.
17. *Memorials*, p. 292.

18. TNA E 101/416/3, f. 20r.

19. Gachard, *Collection des voyages*, p. 424.

20. Chrimes, *Henry VII*, p. 290; *Foedera*, XIII, 123ff.; *The Reign of Henry VII*, III, pp. 83–96; Mattingly, *Catherine of Aragon*, pp. 67–8.

21. Gachard, *Collections des voyages*, p. 426.

22. Aram, *Juana the Mad*, p. 83.

23. *Memorials*, pp. 299, 301–2.

24. Aram, *Juana the Mad*, p. 83.

25. Jones and Underwood, *The King's Mother*, p. 156; SJC D91.21, pp. 99–103; TNA E 36/214, f. 21.

26. *CSPV*, no. 854.

27. Hall, *Chronicle*, p. 501; *Memorials*, p. 292.

28. Gachard, *Collections des voyages*, p. 429.

29. *CSPV*, nos. 867, 869.

30. BL Add. MS 21404, quoted in *LP RIII/HVII*, I, pp. 285–6. For Don Pedro Manrique's role, see *CSPS*, no. 288.

31. Hayward, *Dress at the Court of Henry VII*, p. 92.

32. Machiavelli, *The Prince*, p. 62.

33. Mattingly, *Catherine of Aragon*, p. 71.

34. Vergil, *Anglica Historia*, p. 138; *Chronicle of Calais*, pp. 5–6.

35. *LP RIII/HVII*, I, pp. 273–4.

36. Hampton, 'White Rose, Part 2', pp. 473–4.

37. SJC D91.21, p. 108.

38. TNA E 36/214, f. 32v; Bellamy, *Tudor Law of Treason*, pp. 94–5, 108–15.

39. S. Cunningham, 'Guildford, Sir Richard (*c.*1450–1506)', *ODNB*.

40. *The Pylgrymage of Sir Richard Guylforde, passim*.

41. Jones and Underwood, *The King's Mother*, p. 165; *LP HVIII*, I (i), no. 713.

42. *Select Cases in the Council of Henry VII*, pp. xxix–xxx; Pugh, 'Henry VII and the English Nobility', p. 71.

43. Lander, 'Bonds, Coercion and Fear', p. 289; Cameron, 'The Giving of Livery', pp. 32–3; Pugh, 'Henry VII and the English Nobility', pp. 66–7; Cunningham, 'The Establishment of the Tudor Regime', pp. 259–64.

44. Vergil, *Anglica Historia*, p. 139; Hall, *Chronicle*, p. 502; *Chronicle of Calais*, p. 6.

45. Grummitt, '"Surety for the Towne and the Marches"', pp. 200–202; Luckett, 'Crown Patronage and Political Morality', pp. 592–5.

46. *CCR 1500–1509*, nos. 825 (i–iv); Lander, 'Bonds, Coercion and Fear', p. 289.

47. BL Lansdowne MS 127, f. 19 (Lucy Browne), ff. 33, 34 (Daubeney), ff. 47v, f. 53v (Bergavenny), f. 50v (Northumberland), f. 40v (Nanfan).

10. NEW HEAVEN, NEW EARTH

1. *CWE*, 2, ep. 181.
2. Rundle, '"Not so much praise as precept"', pp. 148–70.
3. *CWE*, 2, ep. 181.
4. *CWE*, 2, ep. 185.
5. MacCulloch, *Reformation*, pp. 97–105.
6. *St Thomas More: Selected Letters*, pp. 4–5.
7. Sowards, 'Two Lost Years of Erasmus', p. 169; Ackroyd, *More*, pp. 66, 103–4.
8. J. B. Trapp, 'Ammonius, Andreas [Andrea della Rena] (bap. 1476, d. 1517)', *ODNB*; Clough, 'Three Gigli of Lucca in England', p. 143 n. 72.
9. ML Add. MS 8441, f. 156, quoted in Chambers, *Cardinal Bainbridge in the Court of Rome*, p. 9.
10. Mattingly, *Renaissance Diplomacy*, pp. 164–5, 169.
11. Mattingly, *Renaissance Diplomacy*, pp. 164–5; Setton, *The Papacy and the Levant*, II, pp. 533–6; Chambers, *Popes, Cardinals and War*, p. 111.
12. Singer, *The Earliest Chemical Industry*, p. 318 n. 241.
13. Mattingly, *Renaissance Diplomacy*, p. 159.
14. Wilkie, *The Cardinal Protectors of England*, p. 29; Underwood, 'The Pope, the Queen and the King's Mother', p. 78; Mattingly, *Renaissance Diplomacy*, pp. 141–3, 158; Clough, 'Three Gigli of Lucca in England', p. 138.
15. Hay, *Polydore Vergil*, pp. 6, 22–3; Vergil, *Anglica Historia*, pp. 144–5.
16. Clough, 'Three Gigli of Lucca in England', p. 144.
17. *CWE*, 2, ep. 198.
18. *Calendar of the Manuscripts of the Dean and Chapter of Wells*, 2 vols., Historical Manuscripts Commission, 12 (1907–14), II, pp. 139–40, quoted in Gunn, 'Court of Henry VII', p. 137.
19. *CWE*, 2, ep. 188.
20. *CWE*, 2, eps. 189, 191–6, 206.
21. Tournoy, 'Two Poems Written by Erasmus for Bernard Andre', pp. 45–51; *CWE*, 2, ep. 191; *CWE*, 10, ep. 1490; *CWM*, 3, 2, no. 148.
22. Vergil, *Anglica Historia*, p. xx.
23. Hay, *Polydore Vergil*, pp. 79–128.
24. Hay, *Polydore Vergil*, pp. 131–5, 143–4.

25. Talbot and Hammond, *The Medical Practitioners in Medieval England*, pp. 179–82, 300–301; *CWE*, 2, eps. 195, 236.

26. Finot, 'Le commerce d'alun dans les pays-bas', p. 425.

27. Setton, *The Papacy and the Levant*, III, p. 49; Tyerman, *England and the Crusades*, pp. 350–51.

28. TNA E 36/214, f. 58v; Chambers, *Popes, Cardinals and War*, pp. 110–12; Mattingly, *Renaissance Diplomacy*, pp. 140–47, 157–8; Currin, 'England's International Relations', p. 27; BL Lansdowne MS 127, f. 52v.

29. *LP RIII/HVII*, II, pp. 167–8; BL Lansdowne MS 127, f. 34v; Hay, 'Pietro Griffo, an Italian in England', p. 120.

30. Underwood, 'The Pope, the Queen and the King's Mother', p. 79; Currin, 'England's International Relations', p. 29.

31. Sicca, 'Consumption and Trade of Art between Italy and England', pp. 7–8.

32. Cellini, *Autobiography*, p. 18.

33. Verdon, *The Art of Guido Mazzoni*, pp. 139–41.

34. Galvin and Lindley, 'Pietro Torrigiano's Portrait Bust of King Henry VII', p. 900; *HKW*, III, pp. 200–201; MS Bodley 488.

35. Verdon, *The Art of Guido Mazzoni*, pp. 137–8.

36. Darr, 'New Documents for Pietro Torrigiani', pp. 108–25.

37. *CWE*, 2, eps. 200, 203, 205.

38. *CWE*, 2, ep. 206.

39. *CWE*, 12, pp. 369–70.

40. *CWE*, 2, ep. 215.

11. EXTRAORDINARY JUSTICE

1. *GC*, pp. 332–3.

2. Cunningham, 'Loyalty and the Usurper', pp. 468–9; Condon, 'Ruling Elites', p. 123.

3. TNA DL 3/4, N1 d. I am grateful to James Ross for an early look at his perceptive article 'Sedition and the King "Beyond the See"?'

4. Horowitz, 'Richard Empson', p. 46.

5. BL Lansdowne MS 127, f. 53.

6. Cunningham, 'Loyalty and the Usurper', pp. 463–4, 470; Horowitz, 'Henry Tudor's Treasure', pp. 562, 568–75; Gunn, *Early Tudor Government*, pp. 124–7; Horowitz, 'Policy and Prosecution', pp. 443–5.

7. Gunn, 'Edmund Dudley and the Church', pp. 523–4; Cunningham, 'Loyalty and the Usurper', p. 480; Gunn, '"New Men"', p. 159.

8. TNA X-2860 (temporary reference). I am grateful to James Ross for

bringing this document to my attention, and for an early look at his article, '"Contrary to the right and to the order of the lawe"', which explores it in depth.

9. *GC*, p. 348.

10. *Acts of Court of the Mercers' Company*, p. 577; Barron, *London in the Later Middle Ages*, pp. 13, 115. Bratchel, 'Alien Merchant Communities', pp. 6–7, 52–5, 129–32, 143–6, 172; Sutton, *Mercery*, pp. 333–51.

11. Sutton, *Mercery*, pp. 343–4; *GC*, p. 348; Dudley, *Tree of Commonwealth*, p. 6; BL Lansdowne MS 127, f. 31.

12. *English Historical Documents*, p. 189; TNA E 154/2/17; Schofield, *Medieval London Houses*, nos. 178, 225.

13. Bellamy, *Tudor Law of Treason*, pp. 85, 125.

14. Grummitt, 'Henry VII, Chamber Finance and the "New Monarchy"', p. 236; *GC*, p. 352; Ives, *Common Lawyers*, pp. 268–9.

15. Arrighi, *The Long Twentieth Century*, pp. 111–29; Vilar, *A History of Gold and Money*, p. 47; Sutton, *Mercery*, p. 114.

16. *GC*, p. 352; Bratchel, 'Alien Merchant Communities', pp. 201–2, 321.

17. *A Relation of the Island of England*, p. 33.

18. *GC*, p. 349.

19. Barron, *London in the Later Middle Ages*, p. 53; Ramsey, 'Overseas Trade', nn. 48, 50, 51, 53; *GC*, p. 349; *CPR 1495–1509*, p. 470; Karras, *Common Women*, p. 28; Pugh, *Imprisonment in Medieval England*, pp. 109–11.

20. TNA E 36/214, ff. 34, 151.

21. 'The Petition of Edmund Dudley,' nos. 12, 58, 63; BL Lansdowne MS 127, f. 49.

22. Sutton, *Mercery*, p. 354; Horowitz, '"Agree with the king"', pp. 352–3; *GC*, p. 336; 'The Petition of Edmund Dudley', no. 75.

23. SJC D91. 19, pp. 8–11.

24. SJC D91. 19, p. 13; Jones and Underwood, *The King's Mother*, p. 198.

25. SJC D91.19, p. 11.

26. Jones and Underwood, *The King's Mother*, pp. 91–2, 159; SJC D91.19, p.9; TNA E 36/214, p. 142.

27. Penn, 'Literary Service', p. 21.

28. Cavendish, *Life of Cardinal Wolsey*, p. 7; Condon, 'Last Will of Henry VII', p. 105 nn. 21, 22: TNA E 36/314, pp. 141, 147, 156; see also Starkey, 'Court and Government', pp. 51–2.

29. TNA E 36/214, f. 74; TNA LC 2/1, f. 63; *The Pension Book of Gray's Inn*, pp. xxiii–xxiv.

30. Horowitz, 'Richard Empson', p. 43; TNA E 36/214 ff. 70, 73, 73v; *GC*, p. 333; Hall, *Chronicle*, p. 502.

31. *CSPS*, no. 511; *CSPS* Supp., pp. 90–91.
32. *GC*, pp. 336, 343; see Horowitz, '"Agree with the king"', p. 354.
33. WAM 13601–2; Horowitz, 'Richard Empson', p. 39.
34. WAM 12249.
35. Horowitz, '"Agree with the king"', pp. 339, 341–2.
36. WAM 9260.
37. BL Lansdowne 127, ff. 46, 48; TNA C 82/307, 24 November 1507.
38. Horowitz, '"Agree with the king"', pp. 363–4.
39. BL Lansdowne MS 127.
40. *GC*, p. 334; Gunn, 'Structures of Politics', p. 88.
41. Roper, *Lyfe of Sir Thomas More, Knighte*, pp. 7–8.
42. *CWE*, 2, ep. 250; Erasmus, *Ecclesiastae*, II, p. 373; *CSPS*, II, no. 44.
43. Marius, *Thomas More*, pp. 51–2, 86–7.
44. Gunn, 'Edmund Dudley and the Church', *passim*; Cunningham, *Henry VII*, pp. 226–7.
45. Jones and Underwood, *The King's Mother*, pp. 83, 92; Gunn, '"New Men"'.
46. Gunn, 'Edmund Dudley and the Church', pp. 515–16; J. B. Trapp, 'Urswick, Christopher (1448? –1522)', *ODNB*.
47. Trapp, 'Christopher Urswick and his Books', *passim*.
48. *GC*, pp. 334–5; TNA C 82/320, 286, quoted in Horowitz, 'Policy and Prosecution', p. 443 nn. 155, 156.
49. Bacon, *History of the Reign of Henry VII*, p. 202; Lander, 'Bonds, Coercion and Fear', p. 293.
50. Harris, *Edward Stafford*, pp. 165–6.

12. COURAGE TO BE BOLD

1. *GC*, pp. 328, 331; *HKW*, III, p. 312.
2. *CSPS*, no. 552.
3. BL Harleian MS 69, ff. 2v–3v.
4. *HKW*, II, pp. 967–9; *HKW*, IV, p. 306; 'Justes of the Moneths of May and June', p. 109; Gunn, 'Chivalry', p. 117.
5. *LP HVIII*, III (ii), no. 765; A. Hawkyard, 'Neville, Sir Edward (b. in or before 1482, d. 1538)', *ODNB*.
6. Gunn, 'Thomas Lovell', p. 120; Gunn, 'Henry Bourchier', p. 138 n. 30; S. J. Gunn, 'Thomas Knyvet (c.1485–1512)', *ODNB*.
7. Gunn, 'Henry Bourchier', p. 137.
8. *Babees Book*, p. 1; 'John Russell's *Boke of Nurture*', in ibid., pp. 162–3.

9. Lander, *Government and Community*, pp. 76–7; Gunn, *Charles Brandon*, pp. 23, 48–9.

10. Young, *Tudor and Jacobean Tournaments*, p. 35; Dudley, *Tree of Commonwealth*, p. 27.

11. SJC D91.19, p. 34.

12. Jones and Underwood, *The King's Mother*, p. 165; SJC D91.19, pp. 80, 92.

13. 'Justes of the Moneth of May', pp. 148–50; Kipling, *Triumph of Honour*, pp. 133–4.

14. 'Justes of the Moneth of May', pp. 148–50; Richardson, *The White Queen*, p. 38.

15. Bratchell, 'Alien Merchant Communities', p. 199; Bernard, 'The Fortunes of the Greys', p. 679; Ives, *Common Lawyers*, pp. 375–6.

16. Bernard, 'The Fortunes of the Greys', pp. 673–4.

17. Pugh, 'The Indenture for the Marches', pp. 437–8; Bernard, 'The Fortunes of the Greys', p. 675 n. 33, citing TNA E 368/290/rot. xlviii–l.

18. 'Justes of the Moneth of June', p. 128.

19. Baker-Smith, '"Inglorious glory"', pp. 135–6; Anglo, *The Martial Arts of Renaissance Europe*, pp. 233–4; Thurley, *Royal Palaces*, p. 180; Dudley, *Tree of Commonwealth*, p. 50.

20. 'Justes of the Moneth of June', p. 126; *LP HVIII*, I (i), no. 880.

21. Bernard, 'The Fortunes of the Greys', p. 676; *Calendar of State Papers, Foreign Series*, I, no. 530.

22. 'Justes of the Moneth of June', p. 129.

23. Hall, *Chronicle*, p. 19; Mancini, *Usurpation*, pp. 79–81; *LP HVIII*, I (i), no. 880.

24. 'Justes of the Moneth of June', pp. 126–7.

25. Stevens, *Music and Poetry in the Early Tudor Court*, pp. 140, 196, 211, 215; TNA E 36/214, f. 14v.

26. For example, Hawes, *Minor Poems*, pp. 90–91, 122; Hawes, *Pastime of Pleasure*, pp. 5, 13.

27. *AR*, II, p. 208; Hawes, *Minor Poems*, p. 97.

28. Samman, 'The Progresses of Henry VIII', pp. 59–74.

29. Thurley, *Royal Palaces*, p. 73; Gunn, '"New Men"', citing TNA PROB 2/199, mm.1–2, 5, 6, 9.

30. Jones and Underwood, *The King's Mother*, pp. 158, 189–90, 194, 217; TNA E 23/3, in Condon, 'Last Will of Henry VII', p. 128.

31. *HKW*, IV, pp. 40, 42.

32. *CSPS*, no. 541.

33. Gunn, 'Court of Henry VII', p. 137 nn. 29, 30.

34. Bernard, 'The Fortunes of the Greys', pp. 673, 677; *CCR 1500–1509*, no. 797.

35. *CPR 1495–1509*, pp. 163–4; TNA C 142/26/21; Cooper, 'Henry VII's Last Years Reconsidered', p. 119.

36. TNA C 82/304, quoted in Horowitz, 'Policy and Prosecution', p. 448.

37. Thurley, *Royal Palaces*, p. 60; *HKW*, III, pp. 349–51.

38. Mattingly, *Catherine of Aragon*, pp. 88–9.

39. *CSPS*, no. 526.

40. *CSPS*, nos. 527, 529, 551; *CSPS* Supp., no. 22; Currin, 'England's International Relations', p. 34.

41. Mattingly, *Renaissance Diplomacy*, pp. 146–7.

42. *CSPS*, nos. 549, 550, 552; *CSPS* Supp., no. 23.

43. *CSPS* Supp., no. 23; *CSPS*, nos. 551, 553.

44. *CSPS*, nos. 511, 525; Mattingly, *Catherine of Aragon*, pp. 76–7.

45. Aram, *Juana the Mad*, pp. 96, 101–2.

46. *CSPS* Supp., no. 19.

47. Mattingly, *Renaissance Diplomacy*, p. 130; *CSPS*, nos. 541, 545, 551.

48. Jones and Underwood, *The King's Mother*, pp. 66, 82–3, 266.

49. *Letters of Richard Fox*, p. 122.

50. *HKW*, IV, pp. 147–8.

13. SAVAGE HARSHNESS MADE COMPLETE

1. BL Add. MS 28623, ff. 11–12; Fuensalida, *Correspondencia*, p. 449.

2. Orme, *From Childhood to Chivalry*, pp. 42–3.

3. TNA E 101/415/11; Hayward, *Dress at the Court of Henry VII*, p. 91.

4. *AR*, II, p. 193; Stevens, *Music and Poetry in the Early Tudor Court*, pp. 244–5, 252, 269, 278, 283, 286–7; Orme, *From Childhood to Chivalry*, p. 200; Bennett, *English Books and Readers*, pp. 150–51.

5. Bernard, 'The Rise of Sir William Compton', p. 755.

6. Gunn, *Charles Brandon*, pp. 23, 49.

7. 'The Most Pleasant Song of Lady Bessy', p. 2.

8. *CSPS*, no. 587; TNA E 36/214, f. 117.

9. Gunn, 'War, Dynasty and Public Opinion', p. 142; *GC*, p. 323; Currin, 'England's International Relations', p. 37.

10. Vergil, *Anglica Historia*, p. 131.

11. TNA DL 5/4, f. 102v; *GC*, pp. 335–6; Horowitz, '"Agree with the king"', pp. 353–5, 361–2.

12. CLRO, *Journal* 11, LMA Col/cc/01/01/011 (thanks to Samantha Harper for this reference).

13. *CSPS*, no. 552; Bacon, *History of the Reign of Henry VII*, p. 199.

14. TNA E 36/214, p. 447; *CPR 1495–1509*, p. 366; BL Lansdowne MS 127, ff. 3v, 31v, 41v; Jones and Underwood, *The King's Mother*, p. 80, pp. 113–15, quoting TNA SC 1/51/179; Starkey, 'Intimacy and Innovation', pp. 74–5; Cameron, 'The Giving of Livery', pp. 26–7.

15. Gunn, 'The Courtiers of Henry VII', p. 30 and n.; TNA PROB 11/16/16, cited in S. J. Gunn, 'Daubeney, Giles, first Baron Daubeney (1451/2–1508)', *ODNB*.

16. *Memorials*, pp. 108–9, 112, 115–16; TNA E 36/214, f. 119.

17. TNA E 36/214, ff. 121v–122; Horowitz, 'Richard Empson', p. 44 n. 85.

18. SJC D91.19, pp. 75–8, 82.

19. Mattingly, *Renaissance Diplomacy*, p. 152.

20. Fuensalida, *Correspondencia*, p. 418.

21. TNA E 36/214, ff. 123–123v; Thurley, *Royal Palaces*, p. 225; *Memorials*, pp. 106, 110; Starkey, *Henry*, pp. 124, 232; Mattingly, *Catherine of Aragon*, pp. 78–91; Fuensalida, *Correspondencia*, pp. 131–5, 194.

22. TNA E 36/214, pp. 252, 254.

23. Mattingly, *Catherine of Aragon*, pp. 84–6.

24. Fuensalida, *Correspondencia*, p. 449.

25. *CSPS*, no. 588; *CSPS*, II, no. 12.

26. Preest and Clark, eds., *Chronica Maiora of Thomas Walsingham*, p. 386; Cunningham, *Henry VII*, p. 116; Kingsford, ed., *The First English Life of Henry V*, p. 18.

27. Stevens, *Music and Poetry in the Early Tudor Court*, p. 2.

28. *CWM*, 3, 2, no. 19; *GC*, p. 373; Anglo, *The Martial Arts of Renaissance Europe*, p. 231. SJC D91.19, f. 94; TNA E 36/214, f. 134; *Memorials*, pp. 120, 124; Young, *Tudor and Jacobean Tournaments*, p. 194.

29. *Memorials*, p. 111.

30. Currin, 'England's International Relations', pp. 24, 27; TNA E 36/214, f. 134v; *LP RIII/HVII*, I, pp. 350–64.

31. *CSPV*, no. 936.

32. *LP RIII/HVII*, I, pp. 363–4.

33. *LP RIII/HVII*, I, pp. 365–6.

34. TNA E 36/214, ff. 136–138v.

35. Horowitz, 'Henry Tudor's Treasure', pp. 563–4, 572 (figure 4).

36. SJC C7.11, f. 40.

37. *CCR 1500–1509*, no. 896; Richardson, 'Surveyor of the King's Prerogative', pp. 65–75.

38. Starkey, 'Court and Government', pp. 38–9; *CPR 1495–1509*, p. 591; Richardson, 'Surveyor of the King's Prerogative', pp. 63–6; Vergil,

Anglica Historia, p. 131; Watts, '"Newe fundacion"', p. 35; Horowitz, 'Policy and Prosecution', pp. 413–15; Cooper, 'Henry VII's Last Years Reconsidered', p. 111.

39. *Memorials*, pp. 126–8; Creighton, *A History of Epidemics in Britain*, pp. 244–5; Samman, 'The Progresses of Henry VIII', pp. 71–2.

40. *GC*, p. 336; Elton, 'Henry VII: A Restatement', pp. 15–23; TNA E 36/214, f. 141.

41. Fuensalida, *Correspondencia*, p. 476; Carlson and Hammond, 'Sweating Sickness', p. 47 n. 116.

42. TNA E 36/214, f. 151.

43. Cavendish, *Life of Cardinal Wolsey*, pp. 7–10.

44. TNA E 36/214, f. 144v, 146.

45. Cavendish, *Life of Cardinal Wolsey*, pp. 7–10; *LP RIII/HVII*, I, pp. 425–52; *Chronicle of Calais*, pp. 48–51; *Memorials*, p. 438; *Foedera*, XIII, pp. 171, 175–89.

46. *Chronicle of Calais*, pp. 54–7.

47. TNA E 36/214, f. 151v; Darr, 'New Documents for Pietro Torrigiani', p. 121.

48. Anglo, *Spectacle*, p. 107; Anglo, 'Court Festivals', pp. 24–6.

49. TNA LC 9/50, ff. 143-47v.

50. Horowitz, '"Agree with the king"', p. 335.

51. Anglo, *Spectacle*, p. 107.

52. *'The Spousells' of the Princess Mary*, pp. 32–3.

53. I am grateful to Steve Gunn for highlighting this point.

54. Mattingly, *Renaissance Diplomacy*, p. 160; Currin, 'England's International Relations', p. 27 n. 72; TNA E 36/214, f. 158; Starkey, *Six Wives*, pp. 102–5.

55. *CWM*, 3, 2, no. 147.

56. *'The Spousells' of the Princess Mary*, pp. 27–8.

14. THE ART OF DYING

1. TNA E 36/214, f. 157v; SJC D102.1, ff. 4–5v.

2. TNA E 23/3 (all references to TNA E 23/3 follow Margaret Condon's edition, in Condon, 'The Last Will of Henry VII', pp. 112–240); *LP HVIII*, III (i), nos. 186–7, 497; Wilson, 'The Functional Design of Henry VII's Chapel', p. 140.

3. Duffy, *Stripping of the Altars*, pp. 344–5.

4. Vergil, *Anglica Historia*, p. 143; Condon, 'The Last Will of Henry VII', p. 105. I am grateful to Margaret Condon for her thoughts on this dating.

5. Gunn, 'The Accession of Henry VIII', pp. 280–81; Cameron, 'The Giving of Livery', p. 25.

6. TNA E 36/214, f. 160.

7. *CSPS* Supp., no. 4.

8. *CSPS* Supp., no. 2.

9. *CSPS* Supp., no. 4.

10. *CSPS* no. 603.

11. TNA E 36/211, *passim*; TNA E 101/517/15, f. 9v; Starkey, 'The King's Privy Chamber', pp. 32–3, 361–5.

12. Starkey, 'The King's Privy Chamber', pp. 49–50.

13. TNA E 36/214, f. 158v; TNA E 101/517/15, f. 9v; TNA E 101/416/7 (unfoliated); Gunn, 'Structures of Politics', pp. 76–82; *CCR 1500–1509*, no. 675 (i); Gunn, 'Court of Henry VII', p. 135.

14. TNA E 36/214, f. 162; SJC D102.1, f. 9v.

15. *Ars moriendi*, p. 17; Duffy, *Stripping of the Altars*, pp. 301–43.

16. *The English Works of John Fisher*, I, pp. 278–9.

17. I am grateful to Rosemary Horrox for her observations on Henry VII's preparations for death.

18. TNA E 23/3, f. 17v; Condon, 'The Last Will of Henry VII', pp. 106, 119.

19. TNA C 67/93.

20. *The English Works of John Fisher*, I, pp. 273–4; *Ars moriendi*, p. 18; for the king's confessor, Stephen Baroms, see *CPR 1495–1509*, no. 568.

21. BL Add. MS 45131, ff. 52v–53, I am grateful to Adrian Ailes for his thoughts on this document; Gunn, 'The Courtiers of Henry VII', pp. 36–7, 44.

22. Gunn, 'The Accession of Henry VIII', pp. 278–9 and *passim*; BL Add. MS 45131, f. 52v.

23. SJC C7.11, ff. 38–40.

24. Fuensalida, *Correspondencia*, p. 513; Gunn, 'The Accession of Henry VIII', pp. 280–81.

25. *Third Report of the Deputy Keeper of the Public Records*, p. 226.

26. TNA E 154/2/17.

27. *Third Report of the Deputy Keeper of the Public Records*, p. 226; GC, p. 365; Gunn, 'The Accession of Henry VIII', pp. 284–6; SJC D102.1, f. 107.

28. BL Add. MS 71009, f. 17; BL Add. MS 45131, f. 52v; *Household of Edward IV*, pp. 114–15.

29. BL Add. MS 45131, f. 52v.

30. BL Add. MS 59899, f. 23; *Receyt*, p. 73; Thurley, *Royal Palaces*, pp. 198–203.

31. BL Add. MS 45131, f. 52v; BL MS 71009, ff. 14v–15; Kisby, 'The Royal Household Chapel', pp. 140–42, 157, 557.

32. BL Add. MS 45131, f. 52v.

33. SJC D102.1, f. 10v; Vergil, *Anglica Historia*, pp. 149, 152; Hall, *Chronicle*, p. 505.

34. *GC*, p. 365.

35. *TRP*, I, nos. 59, 60; *LP HVIII*, I (i), nos. 2, 4–7; Gunn, 'The Accession of Henry VIII', p. 278; Hall, *Chronicle*, p. 505.

36. Febvre and Martin, *The Coming of the Book*, pp. 61–7.

37. *GC*, p. 336; Elton, 'Henry VII: A Restatement', p. 19; *LP HVIII*, I (i), no. 12.

38. *GC*, pp. 351, 337.

39. Fuensalida, *Correspondencia*, p. 516; *GC*, p. 343.

40. Hall, *Chronicle*, p. 505; BL Add. MS 21481, f. 4v; *CWM*, 3, 2, no 19.

41. BL Add. MS 45131, ff. 52v–3.

42. *The English Works of John Fisher*, I, pp. 278–9.

43. Leland, *Collectanea*, IV, pp. 303–9; *The Obituary Roll of John Islip*, pls. XXI, XXII.

44. TNA E 23/3, f. 2, in Condon, 'The Last Will of Henry VII', pp. 113–14.

45. Leland, *Collectanea*, IV, pp. 303–9; Hall, *Chronicle*, pp. 506–7; Kantorowicz, *The King's Two Bodies*, p. 412; Gunn, *Early Tudor Government*, pp. 163–4; *LP RIII/HVII*, I, pp. xvii; Given-Wilson, 'The Exequies of Edward III', pp. 272–4; Sutton and Visser-Fuchs, *Royal Funerals of the House of York*, pp. 41–5.

15. RICH, FEROCIOUS, THIRSTING FOR GLORY

1. Machiavelli, *Lettere familiali*, p. 293.

2. *CSPV*, no. 944.

3. Sutton, *Mercery*, p. 355.

4. *LP HVIII*, I (i), no. 37. Wolffe, *Crown Lands*, pp. 84–7; Horowitz, 'Henry Tudor's Treasure', *passim*; Grummitt, 'Henry VII, Chamber Finance and the "New Monarchy"', pp. 238–43.

5. James P. Carley, 'Marney, Henry, first Baron Marney (1456/7–1523)', *ODNB*.

6. Starkey, 'Court and Government', p. 39; Bernard, 'The Rise of Sir William Compton', pp. 756, 775.

7. *CWE*, 2, ep. 215.

8. *CWE*, 2, ep. 214.

9. *CWE*, 2, ep. 216. For an earlier example of Latin secretaries influencing

their aristocratic masters, see Rundle, 'Humanism Before the Tudors', p. 27.

10. *CWE*, 2, eps. 657, 658.

11. Fuensalida, *Correspondencia*, pp. 516–20.

12. Mattingly, *Catherine of Aragon*, pp. 93–6.

13. *LP HVIII*, I, no. 84; *LP HVIII*, I, (i), no. 119.

14. *LP HVIII*, I, nos. 3, 5, 9; *LP HVIII*, I, (i), no. 39.

15. *LP HVIII*, I, nos. 8, 13, 18.

16. *GC*, pp. 339–40; TNA LC 9/50, ff. 217–18; Hall, *Chronicle*, pp. 505–8.

17. *CWM*, 3, 2, no. 19; Vergil, *Anglica Historia*, p. 151.

18. *CWM*, 3, 2, no. 19.

19. TNA E 36/228, ff. 7–8.

20. Anglo, *Spectacle*, p. 46.

21. Skelton, *Complete English Poems*, IX; *CWM*, 3, 2, no. 23.

22. Hall, *Chronicle*, pp. 505–8.

23. Gunn, *Early Tudor Government*, pp. 163–8; Wooding, *Henry VIII*, pp. 53–4.

24. Hall, *Chronicle*, pp. 505–8; *Memorials*, p. 123; *LP HVIII*, I (i), nos. 211, 213; *GC*, pp. 340–41.

25. BL Add. 12060, ff. 23–23v; Jones and Underwood, *The King's Mother*, pp. 236–7.

26. Hall, *Chronicle*, pp. 510–12.

27. Anglo, *Spectacle*, pp. 110–11.

28. *LP HVIII*, I (i), no. 82/2; Hall, *Chronicle*, pp. 510–12.

29. BL Add. MS 21481, ff. 7, 8v, 10v; *LP HVIII*, I (i), nos. 320, 697; *LP HVIII*, I (i), nos. 158/75, 414/26, 414/58.

30. *LP HVIII*, I (i), no. 94/87.

31. R. W. Hoyle, 'Darcy, Thomas, Baron Darcy of Darcy', *ODNB*.

32. *Letters of Richard Fox*, no. 29.

33. *LP HVIII*, I (i), no. 157; Gunn, 'Structures of Politics', pp. 59–61.

34. TNA C 82/342/1/576, quoted in Elton, 'Henry VII: A Restatement', p. 21.

35. Elton, 'Henry VII: A Restatement', pp. 20–22.

36. *LP HVIII*, I (i), nos. 309, 310, 312, 18 July; see also Richardson, 'Surveyor of the King's Prerogative', pp. 74–5; Starkey, 'Court and Government', pp. 48–50; *Third Report of the Deputy Keeper*, pp. 226–8; Gunn, 'The Accession of Henry VIII', pp. 285–6.

37. Gunn, 'Survival Strategies', pp. 6–7; Anglo, 'Ill of the Dead', p. 31; *GC*, pp. 338–9.

38. 'The Petition of Edmund Dudley, pp. 87–90; WAM 12249.

39. 'The Petition of Edmund Dudley', p. 87.

40. 'The Petition of Edmund Dudley', pp. 85–6.

41. TNA E 154/2/17; *LP HVIII*, I (i), no. 218/13.

42. Wolffe, *Crown Lands*, no. 18, pp. 162–3; Wolffe makes this point in ibid., p. 85; see also Elton, 'Henry VII: A Restatement', p. 23.

43. Fortescue, *On the laws and governance of England*, pp. xxxv, 121; Richardson, *Tudor Chamber Administration*, pp. 164, 184.

44. Grummitt, 'Henry VII, Chamber Finance and the "New Monarchy"', pp. 240–43; Horowitz, 'Policy and Prosecution', pp. 448–52; BL Add. MS 21481, ff. 289–305v, 318–352v; Cavill, 'Debate and Dissent', pp. 173–4; Gunn, *Early Tudor Government*, p. 170.

45. Wolffe, *Crown Lands*, nos. 18–20, pp. 162–70, no. 22, p. 180; Starkey, 'Court and Government', pp. 29, 37, 48–50; Elton, 'Henry VII: A Restatement', p. 23.

46. TNA C 82/343/1/615; *GC*, p. 365.

47. *LP HVIII*, I (i), nos. 559, 381/6, 52; Gunn, 'Structures of Politics', p. 78; Gunn, 'Edmund Dudley and the Church', p. 524, citing TNA C 1/303/62.

48. *GC*, p. 366.

49. Stapleton, *The Life of Sir Thomas More*, p. 25.

50. Dudley, *Tree of Commonwealth*, p. 33.

EPILOGUE

1. Dudley, *Tree of Commonwealth*, *passim*.

2. Howard Leithead, 'Cromwell, Thomas, earl of Essex (b. in or before 1485, d. 1540)', *ODNB*; Gunn, *Early Tudor Government*, pp. 56–7, 149–51; Horowitz, 'Policy and Prosecution', pp. 451–2.

3. *LP HVIII*, I (ii), nos. 2947, 3004, 3029, 3129, 3165, 3240; Hall, *Chronicle*, p. 569.

4. Cecil H. Clough, 'Gigli, Silvestro (1463–1521)', *ODNB*.

5. Sicca, 'Pawns of International Finance and Politics', *passim*; Lindley, '"The singular mediacion and prayers"', pp. 268–74; Wooding, *Henry VIII*, p. 279.

6. Bacon, *History of the Reign of King Henry VII*, p. 3.

Bibliography

PRIMARY SOURCES

Manuscript sources

British Library, London
Additional: 5465, 7099, 12060, 21404, 21480, 21481, 28623, 45131, 45133, 46455, 71009, 59899; Cottonian: Vespasian C XIV, Vitellius C XI, Titus A XIII; Harleian: 69, 78, 283; Lansdowne: 127; Royal: 12 B vi, 16 E xi, 16 E xiv, 18 D ii, 19 C viii; Sloane: 3479

St John's College, Cambridge
C7   Cartularies and registers of college lands and goods
D91   Lady Margaret Beaufort's treasurer: Accounts Various
D102 Lady Margaret Beaufort's treasurer/chamberlain: Accounts Various
D105 Letters to John Fisher, Nicholas Metcalfe and others, 1509–26

The National Archives, Kew
C67   Chancery: Supplementary Patent Rolls
C82   Chancery: Warrants for the Great Seal, Series II
C255 Chancery Files, Tower and Rolls Chapel Series, Miscellaneous Files and Writs
DL 5 Duchy of Lancaster: Court of Duchy Chamber: Entry Books of Decrees and Orders
E101 King's Remembrancer: Accounts Various
E114 Exchequer: King's Remembrancer: Bonds and Obligations
E154 King's Remembrancer and Treasury of the Receipt: Inventories of Goods and Chattels
E23   Exchequer: Treasury of the Receipt: Royal Wills
E404 Exchequer of Receipt: Warrants for Issues
E405 Exchequer of Receipt: Accounts Various

E36   Exchequer: Treasury of the Receipt: Miscellaneous Books

LC2   Lord Chamberlain's Department: Records of Special Events

LC9   Lord Chamberlain's Department: Accounts and Miscellanea

SC1   Special Collections: Ancient Correspondence of the Chancery and the Exchequer

Westminster Abbey Muniments

9260, 12249, 13601, 13602, 16015-16078

Printed primary sources

Acts of Court of the Mercers' Company, 1453–1527, eds. L. Lyell and F. D. Watney, Cambridge, 1936.

The Antiquarian Repertory, eds. Francis Grose and Thomas Astle, 4 vols., London, 1807–9.

Ars moriendi: that is to seye the crafte for to deye for the helthe of mannes sowle, printed about 1491 by William Caxton or Wynken de Worde, London, 1891.

The Babees Book ... The Bokes of Nurture of Hugh Rhodes and John Russell, ed. F. J. Furnivall, EETS, o.s., 32, London, 1868.

Bacon, Francis, *The History of the Reign of Henry VII*, ed. Brian Vickers, Cambridge, 1998.

Bentley, S., *Excerpta Historica, or, Illustrations of English History*, London, 1833.

The Book of Quinte Essence or the Fifth Being; that is to say, Man's Heaven, ed. F. J. Furnivall, EETS o.s. 16, London, 1866.

Burchard, Johann, *At the Court of the Borgia: being an account of the reign of Pope Alexander VI*, ed. and trans. Geoffrey Parker, London, 1963.

Calendar of the Close Rolls, preserved in the Public Record Office ... 1485–1509, 2 vols., London, HMSO, 1955–63.

Calendar of the Patent Rolls, preserved in the Public Record Office ... 1476–1509, 3 vols., London, HMSO, 1901–16.

Calendar of State Papers, Foreign Series, of the Reign of Elizabeth, vol. 1, ed. Rev. J. Stephenson, London, 1863.

Calendar of State Papers, Milan, vol. I, 1359–1618, ed. A. B. Hinds, London, 1912.

Calendar of Letters, Dispatches, and State Papers Relating to the Negotiations Between England and Spain, vols. I & II, ed. G. Bergenroth, London, 1862.

Calendar of Letters, Dispatches, and State Papers Relating to the Negotiations Between England and Spain. Supplement to vols. I & II, ed. Garrett Mattingly, London, 1868.

Calendar of State Papers and Manuscripts Relating to English Affairs, Existing in the Archives and Collections of Venice, vol. II, 1202–1529, ed. Rawdon Brown, London, 1864.

Cavendish, George, *The Life and Death of Cardinal Wolsey,* ed. Richard S. Sylvester, EETS o.s. 243, London, 1959.

Caxton, William, *The Prologues and Epilogues of William Caxton,* ed. W. J. B. Crotch, EETS, o.s., 176, London, 1928.

Cellini, Benvenuto, *The Autobiography of Benvenuto Cellini,* London, 1996.

Chartier, Alain, *Curial . . . translated thus in Englyssh by William Caxton,* EETS e.s. 54, ed. F. J. Furnivall, London, 1888.

The Chronicle of Calais, in the reigns of Henry VII and Henry VIII to the year 1540, ed. J. G. Nichols, Camden Society, o.s. 35, London, 1846.

The Chronicle of the Grey Friars of London, ed. J. G. Nichols, Camden Society, o.s. 53, London, 1852.

The Chronicle of John Harding, ed. Henry Ellis, London, 1812.

Chronicles of London, ed. C. L. Kingsford, Oxford, 1905.

A Collection of Ordinances and Regulations for the Government of the Royal Household, Society of Antiquaries, London, 1790.

Commynes, Philippe de, *Memoirs: The Reign of Louis XI, 1461–83,* trans. M. C. E. Jones, Harmondsworth, 1972.

The Crowland Chronicle Continuations: 1459–1486, eds. N. Pronay and J. Cox, London, 1986.

Dudley, Edmund, 'The petition of Edmund Dudley', ed. C. J. Harrison, *English Historical Review,* 87 (1972), pp. 82–99.

— *The Tree of Commonwealth,* ed. D. M. Brodie, Cambridge, 1948.

English Historical Documents, vol. 5, ed. C. H. Williams, London, 1967.

Erasmus, Desiderius, *The Collected Works of Erasmus,* vols. 1–8, The Correspondence of Erasmus, trans. and ed. R. A. B. Mynors and D. F. S. Thomson, Toronto, Buffalo, 1974–1988.

— *Ecclesiastae sive de ratione concionandi,* ed. F. A. Klein, Leipzig, 1820.

— *The Epistles of Erasmus,* trans. F. M. Nichols, London, 1901.

A Fifteenth Century School Book: from a manuscript in the British Museum (MS Arundel 249), ed. W. Nelson, Oxford, 1956.

Fifty-Third Annual Report of the Deputy Keeper of the Public Records, London, 1892.

Fisher, John, *The English Works of John Fisher,* ed. J. E. B. Mayor, 2 vols., EETS, e.s., 27, London, 1876.

Foedera, ed. Thomas Rymer, 20 vols., London, 1704–35, repr. Farnborough, 1967.

Fortescue, John, *On the laws and governance of England*, ed. Shelley Lockwood, Cambridge, 1997.

Fox, Richard, *Letters of Richard Fox, 1486–1527*, eds. P. S. Allen and H. M. Allen, Oxford, 1929.

Fuensalida, *Correspondencia de Gutierre Gómez de Fuensalida, embajador en Alemania, Flandes é Inglaterra (1496–1509)*, Madrid, 1907.

Gachard, M. M., *Collection des voyages des souverains des pays-bas*, vol. 1, Brussels, 1876.

The Great Chronicle of London, eds. A. H. Thomas and I. D. Thornley, London, 1938, repr. Gloucester, 1983.

Hall, Edward, *Hall's Chronicle: Containing the history of England*, ed. H. Ellis, London, 1809.

Hawes, Stephen, *Stephen Hawes: The Minor Poems*, eds. Florence W. Gluck and Alice B. Morgan, EETS, o.s., 271, Oxford, 1974.

— *The Pastime of Pleasure by Stephen Hawes*, ed. William Edward Mead, EETS, o.s., 173, London, 1928.

Henry VII, The Will of, ed. T. Astle, London, 1775.

The Household of Edward IV: The Black Book and the Ordinance of 1478, ed. A. R. Myers, Manchester, 1959.

'The Justes of the Moneths of May and June', in *Remains of the Early Popular Poetry of England*, vol. 2, ed. W. C. Hazlitt, London, 1866, pp. 109–30.

Leland, John, *Joannis Lelandi antiquarii de rebus Britannis collectanea*, ed. Thomas Hearne, 6 vols., London, 1774.

Letters and Papers Illustrative of the Reigns of Richard III and Henry VII, ed. J. Gairdner, 2 vols., Rolls Series, 24, 1861–3.

Letters and Papers, Foreign and Domestic, of the Reign of Henry VIII, eds. J. S. Brewer, J. Gairdner and R. H. Brodie, 21 vols., with 2 vols. of addenda, London, 1862–1932.

Letters of Royal and Illustrious Ladies of Great Britain, 3 vols., ed. Mary Anne Everett Wood, London, 1846.

The Lisle Letters, ed. Muriel St Clare Byrne, 6 vols., Chicago, 1981.

Lydgate, John, *Stans puer ad mensam: table manners for children*, facsim. and tr. Nicholas Orme, London, 1990.

Machiavelli, Niccolò, *Lettere familiali*, ed. E. Alvisi, Florence, 1883.

— *The Prince*, ed. Maurizio Viroli, Oxford, 2008.

Mancini, Dominic, *The Usurpation of Richard the Third*, ed. C. A. J. Armstrong, Oxford, 2nd edn, 1969.

Materials for a History of the Reign of Henry VII, ed. W. Campbell, 2 vols., Rolls Series, 20, 1873–7.

Memorials of King Henry VII, ed. J. Gairdner, Rolls Series, 10, London, 1858.

More, Thomas, *The Complete Works of St Thomas More*, ed. C. H. Miller and others, 21 vols., New Haven, 1963–97.

— *The Correspondence of Sir Thomas More*, ed. E. F. Rogers, Princeton, 1947.

— *St Thomas More: Selected Letters*, ed. E. F. Rogers, Yale, New Haven and London, 1961.

The Most Pleasant Song of Lady Bessy, ed. J. O. Halliwell, Percy Society, 20, 1877.

The Obituary Roll of John Islip, ed. W. H. St John Hope, London, 1906.

Original Letters Illustrative of English History, ed. H. Ellis, 1st ser., 2 vols., London, 1824–7.

The Parliament Rolls of Medieval England, 1275–1504, vol. 15: Richard III, 1484–1485; Henry VII, 1485–1487, ed. Rosemary Horrox, London, 2005.

The Parliament Rolls of Medieval England, 1275–1504, vol. 16: Henry VII, 1489–1504, ed. Rosemary Horrox, London, 2005.

Paston Letters and Papers of the Fifteenth Century, ed. Norman Davis, 2 vols., Oxford, 1971, 1976.

The Pension Book of Gray's Inn, Records of the Honourable Society 1569–1669, ed. Reginald J. London, Fletcher, 1901.

The Plumpton Correspondence, ed. T. Stapleton, Gloucester, 1990.

The Plumpton Letters and Papers, ed. Joan Kirby, Camden Society, 5th ser., 8, Cambridge, 1996.

Privy Purse Expenses of Elizabeth of York: Wardrobe accounts of Edward the Fourth, ed. N. H. Nicolas, London, 1830.

The Pylgrymage of Sir Richard Guylforde, ed. H. Ellis, Camden Society, o.s. 51, London, 1851.

The Receyt of the Ladie Kateryne, ed. Gordon Kipling, EETS, o.s., 296, Oxford, 1990.

The Register of the Most Noble Order of the Garter, ed. J. Anstis, 2 vols., London, 1724.

The Reign of Henry VII from Contemporary Sources, ed. A. F. Pollard, 3 vols., London, 1913–14.

A Relation of the Island of England about the year 1500, ed. C. A. Sneyd, Camden Society, o.s., 37, London, 1947.

Remains of the Early Popular Poetry of England, ed. W. C. Hazlitt, London, 1866.

Roper, William, *The Lyfe of Sir Thomas Moore, Knighte*, ed. Elsie V. Hitchcock, EETS, o.s. 197, London, 1935.

Select Cases from the Court of Star Chamber ... A. D. 1477–1509, ed. I. S. Leadam, 2 vols., Selden Society 16, 25, London, 1903, 1911.

Select Cases in the Council of Henry VII, eds. G. L. Bayne and W. H. Dunham, Selden Society, 75, London, 1958.

Skelton, John, *The Complete English Poems of John Skelton*, ed. John Scattergood, Harmondsworth, 1983.

— 'The Latin Writings of John Skelton', ed. David Carlson, *Studies in Philology*, 88, 4 (1991), pp. 1–125.

'The Spousells' of the Princess Mary, daughter of Henry VII, to Charles, prince of Castile, 1508, ed. J. Gairdner, Camden Society, n.s., 53, Camden Miscellany, 9, 1895.

Third Annual Report of the Deputy Keeper of the Public Records, London, 1842.

Stow, John, *A Survey of London*, ed. C. L. Kingsford, 3 vols., Oxford, 1908–27.

Tudor Royal Proclamations, eds. P. L. Hughes and J. F. Larkin, vol. 1, New Haven, London, 1964.

Vergil, Polydore, *The Anglica Historia of Polydore Vergil A.D. 1485–1537*, ed. and trans. D. Hay, Camden Society, 3rd ser., 74, London, 1950.

— *Three Books of Polydore Vergil's English History*, ed. Sir H. Ellis, Camden Society, 29, London, 1844.

Secondary Sources

Abulafia, D., ed., *The French Descent into Renaissance Italy, 1494–5: Antecedents and Effects*, Aldershot, 1995.

Ackroyd, Peter, *The Life of Thomas More*, London, 1999.

Anderson, Perry, *Lineages of the Absolutist State*, London, 1974.

Anglo, S., 'The British History in Early Tudor Propaganda', *Bulletin of the John Rylands Library* 44 (1961), pp. 17–48.

— 'The Court Festivals of Henry VII', *Bulletin of the John Rylands Library* 43 (1960–61), pp. 12–45.

— 'The Foundation of the Tudor Dynasty: The Coronation and Marriage of Henry VII', *Guildhall Miscellanea* 2 (1960), pp. 3–11.

— 'Ill of the Dead: The Posthumous Reputation of Henry VII', *Renaissance Studies* 1 (1987), pp. 27–47.

— *Images of Tudor Kingship*, Seaby, 1992.

— 'The London Pageants for the Reception of Katherine of Aragon: November 1501', *Journal of the Warburg and Courtauld Institute* 26 (1961), pp. 53–89.

— *The Martial Arts of Renaissance Europe*, New Haven and London, 2000.

— *Spectacle, Pageantry, and Early Tudor Policy*, 2nd edn, London, 1997.

— 'William Cornish in a Play, Prison, Pageants and Politics', *Review of English Studies* n.s. 10 (1959), pp. 353–7.

— ed., *Chivalry in the Renaissance*, Woodbridge, 1990.

Aram, Bethany, *Juana the Mad: Sovereignty and Dynasty in Renaissance Europe*, Baltimore, 2005.

Archer, Rowena, 'A Skeleton in the de la Pole Closet?' *Ricardian* 13 (2003), pp. 12–26.

Archer, Rowena E. and Walker, Simon, eds., *Rulers and Ruled in Late Medieval England: Essays Presented to Gerald Harriss*, Hambledon, 1995.

Armstrong, C. A. J., 'An Italian Astrologer at the Court of Henry VII', in *England, France and Burgundy in the Fifteenth Century*, London, 1983, pp. 157–78.

Arrighi, Giovanni, *The Long Twentieth Century: Money, Power, and the Origins of Our Times*, London, 1994.

Arthurson, I., 'A Question of Loyalty', *Ricardian* 7 (1987), pp. 401–13.

— 'Espionage and Intelligence from the Wars of the Roses to the Reformation', *Nottingham Medieval Studies*, 35 (1991), pp. 134–54.

— 'The King's Voyage into Scotland: The War That Never Was', in Daniel Williams, ed., *England in the Fifteenth Century*, pp. 1–22.

— *The Perkin Warbeck Conspiracy 1491–1499*, Stroud, 1994.

— 'The Rising of 1497', in Joel Rosenthal and Colin Richmond, eds., *People, Politics and Community in the Later Middle Ages*, Gloucester, 1987, pp. 1–18.

Arthurson, I. and Kingswell, N., 'The Proclamation of Henry Tudor as King of England, 3 November 1483', *Bulletin of the Institute of Historical Research* 63 (1990), pp. 100–106.

Ashmole, E., *The Institutions, Laws and Ceremonies of the Most Noble Order of the Garter*, London, 1672.

Backhouse, Janet, 'Founders of the Royal Library: Edward IV and Henry VII as Collectors of Illuminated Manuscripts', in Daniel Williams, ed., *England in the Fifteenth Century*, pp. 23–41.

Baker-Smith, Dominic, '"Inglorious glory": 1513 and the Humanist Attack on Chivalry', in S. Anglo, ed., *Chivalry in the Renaissance*, pp. 129–44.

Barron, Caroline, 'Centres of Conspicuous Consumption: The Aristocratic Town House in London, 1200–1500', *London Journal* 20 (1995), pp. 1–16.

— *London in the Later Middle Ages: Government and People 1200–1500*, Oxford 2004.

— 'Political Culture in Medieval London', in Linda Clark and Christine Carpenter, eds., *The Fifteenth Century, vol. IV: Political Culture in Late Medieval England*, Woodbridge, 2004, pp. 111–34.

Bellamy, J., *The Tudor Law of Treason: An Introduction*, London, 1979.

Bennett, H. S., *English Books and Readers, 1475 to 1557*, Cambridge, 1952.

Bennett, M. J., *The Battle of Bosworth*, Gloucester, 1985.

— *Lambert Simnel and the Battle of Stoke*, Stroud, 1987.

Bernard, G. W., 'The Fortunes of the Greys, Earls of Kent, in the Early Sixteenth Century', *Historical Journal* 25 (1982), pp. 671–85.

— 'The Rise of Sir William Compton, Early Tudor Courtier', *English Historical Review* 96 (1981), pp. 754–77.

— ed., *The Tudor Nobility*, Manchester, 1992.

Bietenholz, P. G., ed., *Contemporaries of Erasmus*, 3 vols., Toronto, Buffalo, London, 1985–7.

Blake, N. F., *Caxton and His World*, London, 1969.

Bolton, J. L., *The Medieval English Economy, 1150–1500*, London, 1980.

Bowers, Roger, 'Early Tudor Courtly Song: An Evaluation of the Fayrfax Book (BL Additional 5465)', in B. Thompson, ed., *The Reign of Henry VII*, pp. 188–212.

Bratchel, M. E., 'Alien Merchant Communities in London, 1500–1550', unpublished PhD dissertation, University of Cambridge, 1973.

Braudel, Fernand, *Civilization and Capitalism, 15th–18th Centuries*, 3 vols., London, 1981–4.

Brodie, D. M., 'Edmund Dudley: Minister of Henry VII', *Transactions of the Royal Historical Society*, 4th ser., 15 (1932), pp. 133–62.

Bruce, M. L., *The Making of Henry VIII*, London, 1977.

Cameron, A., 'The Giving of Livery and Retaining in Henry VII's Reign', *Renaissance and Modern Studies* 18 (1974), pp. 17–35.

Carlson, David, *English Humanist Books: Writers and Patrons, Manuscript and Print, 1475–1525*, Toronto, 1993.

— 'Royal Tutors in the Reign of Henry VII', *Sixteenth Century Journal* 22 (1991), pp. 253–79.

— 'The Writings of Bernard André (c.1450–c.1522)', *Renaissance Studies* 12 (1998), pp. 228–50.

Carlson, James R. and Hammond, Peter W. 'The English Sweating Sickness (1485–c.1551): A New Perspective on Disease Etiology', *Journal of the History of Medicine* 54 (1999), pp. 23–54.

Carpenter, C., 'Henry VII and the English Polity', in B. Thompson, ed., *The Reign of Henry VII*, pp. 11–30.

Cavill, Paul, 'Debate and Dissent in Henry VII's Parliaments', *Parliamentary History* 25 (2006), pp. 160–75.

— *The English Parliaments of Henry VII*, Oxford, 2009.

Chambers, D. S., *Cardinal Bainbridge in the Court of Rome, 1509–1514*, Oxford, 1965.

— *Popes, Cardinals and War: The Military Church in Renaissance and Early Modern Europe*, London, 2006.

Charlton, E., 'Roll of Prayers Formerly Belonging to Henry VIII when Prince', *Archaeologia Aeliana*, n.s. 2 (1858), pp. 41–5.

Chrimes, S. B., *Henry VII*, London, 1972.

Clough, C. H., *The Duchy of Urbino in the Renaissance*, London, 1981.

— 'The Relations between the English and Urbino Courts, 1474–1508', in Clough, *The Duchy of Urbino in the Renaissance*, pp. 202–18.

— 'Three Gigli of Lucca in England during the Fifteenth and Early Sixteenth Centuries', *Ricardian* 13 (2003), pp. 121–47.

Coleman, C. and Starkey, D., eds., *Revolution Reassessed: Revisions in the History of Tudor Government and Administration*, Oxford, 1986.

Condon, M. M., 'A Kaleidoscope of Treason: Fragments from the Bosworth Story', *Ricardian* 7 (1992), pp. 208–12.

— 'From Caitiff and Villain to *Pater Patriae*: Reynold Bray and the Profits of Office', in M. A. Hicks, ed., *Profit, Piety and the Professions in Later Medieval England*, Gloucester, 1990, pp. 137–68.

— 'God Save the King! Piety, Propaganda and the Perpetual Memorial', in T. W. T. Tatton-Brown and R. Mortimer, eds., *Westminster Abbey*, pp. 59–97.

— 'The Last Will of Henry VII: Document and Text', in T. W. T. Tatton-Brown and R. Mortimer, eds., *Westminster Abbey*, pp. 99–140.

— 'Ruling Elites in the Reign of Henry VII', in Charles Ross, ed., *Patronage, Pedigree and Power in Later Medieval England*, Gloucester, 1979, pp. 109–42.

Cooper, J. P., 'Henry VII's Last Years Reconsidered', *Historical Journal* 2 (1959), pp. 103–29.

Creighton, Charles, *A History of Epidemics in Britain from A.D. 664 to the Extinction of Plague*, 2nd edn, London, 1965.

Cunningham, Sean, 'The Establishment of the Tudor Regime: Henry VII, Rebellion, and the Financial Control of the Aristocracy, 1485–1509', unpublished PhD dissertation, University of Lancaster, 1995.

— *Henry VII*, Abingdon, 2007.

— 'Loyalty and the Usurper: Recognizances, The Council and Allegiance under Henry VII', *Historical Research* 82 (2009), pp. 459–81.

Currin, John M., 'England's International Relations 1485–1509: Continuities amid Change', in Susan Doran and Glenn Richardson, eds., *Tudor England and Its Neighbours*, London, 2005.

— 'Henry VII, France and the Holy League of Venice', *Historical Research* 82 (2009), pp. 526–46.

— 'To Traffic with War', in D. A. Grummitt, ed., *The English Experience in France, c.1450–1558: War, Diplomacy and Cultural Exchange*, Aldershot, 2002, pp. 106–31.

D'Amico, J. F., *Renaissance Humanism in Papal Rome*, Baltimore and London, 1983.

Darr, A. P., 'New Documents for Pietro Torrigiani and Other Early Cinquecento Sculptors Active in Italy and England', in M. Cämmerer, ed., *Kunst des Cinquecento in der Toskana*, Munich, 1992, pp. 108–25.

Davidson, Clifford, *Festival and Plays in Late Medieval Britain*, Aldershot, 1997.

Davies, C. S. L., 'Bishop John Morton, the Holy See, and the Accession of Henry VII', *English Historical Review* 102 (1987), pp. 2–30.

— 'Information, Disinformation, and Political Knowledge under Henry VII and Early Henry VIII', *Historical Research* (forthcoming).

— 'Richard III, Brittany and Henry Tudor, 1483–85', *Nottingham Medieval Studies* 38 (1993), pp. 110–26.

— 'The Wars of the Roses in European Context', in A. J. Pollard, ed., *The Wars of the Roses*, London, 1995, pp. 162–85.

De Roover, Raymond A., *The Rise and Decline of the Medici Bank, 1397–1494*, Washington, D.C., 1999.

Duffy, Eamon, *The Stripping of the Altars, c.1400–c.1580*, London, 2005.

Dyer, Christopher, *Standards of Living in the Later Middle Ages: Social Change in England c.1200–1520*, Cambridge, 1989.

Elton, G. R., *England under the Tudors*, 2nd edn, London, 1974.

— 'Henry VII: Rapacity and Remorse', *Historical Journal* 1 (1958), pp. 21–39.

— 'Henry VII: A Restatement', *Historical Journal* 4 (1961), pp. 1–29.

— *Studies in Tudor and Stuart Politics and Government*, vol. 4, Cambridge, 1992.

— 'Tudor Government: Points of Contact III: The Court', *Transactions of the Royal Historical Society*, 5th ser., 26 (1976), pp. 211–28.

Emden, A. B., *A Biographical Register of the University of Oxford to A.D. 1500*, 3 vols., Oxford, 1957–9.

Emery, Anthony, *Greater Medieval Houses of England and Wales, 1300–1500*, 3 vols., Cambridge, 2000–2006.

Entwistle, W. J., 'A Spanish Account of the Battle of Bosworth', *Bulletin of Spanish Studies* 4 (1927), pp. 34–7.

Febvre, Lucien and Martin, Henri-Jean, *The Coming of the Book: Impact of Printing, 1450–1800*, London, 1997.

Finot, Jules, 'Le commerce d'alun dans les pays-bas et la bull encyclique du pape Jules II en 1506', *Bulletin Historique et Philologique*, Paris, 1902.

Fleming, P. W., 'The Hautes and Their "Circle": Culture and the English Gentry', in Daniel Williams, ed., *England in the Fifteenth Century*, pp. 85–102.

Fox, A. and Guy, J. A., *Reassessing the Henrician Age: Humanism, Politics and Reform 1500–1550*, Oxford, 1986.

Gairdner, J., 'A Supposed Conspiracy against Henry VII', *Transactions of the Royal Historical Society*, n.s. 18 (1904), pp. 157–67.

Galvin, C. and P. Lindley, 'Pietro Torrigiano's Portrait Bust of King Henry VII', *Burlington Magazine* 130 (1988), pp. 892–902.

Gatrell, V. A. C., *The Hanging Tree: Execution and the English People, 1770–1868*, Oxford, 1994.

Given-Wilson, C., 'The Exequies of Edward III and the Royal Funeral Ceremony in Late Medieval England', *English Historical Review* 124 (2009), pp. 272–4.

Goodman, Anthony, 'Henry VII and Christian Renewal', *Studies in Church History* 17 (1981), pp. 115–26.

Goodman, A. and Mackay, A., 'A Castilian Report on English Affairs, 1486', *English Historical Review* 88 (1973), pp. 92–9.

Gransden, Antonia, *Historical Writing in England, 2: c.1307 to the Early Sixteenth Century*, London, 1982.

Griffiths, R. A. and Sherborne, J., eds., *Kings and Nobles in the Later Middle Ages: A Tribute to Charles Ross*, Gloucester, 1986.

Griffiths, R. A. and Thomas, R. S., *The Making of the Tudor Dynasty*, Stroud, 1985.

Grummitt, D., 'Calais 1485–1547: A Study in Early Tudor Politics and Government', unpublished PhD dissertation, London School of Economics, 1997.

— '"For the Surety of the Towne and Marches": Early Tudor Policy Towards Calais, 1485–1509', *Nottingham Medieval Studies* 44 (2000), pp. 184–203.

— 'Henry VII, Chamber Finance and the "New Monarchy"', *Historical Research* 72 (1999), pp. 229–43.

— 'Household, Politics and Political Morality in the Reign of Henry VII', *Historical Research* 82 (2009), pp. 393–411.

Guerrini, P., 'Pietro Carmeliano da Brescia, Segretario reale d'Inghilterra', *Brixia Sacra* 9 (1918), pp. 6–7.

Gunn, Steven, 'The Accession of Henry VIII', *Historical Research* 64 (1991), pp. 278–88.

— 'Anglo-Florentine Contacts, 1485–1547: Political and Social Contexts', in *Henrici-Medici: Artistic Links between the Early Tudor Courts and Medicean Florence*, New Haven and London, 2010.

— *Charles Brandon, Duke of Suffolk c.1484–1545*, Oxford, 1988.

— 'Chivalry and the Politics of the Early Tudor Court', in Sydney Anglo, ed., *Chivalry in the Renaissance*, pp. 107–28.

— 'The Court of Henry VII' in *The Court as a Stage: England and the Low Countries in the Later Middle Ages*, Woodbridge, 2006, pp. 132–44.

— 'The Courtiers of Henry VII', *English Historical Review* 108 (1993), pp. 23–49.

— *Early Tudor Government, 1485–1558*, Basingstoke, 1995.

— 'Edmund Dudley and the Church', *Journal of Ecclesiastical History* 51 (2000), pp. 509–26.

— 'Henry Bourchier, Earl of Essex', in G. W. Bernard, ed., *The Tudor Nobility*, pp. 134–80.

— 'Henry VII in Context: Problems and Possibilities', *Historical Association* 2007, pp. 301–17.

— *Henry VII's New Men and the Making of Tudor England*, forthcoming.

— '"New Men" and "New Monarchy" in England, 1485–1524', in Robert Stein, ed., *Powerbrokers in the Late Middle Ages: The Burgundian Low Countries in a European Context*, Turnhout, 2001, pp. 153–63.

— 'Prince Arthur's Preparation for Kingship', in Steven Gunn and Linda Monckton, eds., *Arthur Tudor, Prince of Wales*, pp. 7–19.

— 'Sir Thomas Lovell (*c.*1449–1524): A New Man in a New Monarchy', in J. L. Watts, ed., *The End of the Middle Ages? England in the Fifteenth and Sixteenth Centuries*, Stroud, 1998, pp. 117–53.

— 'Structures of Politics in Early Tudor England', *Transactions of the Royal Historical Society*, 6th ser., 5 (1995), pp. 59–90.

— 'Survival Strategies: Henry VII's New Men at the Court of Henry VIII', unpublished paper.

— 'War, Dynasty and Public Opinion in Early Tudor England', in G. W. Bernard and S.J. Gunn, eds., *Authority and Consent in Tudor England: Essays Presented to C. S. L. Davies*, London, 2002, pp. 131–50.

Gunn, Steven and Linda Monckton, eds., *Arthur Tudor, Prince of Wales: Life, Death and Commemoration*, Woodbridge, 2009.

Guy, John, 'A Conciliar Court of Audit', *Historical Research* 49 (1976), pp. 289–95.

— 'The Rhetoric of Counsel in Early Modern England', in *Politics, Law and Counsel in Tudor and Early Stuart England*, Aldershot, 2000, pp. 292–310.

— *Thomas More*, London, 2000.

Hammond, P. W., *The Battles of Barnet and Tewkesbury*, Gloucester, 1990.

Hampton, W. E., 'The White Rose under the First Tudors, Part 1', *Ricardian* 7 (1987), pp. 414–20.

— 'The White Rose under the First Tudors, Part 2, Edmund de la Pole', *Ricardian* 7 (1987), pp. 464–78.

Hanham, Alison, 'Edmund de la Pole, Defector', *Renaissance Studies* 2 (1988), pp. 240–50.

— 'Edmund de la Pole and the Spies, 1499–1506: Some Revisions', *Parergon*, n.s. 6 (1988), pp. 103–20.

Harris, B., *Edward Stafford, Third Duke of Buckingham 1478–1521*, Stanford, Calif., 1986.

Harvey, I. M. W., *Jack Cade's Rebellion of 1450*, Oxford, 1991.

Hay, D., 'Pietro Griffo, An Italian in England: 1506–1512', *Italian Studies* 2 (1939), pp. 118–28.

— *Polydore Vergil: Renaissance Historian and Man of Letters*, Oxford, 1952.

Hayward, Maria, *Dress at the Court of King Henry VII*, Leeds, 2007.

— *Rich Apparel: Clothing and the Law in Henry VIII's England*, Farnham, 2009.

Hepburn, F., 'The 1505 Portrait of Henry VII', *Antiquaries Journal* 88 (2008), pp. 222–57.

Hicks, M. A., 'Dynastic Change and Northern Society: The Career of the Fourth Earl of Northumberland, 1470–1489', *Northern History* 14 (1978), pp. 78–107.

— *English Political Culture in the Fifteenth Century*, London, 2002.

— 'The Yorkshire Rebellion of 1489 Reconsidered', *Northern History* 22 (1986), pp. 39–62.

The History of the King's Works, gen. ed. H. M. Colvin, 4 vols., HMSO, 1963–1982.

Home, G., *Old London Bridge*, London, 1931.

Horowitz, M. R., '"Agree with the king": Henry VII, Edmund Dudley and the Strange Case of Thomas Sunnyff ', *Historical Research* 79 (2006), pp. 325–66.

— 'Henry Tudor's Treasure', *Historical Research* 82 (2009), pp. 560–79.

— 'Policy and Prosecution in the Reign of Henry VII', *Historical Research* 82 (2009), pp. 412–58.

— 'Richard Empson, Minister of Henry VII', *Bulletin of the Institute of Historical Research* 55 (1982), pp. 35–49.

Horrox, R. E., 'Caterpillars of the Commonwealth? Courtiers in Late Medieval England', in R. E. Archer and S. Walker, eds., *Rulers and Ruled in Late Medieval England*, pp. 1–16.

— 'Henry Tudor's Letters to England during Richard III's Reign', *Ricardian* 80 (1983), pp. 155–8.

— *Richard III: A Study of Service*, Cambridge, 1989.

— 'Service', in R. E. Horrox, ed., *Fifteenth-Century Attitudes*, pp. 61–78.

— ed., *Fifteenth-Century Attitudes: Perceptions of Society in Late Medieval England*, Cambridge, 1994.

Hoskins, W. G., 'Harvest Fluctuations and English Economic History, 1480–1619', *Agricultural History Review* 12 (1964), pp. 28–46.

Houlbrooke, R. 'Prince Arthur's Funeral', in Steven Gunn and Linda Monckton, eds., *Arthur Tudor, Prince of Wales*, pp. 64–76.

Hoyle, R. W., 'The Earl, the Archbishop and the Council: The Affray at Fulford, May 1504', in R. E. Archer and S. Walker, eds., *Rulers and Ruled in Late Medieval England*, pp. 239–56.

Hutton, Ronald, *The Stations of the Sun: A History of the Ritual Year in Britain*, Oxford, 1996.

Ives, E. W., *The Common Lawyers of Pre-Reformation England*, Cambridge, 1983.

James, Mervyn, 'A Tudor Magnate and the Tudor State: Henry Fifth Earl of Northumberland', in *Society, Politics and Culture*, Cambridge, 1986, pp. 48–90.

Jones, Evan T., 'Alwyn Ruddock: John Cabot and the Discovery of America', *Historical Research* 81 (2008), pp. 231–4.

— 'Henry VII and the Bristol Expeditions to North America: The Condon Documents', *Historical Research* 82 (2009), pp. 1–11.

Jones, M. K., *Bosworth 1485, Psychology of a Battle*, Stroud, 2002.

— 'Collyweston – An Early Tudor Palace', in Daniel Williams, ed., *England in the Fifteenth Century*, pp. 129–41.

— 'The Myth of 1485: Did France Really Put Henry Tudor on the Throne?', in D. Grummitt, ed., *The English Experience in France, c. 1450–1558: War, Diplomacy and Cultural Exchange*, Aldershot, 2002, pp. 85–105.

Jones, M. K. and Underwood, M. G., *The King's Mother: Lady Margaret Beaufort, Countess of Richmond and Derby*, Cambridge, 1992.

Jones, Michael C. E., '"For my Lord of Richmond, a pourpoint ... and a palfrey": Brief Remarks on the Financial Evidence for Henry Tudor's Exile in Brittany, 1471–84', *Ricardian* 13 (2003), pp. 283–93.

Kantorowicz, Ernst H., *The King's Two Bodies: A Study in Medieval Political Theology*, Princeton, N.J., 1997.

Karras, Ruth Mazo, *Common Women: Prostitution and Sexuality in Medieval England*, Oxford, 1996.

Kaufman, P. I., 'John Colet and Erasmus' Enchiridion', *Church History* 46 (1977), pp. 296–312.

Kelly, Henry Ansgar, *The Matrimonial Trials of Henry VIII*, Stanford, Calif., 1976.

Kingsford, C. L., 'On Some London Houses of the Early Tudor Period', *Archaeologia* 71 (1921), pp. 39–42.

— ed., *The First English Life of Henry V*, Oxford, 1911.

Kipling, Gordon, 'The Queen of May's Joust at Kennington and the *Justes of the Moneths of May and June*', *Notes and Queries* 229 (1984), pp. 158–62.

— *The Triumph of Honour: Burgundian Origins of the Elizabethan Renaissance*, The Hague, 1977.

Kisby, Fiona, 'Kingship and the Royal Itinerary: A Study of the Peripatetic Household of the Early Tudor Kings 1485–1547', *The Court Historian* 4 (1999), pp. 29–39.

— 'Officers and Office-holding at the Early Tudor Court: A Study of the Chapel Royal, 1485–1547', *Royal Musical Association Research Chronicle* 32 (1999), pp. 1–62.

— 'The Royal Household Chapel in Early Tudor London, 1485–1547', unpublished PhD dissertation, Royal Holloway University of London, 1996.

Kleineke, Hannes, *Edward IV*, London, 2009.

Knecht, R. J., *The Rise and Fall of Renaissance France*, London, 1996.

Lander, J. R., 'Bonds, Coercion, and Fear: Henry VII and the Peerage', in J. G. Rowe and W. J. Stockdale, eds., *Floreligium Historiale: Essays Presented to Wallace K. Ferguson*, Toronto, 1971, pp. 327–67.

— *Government and Community: England 1450–1509*, London, 1980.

Laynesmith, J. L., *The Last Medieval Queens: English Queenship 1445–1503*, Oxford, 2004.

Leadam, I. S., 'An Unknown Conspiracy against King Henry VII', *Transactions of the Royal Historical Society*, n.s. 16 (1902), pp. 133–58.

Lindley, P., '"The singular mediacion and prayers of al the holie companie of Heven": Sculptural Functions and Forms in Henry VII's Chapel', in T. W. T. Tatton-Brown and R. Mortimer, eds., *Westminster Abbey*, pp. 259–94.

Lobel, Mary D., *The City of London from Prehistoric Times to c.1520*, Oxford, 1989.

Luckett, Dominic, 'Crown Office and Licensed Retinues in the Reign of Henry VII', in R. E. Archer and S. Walker, eds., *Rulers and Ruled in Late Medieval England*, pp. 223–38.

— 'Crown Patronage and Political Morality in Early Tudor England: The Case of Giles, Lord Daubeney', *English Historical Review* 110 (1995), pp. 578–95.

MacCulloch, Diarmaid, *Reformation: Europe's House Divided, 1490–1700*, London, 2004.

— *Suffolk and the Tudors: Politics and Religion in an English County 1500–1600*, Oxford, 1986.

— ed., *The Reign of Henry VIII: Politics, Policy and Piety*, Basingstoke, 1995.

McFarlane, K. B., *The Nobility of Later Medieval England*, Oxford, 1973.

McGlynn, M., ' "Of good name and fame in the countrey": Standards of Conduct for Henry VII's Chamber Officials', *Historical Research* 82 (2009), pp. 547–59.

— *The Royal Prerogative and the Learning of the Inns of Court*, Cambridge, 2003.

Maddison, F., Pelling, M. and Webster, C., eds., *Linacre Studies: Essays on the Life and Work of Thomas Linacre c.1460–1524*, Oxford, 1977.

Mallett, M. E., *The Borgias: The Rise and Fall of a Renaissance Dynasty*, London, 1969.

Marius, Richard, *Thomas More: A Biography*, New York, 1984.

Mattingly, Garrett, *Catherine of Aragon*, London, 1942.

— *Renaissance Diplomacy*, London, 1955.

Morgan, Philip, ' "Those were the days": A Yorkist Pedigree Roll', in S. D. Michalove and A. Compton Reeves, eds., *Estrangement, Enterprise and Education in Fifteenth-Century England*, Stroud, 1998, pp. 107–16.

Nelson, William, *John Skelton, Laureate*, New York, 1939.

Nicolas, N. H., 'Instructions Given by Henry VIII to John Becket the Usher, and John Wrothe the Sewer of His Chamber', *Archaeologia* 22 (1829), pp. 20–25.

Orme, Nicholas, *Education and Society in Medieval and Renaissance England*, London, 1989.

— 'The Education of Edward V', *Bulletin of the Institute of Historical Research* 57 (1984), pp. 119–30.

— *From Childhood to Chivalry: The Education of the English Kings and Aristocracy 1066–1530*, London and New York, 1984.

Payne, Ann, 'Sir Thomas Wriothesley and His Heraldic Artists', in Michelle P. Brown and Scot McKendrick, eds., *Illuminating the Book: Makers and Interpreters*, Toronto, 1998, pp. 143–62.

Penn, T. D, 'Literary Service at the Court of Henry VII', unpublished PhD dissertation, University of Cambridge, 2001.

Pierce, H., 'The King's Cousin: The Life, Career and Welsh Connections of Sir Richard Pole, 1458–1504', *Welsh History Review*, 19 (1998), pp.187–225.

Preest, David and Clark, James G., eds., *The Chronica Maiora of Thomas Walsingham, 1376–1422*, Woodbridge, 2005.

Pugh, R. B., *Imprisonment in Medieval England*, Cambridge, 1968.

Pugh, T. B., 'Henry VII and the English Nobility', in G. W. Bernard, ed., *The Tudor Nobility*, pp. 49–110.

— 'The Indenture for the Marches between Henry VII and Edward Stafford (1477–1521), Duke of Buckingham', *English Historical Review* 71 (1956), pp. 436–41.

Ramsey, Peter, 'Overseas Trade in the Reign of Henry VII: The Evidence of Customs Accounts', *Economic History Review*, n.s., 6 (1953), pp. 173–82.

Rawcliffe, Carole, *The Staffords, Earls of Stafford and Dukes of Buckingham, 1394–1521*, Cambridge, 1978.

Richardson, W. C., *Mary Tudor, the White Queen*, London, 1970.

— 'The Surveyor of the King's Prerogative', *English Historical Review* 56 (1941), pp. 52–75.

— *Tudor Chamber Administration, 1485–1547*, Baton Rouge, 1952.

Ross, C. D., *Edward IV*, Berkeley, 1974.

— *Richard III*, New Haven, 1999.

Ross, James, '"Contrary to the right and to the order of the lawe": New Evidence of Edmund Dudley's Activities on Behalf of Henry VII in 1504', *English Historical Review* (forthcoming, 2012).

— 'Sedition and the King "Beyond the See"? The Norwich Cordwainers, The Prior of Shouldham and Edmund de la Pole, 1504–8', *Ricardian* 21 (2011), pp. 47–59.

Rundle, David, 'A New Golden Age? More, Skelton and the Accession Verses of 1509', *Renaissance Studies* 9 (1995), pp. 58–76.

— 'Humanism Before the Tudors', in J. Woolfson, ed., *Reassessing Tudor Humanism*, London, 2002, pp. 22–42.

— '"Not so much praise as precept": Erasmus, Panegyric and the Renaissance Art of Teaching Princes', in Yun Lee Too and Niall Livingstone, eds., *Pedagogy and Power: Rhetorics of Classical Learning*, Cambridge, 1998, pp. 148–70.

— 'Was There a Renaissance Style of Politics in Fifteenth-Century England?'

in G. W. Bernard and S. J. Gunn, eds., *Authority and Consent in Tudor England: Essays Presented to C. S. L. Davies*, London, 2002, pp. 131–50.

St John Hope, W. H. and Robinson, J. A., 'On the Funeral Effigies of the Kings and Queens of England, with Special Reference to Those in the Abbey Church of Westminster', *Archaeologia* 60 (1906–7), pp. 517–70.

Salter, F. M., 'Skelton's *Speculum Principis*', *Speculum* 9 (1937), pp. 25–37.

Samman, Neil, 'The Progresses of Henry VIII', in D. MacCulloch, ed., *The Reign of Henry VIII*, pp. 59–74.

Schofield, John, *Medieval London Houses*, New Haven and London, 1994.

Setton, Kenneth Meyer, *The Papacy and the Levant, 1204–1571*, 4 vols., Philadelphia, 1976.

Sicca, C. M., 'Consumption and Trade of Art between Italy and England in the First Half of the Sixteenth Century: The London House of the Bardi and Cavalcanti Company', *Renaissance Studies* 16 (2002), pp. 163–201.

— 'Pawns of International Finance and Politics: Florentine Sculptors at the Court of Henry VIII', *Renaissance Studies* 20 (2006), pp. 1–34.

Singer, Charles Joseph, *The Earliest Chemical Industry: An Essay in the Historical Relations of Economics and Technology Illustrated from the Alum Trade*, London, 1948.

Somerville, R, 'Henry VII's "Council Learned in the Law"', *English Historical Review* 54 (1939), pp. 427–42.

— *History of the Duchy of Lancaster*, 2 vols., London, 1953.

— *The Savoy: Manor, Hospital, Chapel*, London, 1960.

Sowards, J. K., 'The Two Lost Years of Erasmus: Summary, Review and Speculation', *Studies in the Renaissance* 9 (1962), pp. 161–86.

Stapleton, Thomas, *The Life and Illustrious Martyrdom of Sir Thomas More*, London, 1966.

Starkey, David, 'The Age of the Household: Politics, Society and the Arts *c.*1350– *c.*1500', in Stephen Medcalf, ed., *The Later Middle Ages*, London, 1981, pp. 225–90.

— 'Court and Government', in C. Coleman and D. Starkey, eds., *Revolution Reassessed*, pp. 29–58.

— *Henry: Virtuous Prince*, London, 2008.

— 'Intimacy and Innovation: The Rise of the Privy Chamber, 1485–1547', in David Starkey, ed., *The English Court*, pp. 71–118.

— 'The King's Privy Chamber, 1485–1547', unpublished PhD dissertation, University of Cambridge, 1973.

— *Six Wives: The Queens of Henry VIII*, London, 2003.

— 'Which Age of Reform?', in C. Coleman and D. Starkey, eds., *Revolution Reassessed*, pp. 13–27.

— ed., *The English Court: From the Wars of the Roses to the English Civil War*, London, 1987.

Stevens, John, *Music and Poetry in the Early Tudor Court*, London, 1961.

Storey, R. L., *The End of the House of Lancaster*, Gloucester, 1986.

Sutton, Anne F., *The Mercery of London: Trade, Goods and People, 1130–1578*, Aldershot, 2005.

Sutton, Anne F. and Visser-Fuchs, Livia with Griffiths, Ralph A., *The Royal Funerals of the House of York at Windsor*, Windsor, 2005.

Talbot, C. H. and Hammond, E. A., *The Medical Practitioners in Medieval England. A Biographical Register*, London, 1965.

Tatton-Brown, T. W. T. and Mortimer, R., eds., *Westminster Abbey: The Lady Chapel of Henry VII*, Woodbridge, 2003.

Thomas, Keith, *Religion and the Decline of Magic: Studies in Popular Beliefs in Sixteenth- and Seventeenth-Century England*, London, 1971.

Thompson, B., ed., *The Reign of Henry VII: Proceedings of the 1993 Harlaxton Symposium*, Stamford, 1995.

Thompson, S., 'The Bishop in His Diocese', in Brendan Bradshaw and Eamon Duffy, eds., *Humanism, Reform and the Reformation: The Career of Bishop John Fisher*, Cambridge, 1989, pp. 67–80.

Thomson, D., 'Henry VII and the Uses of Italy: The Savoy Hospital and Henry VII's Posterity', in B. Thompson, ed., *The Reign of Henry VII*, pp. 104–16.

Thrupp, S. L., *The Merchant Class of Medieval London, 1300–1500*, Ann Arbor, 1962.

Thurley, S., *The Royal Palaces of Tudor England: Architecture and Court Life, 1460–1547*, London, 1993.

Tournoy, Gilbert, 'Two Poems Written by Erasmus for Bernard Andre', *Humanistica Lovaniensia* 27 (1978), pp. 45–51.

Trapp, J. B., 'Christopher Urswick and His Books: The Reading of Henry VII's Almoner', *Renaissance Studies* 1 (1987), pp. 48–70.

Tudor-Craig, Pamela, 'Margaret, Queen of Scotland, in Grantham, 8–9 July 1503', in B. Thompson, ed., *The Reign of Henry VII*, pp. 261–79.

Tyerman, Christopher, *England and the Crusades, 1095–1588*, Chicago, 1988.

Underwood, Malcolm, 'The Pope, the Queen and the King's Mother: or, The Rise and Fall of Adriano Castellesi', in B. Thompson, ed., *The Reign of Henry VII*, pp. 65–81.

Verdon, Timothy, *The Art of Guido Mazzoni*, New York, 1978.

Vilar, Pierre, *A History of Gold and Money, 1450–1920*, London, 2011.

Wagner, Anthony, *Heralds and Heraldry in the Middle Ages*, Oxford, 1960.

Watts, John L., '"A Newe fundacion of is Crowne": Monarchy in the Age of Henry VII', in B. Thompson, ed., *The Reign of Henry VII*, pp. 31–53.

— *Henry VI and the Politics of Kingship*, Cambridge, 1996.

Wilkie, W. H., *The Cardinal Protectors of England: Rome and the Tudors Before the Reformation*, Cambridge, 1974.

Williams, D., ed., *England in the Fifteenth Century: Proceedings of the 1986 Harlaxton Symposium*, Woodbridge, 1987.

Wilson, Christopher, 'The Functional Design of Henry VII's Chapel: A Reconstruction', in T. W. T. Tatton-Brown and R. Mortimer, eds., *Westminster Abbey*.

Wolffe, B. P., 'Henry VII's Land Revenues and Chamber Finance', *English Historical Review* 79 (1964), pp. 225–54.

— *The Crown Lands, 1461 to 1536: An Aspect of Yorkist and Early Tudor Government*, London, 1970.

Wooding, Lucy, *Henry VIII*, London, 2009.

Wroe, A., *Perkin Warbeck: A Story of Deception*, London, 2004.

Young, Alan, *Tudor and Jacobean Tournaments*, London, 1987.

Index